Terry Tarnoff is a screenwriter. He lives in San Francisco, California.

www.**books**at**transworld**.co.uk

# THE BONE MAN
# OF BENARES

## Around the World on the
## Ultimate Drop-Out Adventure

## Terry Tarnoff

**BANTAM BOOKS**

LONDON • TORONTO • SYDNEY • AUCKLAND • JOHANNESBURG

THE BONE MAN OF BENARES
A BANTAM BOOK: 0 553 81668 3

First publication in Great Britain

PRINTING HISTORY
Bantam edition published 2005

1 3 5 7 9 10 8 6 4 2

The names and identifying characteristics of some individuals
depicted in this book have been changed.

Set in 10.5/12pt Sabon by
Falcon Oast Graphic Art Ltd.

Bantam Books are published by Transworld Publishers,
61–63 Uxbridge Road, London W5 5SA,
a division of The Random House Group Ltd,
in Australia by Random House Australia (Pty) Ltd,
20 Alfred Street, Milsons Point, Sydney, NSW 2061, Australia,
in New Zealand by Random House New Zealand Ltd,
18 Poland Road, Glenfield, Auckland 10, New Zealand
and in South Africa by Random House (Pty) Ltd,
Endulini, 5a Jubilee Road, Parktown 2193, South Africa.

Printed and bound in Great Britain by
Cox & Wyman Ltd, Reading, Berkshire.

Papers used by Transworld Publishers are natural, recyclable
products made from wood grown in sustainable forests. The
manufacturing processes conform to the environmental
regulations of the country of origin.

*For my father,*
*who wanted to be a writer*

# Acknowledgements

I am deeply indebted to all the characters of this book, many of whom helped me on my journey, taught me something about life, and opened my mind to a wealth of new possibilities. Retelling this story after so many years became its own adventure and many people added immeasurably to help me to focus on what was important, shape the text, and stay true to the events. Special thanks to Caren Bohrman for urging me to embark on this project; Marc Bruno for his valuable feedback; Michael Danzig for his years of friendship, incredible support, brilliant ideas, and countless hours of creative conversation; Rebecca Heller, my editor at St. Martin's Press, for her boundless enthusiasm and showing me how to make the manuscript better; Seth Jaret, my film manager, for his vision, tireless effort, and profound understanding of what the story was actually about; Angela Lillie for reading every draft and convincing me to go on; Michael Morales for his sound legal advice; Jandy Nelson, my literary agent, for her genius, commitment, encouragement, humor, soul, humanity, friendship, and countless kindnesses; Ivy Ney for providing hope, support, and inspiration at just the right moment; Maya Perez for guiding two rewrites and believing so strongly in the project; Robert Soffian for lending a critical ear, adding his fine touch, and providing thoughtful advice; Kimberly Whalen for her editorial suggestions; and Suzanne Lacey Wisdom for being there all those years, urging me on.

# THE BONE MAN
# OF BENARES

# 1

# The Double

'Psst . . . psst . . .'

I turned from the outer door of Bangkok's Don Muang Airport to see a real mess of a guy calling to me from the shadows. He had a drawn look, with hollow cheeks, straight black hair that hung like vermicelli, and a wandering eye that wandered from my rucksack to my passport to my wallet. 'You wan' taxi?'

Sure, I laughed to myself, I'll go anywhere you want – to your cousin's 'guest house,' where they'll rob me in my sleep, or your mother's 'restaurant,' where they'll slip knockout drops into my tea, or your brother's 'travel agency,' where they'll ship me off to some unknown destination in a teak casket. I'll hop into your old beat-up Toyota, the one belching blue-black smoke, rather than that nice clean Mercedes with the handsome driver and the government-approved seal on the door, or that sparkling minivan with guaranteed rates and air-conditioning, yeah, sure, I'll go with you because I'm some kind of rube with a death wish, or some guy greener than the fresh bamboo that's growing along the runways, or somebody who's been up and back through Asia so many times he'd go with you just for the absolute ridiculousness of it all. I watched him looking at my stuff. He was actually rubbing his hands together like a half-mad wolf licking its chops and I simply couldn't help myself. 'You've got a meter, right?'

'Sure, no,' he said, grabbing my guitar case, and the next

thing I knew we were barreling down the freeway, leaving little vapor trails through the thick smog that hung over the city like a prickly wool blanket. My eyes were watering and I felt a tickling sensation in my throat as we passed a bus, careened around a steep curve, and nearly got run off the road by a gasoline truck that shot out of nowhere with its HIGHLY INFLAMMABLE load leaking a trail behind. My driver lit his seventh match trying to ignite the cigarette that hung low on his lip, Belmondo-like, but the match heads kept zooming by any which way past his ear, past my ear, past the meter stuck on zero, but mostly they made their way right out the window for the ever-growing river of gas that was spewing out of the truck ahead. One little flick, that's all it would take, and the whole road would explode – the gas truck, us, the bus of schoolchildren we just passed, the wall of taxis all heading for the city, the minivans packed with tourists, the military transport snaking along in the slow lane, the official-looking sedan with government plates, the whole lot of us, five hundred, maybe a thousand vehicles, we'd all go up like one enormous Roman candle, all because of one driver with a wandering eye and a box of bum matches. When another ball of sulfur went flying out the window, I finally leaned forward in my seat: 'Hey . . . you gonna turn on that meter or what?'

'Sure, no,' he replied as he struck another match along the fraying side of the box. 'You American?'

I thought for a moment. 'Guess so. It's been a long time.'

'Atlanta Braves.'

Another flaming match head zoomed out the window and I figured go right ahead, toss the whole box out there, what do I care, I *don't* care, not even a little, I don't care if the whole thing explodes. Annika left me. Martine is dead. You really think I give a shit if it all ends on this piece of crummy road under a piss yellow sky? I caught his blank stare in the rearview mirror and nodded to him. 'Yeah, Atlanta Braves.'

He finally caught an ember on the edge of his cigarette and took a deep drag. 'Bangkok too hot. Too much car. Too much people.' My shirt was already drenched with sweat –

this with a breeze coming through the windows, a breeze that did nothing but radiate big waves of heat that rolled in as if being fanned by a convection oven. Oh, this is an ugly city, I thought, not that all cities aren't ugly coming in from the airport, but this one has a particular edge to it, a certain harshness, the cars are moving too fast, the motor scooters are too reckless as they weave in and out of the lanes, the buses are coughing up clouds of smoke too toxic to be believed, and the people are, well, I don't know exactly, they're hard to get a feeling for, the passengers in the plane and the people in the airport and the guy in the front seat, there's no connection there.

We crossed over the Chao Phraya River, got off the freeway, and headed for the center of town. The city was big and sprawling, a little like Los Angeles, and more modern than I'd expected, but the architecture was bland, offering a few curlicues and swirls to the past but not much more. Other than the odd sharply slanted roof and carved door, it could have been downtown anywhere. We passed Siam Square and its neon signs for American Express, Lufthansa, and Nikon, and all I could see was a sea of Westerners, all of them white and pudgy and sweating, mugging for their cameras and smiling ear to ear, but hating every minute of the journey, as all tourists do, hating the planes and the food and the hotels, hating the sites and the hustles and the knick-knacks, hating every goddamn minute of it and just counting the hours before they could get back home and tell their friends what an incredible time they had. The driver turned up Rama I Road, which became Phloenchit Road, which became Sukhumvit Road, which turned into Rama IV Road, all broad expanses of endless traffic and wall-to-wall shops, and then the Sois began, Soi 4, Soi 5, Soi 6, little cross streets that offered some hope of relief from the cars and buses. He finally turned on Soi Ngam Du Phli and sped down a non-descript residential street that was interspersed with a few travel agencies and clothing shops that spilled over from the boulevard. A couple of blocks down, he wheeled too quickly into the parking lot of a hotel, scraped the bottom of the car

13

on a dip in the road, and sent a clanking shiver up my spine. 'Hotel Malaysia,' he said, with what I thought was a little smirk to his voice. 'You sure you wan' this hotel? This real cheapie hotel.'

I glanced up at a ten-story block of cement that reminded me of Sellery Hall, my dorm back at college. *Hmmm*, where did that come from? I hadn't thought about my college days in – 'This'll be fine.'

'Okay, you save money, you smart.'

'It must be my lucky day. The meter says zero.'

The driver got a good laugh out of that. In between his gasps and guffaws, he managed to spit out: 'Sure, no . . . meter for locals only.'

'Uh-huh. So, how much?'

'Two hun-ned baht.'

Ho. Ho-ho-ho, I thought to myself. Let's see, at five baht to the dollar, that's – 'I'll give you ten baht.'

The driver swung around in his seat and stared at me, at my worn rucksack, and at my beat-up guitar case. The laughter stopped. 'Okay, one hun-ned baht.'

'Eleven baht.'

'Fit-ty baht.'

'Twelve baht.'

'Twen-ny baht.'

'Thirteen baht.'

'Okay-okay,' he screamed. 'Fi-teen baht!'

'Fine!' I yelled back, too hot and tired to argue. 'But you're screwing me . . .'

He sat back in his seat and smiled. 'You need girl?'

Annika's face suddenly came to me clear as day, as if she were sitting right beside me. Martine's then appeared, a little less clear: Was I already forgetting what she looked like? 'Yeah, I need girl.' Seeing his eyes light up, I quickly added: 'But you won't be able to help.'

'Sure, no,' he said, not understanding. 'Too many Thai girl.'

'Maybe next time,' I said, opening the door onto the baking hot asphalt of the parking lot. The driver slid the guitar case across the backseat and I was beginning to walk toward the lobby when another cab came roaring into the lot. It made a sharp turn around a dried-up fountain, came flying back in reverse, nearly hit a maid carrying an armful of supplies, and screeched to a halt. The driver hopped out and opened the trunk, and he was beginning to pull out suitcases when a voice called from the backseat, 'Hey! Wait a minute! I said Hotel Asia, not *Mal*aysia.'

The driver came around to the side of the car. 'Eighty baht.'

'No, no, you don't understand. This is the *wrong* hotel.'

The driver, a short, squat man, didn't understand a word. He understood the tone, though, and he didn't like it. 'Eighty baht,' he reiterated, narrowing his eyes.

The door creaked open and the passenger pulled himself out of the car. He wasn't much taller than the driver, but was leaner, quite handsome, and had the blackest hair I'd ever seen. He held a business card in his hand and shoved it into the driver's face. '*Asia*, you get it?' he said, in an accent I couldn't quite place. Then, with each syllable, he poked the card with his finger. '*As–i–a*.'

The driver glanced at the card, then shook his head with one quick jerk. 'You pay.'

The passenger looked at the driver in disbelief. 'I'm not paying you until you take me to the right hotel.' He held his ground as the driver turned and walked to the rear of the car. A couple of hotel employees and a traveler or two edged closer, wondering what the disturbance was all about. 'What kind of an asshole is this guy?' the dark-haired foreigner asked of no one in particular.

The driver reached into the open trunk, pulled out a thick rubber baton, came back around the side of the car, and then, in the flick of an eye, smashed his passenger across the chest with a vicious blow. It propelled the foreigner right off the ground, buckled his knees, and left him gasping for air in the middle of the parking lot, his question answered. He finally pulled himself up with his elbows and stared at his attacker, who stood over him like a kickboxer, his arms outstretched, his feet coiled into tight explosive balls. 'Eighty *ba-a-a-ht*,' demanded the driver, leaning over him with a malevolent leer. He strung out the last word a little too long, as if to rub it in, until the name of the currency itself took on an ominous sound. 'You *pa-a-ay*.' The passenger struggled to his knees, dug into his wallet, and handed over a hundred-baht note without another word.

The driver tossed out a last piece of luggage, slammed the trunk closed, and drove off into the late-afternoon heat. The passenger waited until the driver was safely out of earshot, then yelled after him, 'Keep the change, motherfucker!'

I took a few steps toward the guy – he was still crouched on the pavement, his shirt wringing with sweat – and called to him. 'You okay?'

He looked at me for a moment and rubbed his chest. 'It hurts like hell.' The pain only reminded him of his anger, and he pulled out the business card once again. 'What does this say? "HOTEL ASIA" right?' He began poking the card again with his finger as he drew out each syllable, still unable to let go: '*As–i–a.*' He shook his head as he stared at the card, where the proof was there for anyone to see in full-color black-and-white. 'Fucking place.' He reached over and grabbed one of his suitcases, then pulled himself to his feet. 'You know where to score?'

'What, you mean—'

'You know what I mean. Powder.'

'No, no . . . I just got here.'

He rolled his eyes and turned to a couple of locals who were watching the action. 'Does *anybody* know where to score?'

'Be *cool*, frien',' someone whispered as they all turned away, but then a skinny man in tight polyester pants appeared from the shadows and pointed to the broken-down fountain, where a thin stream of water trickled out. 'Over there,' he said. 'One hour. Best stuff.'

The black-haired guy nodded, then looked up at the facade of the hotel. Since he'd so easily made a connection, the place suddenly looked a whole lot better to him. 'Guess

16

this hotel is as good as any,' he said, picking up his suitcases. 'I'm Zed Habib.'

As he turned toward me to shake my hand, I noticed a small Star of David hanging against his bronze skin. 'You're—'

'—Turkish. Ankara. You been there?' I shook my head. 'No matter. Real dump of a town.' As we headed for the lobby, I thought about the cab driver, how I'd never seen a local go after a foreigner like that, how this whole place made me feel uncomfortable. I wondered what exactly I was doing there, me and this Turkish Jew in Buddhist Thailand checking into the Malaysia Hotel.

The elevator to the fifth floor jarred me. I hadn't been in an elevator for two, maybe three years, and I wasn't all that comfortable being cooped up in a creaking, rickety cage. The music being piped into the elevator jarred me, too. It was some kind of Thai pop music that would have made a good score for an old film noir set in the mysterious Orient. The fifth floor itself jarred me, as I hadn't been that high off the ground in a very long time, the hallway and its fluorescent lighting jarred me, the room jarred me, the air-conditioning jarred me, the Western-style toilet jarred me, and, an hour or so later, the knocking on my door jarred me.

It was Zed. He invited himself in and made himself at home on a corner of the bed. He sat cross-legged, spread a newspaper over his lap, opened a pack of 555s, and emptied all the tobacco from a filtered cigarette into a neat little mound. He then pulled out a vial of heroin, poured some onto a pocket mirror, and began chopping it up with a razor blade. I watched him out of the corner of my eyes, wondering what would happen if some maid barged in with complimentary mints. Then I glanced at the ripped pillow-cases and discolored sheets and realized that was pretty unlikely. Still, what's with this guy? He just walks right in and starts chopping up heroin? What if he OD's right on my bed? For sure the maid would notice that – *wouldn't* she? – then they'd haul me downtown, like in one of those noir films, and now they've got a bare bulb shining in my face and exaggerated shadows on the walls and everything is black-and-white and a little grainy and some Thai detective leans into my face like he's Humphrey Bogart and says, 'Okay, bud, why'd ya kill the Turk,' and now there's a close-up on me, I'm sweating under the lamp, my eyes are darting back and forth and I'm thinking yeah, if I tell them what they want to hear, maybe they'll go easy on me, okay, I admit it, I killed him, just turn off the damn – 'Can you believe it?' said Zed, looking around at the tattered drapery, worn carpet, and mismatched furnishings. 'Five bucks for this dump! It took me ten minutes to get a 7-Up from room service.'

'They've got *room* service?' I asked, hardly able to conceive of such a thing. I was still trying to get used to the idea of an actual room, period.

Zed looked at me like I was some kind of hick from the country. 'Where'd you say you were coming from?'

'Calcutta.'

He stopped chopping for a moment. 'I'm not going to catch anything from you, am I?'

'Hard to say. You've got your typhoid shots, don't you?'

Zed leaned away from me. 'Typhoid? Are you shitting me? How can they still have typhoid? It's 1974, for Chrissakes, not the Middle Ages.'

'Typhoid, cholera, plague, take your pick.'

'Fucking India,' he said, shaking his head as he turned back to the mirror. He mixed the heroin and tobacco together, funneled the mixture back into the shell of the cigarette, then tamped it down until it was nearly perfect. 'Poppies growing out of their asses, but you think they could ever come up with something like this? Never!' Zed tapped the vial with admiration. He was obviously a connoisseur in these matters, which made it all the more obvious that it was time to send him on his way, I mean, sure, one of the benefits of traveling is the ease with which one meets strangers, but this was just a little *too* easy – how did he even know what room I was in? – no, off you go my friend, it's not that I'm a prude or anything, hell, I even snorted a couple of lines in San Francisco and smoked a bong or two in Amsterdam, but that was just youthful-indiscretion stuff, believe me, it was no big deal, the powder was cut with so much baby laxative I didn't get much more than a case of diarrhea, but this stuff, damn, this stuff looks deadly just lying there on the news-paper, no, this is the real deal, 90 percent pure China White, and I have no intention whatsoever of messing around with it, the fact is, I don't even take aspirin anymore, and in any event I'm just in transit, this is a quick stopover on my way from somewhere to somewhere else, whereas you, Zed, I'm getting the sneaking suspicion that this is your final desti-nation, well, best of luck to you, but I'm just a little tired from the journey and maybe I'll see you in the lobby or something – 'In transit, huh?' said Zed, lighting up the loaded cigarette.

'Yeah. What about you?'

'Me? I'm an economist,' he said, taking a deep drag, 'or a biologist.' He held it in for a long moment, then let out the smoke before finishing his thought – 'or a dental technician.'

'Uh-huh. Lots of latitude there.'

'Whatever works at customs. Of course, a hundred-dollar bill slipped inside your passport doesn't hurt matters. The guy gave me six months. Mighty generous of him, don't you think?'

'Mighty.' Zed shot me a knowing look, then handed me the cigarette. I stared at it a moment, thinking how, deep down, I always knew I'd never get out of Southeast Asia without at least trying the local stuff – when in Rome, after all – but I certainly hadn't planned on trying it quite *this* soon. No, that would be ridiculous. 'So, this, uh, this cigarette of yours, you've tried this brand before?'

'Yeah, yeah,' said Zed, watching impatiently as the joint burned down. I was about to hand it back to him when a crazy impulse overcame me, I glanced at the long ash at the tip of the cigarette – heroin makes the tobacco burn irregularly so a lip of paper just hangs there – and it some-how reminded me of, well, a diving board, maybe it was the heat or the humidity or the smell of chlorine in the air, but that's what I was thinking as I stared at that joint, a diving board, and the next thing I knew I was at the edge of that board, my toes curled around the plank, and it was firm and springy as I bounced, once, twice, then up and over, I executed a beautiful triple-double, lips loose, cheeks tight, tongue relaxed, and I dove right in, that's right, I took a quick hit, just like that, I sucked it in, held it for a moment, felt something metallic in my blood, pulled it out, and passed it back to Zed. Okay, so I did it. I tried the local stuff. An hour after arriving in Bangkok. Big deal.

I'm a little inconsistent sometimes.

Zed rolled his eyes at my meager puff, then inhaled so deeply that the joint burned right down to the filter. He crushed it out, chopped some more powder, then picked up the phone and dialed the lobby. It rang and rang. Growing impatient, he unbuttoned his shirt and fanned his chest. 'Hey, what's with the air-conditioning?'

'What, you're warm?'

'Yeah, turn it up, okay? Five bucks a night, at least they could keep this dump cool.' I went over to a clunky old unit that was jammed into the window and I tried to figure out the dials. Everything seemed to be on full blast. Then I heard Zed on the phone. 'Room service? About time. Why's it take you so long to answer? – What? – *What?*' Zed held the phone at arm's length, just shaking his head. 'Look, I don't know what you're saying. English, okay? *English*. I want four 7-Ups, with plenty of ice, no, better make that five, with *ice*, understand?' Zed snapped his fingers at me to see if I wanted anything. I shook my head, and he returned to the phone. 'And a pack of 555s, okay? I'm in room 512 – what? No! Not *room 555*, a *pack* of 555s! Shit. And don't forget the ice. Lots of ice. Chop-chop.' Zed rolled his eyes, hung up the phone, and returned to the mirror. 'Fucking place.'

I stood there for a moment, wondering how I was going to get Zed out of there. 'How about we go out for some dinner?'

'What d'you think I just ordered?'

'Seven-Up and cigarettes? I was thinking maybe a little

soup or something. The food's supposed to be great—'

'Yeah, sure, the food.' Zed funneled his tobacco-heroin mixture into the cigarette and lit up. 'You mind if I stay here? If I call room service again, they'll never figure out where to send it.'

He passed me the joint, and I took a hit for the road, just to show him I had the strength to say yes. 'That's fine. Just don't burn down the hotel while I'm gone,' I said, heading for the door.

'Fucking place. I'd be doing them a service.'

I closed the door behind me and headed down the hall, feeling stoned and light-headed. Here I was, leaving a total stranger in my room, going out into Bangkok for the first time, feeling a tingling in my fingertips, and waiting for that godforsaken elevator. As the doors opened and the film noir pop music dripped out of the speakers, I thought about what a pain in the ass Zed was, but found myself somehow smiling at the thought of him waiting there endlessly for the room service that would never come. Zed was okay.

The elevator jerked to a stop on the ground floor. I walked gingerly across the lobby and stepped out into the Bangkok night, where I was hit by a wall of hot, humid, impenetrable air. I leaned against the side of the building, then finally gathered myself and turned up the street, in search of a bowl of soup.

I had always been fascinated by the idea of the doppelgänger, even if I never quite accepted what it was. To most people, the doppelgänger is a double-somebody on the planet who looks just like you, whom maybe you see one day walking toward you on the street and you think you're looking into a mirror, but it's no mirror and the person is not you, it's somebody just *like* you, maybe more you than you, maybe the you you always wanted to be, maybe the you who turned right instead of left one day and became successful, the you who is happy, the you who exercises regularly and knows that too much of a good thing is too much of a good thing. I never encountered my doppelgänger – well, once maybe, but that was far too disturbing an event to even consider – and I figured I was probably the better off for it. So, instead, I decided to just change the meaning. After all, the word *doppelgänger* is so deliciously German I figured it could sustain at least a few levels of interpretation, German being nothing if not mind-boggling. I started thinking of my doppelgänger as kind of a *gang of doubles* – a gang that, I decided, was invisible and existed as a protective shield around me. It was essentially a giant guardian angel, for those seeking a simpler explanation, but thinking of it as a doppelgänger gave the necessary weight I was looking for. Guardian angels are for sissies. I needed something more formidable.

It was reassuring to think there was a gang looking out for me, a gang that woke me up in time to escape a falling tree in Greece, kept me from being bitten by a snake in Africa, and helped me escape an angry mob in India. Yes, it had saved my life and gotten me out of some serious scrapes. My doppelgänger was pretty darn terrific, except for one thing: It hated heroin. All doppelgängers do. I have no idea why, but I'm convinced that the moment you do a line, your doppelgänger takes a powder. And then it's just you, all alone, no one to watch your back, it's just you against the world, and that's when you discover just how nasty things can get. It's just you saying the wrong thing to the wrong person, it's just you showing up in the wrong place at the wrong time, it's just you standing on the corner, afraid to cross the street.

I stood on the corner of Rama IV Road, afraid to cross the street. Four lanes of traffic were speeding by in each direction, separated by a narrow pedestrian island. My pupils, pinned by the heroin, let in too much light and it was hard to distinguish the speed and distance of the oncoming headlights. There was finally a break in the stream of cars and I hurried to the halfway point. Now I was really in it, with cars whizzing by on both sides. Why did I ever leave Calcutta, I wondered. Well, I knew why I left Calcutta. But why did I ever leave Kathmandu? More cars passed me in these last few minutes than I'd see in a whole day in Kathmandu.

Ah, Nepal. Walking through the White Machendranath Temple at sunset, wandering down the deserted streets of Asan Tole, stepping over the sleeping cows of Durbar Square, crossing the swing bridge over the Bishnumati, heading through the rice paddies for Swayambhu, hearing the sound of Tibetan horns floating down from the stupa, those deep, spine-chilling tones, and oh, shit, Martine, look at you now, the monks chanting for you on the twenty-fourth day of the *bardo*, where are you now, is it a better place, a place where you can finally relax and listen to the laughter of children and feel the grass between your toes and let your hair blow in the soft fragrant breeze are you feeling a little like I'm feeling right now disembodied & floating & carefree I can almost feel you at this moment I can almost touch you I can almost hear your laugh . . .

A car barreling down the street grazed my pants and I jumped back, discovering I was two feet off the island without even realizing it. I shaded my eyes from the headlights, saw an opening, and darted across the street to a cacophony of car horns and bicycle bells. I slipped into a restaurant on Soi Saphan Khu and sat at a table near the door. The place was cool, thank God, without too many customers. Perfect. I could fade into the woodwork, eat a little something, and get back to my room before Zed did anything stupid. Then I heard the music again, that same music from the elevator, and I began to realize it was the soundtrack to the whole country. It sounded vaguely Western – the arrangements could have been from some 1940s Sinatra ballad – but then the singing began and it was as *un*-Western as you could get. The music and the vocals collided into each other, creating an effect that was strangely mellow and malevolent at the same time.

I glanced around the restaurant. It was strangely mellow and malevolent at the same time. The waiters looked at me with pleasant-enough expressions but no one made a move to come over with a menu. I waved to one of them. He waved back. My mouth was dry and I motioned for some water. The waiter nodded, went into the kitchen, and returned with a plate of peanut sauce. Okay, so this was how it was going to be. I'd been on the road for nearly four years, had been to maybe twenty-five countries, and knew a few things. Like the international sign for water is you cup your hand and bring it to your mouth as you throw back your head. The Masai tribesmen in Tanzania knew what it meant. The goatherds on Crete knew what it meant. Even the waiters in Paris knew what it meant. So what, exactly, was it that this guy didn't understand? Another waiter came by and I motioned for a fork. He gave me a napkin. I ordered soup, they brought noodles. I asked for salt and got pepper. What the hell was going on here? There was only one possibility.

They were fucking with me.

The Thais are the tough guys of Asia. They're the only people never to have been conquered or colonized by the West and are rightfully proud of that fact. They protect their honor jealously and look upon foreigners with a good deal of suspicion. I thought this was all pretty wise on their part, but something else was going on here, something unintentional and beneath the surface. It was like a sixth sense. I don't think they actually knew I was stoned, but they sensed I was weak and knew they could take advantage of that weakness. They recognized, in some murky, subconscious way, that I had no doppelgänger.

A TV with the sound turned off flashed images of an explosion somewhere near the royal palace. People were being carried off on stretchers and a couple of guys wearing red bandannas were being shoved into an army truck. Those shots segued into footage of American jets strafing communist positions in North Vietnam, Cambodia, and Laos, then back again to film clips of the building insurgency in Thailand. All the while, the national soundtrack kept wafting in over unseen speakers, laying down the perfect discordant background to all those arms and legs being blown apart.

I guess the noodles were good. I couldn't really tell since my appetite had gone up in smoke and I was feeling nauseous. I found myself nodding just slightly, well, maybe more than slightly as I was halfway into the bowl when there was a commotion at the door. I pulled myself upright to see a half-dozen Thai soldiers swaggering in. They glanced at the TV, yelled some obscenities at the screen, then ordered some beers from the bar. One of the soldiers, a short, squat guy with puffy cheeks and a crew cut, noticed me at the table and came right over. 'American?' I nodded. 'Hippie?' I shrugged. 'Commie?'—

I thought about Sellery Hall again and my dorm room filled with posters of Marx (Karl) and Lenin (Vladimir) and Marx (Harpo) and Lennon (John). I had a Lyndon Johnson dartboard, a Richard Nixon toilet seat, and a banner that read: WHERE IS LEE HARVEY OSWALD NOW THAT WE NEED HIM? But, commie? Gee, I dunno – 'Listen, I'm not all that into politics. Not anymore.'

He leaned over so close that I could smell the beer on his breath. 'Fuck you.' I was half expecting a rubber truncheon to come flying out of his back pocket, but when he said, 'Fuck you,' I felt a little better, since it seemed more like the end of something bad rather than the beginning of something *really* bad.

'You're welcome,' I replied. The soldier turned to his friends, not sure if he heard right. I turned to his friends also, not sure if *I* heard right. '*You're welcome?*' Did I really say that? Doppelgänger! C'mon! Gimme a better line than that!

Nothing.

The soldier turned back to me, held up his hand as if it were a gun, aimed for my heart, and pushed down his thumb as if to fire. I could feel the invisible bullet tearing into my body, blasting through muscle and tissue and bone, and I was thrust clear back in my chair. A waiter arrived with a beer, and the soldier aimed again, and then again, and again, until I finally realized the beer was for me, and the thumb gesture was to indicate it was a twist-off cap. What's *with* these people? Don't they understand the international sign language of travelers?

The soldier either smiled or frowned, his buddies either saluted or threatened me, the waiter either got a very small payment or a very large tip, and I got the hell out of there. All I wanted was to be back in my hotel room, shut off from the outside world. I didn't want to be prey to these waiters or these soldiers, to the American jets or the guerrillas in red bandannas, to the cars on the street or the taxi drivers at the airport. I just wanted to enter my own little dream world where no one was looking for trouble.

# 2

# Trouble

The days passed, slowly at first, then more slowly still, until finally they pretty much stopped moving altogether. Zed never left the hotel except to score, and that was just down to the fountain in the parking lot. He'd come back as if he'd just swum the South China Sea, flop onto the bed, and treat himself to a double for a job well-done. I wasn't doing a whole lot more. I made a couple of forays to the Emerald Buddha, the Reclining Buddha, and the Weekend Market, but as I gazed out over the sweltering, polluted city, I realized I was entering a state of suspended animation. Bangkok didn't interest me, the weather was getting hotter by the day, and it was hard to muster up the energy to think, much less to make plans. All I knew was that it was time to get out of there before I succumbed to the temptation of Zed's endless joints. When I told him I was going to Chiang Mai, a city in the north, he thought I was crazy. Leave this paradise of cheap drugs and all-night room service? What for?

I arrived at the bus station early the next morning and immediately felt better. Chiang Mai, after all, was sure to be the real Thailand, not this soulless city that reminded me too much of the West. While waiting to leave, I heard a terrible commotion from inside the terminal. Amidst a great deal of pushing and shoving, a cart full of suitcases suddenly came careening through the doorway into a crowd of people. A porter yelled at the top of his lungs and other voices yelled back as the cart jerked this way and that, through the crowd, across the landing, and straight over to the baggage door of the bus I was about to board. The porter roughly threw the luggage into the hold, which only set off a new round of screaming. From behind the cart I could see some hands wildly gesticulating until, finally, the porter crawled into the hold, arranged the bags neatly in order, and climbed back out. Some money exchanged hands, the porter stared in disbelief, and a whole new argument broke out. Finally, a few more baht were begrudgingly slapped down and the porter ran off. A voice, clearer now rang out. 'Keep the change, motherfucker!'

'*Zed?*'

'Fucking place!'

'What are you doing here?'

'I looked at a map. You know where you're going?'

'Of course I know where I'm going. Chiang Mai. Like I told you.'

'No. You said Chiang Mai, some little city up north. You didn't say Chiang Mai, fucking capital of the *Golden Triangle.*'

'What's the big deal? A bunch of poppy fields?'

'That's right, *poppy* fields. Why should I sit in this miserable place when I can go right to the source?'

I glanced at Zed's bags in the hold of the bus. 'Look, I don't know about this.'

'They'll eat you alive up there. You need somebody with experience around. This isn't fucking India, you know.'

'No, it certainly isn't,' I said, wishing I'd never left. And so, we climbed onto the bus, me to get away from the city and the smack, Zed to dig himself in deeper. I somehow convinced myself that these two paths weren't necessarily contradictory.

The Vietnam War, which was supposedly winding down, had been a huge boon to Thailand. Bangkok was a major R&R center and dozens of cheap, American-style hotels had been built to accommodate the soldiers. An army of women had migrated from the countryside to service the servicemen, and it was said that Bangkok in its heyday had more prostitutes than any other place on earth. Add to that a flourishing drug trade and it had the makings of one very wild town. But this was not the heyday. This was one year after the heyday. The last American ground troops had been pulled out of Vietnam in the spring of 1973, and all that was left were some pilots conducting a few thousand more secret bombing raids. I'd spent no small effort trying to stay as far away from Vietnam as possible, but now I was there, right on its doorstep, rubbing shoulders with the ghosts of soldiers who'd walked these same streets, eaten in these same restaurants, and slept in these same beds. I was stepping into the vacuum left by their sudden departure, a big whooshing void of uncertainty and regret, but if America had drawn one final, absolute line in the sand, it was Thailand. Vietnam was a lost cause, Cambodia was iffy, and Laos was teetering, but Thailand, they decided, was not going to fall. So what did they do to stop the communists? They built freeways.

Big, sweeping four-lane roads that banked gently over the rice paddies, then roared in straightaways out to the plains. The freeways crisscrossed the country, sometimes connecting the bigger towns, but more often going from nowhere to nowhere else. The politicians decided there weren't going to be any Ho Chi Minh Trails in Thailand, any secret tunnels or hidden caves. If the commies were going to show their faces, the Thai army would speed down one of those freeways and be there in no time. The amazing thing is, it worked. Americans can't fight worth shit in jungles, but give us a freeway to build, and we'll kick ass every time.

Our bus flew down the freeway doing seventy, with pretty much the whole road to ourselves. Zed nodded out before we even left Bangkok, but he awoke every forty-five minutes like clockwork. He came out of his first nod somewhere around Ayutthaya and pulled out a pack of 555s. I was nervous that the mirror and razor blade would appear next, but Zed wasn't that crazy – not yet, at least. No, Zed had actually loaded up the whole pack and, I had to admit, they looked perfect. He lit up a joint, inhaled deeply, and offered me a hit.

Refusing Zed was becoming a problem. It seemed like every two minutes he was waving a joint under my nose, and I was in danger of becoming addicted to the air that swirled around him. As the bus headed north, a cloud of heroin-laced smoke hung over the rear seats, and I noticed the passengers getting mellower with each passing mile. After Zed finished off his fourth or fifth joint, a man leaned over from across the aisle holding an empty, crumpled-up cigarette pack. 'You cig'rette for me?' Zed looked at him sideways and shook his head. 'One cig'rette,' the man repeated, pointing to Zed's shirt pocket.

I could see Zed was getting bugged. I decided to intercede before we had an international incident. 'Just give him one, why don't you?'

'Because I don't *have* a fucking cigarette. I loaded them all up.'

I glanced over at the Thai man and saw he was getting agitated. 'This *English* cigarette,' I told him. 'No good.'

'Okay, sure,' he said, reaching out his hand. He stared at us for a long moment, then dug into his pants, found a one-baht coin, and held it out to Zed. 'One cig'rette.'

Now we were in whole new territory. The Thais had all sorts of weird social customs, with a list of dos and don'ts a mile long. Things like you don't show a Thai the bottom of your foot unless you're ready to fight to the death. I had a feeling that this was one of those taboos. 'Give him a cigarette.'

Zed looked at me like I was crazy. 'No fucking way!'

'Zed, give him a cigarette, offer him a light, and do not, repeat, do *not* accept the money. Just do it.'

Zed glared at me for a moment, but did as I said. The man leaned back in his seat, drawing deeply from the joint, savoring the taste. '*Ennnnglish* cigarette,' he said, nodding his approval. I watched out of the corner of my eye as he finished it off and sat there with this odd, happy expression. He began humming the Thai film noir soundtrack and giggled a little. Then the bus hit a little dip in the road and he vomited all over himself.

Zed barely moved a muscle. 'Fucking place,' he said, 'fucking, fucking place.'

If Bangkok is Los Angeles, Chiang Mai is Santa Barbara. It's much smaller, quieter, and almost – if not quite – livable. The weather was still hot, but not oppressive, and a slight breeze welcomed the bus as we pulled into town that evening. Still, Zed was getting cranky. He'd finished off his last joint more than an hour ago and insisted we check into the first hotel we saw so that he could roll up a double. The Ratchamankha Guest House was nice enough, with good-sized rooms, attached bathrooms, and narrow little balconies. I was enjoying the cool air wafting in from the window when there was a sharp rap on my door. 'My room's fucked-up!' cried Zed, pushing his way in as I opened the door a crack. 'There's no air-conditioning – are they *crazy*? – and no room service!'

'Listen, we're gonna have to rough it,' I said, thinking how in Calcutta this hotel would have seemed like a palace. 'We're not in the big city anymore.'

'Fuck, man,' said Zed, plopping down on the edge of my bed to roll a joint, 'I can't believe you dragged me here.' There was a look of panic in his eyes, as if the thought of actually having to go out for his 7-Ups might be the end of him.

I escaped to the balcony for a moment's peace. It grew quiet in the room. Too quiet. I had learned that not hearing Zed complain about something for five minutes was grounds for concern and sure enough, as I glanced inside, I saw him nodded out against the backboard, a joint slipping out of his hand, burning a hole in the bedcover. 'Zed, goddamn it!'

'What? What?' he said, his eyes snapping open.

'Will you *please* watch out?'

'It's too hot in here, you got something cold to drink?'

'Oh, Christ . . .' I knew Zed would drive me crazy if I stayed in that room one more minute. 'I'll go out and get something, okay? Just promise me you won't light up again before I get back.'

31

'I'll give you twenty minutes.'

'That's very generous of you,' I said, fleeing the hotel for a little grocery shop down the street. Along the way I came upon a wooden placard advertising private tours of the area. Pasted onto the sign was the photo of a 1959 Chevy Biscayne, the one with the crazy Flash Gordon fins, and the exact model car I had owned in Berkeley before I left America.

'You wan' tour?' came a voice from over my shoulder.

I turned to see a man in his early twenties standing there, eagerly rolling a set of car keys between his fingers. I took a long look at him. 'Do you go, you know, out to the fields?'

'Hill tribe, Doi Inthanon, paddy tour, go everywhere.'

'Okay, but, you know, the *fields*?'

The guy looked at me knowingly and smiled. 'Fast car, cheap price. Siritep give best tour.' I remembered that Zed was alone in my room and made some quick arrangements. We agreed to meet at eight the next morning outside the Ratchamankha. I returned to the hotel fifteen minutes later with a couple of 7-Ups and a bag of ice. Zed was nodded out and didn't even hear me come in. A half-burned joint was dangling from his fingers – needless to say, he hadn't kept his promise – and was ready to fall onto the bed. I slipped it out of his hand and figured I'd better take a hit before I completely flipped out.

'You gonna smoke *all* of that?' Zed asked as he suddenly reached out his hand. His eyes were still closed tight.

'Now, listen, Zed—'

'You're slower than room service. You got ice, I hope.'

I just stared at him lying there on my bed, reaching out for the joint with one hand, waiting for the 7-Up in the other, his eyes still closed, living in a magnificently insane fantasy world. How could I be mad at him? 'We're going to the poppy fields tomorrow.'

His eyes snapped open. 'Yeah?'

'Yeah. Eight o'clock sharp. I hired a driver.'

Zed sat up on the bed. He actually looked excited. 'No shit?' He knocked back both 7-Ups, rolled a quick joint, and headed for his room. 'See you at nine.'

\* \* \*

Ten o'clock the next morning, Zed showed up outside the hotel. It was already hot and muggy, the skies were overcast, and it felt like rain. Siritep and I were hunched over a map that highlighted all the places of interest. Whenever I'd point to some nearby village on the map, he'd shrug noncommittally, then point to some faraway hill tribe near the Burmese border and give me a big wink. It all made sense. To get something good, it figured we'd have to work a little for it. So, off we went, due west, to the heart of the Golden Triangle.

The backseat of the Chevy Biscayne was even bigger than I'd remembered and looked like it had been through its own wars. I found a spot between two broken springs and leaned back for the ride. Zed, meanwhile, came prepared. After the fiasco on the bus, where he was left empty-handed for an entire hour, he now had two full packs of 555s loaded up. As for me, I'd rolled up some Thai sticks, the strongest pot I'd ever smoked, just to keep me occupied.

Half an hour later, zoned out in the backseat, I had the unusual feeling of hurtling through space and opened my eyes to see that Siritep was barreling down the freeway at ninety miles an hour. 'Hey, slow down!' I yelled, pointing to the speedometer. Siritep looked at me with puppy-dog eyes and slowed to sixty. Ten minutes later, I felt the old clunker shaking at every imaginable joint and saw the speedometer needle pushing far into the red again. 'Too fast, Siritep, *too fast.*' Siritep nodded and slowed down. A short time later, we were back at warp speed. '*Siritep!*' He glanced at me in the rearview mirror and waved. I was certain he was just waiting until my eyes closed before he revved it up again. The next thing I remember was an explosion, the sound of metal on concrete, sparks flying, the car pitching like a boat in a hurricane, and a sickening feeling of moving sideways along the freeway. The car screeched, groaned, rolled and tumbled, then skidded to a stop in a field of dandelions off the road. Siritep held onto the steering wheel as if letting go would be the end of the world. I sat there in stunned silence. Zed barely moved.

I got out of the car and saw that the tire was not only flat, it was *gone*. The wheel was all bent out of shape, the underside of the fender was beat-up, and the side of the car was dented in. Then I looked at the other tires. There wasn't even the hint of tread on any of them. They were absolutely stark-raving bald. '*Ninety miles an hour on these?*' I screamed at Siritep. '*Are you mad?*' Siritep finally pried his fingers off the steering wheel and got out to inspect the damage. I took a closer look at the Chevy and realized what a total piece of crap it was. The whole car was held together with paste and glue. Siritep shrugged, opened the trunk, and pulled out a spare with so many patches on it, it looked like an old, moth-eaten quilt. He jacked up the car, took out a mallet, and started pounding the rim of the wheel into shape.

Zed finally rolled out of the backseat, completely oblivious to what was going on. He stood looking out over the field of dandelions and – thinking it was opium – nodded his approval. 'About time,' he said.

An hour later, we were back on the road. 'Fucking place,' Zed kept muttering after I told him what had happened. A few minutes later, he was nodding again, a few minutes after that, I was zoned out again, and a few minutes after that, Siritep was driving ninety again. I woke up sometime later to the mountains of Burma just ahead of us – the center of the world's opium trade. The border was sealed tight and the Red Karens, the tribe that populated these hills, didn't seem all that thrilled to see us when Siritep pulled up in a cloud of dust. They smiled uneasily and brought out a few pieces of jewelry to sell, but Zed wasted no time: 'Who's got the opium?' He was met with silence. 'Opium, you know, *poppies*, for Chrissakes.' There was still no response. Annoyed, he turned to Siritep. 'Hey, race-car driver, what's Thai for opium?'

Siritep looked at him blankly.

'C'mon, Siritep,' I interjected. 'Poppy fields, like we talked about.' I made the international sign of opium smoking –

sucking on an open thumb outside a clenched fist – but Siritep just shifted uneasily.

'I thought this guy knew where to score,' said Zed through clenched teeth as we drove further into the hills. We looked for fields, for little puffs of smoke, for anything at all, as we pushed down lonely stretches of road far from the freeway. The skies, which had been threatening since we left Chiang Mai, finally erupted. We were caught in a deluge, a sheer wall of rain that came at us from all sides. I tried to roll up my window, but the handle just flopped around and around. Zed's handle worked fine, but his window frame turned out to have no glass in it at all. Despite getting drenched, Zed still managed to keep his pack of 555s and a box of matches dry. He somehow got a joint lit and smoked it down in between the sheets of rain. Siritep, meanwhile, just kept driving – God knew where – and in between the irregular sweep of the windshield wipers, I could hear him humming to himself. It was the Thai film noir soundtrack.

The rains stopped as suddenly as they had started. We checked the map, got a general sense of where we were, and discussed heading back to Chiang Mai, but then we noticed a tiny village, far from any other town, that was just a few kilometers down a dirt road. If any secluded village in the Golden Triangle was going to be growing poppies, this had to be it. Siritep went tearing down the road – he was unstoppable – and we just held on in the backseat. The Chevy hit pot-holes, boulders, vegetation, and anything else in its way as we drove deeper into the interior. Then, about halfway to the village, we hit a big patch of muddy road. Siritep managed to jam on the brakes before getting stuck. '*Slooow*,' I said, drawing out the word, 'go ve-ry *sloow*.' Siritep studied the terrain and nodded. Then he floored it. The engine roared, the bald tires squealed, and the fins fishtailed all over the place for about a hundred yards. That's where we wound up, a hundred yards down the road, mired in the mud. 'Siritep,' I said with an even tone, 'I know you don't understand a word I'm saying, but I just want to tell you that if we ever get out of here alive,

I'm going to cut out your heart and feed it to the snakes.'

Siritep smiled and said, 'Push car.'

For Zed this was the final straw. 'I've got a bad heart,' he said as we stood ankle-deep in mud. 'I'm gonna fucking die here, I'm gonna have a heart attack in this hellhole.'

I couldn't listen anymore. 'On the count of three. One . . . two . . .' Zed, a heroin-laced 555 dangling between his lips, begrudgingly leaned against the rear of the Chevy. I pushed on the other side and yelled so that Siritep could hear. '*Threeee!*' Zed pushed, I pushed, and the tires spun. The Biscayne rocked a little, edged forward an inch or two, then spit up a new pool of mud. Zed and I were covered in muck. The car was entrenched even further. Siritep got out and, for the first time, looked worried.

'That's it. It's over,' said Zed as he collapsed against the trunk. 'I can't breathe. My arm is numb. You killed me, the two of you.'

I pulled the joint out of Zed's hand and took a quick hit. At that instant, a farmer and two water buffaloes appeared at the horizon. 'Siritep!' I yelled, grabbing his shoulders. 'Get man! Get buffaloes! Get going!' I pushed him toward the farmer, then turned to Zed. 'C'mon. Let's walk to the village. We can make it.' Zed looked at me as if I were crazy, but he was too far gone to argue. As we set off the skies cleared, the sun pounded down, and the mud quickly caked into our skin and hair. We stopped for another joint and looked at each other. Wearing a hodgepodge of Western and Eastern clothing – all ratty and torn and disheveled – we looked like absolute wild men. With Zed's pinned pupils poking out of his mud-encrusted face, he could've been some Stone Age tribesman. As for me, I was beginning to look like one of those ash-covered holy men I'd seen on the banks of the Ganges. 'Zed?'

'What!'

'You look great.'

We came upon the village an hour later, burning hot, exhausted, and dying of thirst. These were hill people we were visiting, the kind that anthropologists and ethnologists still studied for their unusual ways. They took one look at us and panicked. Doors slammed tight. Windows shuttered closed. Children hid under tables. Animals retreated into their pens. In a matter of moments, the entire village was a ghost town, and we were the ghosts.

'Fucking place,' said Zed between his parched lips. We walked down the main path of the village in search of water. Every once in a while, I'd turn to see a dozen eyes disappearing behind some darkened window. Then we came upon a house on stilts just off the path. I motioned for Zed to be quiet as we tiptoed over to the landing. There, sitting on a porch, were three old men who hadn't heard about the wild-man invasion. We climbed up a ladder on one of the stilts and stepped behind the men, blocking the doorway to the house. After a moment, one of them turned.

'*Hoi-hoi-hoi!*' he screamed, rubbing his eyes.

'*It-sip! It-sip!*' hollered another, pointing at Zed in fear.

'*Fuuuuuuck!*' yelled Zed, clenching his heart.

The men jumped up and huddled in fear. There was nowhere for them to run to since we had the exits blocked, so they moved toward the edge of the landing. Afraid they were going to jump, I held my hand up in the international sign of peace. This only frightened them more. They looked at me in a funny way. I think they realized I had no doppelgänger. 'Friend . . . friend . . .' I said soothingly, sounding like Frankenstein greeting the townsfolk.

'Water . . . water . . .' begged Zed, making the international sign of thirst.

I saw a clay pot at the corner of the landing and made the international sign of drinking. As usual, I got nothing but blank stares. Finally, I said, 'Fuck it,' went over to the pot, dipped in a coconut cup, and pulled out some water. The men did nothing to stop me. Zed found his own ladle and drank cup after cup until I thought he would capsize. The men looked at him like, What kind of man could have such capacity? I just shook my head as if to say, You should only know. Finally, everyone more or less relaxed and we sat down to rest. Zed wiped some of the mud off his face and said, 'Opium? You sell?' Getting no response, he made the international sign of opium smoking but, as expected, it got us nowhere.

I noticed that the men had been sharing a water pipe when we arrived, and I decided to give them a hint. I filled the bowl of the pipe with one full Thai stick, tamped it down, and offered it to the oldest of the group. He was wary at first but finally took a monster hit off the hookah. The other men followed, then Zed and I. Moments later, our captive hosts were totally zonked out. They began giggling, singing, and telling endless stories to one other. They even brought out some sickly-sweet coconut candies, which we polished off in no time. I made one final attempt at the international sign for opium, but the men just smiled, pointed to the rest of my pot, and held out the bowl of the pipe. Sure, I figured, why not? They'll probably wake up tomorrow and think they hallucinated the whole thing.

With the sun about to set, we bid the village elders a fond farewell and headed back down the road. When we arrived at the patch of mud, I was amazed to see that the Chevy Biscayne was miraculously turned around and facing the road to Chiang Mai. Zed and I piled into the backseat, Siritep started up the engine, and we headed out of the Golden Triangle. Zed pulled out a 555, took a couple of hits, and started nodding out. I pulled the joint out of his fingers before it fell on the floor and took a couple of hits myself. Siritep watched in the rearview mirror and, a few moments later, was flying down the pitch-black freeway, going ninety miles an hour.

We arrived at the Ratchamankha Guest House around midnight. I paid off Siritep and even gave him a nice tip. He smiled and asked if we'd like to take another tour tomorrow. Ho. Ho-ho-ho. Zed and I trudged through the lobby with thoughts of nothing but a nice, long shower. Suddenly, the hotel manager came running out of his office with blazing eyes. He grabbed Zed's shoulders and began shaking him violently. 'You pay! You pay!' he screamed.

'Hey! Fuck off! What're you talking about?'

The manager pulled Zed out the back door to a small garden. There we saw a mattress propped against the wall, still smoldering. 'You wan' burn down hotel?'

'Now, wait just a minute—' said Zed, indignantly.

'How much?' I asked, cutting him off.

'Four hun-ned baht!'

'*Wha-a-a-t?*'

'He'll pay.'

I'm not sure where Zed slept that night, but the next morning he was at the bus station bright and early, throwing his bags into the luggage rack of an air-conditioned minivan. 'You're really going to stay here?' he asked for probably the fifth time that day.

'Yeah, I'm gonna head farther north in a few days.'

'I don't know why you do it. Bangkok's got it all.'

'I'll catch you on the rebound.'

Zed climbed into the van, checked to make sure he had his 555s, and leaned out the window for one last look. 'Fucking place.' We shook hands, and I watched as the van pulled onto the highway. It would be months before I realized how closely our fates were entwined – and how differently things might have turned out had we traded itineraries at that bus station in Chiang Mai. But I was going north and Zed was going south, and I wondered if I'd ever see him again. As the van disappeared around a bend in the road, it was funny how I almost couldn't remember his face anymore.

# 3

# The Toxic Trampoline

I spent a few days resting up from the ill-fated trip to the Burmese border and a few more resting up from my two weeks with Zed. Without those 555s constantly passing my way, it was amazing how much better I felt. So much better that I actually had time for my guitar. Yes, my guitar – and my harmonica – well, sixteen harmonicas, actually, the central reasons for my existence. I wasn't like Zed or the junkies in Bangkok or the hundreds of other travelers passing through these parts. I had a *reason* for being here, a reason beyond just experiencing the world, or getting my head together, or exploring far-off places. I was a musician, and a pretty good one at that. Among the best, that's what some people said, and if my arguments against such praise were a little insincere, well, so what? I mean, of course it wasn't true – there was Paul Butterfield and Charlie Musselwhite and James Cotton and Big Walter Horton, for God's sake – but on a really good night maybe I was in their ballpark. Or maybe not. Who knows? It's a subjective thing. Still, I was trying to take the harmonica somewhere new, and maybe the guitar too. I wanted to add the sounds of these strange corners of the world, these crazed cacophonies from the streets of Mombasa and the back alleys of Bombay and the bazaars of Kathmandu, and transform them all through my own prism of metal reeds and steel strings.

I tuned the guitar, strapped the harmonica brace around my neck, and strummed a few chords. It didn't really sound right – was it the air? The humidity? The barometric pressure? – then looked around at the matted floor, bamboo walls, and corrugated ceiling and realized the room was an acoustic nightmare. Ah, so that's it! Relieved, I put away my guitar. Soon enough I'd be in more conducive surroundings.

After a good night's sleep and a hearty meal, I was ready to continue my journey. I checked out of the Ratchamankha and was about to head for the bus station when I ran into a couple of fresh-faced Australians outside the lobby. They were wearing hiking boots and small day packs. 'Hey, mate, wanna hit the poppy fields?' one of them asked.

I looked at these novices and couldn't help feeling sorry for them. Did they think this was some little jaunt outside Melbourne? Their naïveté was almost scary. 'Listen, guys, I don't think you understand—'

'We've been to three already just outside town. Doesn't take but an hour on the trail.'

'What? – *What?*'

'That's on the west side. They say if you walk north, there's one in twenty minutes.'

I just stared at them, then begged off. I had a bus to catch.

The ride to Chiang Rai was uneventful. I had no idea why I was going to Chiang Rai except that it was north and near the Mekong River. The bus pulled in that night, kicking up dust on the main road through town. The passengers getting off kicked up some more dust, and the jitneys cruising for fares kicked up still more. The whole town, in fact, was covered in dust, which was maybe why I'd never seen any tourist brochures for the place. I wheezed my way to a modest hotel and considered my options. Chiang Rai, for sure, was a one-night town, but where to next? The choices were limited. I was once again only miles from Burma – Burma wraps around Thailand from the west to the north – but Burma was off-limits. The only other option, besides returning to Chiang Mai, was to cross the Mekong into Laos. Unfortunately, Laos was in the middle of a war, the communists had taken over most of the country, and the whole place was ready to topple. Laos was clearly out of the question. Only somebody with a death wish would go to Laos.

The next morning, I headed for Laos. After taking a jitney to the Mekong, I boarded an old wreck of a ferry that slowly trudged across the water. The river was maybe a mile wide at that point and snaked along the fat terrain separating the two countries. The Mekong was muddier than I'd expected and Ban Houayxay – the village where the boat was headed – looked like a steaming, tropical nightmare. The captain of the boat told me there were only two flights a week out of the village but luckily one of them was leaving in forty-five minutes. As we neared the port, I thanked my lucky stars for that flight. The place looked like a real dump, even hotter and dustier than Chiang Rai. That's when I heard the sound of propellers. I looked up and saw an airplane climbing into the sky. I ran over to the captain. 'That's not the plane, is it?'

He looked up at the Royal Lao insignia and nodded his head. 'Very sorry.'

'But they can't *do* that! It doesn't leave for another thirty minutes.'

The captain watched the plane disappear into a cloud. 'No, it doesn't.'

I plunked my bag onto the narrow cot of some fleabag guest house, looked around at the spartan surroundings, and shuddered at the thought of four days in this place. The air was feeling heavy and still when the quiet of the room was suddenly shattered by the sound of giant propellers. My eyes widened with excitement. What luck! The plane was coming back! Just for me! I ran out into the courtyard and saw it was a plane all right, but nothing that Royal Lao would be flying. No, this was a giant military cargo – a C-130. As the plane banked down toward the airport, I got a clear view of its underbelly. Strange. There were no markings anywhere on the wings or fuselage.

I returned to my room and came upon something unfamiliar in my rucksack. I pulled out a small bottle, inside of which was maybe half an ounce of white powder and a note in Zed's herky-jerky style of handwriting: 'Just in case you get lonely.' Was he completely crazy? What if there'd been customs inspections at the Mekong? I dumped out the rest of my belongings to make sure there were no more surprises and was looking for somewhere to throw away the heroin when I heard a soft tapping on the door. I opened it to find the manager of the hotel standing there, a middle-aged woman with soft eyes and an easy smile. 'Is okay?' she asked, pointing to the room.

'Is okay,' I said, quickly burying the vial of powder beneath some clothes.

She inquired if I needed anything, and I made the international sign of drinking, wondering what my latest miscommunication would bring. When she returned a moment later with a pitcher of water, I could barely contain my joy. I was really out of Thailand.

Ban Houayxay was unbearably hot. The days crawled with bugs, the nights buzzed with mosquitoes, and the constant sound of C-130s filled the air. Where the hell was I? The flimsy walls of the guest house rattled as the propellers ripped through the dense air, sending thunderous vibrations throughout the village. I spent most of my time alongside the Mekong, where the temperatures were maybe a degree or two cooler. A few times, when I really couldn't stand it anymore, I jumped into the muddy water. Everything about the Mekong spelled trouble to me: It flowed too slowly. It was grossly polluted. It had an unnatural color. But the worst thing about the Mekong was the story I heard the night I arrived in Laos. The locals claimed to have seen the bodies of two Westerners, their heads severed, floating down the river just a few days earlier.

I felt trapped. I lay on the bed, unable to sleep, thinking of Martine, thinking of Annika, thinking of the two headless bodies. After a miserably hot night, I wanted nothing more than to get out of town. I didn't care how – road, boat, it didn't matter – but with 90 percent of the countryside controlled by the Pathet Lao rebels, the only way out was by plane. So, I waited. My skin was swollen from the heat, my appetite had deserted me, and I was too dizzy to read. Time hadn't merely stopped, it seemed to be moving backwards. That's when I remembered the little vial at the bottom of my rucksack. What would be the harm in snorting a line or two? Sure, it's more addictive that way, but it was too damn hot to even think about rolling a joint. I knew I'd be out of there in a couple of days, anyway.

Lying on the bed, staring at the ceiling, my mind became pleasantly unfocused. Rather than the sleeplessness unleashing all sorts of tortured memories, I found the hours just kind of floating by. Martine's image retreated into the background until there was nothing left but vague shadows. I thought about Annika once or twice, but her face was strangely indistinct. I couldn't quite picture her eyes. They were blue, weren't they?

I did another line and forgot all about it.

On the fifth morning, I threw my belongings into the rucksack and double-checked everything before heading for the airport. I had my passport, health certificate, ticket, money, heroin . . . *hmm*, what to do with the heroin? Even though I was traveling within the country – thus, no customs inspections – I had a funny feeling about just carrying half an ounce right on me. At the last moment, I decided to shove the vial inside some dirty old socks.

The airport wasn't much more than a low, flat building with a counter and a couple of desks. I glanced outside and saw one unmarked C-l30 after another lined up along the runway. 'What the hell is this place?' I wondered again. A moment after checking in, I found out. The ticket agent pointed to a long, narrow table on the other side of the room. 'Inspect bag,' he said.

I stood there, hoping I hadn't heard right. 'No, no, I'm going to Luang Prabang.'

'Inspect bag!' he said again, more firmly this time. Okay, fine. I walked over to the table and waited until a guy appeared wearing casual slacks and a short-sleeve shirt open at the neck. The lack of a uniform was strange, but there were at least three other things *really* wrong with this guy: He was white, he had a crew cut, and he wore shiny black shoes. I'd been in Southeast Asia long enough to know what that meant: He was with the CIA.

'How ya doin', bud?' he said, looking at me with an icy stare. My days as a war protester at the University of Wisconsin flashed before my eyes. Sure, now it all made sense. They'd been following me ever since that speech I made. The guy on the train to Marseilles. The woman in the hotel in Stockholm. The researcher at the bar in Nairobi. Now, this guy – this ramrod-straight, uptight jerk of a spy – was finally gonna nail me. HEADLESS BODY OF WAR PROTESTER FOUND FLOATING IN MEKONG, that's how the headlines would read. I decided I wouldn't go without a fight. I figured if I could surprise him with a quick diversionary tactic, I'd be able to reach into my bag for the hunting knife I always carried. I'd hold it to his throat and draw just a little blood to show him I wasn't kidding, then the two of us, real nice and easy, would back our way out of the terminal, onto the tarmac, and into one of those big C-130s. I'd kick his ass out the door just as we were ready for take off, then I'd commandeer the plane back to Nepal because – *oh, shit!* Why did I ever leave Nepal!

'Just fine, thanks,' I replied, in my most respectful voice. 'How are you?'

'Got any contraband?'

'Me? Why . . . no.'

'Okay, just dump out all your stuff on the table and we'll take a look-see.'

I gulped the gulp of the terminally guilty as I began removing my things one by one from the rucksack. The CIA agent watched me for a moment, then grabbed the bag and turned it upside down. My whole life poured out onto the table.

A Benares prayer shawl. A tattered copy of the *I Ching*. A checkered Kenyan *kikoy*. Sixteen harmonicas. A pair of pajama pants. An embroidered shirt from Manali. A bag of beads and stones. Two bars of Chandrika Ayurvedic soap. A book of guitar chords. An eight-yard-long silk sari border. A miniature bronze statue of Ganesh, the Overcomer of Obstacles. Two shredded flip-flops. A pair of Thai coolie pants. A bottle of adulterated Indian shampoo. A tape of Van Morrison's *Astral Weeks*. A poster of Brahma, Vishnu, and Shiva. A pair of crusty old socks.

The CIA agent stared at the display on the table and, truth be told, I think he questioned for the first time in his life what the hell he was fighting for. He was making the world safe for *this*? 'Get out of here,' he said, as he turned on a dime and left.

Flying from Ban Houayxay, the biggest CIA outpost left in Southeast Asia, to Luang Prabang, the ancient royal capital of Laos, was a relief. The city, high in the hills, was dotted with hundreds of stupas and other remnants of a once-thriving culture. The people seemed friendly enough, but behind their eyes I could sense a feeling of fear and uncertainty. In another time, Laos might have been a paradise, but now it sat in the crosshairs of history, lost amidst its neighbors, landlocked, weak, a forgotten land. I remembered early in the Vietnam War hearing about the bombing of the Plain of Jars, but I never could quite place it. Now I was almost there. The Plain of Jars extends east from Luang Prabang to the Vietnamese border. It incorporates nearly half the country and was, by all accounts, a vast wasteland, leveled by wave after wave of American bombers. I looked into the faces of the locals and wondered how many of them were refugees from the eastern villages. There was a sadness in Luang Prabang, a feeling of doom. The city was run by both the government and the Pathet Lao, and there had been endless negotiations between the rival forces, with cease-fires here, liberated zones there, and all sorts of other combinations. There were camps of soldiers from both sides within the city limits, but they were rarely seen, and certainly not together.

While visiting some ancient temples just outside town, I

walked among the stone Buddhas of a lotus garden. Transported back in time by the grace of the images, I turned onto a path and came upon a ragtag unit of Pathet Lao soldiers marching right toward me. There were maybe eight of them and they all appeared to be teenagers, some no more than twelve or thirteen years old. They carried machine guns as big as their bodies, wore red bandannas wrapped around their foreheads, and lugged belts with bullets and grenades. They saw me and stopped marching.

'Look at this guy, walking around out here without a care in the world,' I imagined one of them saying.

'He doesn't even have a doppelgänger.'

'He must be very brave.'

'Or very stupid.'

'Let's shoot him.'

'Okay.'

HEADLESS BODY OF WORLD TRAVELER FOUND FLOATING IN MEKONG. As the conversation grew more heated, I decided to prove to them that I wasn't the enemy. 'Hey, I'm with you guys,' I said, speaking slowly in case they might understand. 'I've always been pretty much of a communist myself, it's just that I'm exploring some other interests these days.' Then, I did the only other thing I could think of. I flashed them the international symbol of peace, the hippie 'V.' They looked at me like I was crazy, then quickly marched off. 'Hey, wait a minute . . .' I called after them, 'where you going?'

When I got back to my guest house, I snorted a line that would've done Zed proud. It was funny about the heroin. I was starting to snort it more and more often. I snorted it in the morning, in the afternoon, at night, and whenever I got the hankering in between. It was instant oblivion, extra-strength aspirin for the soul. It was very easy, really. Just chop a little up, roll up a thousand-kip note, and inhale. I got a kick out of kip, the Laotian currency. The economy was in free fall, inflation was astronomical, and the money was nearly worthless. When I exchanged ten dollars at the bank, I walked out with an enormous wad of money that barely fit into my pocket. Not only was there a lot of it, it was *big*. These enormous bills, all different sizes and denominations – who knew what anything was worth? The best thing was the name. I could never get out of my mind that, in Dutch, *kip* means chicken. Whenever I bought something, I had this image that I was paying in chickens. Tens of thousands of chickens.

The days began to blur together. There were rumblings that the country was about to fall, that it wasn't really safe to be there anymore, but I found the whole thing too exotic to leave. I decided to just stay on, getting higher and higher, while everything crumbled around me. Then, one morning, I pulled out my guitar and tried to run some scales. I hadn't been practicing much lately, but I was disturbed to see just how much my playing had deteriorated. I figured it was an off day, but the next two mornings were even worse and I could no longer deny what was happening to me: I was sliding back in my playing. Music was no longer the focus of my day – heroin was, and that scared the hell out of me. After all, I wasn't one of those Bangkok junkies just wasting away in some hotel room. I was *doing* something in Asia. Still, what was I doing here, in Luang Prabang? Waiting to get shot? I looked at my stash of powder and saw that it was nearly finished. Another few days and I'd have to score again. This was the perfect time to quit.

There's this thing about heroin users: The amount they use is in inverse proportion to the amount they *claim* to use. Stone-cold junkies are convinced they're only dabbling in the drug, while dilettantes would have you believe they're strung out to the eyeballs. This is one of the irrefutable laws of junk. People who tell you years later how strung out they were in Asia are lying. They probably got loaded a few times for the thrill, but stopped at the first sign of trouble. It's the ones who say they only fooled around a little that you have to watch out for. In all my time in Asia, I only met one person who told the truth about how much he used. That person was me. I only fooled around a little. I made a plane reservation for Vientiane, the capital, deciding that would be the best place to kick. I had three days of smack left and portioned out the powder so that I'd have just enough to get me on the plane the third day. There's something un-equivocal about that word – *smack*. You can smack someone upside the head. Someone can smack you down. Sometimes you can land smack – dab in the middle of nowhere. It's not the kind of word that elicits a real warm feeling. It's a no-nonsense kind of word – one cold, hard syllable that kind of dies on your lips before you've even finished pronouncing it.

On the morning of my fight, I snorted a line, gathered my things together, snorted another line, had a cup of coffee, and snorted yet another line. That should have been it, but there was still some powder at the bottom of the vial. I had about an hour before catching a bus for the airport and sat in the hotel room waiting. I glanced over at the vial and figured maybe I'd take just one more line, then toss away the rest. I emptied it onto a mirror, chopped it into five lines, snorted one of them, and felt a burning sensation in my nostrils. I then opened the door, made sure no one was looking, and headed for the bathroom. I was about to dump the powder into the toilet when a crazy urge came over me. This was my last high, why not do it right? Why not push things to the edge? I pulled a ten-thousand-kip note from my pocket, rolled it up, and snorted all four lines.

Ten thousand chickens flew through my brain. They scratched at my hypothalamus and pecked at my frontal lobe. They squawked and danced and stared at me with their beady little eyes. They flapped their wings and left coarse, jagged feathers all over my cerebellum. They fought and clawed their way through arteries and synapses and nerve endings. They came rushing through my skin – ten thousand chickens in the form of little beads of sweat, rushing through my pores. I fell against the wall of the bathroom and could feel myself slipping to the floor.

'Walk!' a voice screamed to me from miles away. I some-how managed to prop myself up against the wall, but my legs wouldn't move. My eyes flickered open for a second, and I could see pieces of broken mirror on the floor and the ten thousand kip floating in the toilet. I felt my eyes closing and everything seemed to be moving in slow motion. My heart beat slowly in my ears . . . *ka-thump* . . . *ka-thump* . . . *ka-thump* . . . *ka-ka-ka* . . .

'*Walk!*' screamed the voice again, and I felt myself pushing up against the wall. I made it a step or two, crashed into the door, then somehow found myself floating down the hall to my room. I was so far beyond stoned that I wasn't even high anymore. I was on some kind of toxic trampoline that kept pushing me from one ether zone to another.

Next thing I knew I was outside on the street, rucksack over my shoulder, guitar case in my hand, forcing myself to the bus stand two blocks away. The morning sun beat down upon my face in little pinpricks of torture and I felt as if my insides were going to explode. I stopped alongside the road and tried to vomit, but couldn't. Somehow I made it onto the bus, where I sat with my head near an open window. The driver pulled out, and I was sure I would heave all over the place as the heroin broke down in my blood and the toxins built up in my body.

The airport was a surreal vision of soldiers, ticket agents, and passengers, all shimmering figures and echoing voices. When another wave of toxicity hit me, I found myself in the bathroom with a finger down my throat. Still, I couldn't vomit. '*Passage pour Vientiane, numéro vingt-sept,*' came a voice over the loudspeaker. I floated out onto the boiling runway, where an old French prop-jet was waiting. '*Bienvenue,*' said an attractive Laotian flight attendant. I nodded, located my row, and eased my way into the seat. My stomach was clenching up, my breathing was forced, and my skin felt like cold pasta. The plane taxied down the runway, and I held on for dear life. Then, suddenly, we were airborne. I felt better as the plane climbed. Maybe it was the atmosphere, or the air pressure, but for the first time I actually thought I might make it out of there alive. I leaned back against the seat for what was to be only a forty-five-minute fight. I could do it. I could last. I knew it. That's when the plane hit an air pocket.

I vomited. Green-yellow-red-brown projectiles spewed forth with unbelievable intensity. I grabbed for an airsick bag and managed to get most of it inside. The rest wound up on me, the seat, the floor, and the poor guy sitting next to me. Then, miraculously, I felt better. My mind cleared slightly. I was even able to ponder the immediate future.

I wondered what Vientiane would be like, now that I was off heroin.

# 4

# Hotel Lido

Arriving in Vientiane was like entering an old French movie set in colonial Indochina. The streets were wide and tree-lined, the buildings imposing, the shops and restaurants sophisticated. Still, upon closer look, there was a definite sense of decay. The facades might have been French, but chip away at the paint and it seemed the whole place might crumble. Like former French colonies everywhere, Laos was either very expensive or very cheap. Even second-rate hotels were much more than those in Thailand, as were the restaurants and coffee houses. I told my cab driver to take me to a hotel *moins cher*.

'*Etes-vous certain, monsieur?*' he asked, unused to taking Westerners anywhere but to the Central Plaza.

'*Je préfère un hotel locale,*' I said, hoping that my paltry French made sense.

He turned down a crowded street, drove through a marketplace, pulled into a cul-de-sac, and stopped in front of what had once been a government office building. The flimsy structure was three stories high, had wood-slatted walls, and looked as if a good wind could topple it over like a house of cards. '*Hotel Lido, monsieur.*'

I paid the driver and trudged up the stairs with my bags. I still felt weak from my experience on the plane and had yet to come down from all those hits. All I wanted was a decent room, a shower, and a glass of orange juice. The room was cheap enough, only forty-five-thousand kip, so I took it sight unseen. I lugged my stuff up to the third floor and found Room 312 at the end of the hall. The door creaked open upon a semi-darkened room. I flicked on the light switch and was nearly blinded by the single bare bulb, which hung on a tattered wire. When my eyes finally adjusted, I saw a narrow steel cot with rubbery springs and a lumpy mattress, a chair that teetered on three and a half legs, a dresser with one drawer missing and one that didn't open, and a ceiling fan with five settings, none of which worked except 'slow.' That was it.

I turned off the light and stretched out on the bed. Sunlight streamed in through the slatted walls and gave an Expressionist, Venetian-blind look to the room. The shadows angled up from below, creating a dramatic, if creepy, chiaroscuro effect. Okay, I thought, it's a little weird. I can live with it. I lay there in kind of a partial dream state, half-stoned and half-sick, trying to block out the sounds of slamming doors, blasting radios, squeaking bedsprings, heated arguments, raucous laughter, and crying babies. An hour later, I unconsciously reached over for my rucksack and dug through it for some heroin.

Oh, right . . . I don't do that anymore.

It didn't really matter, since I was still a little high anyway. I figured a cool shower would take the edge off things, so I wrapped a towel around my waist, slipped into my flip-flops, and headed down the hallway. The bathroom was tiny, with the shower and toilet occupying the same space. The toilet was a hole in the floor and also served as the shower drain, but as my eyes adjusted to the dim light, I noticed there was still shit in the hole. There was also shit on the floor. There was shit floating in little pools of water that hadn't drained. There was shit on the walls. There was shit on the shower handles. There was shit on the ceiling. There was a river of shit, an ocean of shit, a tsunami of shit, and damned if I was going to ride that wave.

I backed away from the bathroom, careful not to touch anything. As I made my way down the hall, I heard a door open and turned back to see a guy heading for the very same room with a bar of soap and a bottle of shampoo. He opened the door and flicked on the light. I could hear a latch closing and then the sound of water from the shower, and then . . . the guy started *singing*.

Back in my room, I lay down on the cot and watched the ceiling fan slowly cutting through the thick air. The fan didn't really move the air, it just kind of shoved it over a few inches. I reached over for my vial of heroin, then remembered again. 'No problem,' I said to myself, 'just the force of habit.' Instead, I smoked a Thai stick, which only made me more acutely aware of my surroundings. There was an endless stream of voices, footsteps, and slamming doors. As the sun set, I just lay there on the cot, watching the fan, listening to the noise, reaching over occasionally for the heroin that wasn't there.

I slept fitfully that night, waking up at all hours to strange sounds from the hotel, the street, and the room itself. When the sun filtered through the slats of the walls early the next morning, I forced myself to get up. I made it down to the lobby, where a dozen women with thick lipstick, lace stockings, and incredibly short skirts were showing their wares to a stream of prospective clients. I watched the negotiations for a few moments, until a wave of withdrawal sickness forced me back to my room.

It had been nearly twenty-four hours now, and I felt I was holding up reasonably well. I'd heard that it took five days to get heroin out of your system, but that the first three days were the worst. The desire lasts longer than that, but as far as the actual physiological need, it wasn't much different than quitting cigarettes. I lay flat on my back, watching the fan make one painfully slow revolution after another. Suddenly, I had an insatiable desire for a line. My muscles tightened, my head throbbed, and my skin got clammy with sweat, but then, a few minutes later, the craving passed, and I felt better again. I managed to get a basin and a pitcher of water for my room, so I could wash myself down every couple of hours without going near the bathroom. The one benefit of kicking was constipation, which I welcomed in this case with open arms.

In between the pangs of withdrawal, the biggest thing I had to fight was boredom. I tried reading, but couldn't concentrate. I tried exercising, but was still too weak. There was only one thing left. I tuned up my guitar, strummed a few chords, and managed to get a decent sound. Then I strapped on the neck brace, slipped in a harmonica and began playing a tune I was working on. Despite the slatted walls, the acoustics were good and the sounds of the reeds and strings blended together well. I closed my eyes and started getting into it, feeling the music for the first time in weeks, realizing how much I'd missed it. I played the chorus over and over, bending the notes a little differently each time, pushing the rhythm, giving it a jazz syncopation.

When I finished the tune, I heard someone call out: 'More! More!' I glanced up to see a dozen people standing in the doorway, and the moment our eyes met, they burst into applause. I felt embarrassed, but a little pleased all the same. 'Music! Music!' they chanted, and I couldn't help but invite them in. There were two guys from down the hall, three or four hotel employees, a couple of tribesmen from out of the hills, and four prostitutes from the lobby. They sat on the bed along the floor, and on the broken-down chair, waiting for more. I played another song, glancing up from time to time to check out their faces. They all seemed transfixed, this rather unsavory lot, and I only hoped it was by the music. I was pretty sure at least some of them were as wasted by drugs as I was. I was drawn to two piercing black eyes across the room. The Expressionist lighting from the slats illuminated the face of one of the prostitutes, and her eyes glowed through the shadows, reminding me of Marlene Dietrich in *Shanghai Express*. I looked away, but seconds later I was drawn back. She was still staring at me, unblinking, and as I followed the contours of her face – the rounded forehead, the high cheekbones, the small straight nose, the perfect lips – I saw that she was absolutely beautiful.

A wave of withdrawal suddenly retched through my body,

my hand froze on the fret board, and the music abruptly stopped. My guests applauded again and chanted for more, but I waved them off. 'Maybe later,' I said as the guitar slipped onto the bed. They slowly filed out of the room until only one person was left. It was her. She just stood there, still staring at me, until one of the other prostitutes called to her from down the hall. She walked to the door, turned back one more time with those big, wide eyes, and vanished out of the room.

I fell back onto the bed, my muscles throbbing in pain. If only I had a hit, just one hit, I'd pour a small amount onto a mirror, chop it up with a razor, roll up ten thousand chickens, and take a quick snort. Just to take the edge off. I watched the blades of the fan, wondering how they could move so slowly. Just one hit and things would be much better.

That night I made a quick foray outside for some food and found a soup vendor at the Central Plaza who agreed to let me take the bowl away. As he ladled out some milky liquid, I noticed my first Westerners. One look into their eyes told me they were as messed up as I was, maybe worse. No foreigners were in Laos anymore except for junkies and war correspondents. Sometimes they were one and the same. A skeletal German guy and his black girlfriend shuffled over. 'Far-out, man, far-out,' was all they could say as they stared blankly into the soup. I wondered if these were the two headless bodies they'd found floating down the Mekong.

Back at the Lido, I managed to eat half the soup. The hot liquid toned down my muscle spasms for a while, but as the night wore on, I again awoke to throbbing muscles and a pulsing headache. I was lying there watching the fan slowly rotate, around and around and around, when there was a knock at the door. I switched on the light – the bare bulb again almost blinded me – and stumbled to the door, expecting to find some drunken john trying to get into the wrong room. I yanked open the flimsy door and was surprised to find the prostitute from that afternoon standing in the hallway. 'You play?' she asked shyly, making a strumming motion with her hand.

I'd forgotten how beautiful she was, but even in this stark light she was stunning to look at. I could hardly take my eyes off her. 'Sure, I play.'

She walked in and stood against the wall. 'I am ... Emmanuelle,' she said, pausing slightly to pronounce the word correctly. I smiled to myself, wondering who had given her that name. I turned off the bulb – an outdoor streetlight cast enough light through the slats for us to see – and motioned for her to sit. She watched from the edge of the bed as I played a few chords, then made a motion of blowing into her hand. She wanted to hear the harmonica. I hooked up the neck brace, slid in a harp, and played a quiet blues. I glanced over at her and saw that she was staring at me again, just like before, but as I continued playing, something happened. I noticed tears in her eyes. She did nothing to hide them or wipe them away, but just sat there listening to the sad tones of the harmonica and cried along. I couldn't remember ever connecting quite so strongly with anyone through my music before and, as I looked at her, I realized it wasn't just her face that was beautiful. Her *soul* was beautiful. She understood every emotion behind the music – the joy, the pain, the longing – and that's when our eyes locked together in an endless gaze. I didn't care if this woman was a prostitute, I didn't care if her name was Emmanuelle, I didn't care if we couldn't speak the same language, this was someone who understood something deep and important inside me. I took off the neck brace and put down the guitar. Still she stared at me, the tears welling up in her eyes. She slid closer on the bed, and now the light from outside hit directly on her face. Shadows of light and dark crisscrossed her eyes and nose. I leaned over and kissed her. Her lips opened slightly and I felt her tongue, small and thin and cool, as it moved into my mouth. She brushed against my cheek, curled around, then withdrew, delaying slightly as if to draw me along inside her. As my tongue followed past her lips, she bit down gently, then playfully darted her tongue back and forth against mine. I followed deeper and she began sucking me in, deeper and deeper into her mouth.

We kissed for an eternity. We kissed while China massed troops on the border. We kissed while America bombed the villages. We kissed while the government fled to the highlands. We kissed until oblivion. And when we finally broke apart, I was in love. We'd find a way, she and I, we'd find our place in the world, we'd find some village in the hills or some island off the coast or some clearing in the forest, but we'd be all right, we'd kiss like this forever, and we'd be all right. Emmanuelle picked up the harmonica and held it to her heart, then took my hand and drew it to her breasts. They were round and firm and I could feel her nipples pressing against my skin. I ran my fingers over her blouse and squeezed gently. She took a quick breath as her nipples hardened. We sat like that for what seemed like hours, just kissing and touching each other, savoring every moment. Finally, I ran my hand along her waist and unfastened her skirt. Her breathing quickened and her body moved toward me in encouragement as my fingers touched the edge of her undergarments. Emmanuelle thrust her tongue into my ear, and I felt a chill run down my spine. She held me tight, rubbed her body against my chest, and whispered, 'You pay.'

I was sure I hadn't heard right. 'Wh-what?'

'You pay. Hun-ned thousan' kip.'

I pulled away from her in shock. 'I-I can't pay you. I thought—'

'Okay, fit-ty thousan' kip.'

'You don't understand—'

Emmanuelle stared deeply into my eyes. 'Me love you,' she said. 'Twen-ny thousan' kip.' I began feeling sick to my stomach. My head throbbed and my muscles ached. My withdrawal was hitting again – worse than ever – and all I wanted at that moment was to withdraw from her, from my mind, from my skin, from everything. I went to pull my hand from under her skirt, but she held it there. 'Okay, fi' thousan' kip,' she said.

Everything seemed irrevocably demeaned. Me, her,

the moment itself. I tried to speak. 'Emmanuelle—'

'You *pay*,' she said, tearfully. 'One thousan' kip.'

That's only *six cents*! All I'd wanted a moment ago was to shower her with gifts, take her to fine restaurants, treat her like a princess. But *pay* her for sex? I couldn't. Not even if she did love me. Not even if this was just some weird cultural thing. Every joint in my body felt raw. I pulled my hand away and collapsed back against the mattress. She stared at me for a moment, then straightened her back and held her jaw firm as she got up from the bed, walked to the door, and turned back to face me. 'Bastard,' she said. And then she left.

On the third day, it really hit. I hadn't slept in two nights, the temperature in the room kept rising, the air was getting thicker, and the fan was moving more slowly than ever when I saw something crawling on the wall. I flicked on the light. Maybe it was nothing, just the shadows, but wait, over there, what's that on the ceiling? I got up on the bed to look more closely, but then it moved to the side of the dresser. My arm brushed the lamp wire, and the bare bulb began swinging back and forth, casting hellish shadows from one corner of the room to another. Fuck this room! Fuck this light bulb! Fuck this fan! One line of heroin, that's all it would take to end the misery.

The bulb swung slower, the fan spun slower, and the walls crawled more slowly still. The light from the slats angled upward and focused on me like klieg lights. There I was, the star attraction: Thank you very much ladies and gentlemen, for my next number I'd like to writhe on the floor, vomit a little, and scratch my skin until it bleeds. Then, for your listening pleasure, I'll howl like a banshee under a jagged moon. Thanks for coming, drive safely, and be sure to come back tomorrow when I'll do a swan dive into the toilet of Vientiane's most illustrious hotel.

A sudden moment of lucidity overcame me. I'm in Vientiane, Laos. I'm trying to kick heroin in a room that even Dante couldn't have dreamed up. The communists are about to take over the country. I'm crazy in love with a prostitute whom I won't pay six cents to sleep with. And, I haven't even sent my parents a postcard since I got here.

> Dear Mom and Dad. Having a wonderful time. Weather's a little hot but not much worse than Milwaukee in August. Ha ha. Good food, nice people, and, boy, the scenery. Mom, you'd love shoes. Dad, how about a steak for two dollars? Ha ha. Wish you were here.
> Love.

I tossed and turned all night. Why couldn't I pay Emmanuelle six cents to sleep with her? Because I had a twisted sense of morals. There is nothing more debilitating, more self-defeating, more *ridiculous* than a druggie with morals, but this was the curse I'd carried around for years: I knew right from wrong. This condition, this tragic, unfortunate condition, led directly to one of the three cornerstones of my philosophy.

*Guilt is good.*

Since I *knew* what was right, I felt I had a responsibility to *do* what was right. Of course, with the rules of society all being upside down, I felt I needed to challenge all my assumptions, but in challenging everything, I found that nothing really seemed wrong anymore. If nothing was really wrong, then nothing could really be right, either – a sticky situation for a moralist to find himself in. There was, in fact, only one ethical test that I could rely on: looking into the mirror. The mirror never lies. The mirror knows. The mirror tells all. You were a jerk! You did wrong! You need to suffer! Which leads to the second cornerstone of my philosophy.

*People don't know what jerks they are.*

Nobody wakes up in the morning, looks into the mirror, and says, 'Hey there, badass, you're an evil son of a bitch, let's go out and fuck up the world.' The fact is, of all the people who have screwed you over – the boyfriends and girlfriends, husbands and wives, teachers and bosses – *not one of them* realizes what a jerk he was. Rapists, murderers – it doesn't matter who they are, they've explained away all of their actions, justified their behavior, and twisted events to fit whatever loony scenario their brain has dreamed up. Hitler might've had a mean mother, Stalin an abusive dad, Nixon a clubfoot – whatever it was, there was surely a ready explanation at hand. Which leads to the third – and only other – cornerstone of my philosophy.

*Everyone is wrong about everything.*

E does not equal $mc^2$. Gravity is not proportional to the product of two masses. Speed does not equal distance times time. There is no such thing as id, or ego, or superego. Time is not the fourth dimension. Change is not the only constant. Might does not make right. Vitamin C will not cure cancer. Vitamin C will not cause cancer. Trust me on this. This is the way things are.

And so, I tossed and turned. I craved heroin and I craved Emmanuelle, but I knew that paying six cents for either of them would be wrong. This is the way things were.

The night wore on and insane memories of the past forced their way into my mind. All I wanted was to sleep, but the muscle spasms were almost constant now. I thought I'd hit rock bottom a couple of times already, but the bottom kept falling out. Oh, what an asshole I was to have kept snorting week after week in Luang Prabang! Beads of sweat ran down my face. My muscles felt like they would tear out of my arms and legs. My throat felt copper plated. I kicked the bed frame, swatted wildly at a mosquito, then flung a coffee mug at the dancing shadows on the wall. The mug, the wall, and the room exploded into a thousand shards of glass.

When I wiped my eyes, the chiaroscuro on the wall was more pronounced than ever. White was white. Black was black. There was no in-between. A movie was playing on the wall, throwing back my past, flickering from scene to scene. Was this it? Was I dying? Were these the images of a drowning man going down for the last time? The bare bulb slowly swung back and forth to the movement of the fan and a recurring thought hit me again: I'm kicking heroin. I'm in Vientiane, Laos. I'm in the worst flophouse I've ever seen.

There's a war going on all around me. I'm on the doorstep of the country I swore I'd never enter. Annika left me. Martine is dead. How in God's name did I ever get to this place? I turned back to the wall and watched it all unfold . . .

A modern 1950s ranch-style home. There I am, in the living room, I must be nine because some of the furniture isn't there yet and we just moved to Milwaukee from a little town up near the Canadian border. I'm watching TV with my older brother, Ed, he's fourteen and really skinny, and with Mom, but she's not really watching, she's paging through *Life* magazine, taking a load off. Everything's pretty cool until – oops – here comes Dad, what's *he* so happy about? Yapping, yapping, yapping – I wish he'd shut up so we could just watch the show, but he's going on and on until Mom finally asks him to sit down, but he doesn't want to sit down, he wants to stand he wants to walk he wants to dance he wants to go to the theater he wants to throw a party he wants some new friends he wants to finally live a little, goddamn it doesn't she understand? Dissolve to a 1956 Oldsmobile speeding down the highway, Dad's at the wheel, the windows are all open, the wind is blowing through his hair, the radio's on full blast, and the speedometer is way in the red at 112. Whoa, *cool*. Well, maybe not. St Michael's Hospital, the psychiatric ward, and there's Dad, he's tied down to this gurney with leather straps around his arms and legs and these weird metal things attached to his head and then they wheel him into this room and we're out in the hallway, and it's like one of those prison movies where there's an execution and the lights dim when they turn on the juice. Now they wheel him out and his eyes are all funny and Mom kisses him on the cheek but he doesn't know who she is and he doesn't know who I am and I don't think he even really knows who he is. Back to our dining room, we're having dinner, Dad's back and back to normal, which means so long manic, hello depression, he hardly says a word, he just sits there all glum and bummed out, his eyes are kind of glassy, I guess it's the medication, but boy is it quiet, he doesn't like it when any of us talk, so we just sort of sit there eating and trying to pretend that this is the way it's supposed to be. Close-up on Ed, poor Ed, Ed hates him and thinks it's all Dad's fault, even though Ed's got a lot of problems of his own, he's failing his classes, he's sick all the time, and he's developed this really terrible stutter. Suddenly, it's the next spring – spring was always the worst – Dad's at the Milwaukee Symphony, cheering too loud and applauding too long. He brings three hoboes home to dinner and regales them with endless stories, then he's up all night and running around all day and up again the next night and Mom is closing the blinds hoping the neighbors won't see and Dad's yelling at her and Ed is cowering in his bedroom and I'm try- ing to reason with him but I'm just a kid what the hell do I know? Back to St Michael's Hospital, the 'closed ward' for the really serious nuts and, let me tell you, we've got the whole mixed assortment here, the cashews and the pecans and the filberts, and Dad is going in and out on that gurney every day – the electric bill's gonna be a killer – and Mom's looking really frail lately and Ed's hanging back near the door, and those *other* people in the ward, talk about weird, Dad doesn't seem *that* bad, but I'd just as soon not have to visit, I mean I love him and all, but I don't like how we have to get them to unlock the doors when we want to leave and I start worrying that one day they'll forget and I'll have to spend the night there with all those people who are always laughing and crying and dribbling onto their chins. Dissolve to my bedroom, and it's really neat, Mom's a little crazy about keeping things neat as a pin because what would people say if they saw a mess, but we never have people over anyway so what's the difference? I couldn't wait to have my own place someday so that I could live like a pig, but for now I'm staring endlessly at a map of the world, imagining my escape. There are lines drawn all over the place, travel routes planned, changed, and rerouted, the plains of Andalusia, the Mongolian steppes, the savannas of East Africa, the valleys of the Himalayas, the Hindu Kush. Now the flickering images on the wall begin to move faster as we cut to the University of Wisconsin in Madison and there I am, moving

63

into Sellery Hall – *I'm free!* – and there's my first psychology class and my first date and my first sit-in against the war and – uh-oh – here come the cops, they're dressed in riot gear, swinging their nightsticks, pulling girls by their hair, smashing guys over the head, there's blood all over the place and everyone's screaming and teargas canisters get shot into the air and there's Trudy, my first love, and she's crying – how could they *do* that to us? – and man, is it unraveling, and then, somehow or other four years pass and it's Graduation Day, but I'm not there, none of us is, we're laughing at our diplomas and rolling them into joints and smoking our whole educations away. I move to Berkeley, the only city in America more radical than Madison, and I'm angry – oh, *God*, am I angry – it's really getting ugly, the teargas is hanging in the air and I've got a brick in my hand and I'm ready to take out a police cruiser or the window of a bank or maybe even my own front door. The sound of a harmonica echoes through the streets, a wail that comes straight from the soul and shoots right up my spine, and I'm being split right in two, half of me wants to join the revolution and half wants to get out. And then I hear gunshots. Somebody falls to the ground, and I've got a decision to make, the biggest decision of my life, for to choose the wrong path could be fatal. I flip a coin and it turns into a two-headed snake. I stare at it for a long moment as it twists and turns in the air, I'm getting lost in it and transported, as if on a cloud, and then I awake in a smoky club in London, there's a singer, a drummer, and a harmonica player – it's me – and then I'm in Amsterdam, a little hole-in-the-wall club, just me and a guitarist and the place is filling up, and it's beginning to make a bit of sense, yes, maybe I can live like this from one day to the next, and now I'm heading north to Scandinavia even though winter's approaching, there's a snowy landscape, the flurries are swirling around and around, and then—

# 5

## Annika

A freezing gust of wind blew through the crack of the window and sent an icy shiver down my spine. My hands were wrapped around the steering wheel of an old VW van, the heater had given up long ago, and my feet were like blocks of ice. Sweden was blowing and howling right outside my windshield, and it was not the best time to be driving with bald tires, a bent steering rod, and a slipping transmission. The gray sky blended into endless snowfields at the horizon and it was as if the terrain had neither beginning nor end, it was just a long interminable expanse of road upon which my beat-up van creaked and groaned, like a freighter brushing against the ice floes of the North Atlantic. What was I doing here, all by myself, driving from Oslo to Stockholm in mid-November? What idiocy led me to this place, what made me go north instead of south, like any sane person? The tires slid along the frozen road, and I took my hands off the wheel for a moment and realized it didn't much matter whether I steered or not. The vehicle was moving on its own inertia, and I was just along for the ride. Go wherever you're going to go, down the road, into a snow-drift, wrapped around a telephone pole, upside down in a gully, what's the difference anyway? HERE LIES A POOR BOY FROM WISCONSIN, DIED 1971, AFTER TEN LONELY MONTHS IN EUROPE, that's how the markers would read, a boy who lost his way, a real idiot from all accounts who hit the road in search of himself only to discover his soul was as frozen as the fjords in which he met his untimely demise. 'Fjord Motors.'

'*Hmm?*'

'That's what they should call the car company up here.'

'*Um-hmm.*'

I turned away from my imaginary friend – she was incredibly beautiful, and sweet too, and laughed at all my jokes – and stared again at those barns in the distance, they look exactly like the ones on the road from Milwaukee to Madison, and the fields, they're flat and unrelenting, and the sky – did I mention the sky? – it's big and oppressive and scarily familiar. Oh, God, I'm alone, what kind of fool leaves his homeland only to visit its exact duplicate in the dead of winter? Why, for that matter, did all those Swedes pick up and leave here a hundred years ago only to seek a similar hell in Wisconsin? A gust of wind, bigger than before, blew across the highway and sent the van careening into a lane of oncoming traffic. LONG-HAIRED AMERICAN DIES IN HEAD-ON COLLISION. They'd give me a pauper's funeral, nothing religious I hope, with a constable and a medical examiner and maybe a pretty local girl in attendance. She'd just be walking by, wonder what all the activity was, and see some guy laid out in a leather vest, jeans, and Frye boots. She'd lean over the coffin, stare a moment, and then a single tear would fall onto his face and I'd think to myself, Why weren't you there when I needed you, with those buxom breasts and blue eyes and that blonde hair, why weren't you comforting me in Oslo, or in Amsterdam, or in London? Is this when you make your appearance, when they've got me laid out here like a pickled pig farmer? I felt another tear, then another – what? Wait a minute! Those aren't her tears, she's not even here! Okay, let's get something straight. I don't care how cold it is or how alone you are, you *don't* cry, understand?

I drove on silently, cursing the Norwegian club owner who'd heard me playing in Amsterdam and offered me a gig in Oslo. It seemed like too good an offer to refuse, but when I arrived, I discovered that the club was closed, the guy was gone, and the gig was deader than the whale blubber that was hanging all over town in the markets. I knocked around for a couple of weeks, watched the weather getting colder by the day, then finally decided to get out while the getting was still good. Now, here I am, under this low and somber sky, watching Stockholm take shape in the distance, wondering what in the name of all that's Ole I'm doing here. Just get me there, okay, and I'll even stop with the stupid jokes. 'Yes,' sighed my imaginary friend as she cuddled into my arm, 'you'd really better.'

I awoke in the parking lot of the Museum of Modern Art the next morning to a sheet of ice covering the inside of the van. The Oriental carpets hanging from the ceiling were frozen stiff. The twelve candles lodged into the inside walls were like rocks. Even the outside of my sleeping bag crackled when I moved. I tried opening the side doors, but nothing budged. Finally I climbed over the front seat, crawled out the window, and fell straight into a three-foot snowdrift.

The Modern Museum was an outpost of warmth in a sea of icicles. The hallways were warm, the cafeteria was warm, even the Kandinskys and Pollocks were warm. I ducked into the bathroom, had a quick shave, combed out the glacier forming in my hair, and treated myself to ten minutes under the electric hand drier. Then I trudged back to the van, where I decided to cook up some vegetables on my butane burner. I had a whole kitchen set up on the 2.3 square feet of space over the rear wheel well. There was a double burner/dish drier, a sci-fi novel/cutting board, a steak knife/nail file, a stew pot/sock drawer, and a very large refrigerator exactly the size of my van. I pulled on some gloves, wrapped a scarf around my neck, zipped up my jacket, and began cutting up potatoes, mushrooms, carrots, and onions. When I discovered that my Jeri can was frozen solid, I filled a pot with snow instead and turned on the burner, and in no time the vegetables began cooking. God, I was clever. Not only was I making a hearty meal, not only was I saving a ton of money – Stockholm was insanely expensive – but I was also warming up my van so nicely that I was even able to take off my gloves a few minutes later. Things were definitely looking up. There is nothing quite like the aroma of potatoes cooking on a chill morning, nothing better to get the olfactory glands stimulated than onions simmering away, nothing likelier to bring a little song to the heart and a whistle to the lips than the sense of man conquering nature.

That's when it started raining. Not outside – rain in Stockholm would've seemed downright tropical – no, it started raining *inside*. The layer of ice that had formed overnight on the walls and ceiling was now melting as if the van had been turned into a Swedish sauna. Which, in fact, it had. The ceiling opened up with a great cloudburst of rain, a veritable downpour that was soaking me, my clothes, the sleeping bag, and anything else unlucky enough to get caught in the squall. Oh, God, how I hate life! Is this really how it's all going to end? Drowning in my own van? FOREIGNER FELLED BY MYSTERIOUS FLASH FLOOD.

No, this simply will not do. I escaped back into the museum, crouched under the hand drier, and thought about Plan B. Oh, right. There is no Plan B. Plan C entailed sneaking into a local supermarket and shoplifting enough cold cuts, cheese, and Swedish rye to get me through the next eight or ten meals. Plan D involved eating quickly enough so that my jaw wouldn't freeze. Plan E centered around coming up with a Plan B.

And then my mouth started to hurt. First it was a general discomfort of the teeth, then sensitive gums, and then excruciating pain in the middle of the night. If I so much as touched my gums with the tip of my finger, they started bleeding profusely and throbbing with pain. 'Oh, God, what am I doing here?' I moaned. I could have gone to Spain or Italy or Greece, like a sensible person, but no, I had to go against the grain – like always – and wind up trapped in Stockholm. I was stuck in a snowdrift called Sweden, and all I could do was dream.

Blue waves gently lapped against the white sands of the

Swahili coast. The sun beat down upon my body and I rolled over for M'bilia to rub a little more coconut oil onto my back. More mango? Sure, I'd love some. See if you can cut the pieces just a little thicker this time. Oh, and the pineapple slices were just divine. We really must take some with us on the sailboat. *Mmmm*, let me just have another bite of passion fruit . . .

'*Aaaaaaaah!*' I screamed as my teeth bit together, sending a jolt of pain through my gums. I awoke to the howling winds of yet another blizzard tearing through the parking lot, then turned on the dome lights and looked into the rearview mirror. I pulled back my lips to see that my teeth were drenched in blood. 'Get me out of here!' I howled, looking like an insane vampire who'd just ingested the wrong blood type.

The next morning, just like every other morning, I stood at the door of the museum, nine o'clock sharp. 'What a devoted lover of the arts!' the staff must have thought as I pushed my way into the exhibits. Truth be told, I'd found an especially warm spot right near a Klee and a heating vent next to a Miró. I slipped into the bathroom, shaved, combed my hair, and tried to brush my teeth, but the bristles of the toothbrush were beginning to feel like a hundred daggers. After the pain died down, I headed for the warmth of Swedish modern art. The ticket clerk greeted me, the guard tipped his hat, and the curator smiled. It was almost like going to work.

I made occasional forays into other parts of town and found a warm bookstore, a cheap coffee spot, and a toasty Christian Science Reading Room. One day, while walking along the cobblestone streets of Gamla Stan, the Old Town, I followed a side street past an ancient fortress, turned down an alleyway, and came upon a pub called Magnus Ladulås. Inside, there were a couple of sad-eyed guys leaning into the bar, nursing beers. One of them looked up at me when I came in. 'How's it goin', bub?' he said with a flat, Midwestern accent.

'Okay, I guess. I'd rather be in Mombasa.'

'You and me both. Anywhere but here.' He put out his hand to shake. 'Curt Lester. One Hundred-Eighth Army Airborne Division. Da Nang. Deserter.'

'Ah,' I said, shaking his hand. 'Glad to meet you.' Sweden was home to several hundred American deserters and draft dodgers who'd been welcomed in protest against the war, and maybe that had something to do with why I was there, to see what kind of country had the guts to stand up to the American war machine.

'Now that you know my whole story, what're *you* doing here?'

'Just traveling, I guess, checking it out.'

'Checking it out? *Hmm*. Have you looked outside?'

'Yeah, it's a little snowy.'

'No, I mean at the people. Have you looked at the people?'

'Well, sure, I mean—'

'Nah, you haven't really looked, I can tell. You haven't looked into their eyes. They're not human, you know.'

'Not human? Who?'

'The Swedes. They're from some alien planet, some piece of jagged rock out past Pluto where the sun never shines and the body temperature is sixty-point-two and the words *love*, *compassion*, and *human kindness* have no meaning.'

'But I thought—'

'Yeah, we all thought. It's bullshit. Hell, I shoulda stayed in the jungle. The Viet Cong at least show a little emotion when they kill you. Here it's just a slow death, living on the dole, sweeping up shit in the subways, bowing and scraping all day long.'

'How can they do that? You're a political refugee—'

'Not to them I'm not, to them I'm nothing but cheap labor. The self-righteous assholes, it's got nothin' to do with morality, it's all political posturing. Hell, the jails are full of Swedes who refused to be inducted into their *own* army.' Curt poured me a beer, and we clinked glasses. I brought the glass to my lips, then recoiled in pain when the cold liquid hit my gums. 'Hey, I know it ain't Heineken,' he said, 'but it ain't *that* bad.'

70

'No, no, it's my gums.' I pulled back my lips for him to see.

'Shit! You been in Nam? You got scurvy, friend.'

'Scurvy!' I said in horror. I didn't know what scurvy was, but it sounded unimaginably horrible. I envisioned my mouth dripping out of my jaw into a pool on the floor, like one of those Dalís in the museum.

'Relax,' said Curt. 'Get some vitamin C in you, and you'll be rid of it in no time.'

'Oh, right,' I said, sucking my mouth back off the floor. 'No big deal.'

A tall, lanky Swede lumbered in, ordered a pitcher of beer, and knocked back a glass in one gulp. He poured a refill, then made his way to a stage at the front of the room, where he sat down at the piano and pounded out a slow blues. I turned to listen. 'That's Per,' said Curt. 'Sweden's Elton John.'

'He's not bad.'

'He's still sober. Come back some night when he's performing and see what you think.'

I glanced around the room, realized that the acoustics weren't half-bad, and decided that's exactly what I would do. I'd come back here and check it out. Just as soon as I stopped bleeding to death.


Three nights later, my gums miraculously healed, I was onstage at the Magnus Ladulås with a ragtag bunch of Swedish musicians. Sten was playing a blues on his Fender Stratocaster, counting out the pattern over and over so as not to miss any of the twelve bars. Jan stood over his stand-up bass, filling in licks that never quite fit. Tomas sat behind the drums, looking terrified, praying that the tempo wouldn't completely escape him. Per was drunk at the piano, playing a few inspired riffs, disappearing into an alcoholic haze, then adding a few chords at just the wrong moment. I held a harmonica against the microphone, waiting for a spot to come in. The club was crowded, and the patrons leaned forward with anticipation. I was, after all, an *American* musician, and they were there to hear the blues the way they were meant to be played. That's right, straight from the cotton fields of Milwaukee, let's give him a big welcome ladies and gentleman, and off I went on a solo. Oh, God, this is horrifying, the rhythm is wrong, the chorus just came in too soon, and Per, what the *hell* is Per doing, that doesn't fit! I closed my eyes, hoping I'd wake up from this nightmare in some nice, cozy bed, but no, this was no dream, I was actually standing there in front of two hundred people, making a total fool of myself.

When the song ended, I cringed, thinking we'd be the targets of boos, catcalls, and perhaps a few empty beer bottles. Instead, there was a moment of silence, then a roar of applause. I looked out at the faces of the audience and couldn't believe what I saw: a roomful of tone-deaf Swedes beaming with joy, stomping their feet in unison, begging for more. I picked up the microphone, waited for the applause to die down, and said, with a bluesman's typical big heart, 'Ladies and gentlemen, that's Tomas Jenson on drums.' Tomas, counting in the next tune, smiled with embarrassment and completely lost the beat. Jan jumped in with a bass line, Sten overlaid a rhythm, Per tossed me a beer, and on we went, playing eleven-bar blues, thirteen-bar blues, getting drunker, missing solos, getting sloppier and sloppier still. By the end of the set, I had nearly collapsed under the piano in a drunken stupor, but this only inspired the audience more. It was just as they'd imagined American blues – a little rough, a little raw, and totally out of control.

I stumbled off the stage and made my way between some tables toward the bar. Per was already there, knocking back yet another beer. When he saw me, he raised his pitcher in a toast, then fell straight backwards off his stool. I leapt over a chair and caught his head just before it hit the floor, but Per looked at me like I was some kind of intruder at a party to which only he had been invited: 'What are you *doing*?' he demanded.

'Trying to save your skull.'

'I *like* to hit my head on the floor,' he said, the words dripping out of his mouth like slow molasses. I saw he was dead-serious and let go. Per's head smashed against the floor. He gurgled a few grunts of appreciation and immediately passed out.

'Here, you'd better put this under him,' came a voice from the next stool over. I looked up to see a woman holding a sweater folded up like a pillow. 'It'll help him sleep it off.'

'You think?'

'No, not really, but at least he might have nicer dreams. You blues musicians don't mind nice dreams, do you?'

'Dreams are okay,' I said, 'we just have to keep reality bleak and hopeless.'

'Yes, I see,' she said, 'that's very healthy.' I raised Per's head, and she propped the sweater underneath. When she leaned down into the light, I could see how pretty she was. She had dark hair, luminous blue eyes, silky skin, and the most perfectly formed head I had ever seen. She held it at just a slight tilt, which gave her a look of inquisitiveness and made her look all the more stunning. Emboldened by the alcohol, I said the first thing that popped into my mind.

'You've got the most beautiful head I've ever seen.'

'What *do* you mean?' she said, raising an eyebrow.

'No-no, it's a good thing,' I quickly added.

'Well, in that case, thank you.'

'And your English, it's nearly perfect.'

'I lived in New York for a while.'

'You know the East Side Bookstore?'

'Sure, on St Mark's Place. I think I've still got a book on hold there.'

'I used to work at the counter.'

She looked at me more closely in the light. 'Funny, you don't look familiar.'

'That's what I said when I looked in the mirror this morning.'

She laughed a little, which I took as a good sign. My fumblings with sophisticated European women, after all, rarely got this far. 'So . . . the blues,' she said. I couldn't quite get a read on what she was thinking.

'Not your cup of tea?'

'No-no, I like all kinds of music. Music that makes me think. Music that connects me to something higher.'

'That's what music does. It gets you high.'

'Yes, it opens something up deep inside,' she said, moving a little closer.

'Sometimes I get so high, I almost fall off the stage.'

She looked at me, disappointed: 'That's not exactly what I meant.' Then, before I knew what happened, she was gathering up her scarf and buttoning her coat. 'Better check on your friend,' she said. By the time I glanced back at her, she was gone.

The van was warmer that night, perhaps because there was more alcohol in my bloodstream than in the antifreeze. I slept so soundly that I missed the opening of the museum. When my eyes popped open at nine-fifteen, I leapt from my sleeping bag and hurried for the door, afraid I might be reprimanded for being late. The ticket taker mumbled something, the security guard furrowed his brows, and the curator *tsk-tsked* as I hurried for the warm Miró. After performing my morning rituals, I made my rounds for the day. First was Konsum Supermarket, where I purchased twenty-four kronor worth of Swedish rye and mayo, and shoplifted sixteen kronor of salami and cheese. With the government tax at 40 percent, I figured we were breaking even. Then it was on to the Christian Science Reading Room to warm my feet, over to the Swedish House of Pancäken for coffee, and back to the museum for the afternoon shift. It seemed like no more than the blink of an eye before I was back on stage at the Magnus Ladulås, only a few blinks more before I was picking Per off the floor again, and another couple of blinks before I was staring at that same pretty girl at the bar. 'Listen, about last night, I'm—'

'Your harmonica playing, it's very good.'

'Yeah, thanks, but I just wanted you to know—'

'That you're not really like that? You shouldn't be ashamed.'

'I'm not ashamed. But I'm not a drunk, either.'

74

'No, I can see you have another side. I can hear it in your playing.'

'I played that last song for you.'

'But how did you know—'

'I saw you sitting over here.'

'In that case, I like your playing *very* much.' The band began tuning up, and the sound of jangling guitar strings reverberated from the stage. 'You'd better go,' she said.

'Will you be here?' I asked. She gave me a quick nod as I headed for the stage. I could no longer see her across the crowded dance floor, but I saw her face every time I closed my eyes to take a solo. I found myself playing a bit faster, as if trying to get through the set so that I could talk to her again. Fifty minutes later, I returned to find nothing but an empty stool at the bar.

I stared into the bathroom mirror of the museum and saw that it was time for drastic action. I hadn't shaved in several days, my hair was getting matted, and the sweat from playing under the hot stage lights was beginning to cake on my forehead. I took a subway to the central station, headed over to the main square, and checked out a few tourist hotels. In the lobby of the Scandic Continental, I slipped between two tour groups and asked the concierge if I could see one of the rooms. He barely looked up as he tossed me a key. I headed straight for the sixth floor, snuck into the room, took a hot shower, and slipped down the back stairs before anyone noticed. Then it was over to Konsum for eighteen kronor to the government and twelve kronor to me, lunch in the van, coffee at the S-HOP, and back to the club. She was there again. 'So, when did you come back to Sweden?' I said, continuing our conversation from the night before as if there hadn't been a moment's break.

'Last year. New Year's day.'

'You're kidding. That's when I left.'

'I flew from New York. There was a big snowstorm—'

'—the biggest in fifty years—'

'—and the flight was twelve hours late—'

'—mine, too—'

Her eyes widened with surprise. 'Not to *London*?'

'TWA to Heathrow. They served weird little dumplings.'

'And Chicken Kiev.'

We sat there quietly for a moment. I knew there was something special about this girl the moment I saw her, but now it was getting downright spooky. How could I have missed her on that plane? Look at all the time we could've been together. 'It seems we have a similar itinerary.'

'Perhaps,' she said, taking a moment to answer before wrapping a scarf around her neck. Then I noticed that she was gathering her coat and purse. She buttoned her coat to the top and turned to me. 'The band is getting better.'

'You think?'

'Maybe I'll come again sometime.'

Our eyes met for a brief second, but I couldn't tell what she was thinking. What was her rush? Did she really have to go? Was there a boyfriend waiting? She gave no clue whatsoever as she headed for the door.

'Who is she?' I wondered as I stood in the checkout line at Konsum the next day. I found myself thinking about her from the moment I awoke that morning. There was something mysterious about her, the way our conversations would start and stop and kind of vanish into thin air. More often it was she who vanished, always without a goodbye, one minute she's there, the next she's not, I don't even know her name, yes, that's my goal for tonight, tonight I'll find out her – '*Ursäkta mig*,' came a voice from behind the counter. '*Jag vill se vad du har i fickorna*.' My reverie was punctured by a stern-faced grocery clerk who stood there staring straight into my eyes. I stared back, uncomprehending. 'Your pockets, I have reason to believe—' Oh, God, I feel small, my parents are watching, I'm sure of it, I have shamed them beyond belief, is this the way I was brought up, to be a common thief, is this why they put me through four years of college, oh, this is really disgusting, I've got nothing to say for myself, well, except for that 40 percent tax thing, but no, he's not gonna buy it, I'm not even sure *I* buy it, okay, I have really fucked up, what do I do now, wait, I've got an idea, I'll run, I'll run like the wind, out that door, across the parking lot, and straight into that snowdrift in the distance, they'll never find me, not until spring, at least, when my body thaws out like some smelly carcass that fell off a meat wagon – CRAZED CRIMINAL CAPTURED IN CHEESE CAPER – okay, think, why don't you, you've got to say something, just standing here in total silence is getting you nowhere, just say something, maybe he's a liberal, he's against the war I'll bet, I'll tell him I was a leader of the protests, the FBI has a file on me a mile long, that's why I did it, it was the FBI, and Richard Nixon, that bastard, that's what made me do it, Nixon and the war and civil rights and marijuana – yes! – I'm a drug fiend, I need help, marijuana, LSD, you name it, they forced me to do it – who? – why, all those out-of-state students in Madison, that's who, I *knew* pot wasn't harmless, look what it's done to me, I swear, this isn't me, not the real me, the real me would never shoplift, the real me would say I need to be punished, the real me would say lock me up and throw away the key, the real me would say: 'Do you take a check?'

The clerk reached into my coat pocket and pulled out a round of creamy Havarti cheese, a bit aged but not too strong, and a firm but not too chewy salami (my teeth, after all) and said: 'I will have you deported!' Okay, maybe that's not so bad, maybe they'll pay, maybe they'll even give me a choice of spots, how about the Swahili coast of Kenya, sure, I could deal with that, except – that girl! The one at the club! I'll never see her again! I don't even know her name! – 'You will be deported and never allowed back into Sweden!'

'Listen, I'm not going to lie to you,' I said. 'I took the cheese, I took the salami, I have no excuse, I'm sorry, I really am, but I think I'm in love with a girl, a Swedish girl, and if you turn me in to the police, you'll be ruining my life and maybe hers, too.'

He stared at me a long moment, glanced at the line of customers who were waiting impatiently, and rang up my bread and juice. 'Enjoy your sandwich,' he said, tossing the cold cuts into my bag.

It took at least fifteen minutes before my knees stopped shaking in my van. All I could think about was that girl, about how close I'd come to never seeing her again. Finally, I started up the engine and drove across town to another supermarket. I walked in, bought twelve kronor worth of food and shoplifted eight, then got out of there as fast as I could. Good, I'd proven to myself that I could still do it. From that moment on, I never shoplifted anything, not even a paper clip, and I never will.

'Listen, I need to know something,' I said to her at the bar that night. 'I need to know your name.'

'Oh? Why is that so important?'

'Because I almost got thrown out of the country today, and I don't even know who you are.'

She looked alarmed – as if maybe she actually cared if we ever saw each other again – but before she could respond, everything around us dissolved in a blur. There was a sudden whoosh of activity, and I don't know how it happened exactly, but we were carried along by the crowd, as if on the crest of a wave, and wound up at the other end of the bar, where Curt was filling our glasses. Then Per rolled down from the stage with another pitcher, and the door burst open as Eva, her best friend, showed up with reinforcements, and then we were dancing and then some more people arrived, Pia and Sigrid from work, Gunnar and Anders from across the street, Tobias and Tilda from I didn't quite catch where, and now we're all dancing and the pitchers of beer are flowing nonstop and I keep looking at her and I think she's looking at me, and now the place is closing and the bunch of us are singing in the street and some are going here and some are going there and Eva's place is free that night and a key is exchanged and the next thing I know I'm driving over a bridge to the south part of the city, turning down a couple of quiet streets, and pulling up in front of Number 7 Svartensgatan.

We barreled in through the doors, trying not to wake the neighbors, and suddenly our conversations of the past several nights all rolled into one and it was as if we'd met for the first time only moments ago – '*Sssssh!* Oh, God, that's the funniest thing I ever saw, you rang the *wrong* doorbell!' 'It's not possible, the *East Side Bookstore*? No, really, sssssh!' 'The shape of my *what*? What *do* you mean?' – we somehow found the apartment, discovered that Eva's key worked much better in her lock than did my car key, and wound up almost immediately in the bedroom. There was a single lamp in the corner of the room with a scarf thrown over it to diffuse the light, and now that we were there, in a quiet room, away from the drunks and the music and the neon signs, the laughter stopped and we stood there just looking at each other. We edged closer and our hands touched slightly. Her fingers were long and thin and fit perfectly inside the palm of my hand. I pulled her toward me and felt the touch of her shoulder along my arm. She looked up slightly. The lamp cast a soft haze over the room and her face looked almost milky, like Ingrid Bergman's in one of those old Swedish black-and-white movies. I suddenly got an insatiable urge to lift her in my arms. 'Oh, my God, what are you doing!' she laughed as I swung her around.

'I don't know. I just have this feeling like I want to carry you somewhere.'

'You're not going to drop me, are you?'

'What do you think?'

'No, I don't think you would. Okay, let's look at Eva's kitchen,' she said, pointing to the door like a scout for the cavalry. I swooped her out of the room and she laughed like a little girl as we headed down the hallway. We dipped through an archway, passed a table and chairs, and swung around the counters. '*Um-hmm*,' she said as she pulled her arms a little tighter around my neck. 'Nice pots, cast-iron pans, clean dishes, very nice indeed.'

'Where to next?' I said, twirling her around.

'I'm not too heavy?'

'You're like a feather.'

'All right, then I'd like you to do something.'

'Name it.'

'I'd like you to pull off my sweater.'

'Without letting you down?'

'Can you do it?'

'Of course I can do it. I'm a harmonica player.'

She lifted herself higher in my arms until I found a button, which I maneuvered with my tongue until it popped through a hole. '*Ooooh*,' she purred, 'you *are* good!' Once I had the buttons undone, I slipped the sweater over her shoulders and let it fall to the floor. She leaned into me at that moment and seemed even lighter than before. I felt I could hold her like that forever as we kissed deeply. She then pointed down the hallway and said, 'Bathroom.' My arms were starting to tire, but I found a second wind as we headed back down the hall. We slipped through the bathroom door and turned so she could inspect everything. '*Um-hmm*,' she said, 'fresh towels, clean tub, lavender soap.' She then grabbed a perfume bottle off a shelf and sprayed some mist into the air, and we kissed again as the tiny droplets descended onto our skin. I started to edge toward the door, but she stopped me. 'Not yet. There's something else you need to do.'

'What's that?'

She motioned to her skirt. I ran my hand up around her waist and over to a zipper, which opened halfway down the back. I slipped my fingers inside a pleat and could feel her skin against my hand as I slowly pulled the skirt down around her hips. 'Bedroom,' she called out with a muffled voice and I could see her pointing again, like a general leading the charge. I carried her back across the hall, kicked the door closed with my foot, and fell onto the bed.

'Any more requests?' I whispered to her.

'Can you play something in A-flat?'

'I don't have my harmonicas with me.'

'I didn't mean on the harmonica.'

I kissed the back of her neck and the inside of her thighs, the strands of her hair and the curve of her breasts, and I began to understand something: This is why I went north instead of south, this is why I drove on icy roads and slept in a freezing van. And now, as she pulled me closer, it felt as if ten months of loneliness were being washed away in one night, as if destiny were interceding on my behalf, as if two pieces of some grand puzzle were miraculously fitting together.

'Annika,' she said.

I looked up at her, not sure what she meant.

'My name is Annika.'

# 6

# Defying Gravity

And that was it. I wound up moving into Eva's spare room, rehearsed with the band most afternoons, played a few nights a week, and spent every other possible minute with Annika, every minute that we could steal from the day. I picked her up at the hospital where she worked, or met her in Gamla Stan, and always felt that same rush of desire whenever she came near. It was as if there were an aura around her, a warm golden field that welcomed me in. 'You're the most beautiful woman I've ever seen,' I would whisper to her. 'You don't mean that,' she would say, turning her head just slightly so I wouldn't see her blush. 'Of course I mean it,' I would insist. 'Well, I'm glad you feel that way, because you're the handsomest man in Sweden,' she would say. 'I'm not even the handsomest man in the band,' I would protest. 'No, but they're all *blondes*,' she would remind me. I'd laugh, she'd give me an exaggerated wink, and we'd kiss again. 'I just can't believe how lucky we are,' I'd whisper to her. 'Look what we've been missing all these years,' she'd whisper back.

The world loves a lover, so the saying goes, but really it's a lover who loves the world. I felt guilty that not everyone could share my joy, because that's what I wanted, I wanted the whole world to feel that tingling sensation, I wanted the whole world to blush slightly, I wanted the whole world to wake up a little late one morning and not care if it was late for work, I wanted the tides to ebb a little later, for the sun to sleep in, for the fields to lie patiently in wait, for the rivers to stretch out and dangle lazily like toes hanging over the edge of a bed.

'Tell me about the town where you were born,' Annika said one day.

'Rice Lake? There's not much to tell. It's a little dot on the map, a hundred miles or so from Canada. I guess it's kind of a vacation spot – fishing and boating, that kind of thing. I don't really remember much about it.'

'It sounds like the countryside in Sweden.'

'Yeah . . . or Russia. That's where my parents were born. My mother's family was supposed to take the *Titanic*, but she got scalded by a pot of boiling water at their going-away party. She was just a baby, so they had to postpone the trip, but it probably saved her life—'

'And yours too.'

'Yeah, maybe so.'

'So, why Rice Lake?'

'Her dad wanted to go to Argentina. He was a carpenter, and his boss had already emigrated and wrote back saying there was good work for skilled craftsmen, but my grandmother had America in mind and said it made no sense to leave Russia if he was just going to become a carpenter again. Plus, she had some cousins who had found a place just like Russia, which turned out to mean that it was cold and snowy and had absolutely nothing going for it.'

'So, let me guess. He became a prominent brain surgeon?'

'Nah, a carpenter. Didn't much matter, though. He died a few years later, anyway. So, now my grandmother's got a couple of kids and no money, and she winds up starting this trapping business. Minks and otters and beavers – she damn near forced an ecological disaster. Those minks didn't know what hit them. They were used to weekend hunters, not this crazed Russian Jewish woman who took no prisoners. You go up to Rice Lake these days, you know what you find?'

'What?'

'No minks.'

83

'I'd like to go there someday.'

'To Rice Lake?'

'Sure.'

'What, with me?'

'Well, I probably wouldn't go up there by myself—'

'No, no, of course not.'

'You really get to know someone when you're on the road. Just being together all the time, it's more intense.'

'Maybe we should go somewhere.'

'I think I'd like that.'

'Then that's what we'll do. We'll go somewhere. Somewhere faraway.'

'Okay.'

Eva had a boyfriend, Jerry, an English musician who played in the subway tunnels, one of those voluble Brits whose ready laugh and quick wit barely disguise an inner rage boiling just beneath the surface. Jerry ostensibly lived with Eva, but he was there less than half the time, and she had long ago stopped asking where he spent all those other nights. Eva didn't have the looks to be choosy and Jerry reminded her of that fact at every possible opportunity. In a joking way, of course, always in a joking way. 'Eva, you old hag! Where's me tea then?' he'd roar.

'Now, Yerry,' she'd laugh in her singsong accent, 'a little patience goes a long way.'

'Eva, old girl, a little of *you* goes a long way, and if you don't shape up, a long way away is where you'll find me.'

'Oh, Yerry, who else would have you?'

'In this frozen hell? They're lining up for a warm body like mine.' Eva laughed as she poured his tea and stirred in a dollop of honey. 'Come then, give us a little massage, will you, pet? Least that way I won't have to see your face over me breakfast.'

Eva looked at me, trying to hide her embarrassment with more laughter. 'Have you ever seen such a demanding man?' she crowed as she began kneading his back.

Jerry suddenly jerked forward. 'Christ! Go easy there,

girl, that's not a load of laundry you're wringing out.'

'Oh, Yerry, Yerry, Yerry . . .'

This would go on for fifteen minutes or so, Jerry would finally make up some excuse to leave, Eva would sing a lilting melody while doing the dishes, then disappear into her bedroom and sob quietly behind the locked door. Eva's one great joy in life was Frederick, a three-foot-long boa constrictor whose cage was the centerpiece of her bedroom. Frederick was in semihibernation and did pretty much nothing except lie there, which was fine with me since I was terrified of snakes. His only exercise, in fact, was on every second Friday when Eva brought Frederick a little snack. I was unlucky enough to be around one day when she arrived with a Chinese take-out carton, opened the flap, and exposed a little live mouse. 'Frederick,' she cooed, 'it's Friday.' She pulled back the glass top of the cage, reached in and petted the snake, made a little space near its head, and dropped the mouse inside. It took Frederick a moment to realize what was afoot, but when he did, all I noticed was a slight widening of his eyes. The mouse, meanwhile, had no idea whatsoever what was going on, and pranced around the cage as if it were checking out its new home. *Hmm*, it seemed to say, that's an interesting pellet over there, a nice little warm spot here, a curious long green thing right there . . .

'Get away!' I whispered to the mouse as it started moving toward Frederick's head. Rooting for the little guy was utterly pointless, of course, as it had no possible escape. I wished for at least one way out, even a million-to-one chance, but Eva wasn't sporting in that way. The mouse turned away and checked out a glass wall, *hmm*, that's awfully smooth, and what's this little twig here, and that little leaf there, and then – *fwap!* – Frederick grabbed the mouse's throat with his fangs, wrapped his coils around its body, and squeezed until the little guy's eyes almost popped out. '*Uggggh* . . .' I groaned, feeling queasy, as Frederick opened his trapdoor of a mouth and slowly began to ingest the mouse. It took a long time going down, first the front feet, then the head, then the body, until there was nothing left but the mouse's tail hanging out of Frederick's mouth like an after-dinner cigarette.

Eva beamed at the snake and either said, 'Very good,' or 'Yerry good,' and I flashed forward a few years, imagining an eight-foot Frederick wrapped around a gasping Jerry, then watched as Eva replaced the lid on the cage, checked the heating coil, and turned off the lights.

Sweden has the highest suicide rate in the world and, as the winter wore on, I began to suspect why. Maybe it was because the sun rose at 10:30 in the morning and set at 10:35. Or because the snow kept piling higher and higher until the sidewalks were four stories high. Or because the temperature is in centigrade, which makes it that much colder. Whatever the reason, as November became December, the Swedes started dropping like flies. One day, when I didn't have exact change at a bakery, the counter girl took out a revolver and shot herself in the head. When I tried to pump my own gas, the guy at the station sucked on my exhaust pipe. When I asked someone directions, he threw himself down an escalator. The whole of Sweden became the set of an Ingmar Bergman film. Wherever I looked, I saw Death with his black cape and gaunt face, Liv Ullmann having a spiritual crisis, and Max von Sydow reliving his tortured past. Now, I understood why Bergman filmed in black-and-white. During winter in Sweden, there are no other colors.

Except for me and Annika. We were bright swatches of red and yellow twirling on the ice. We were a warm cocoon rolling in the snow. We were joy and laughter riding a toboggan that never tumbled.

Not that I exactly knew her. Annika didn't really talk very much and I saw no reason to push things. Talking is over-rated, anyway. It usually leads to more talking, which often leads to much more talking, which frequently leads to arguing, which often leads to yelling, which generally leads to silence, then strained silence, and eventually total silence. No, there was something far more important between us than words: What we had was destiny, this destiny that had brought us together, this destiny that put us in New York together, this destiny that put us on a plane together, this destiny that put us in a little bar in Stockholm together, and if destiny didn't care about all the little details in a person's life, I sure as hell didn't either.

The first time I picked her up from work, Annika glanced around at my harem room on wheels and smiled slyly: 'So, you're into Scheherazade?'

'I'm pretty sure I was an Arab serf in a past life.'

'Why a serf? Why not a king or a prince?'

'Everybody always thinks he was royalty in a past life. I'm more of a realist.'

'Yes. Indeed. A realist . . . I like the rugs. They're on the ceiling, you know.'

'Yeah, I noticed.'

'And the candles, they're in the walls.'

'Right.'

'Should I assume the ceiling fan is on the floor?'

'Only in the summer.'

Annika nodded, as if anticipating that one. 'It's just a wee bit, well, upside down in here.'

'Unless you're lying on your back.'

'*Um-hmm*. That makes sense. I think.'

'Want to see?'

'Okay.' Annika climbed over the seat and plopped down on the bed behind me. 'You're right. It does almost make sense. There's just one thing.'

'What's that?'

'It's a little lonely back here.'

'How about we find a nice quiet spot?'

'How about right here?'

'In the parking lot? What if somebody came by?'

'Yes. What if?' By the time I crawled over the seat, Annika already had her blouse halfway open. 'Warm me up, sweetheart,' she said as she pulled my head to her chest. 'You know what I feel like?' she whispered into my ear. 'Like we're defying gravity.'

'It's like that back here.'

'I wish we could just float away.'

'Maybe we can.'

'Yes,' she said, pulling me closer, 'maybe we can.' Annika ran her fingers over a cloud design on the carpet. 'Look at the sky, it's the color of a ripe peach, all reds and yellows and oranges mixed together, it's like a painter's palette gone drunk from too much sun—'

'The whole world is in these clouds, there's no up or down, no beginning or end—'

'I wish we could live like this forever, just floating and floating, defying gravity—'

'That's why we met—'

'I'm sure of it—'

'On the wisp of a cloud.'

The holidays were upon us. It was a psychological national emergency, with the entire country on suicide watch. Eva was taking things especially hard now that Jerry was showing up less frequently and treating her worse than ever. On Christmas Eve, Annika went to spend the night with her grandmother, and Eva and I were left alone in the apartment. We listened to some Miles Davis and had a few beers, but I could see she was growing more melancholy with each sip. Finally, she retreated into her bedroom, where, a few minutes later, I heard her quietly sobbing. I stood outside the doorway, feeling bad for her, as I had on other occasions, but tonight it seemed worse, with Christmas so close and all, and I decided to try to soothe her feelings. 'Eva, c'mon, don't cry,' I called through the door. 'Things will get better.'

There was a sudden silence, a moment's pause, and then the door opened. Eva looked at me with flushed cheeks. 'You can hear me?'

'No-no – I mean, just a little.'

'I didn't know. I am so embarrassed.'

'There's nothing to be embarrassed about. Lots of people get down at the holidays.'

'Yerry is terrible! How can he disappear like this?'

'Well, you know musicians.'

'But you're not like that.'

'Yeah, well, I've screwed up plenty, believe me. Jerry's, you know, Jerry's a little—'

'Yerry's a shit!' she blurted out. 'He eats my food, he drinks my beer, he spends my money, and he gives nothing in return!'

'Listen, maybe you should think about—'

'Somebody else? Who would have me?'

'That's crazy.'

'Is it? Would you have me?'

'I've got a girlfriend.'

'And if you didn't?'

'I don't know, Eva, I mean, we're friends. . .'

Eva burst into tears. 'You see? Who would have me but Yerry – and Yerry won't even touch me!' She wobbled a little, then fell against my chest. 'I just need someone to hold me—'

'It's okay. I'll hold you,' I said, putting my arms around her.

'Yes, thank you, it feels so good,' she said, snuggling closer. 'You're so kind . . . so understanding.' I felt Eva's hands moving up my back, then brushing against my neck. 'Make love to me,' she whispered. I hoped to hell she was kidding. She pulled closer still. 'Please.'

I immediately pushed her away. 'C'mon, Eva, you know I can't do that.'

'Annika wouldn't mind. She's slept with plenty of guys at the club.'

'What?' It took a moment for the words to register. 'What do you mean?'

'Haven't you heard about Swedish free love?'

I just stood there a moment, imagining Annika in the arms of every guy I ever saw at Magnus Ladulås. 'Maybe I'm not so free.'

'No, but your room in my apartment is free, isn't it?'

'I *thought* it was,' I said, stepping back. 'I can leave anytime.'

'No-no, I didn't mean that.'

'Listen, I'm gonna take a walk——'

'No, please, why not have another beer? Maybe I won't look so ugly.'

'You're not ugly.'

'Of course I am. Yerry can't stand to even look at me anymore. Maybe if you drank all the beers, you could pretend I was Annika.'

'Eva, go to bed. You'll feel better tomorrow.'

'Please,' she said, tugging at my arm, 'just stay with me a few minutes.' She pulled me toward her room and I finally decided to lie next to her until she fell asleep. Once we were on the bed, however, I noticed her breathing getting heavier.

'Listen . . . I'm going to say good-night now,' I said, moving away.

'You can't go!' she said as she moved her hand up my leg. 'Please . . .'

'Eva, I already told you—'

'Must I *beg* you?'

I felt something cold at the pit of my stomach, the cold of Eva's loneliness, the cold of her desperation, and then I felt her lips against my neck, heard her whispering into my ear, and I glanced out the window and saw snow falling against a tree and thought about Annika and thought about Annika and thought about Annika . . .

# 7

## Timing is Everything

'*Fem! Fira! Tre! Tva! Ett!*' everyone screamed as the clock ticked down to midnight. 'Happy New Year!' Annika and I kissed, finished off our second bottle of champagne, and kissed again. Then, before I knew what happened, somebody grabbed her arm, she grabbed mine, I grabbed someone else's, and off we went running like crazy through Sten's apartment. It's a New Year's tradition among Swedes to run through every room in the house in a snake dance, faster and faster, through every door and archway, around and around, back and forth, until suddenly everyone gets tired, and then it's all over, and that's that. Nobody seemed to know if we were casting out spirits or shedding our skins or just getting a year's worth of exercise, but for the Swedes, this constituted some kind of connection with their ancestors, so who was I to question it? We flew through the kitchen and into the living room, the whole bunch of us – Per, red-faced and drunk, Tomas, sweating like crazy, Jan, howling like a banshee – faster and faster we ran, our feet stomping against the hardwood floors, Annika holding my hand, glancing back at me and laughing, and the snake dance sped up even more, we spun around through an archway and Annika turned away and then she turned back and exactly at that instant, as we charged into another room, her head smashed into the door, her knees buckled, and she fell over, unconscious.

I caught her before she hit the ground, but it was ten long

seconds before her eyes blinked open. 'Happy New Year, sweetheart,' she said in a slurred voice. 'Are we home yet?'

'Almost, baby, almost.'

Annika leaned up in my arms, and her eyes cleared a little as she looked around. She then pulled herself closer still, as if to block out everything in the room but her and me. 'Look at the two of us,' she said, 'look how a year ago today we were getting on a plane, and look how something brought us together. I believe in those things, that things happen for a reason, and I don't know why we had to wait all these years before finally crossing paths, and I don't know why I had to come back to Sweden for it to happen, but I think that's why I'm here and I think that's why you're here, and I just want to thank destiny or fate or God or whoever for bringing us together, and that's all I want to say.'

'I love you, Annika.'

'I love you, too,' she said. And then she passed out.

As we crossed the bridge that night through a light sprinkling of snow, I thought about how lucky I was, how this tumultuous year in Europe had all been worth it, how I was happier than I could ever remember. Images from the past twelve months flickered between the irregular swipes of the windshield wipers – images of New York receding from an airplane window on New Year's Day, of London yawning in an endless sprawl, of Amsterdam awakening to the spring thaw, of Oslo nestled into the rolling hills. Annika was sound asleep in the seat next to me, her head snuggled into my arm, and I thought about how life was suddenly promising, how leaving Berkeley had been the right decision, how the future was looking better than ever. Europe had shown me another way to live, a more humane way, and the protests and the riots and the smell of teargas were now nothing but remote memories. I kissed Annika's forehead, thanked my lucky stars, and drove off into the beautiful snowy night.

I dropped Annika off at work early the next morning, stumbled into Eva's apartment, and glanced into her room.

Something seemed wrong. Very, very wrong. '*Where's Frederick?*' I screamed.

The panic in my voice awoke Eva from a deep sleep. 'What? What?' she said, trying to focus her eyes.

I stood outside her room and pointed in panic. 'The cage! It's open! The top is pushed back!'

Eva didn't seem all that concerned. 'Bad boy, Frederick,' she said in a scolding voice. 'Where have you gone *this* time?'

'This isn't the *first* time?'

'No, no, he pushes the glass back when he gets curious, or bored, or . . . *jealous*,' she said, playfully grabbing me.

'Don't fuck around, Eva. You gotta find him.'

'He'll turn up. He's probably wrapped around a warm pipe somewhere.'

'Shit. You see, this is what we get. It's like Adam and Eve or something. I can't believe I cheated on Annika.'

'You think God is punishing us? You think God pulled back the top so that Frederick could come out and kill you?'

'Yes, Eva, that's *exactly* what I think.'

'When I was a child,' said Annika, 'I found a little sparrow right over there with one of its wings all crushed.' We were walking through her favorite park and had stopped at a clearing beneath some conifer trees. 'It looked at me with panicky eyes as I picked it up, but then, when I cupped it into my hands, it relaxed and no longer tried to get away. I carried this little bird all the way home, then snuck it into my room and laid out a little thimble of water and a few crumbs of bread. When my mother came home, she heard a strange peeping sound and found the sparrow under my bed and said, 'Who knows what diseases it might have?' When I held it in my palm, she finally relented and helped me make a little bed with soft cotton and a place for the bird to rest its wing and even a little pillow for its head. When I awoke the next morning, the bird was chirping, and I could tell how happy it was to be with me, and I gave it more bread and filled the thimble with water and told it to be good while I was away at school. I ran home as fast as I could that afternoon and rushed into my room, and there was the bird, lying in its bed, its wing rolled back under its side, its head against the pillow, dead. When my mother came home to find me crying, she couldn't explain why the sparrow had died or why everything was so unfair or why God would hurt something so innocent. She came with me as I cupped the bird in my hands, retraced my steps to this spot, and buried the little sparrow under a few feet of dirt, just where I'd first found it. I tried to sing a hymn from church, but I couldn't remember the words so we just hummed the melody until it got dark, and then she said, 'Honey, we have to go,' and we walked across the park, turned up the street, and took the long way home.'

'Are you a little sad, Annika?'

'Maybe a little.'

'God, this is a long winter.'

Stockholm became as quiet as a Swedish joyride. The days became shorter, the nights longer, and I began succumbing to the inevitable darkness. On one particularly dreary morning, I awoke to a strange sensation, a throbbing, existential angst that reached right down to the tips of my toes. I wearily opened my eyes. *Aaaaaaaaah!*' I screamed. Frederick was wrapped around my foot, his tongue flicking against my big toe, and he was getting ready to ingest me, that's what he was doing, he was opening that big gaping mouth of his and planning to suck me down whole, from the big toe on up. THREE-FOOT SNAKE EATS SIX-FOOT FOREIGNER. '*Evaaaaaaaaaa!*'

'What! What!' she yelled, rushing in. When she saw Frederick, she jumped for joy. 'Frederick! Thank God! Where have you been?'

'Get him off me!'

'Don't be so nervous. You're scaring him,' she said as she bent down to pet him. '*Oooh*, Frederick, you're so smart. How did you know it was Friday?'

Frederick glared at me, still clinging onto my foot for dear life, while his tongue darted back and forth, leaving little word balloons in the air: 'Repent!' 'Adulterer!' 'Repent!'

I couldn't believe it. The little jerk had digested my guilt and was throwing it up right into my face. 'All right! Get off of me!' I beseeched him. 'I'll do anything!' Eva finally pried him off my foot, hugged him like a favorite child, and coiled him back into his cage. I waited until she left for work, then snuck into her bedroom, checked to make sure the glass top was closed tight, and tapped on the side. '*Ohhh*, Fred-er-ick,' I cooed, bending down to get eye to eye with him. 'C'mon, shithead, wake up and listen to me. Okay, I was wrong to sleep with Eva, I admit it, and I promise – oh *boy*, do I promise – to never sleep with her again. And I just want you to know that I'm gonna tell Annika everything, deep down I always wanted to tell her anyway, I'm actually looking forward to clearing the air, I owe it to her, I owe it to the relationship, if I've learned one thing, it's that relationships are doomed without honesty, so this little thing between us, Fred – can I call you Fred? – this *pressure*, this *tension*, this scaly, reticulated, all-consuming *hatred* that you have for me, maybe we can just cool it, know what I mean, 'cause I'm gonna do what's right, I'm gonna tell her what happened. Okay? – Fred?'

'Flowers? For me?' said Annika when I picked her up from work that night. 'How nice!'

'They're tulips. From Holland.'

'Yes, I see. There's a little tag here that says: TULIPS FROM HOLLAND.'

I pulled onto the road and headed for Gamla Stan. 'Do you like tulips?'

'Of course. Who doesn't like tulips?'

'I don't know. I suppose nobody. They're from Holland.'

'Yes, so they are. So . . . what's the occasion?'

'No occasion.'

'I see. Well, that's kind of an occasion in itself, your buying me tulips for no occasion.'

'Yeah, it's a good thing I don't do it too often—'

'—because then it wouldn't be an occasion.'

'Did I mention they're from Holland?'

'I thought you said Yugoslavia.'

I impulsively pulled over to the side of the road. 'I have to tell you something.'

'Yes, I thought so.'

'I slept with Eva.'

Annika didn't react for a moment. She just sat there, staring straight ahead. 'I see,' she finally said. 'You make an interesting couple.'

'Annika, please, it's not like that. She needed somebody. It was just before Christmas, she was completely bummed out—'

'And you were nice enough to volunteer? That's very generous of you.'

'C'mon, you know I'm not attracted to her. The only way I could even do it was by pretending she was you.'

'*Jävla förbannade*,' she said under her breath. I didn't know what that meant exactly, but I remembered her saying it once when she accidentally cut herself with a knife.

'It was a stupid thing to do.'

Annika shook her head, then shrugged. 'It's okay. It just teaches me where the limits are.'

'What do you mean, limits?'

'To how far I can trust you. To how far things can go between us.'

'Annika, I don't want there to be limits—'

'Here,' she said, handing me the flowers, 'you didn't need to give me these.'

'I *wanted* to give you these.'

'No, you wanted to soften me up.'

I leaned back in the seat, feeling lousy, looking out at the dreary sky. It was nearly pitch-black. 'God, this is a grim place.'

'Is it finally getting to you?'

'I don't know, sometimes I wonder what I'm doing here.'

Annika looked at me coldly. 'I figured it was only a matter of time. Isn't that what always happens? Things start to go bad?'

'Yeah, I guess so,' I said, suddenly feeling like I was walking into a trap. 'We're, uh, talking about Sweden, right?'

'You tell me.'

'Wait a minute, you're twisting everything around. I just wanted to have a clean slate.'

'So, now it's my fault?'

'Of course not. I didn't say that.'

'Am I not being understanding enough?'

'C'mon, Annika,' I blurted out, 'it's not like you haven't slept with half the guys at the club.' There was an instant of silence in which I could see the words crashing into each other like a ten-car pileup.

Annika slowly turned and fixed me with a stare. 'Not when I was *with* somebody.'

I avoided her gaze and backtracked as best I could. 'Look, I don't even know how we got into this argument.'

'Then let me remind you. You were saying you weren't sure what you were doing here. So, maybe you should leave.'

I felt things spinning out of control. I was a kid in the schoolyard being challenged to a fight. I had to defend myself. I heard myself saying: 'Yeah, maybe I should. If I wasn't snowed in—'

'There's always the train.'

'Believe me, if I had the money,' – I glanced at the tag on the flowers and blurted out the first place that came to mind – 'I'd be on the first train to Amsterdam.'

Annika dug into her purse and pulled out a wad of bills. 'Well, now you do.'

'*What?*'

'I just got paid. Buy yourself a ticket.'

I pushed her hand away. 'C'mon, Annika—'

She shoved it back. 'Take it. I insist. We *both* need a vacation.'

'Annika, I am *not* going to Amsterdam.'

# 8

# One-Upmanship

The train to Amsterdam plowed through the snowdrifts of Sweden, across the ferry to Denmark, and into the industrial valleys of Germany. I ran over and over in my mind what had happened with Annika, and not a bit of it made any sense. Could she really be jealous of Eva? It wasn't possible. All I knew was that those feelings of love and warmth and belonging were suddenly replaced by belching black clouds of waste spewing from the smokestacks outside my window. The Ruhr Valley reminded me of World War II, World War II reminded me of Vietnam, Vietnam reminded me of Berkeley, and suddenly I felt cold and alienated and not quite so welcome in Europe anymore.

When we pulled into Amsterdam, it was still the dead of winter, but for the Dutch that was just a little blip on the horizon. They were as exuberant as ever, drinking, screwing, getting stoned, sprucing up the red-light district for the spring tourists. I headed for the Oudezijds Achterburgwal, a canal running past the whorehouses, a scruffy canal upon which my friend Robert had recently purchased a fixer-upper houseboat. The water was frozen solid, and the boat just sat there like a hulking piece of iron crammed into the ice. The pipes were cracked, the toilet didn't work, the heater was broken, and the windows in the steering cabin wouldn't close. When I arrived, Robert was in his usual panic, trying to fix something – *anything* – on the boat before his whole life sank. 'Quick, throw me that bar!' he barked as I climbed down a ladder from the captain's quarters.

'What, this one?'

'This one, that one, it doesn't matter, c'mon, hurry up, before the wall caves in.'

'Shit, okay, here.'

'*Fuck!*' he screamed as he tried jamming it into a space half the size of the bar.

'Try this one!' I yelled, tossing him a shorter length.

'No-no-*no*!' he cried out, slamming the bar against the floor.

'Maybe this'll work,' I called to him, throwing him yet another length.

Robert let the bar sail right past him. It clanked against the steel hull, sending an echoing tremor through the boat. 'Fuck it, it doesn't matter,' he said, dropping the original bar from his hand. 'I think it's stabilized for now.'

I looked around the creaking hull. 'You sure?'

'Nothing on this boat is sure. What are you doing here?'

'Well, I thought if you had the room—'

We heard a sizzling sound on the other side of the boat. '*Fuck!*' yelled Robert as he lunged over to a double burner that was precariously balanced on some boxes. On the burners were two huge vats of wax that were in danger of igniting. 'Quick, throw me that mold!'

'What, this one?'

'This one, that one, it doesn't matter. C'mon, c'mon—'

I shoved an oblong, star-shaped mold beneath the burner as Robert grabbed the sides of a pot. He poured some wax into the mold, splashing half of it onto the floor, then jammed a wick down the middle.

'You're making candles?'

'I gotta pay for this tub of rust somehow, don't I? I'm glad you're here. You can help.'

'Yeah, well—'

'It's a rough business, this candle thing. They're busting my balls on the paraffin, the dyes can kill you, and the competition is murder.'

'Really? Who'd of thought—'

'I either gotta scale down or go really big. What do you think? You were always good at business.'

'I don't know, going big looks iffy, and scaling down, well—'

'The funny thing is, I really like doing it. I mean, sure, I get my share of rejects—'

'You're making bum candles?'

'Who cares? I just remelt them. Just so long's they don't explode.'

'Uh-huh, well, I've got to say, you do look happier than before.'

'You think?'

'No question about it.'

'You like the boat?'

'Yeah. It's you.'

'Really?' Robert smiled, then thought things over. 'Fuck you. You can stay one week.'

Robert had a little thing for Kathy, whom he knew from college, but Kathy was married to Jerry, so that made it difficult. Jerry and Kathy were one-third of a roving light show that backed up all the bands that came through Amsterdam. Jerry had a little thing for Lois, but that was also tricky because Lois was married to Michael and they were another third of the group. Michael, in turn, had a thing for Leila, but that was *really* tricky because Leila was married to Walter and together they made up the final third of the light show. Not that the six of them were elitist, no, they each had other little things for people outside the group. Michael was quite taken by an Israeli beauty who hung around the projectors, while Lois had a fling with Robb, a surrealist/anarchist/dadaist poet. Then there was Fantuzzi, a Puerto Rican musician who blew through town, Charlie, Luek, Victor, and God-knows-who-else on the fringes of the circle. This is where I went – to this incestuous cesspool, this pit of sexual intrigue, this cauldron of roiling emotions – this is where I went to figure things out.

\* \* \*

Robert's boat used to haul coal, shanks of meat, and wheels of cheese through the canals, but now, with its engine kaput and its body less than seaworthy, the captain of the *Wilhelmina* was happy to part with it for five thousand gulden. Thrilled beyond belief, in fact. He convinced Robert how comfortable the old tub could be once a nice floor was laid and walls erected, yes, the place could be absolutely *gezellig*, warm and cozy and romantic, and that sold Robert, who was surely a romantic at heart, and he went right out and bought some Belgian rugs. The rugs added such a nice touch, he forgot all about the floor and walls, not to mention the cheese rinds and meat hooks that were hanging all over the place. Lying there in the soot-filled corner of the hull, the boat creaking in the ice, I was reminded of my van in Stockholm and a tremor rushed through my body – shit, I'm *alone* again – and for a moment I wondered if Sweden had been just a dream, that girl, the one I met one night in that club, she never really existed, did she, of course not, that kind of happiness never happens in real life, I should've known, I'm not destined for that kind of happiness, I'm basically a loner at heart, only in some cruel dreamworld would I meet a girl like that – *wait* a minute, that wasn't a dream, wake up, why don't you, she was real, she was there, she's there right now, she's waiting for you, you should call her, you should send a telegram, you should write, you should apologize, you should beg her forgiveness, you should be on the next train back, you should get down on your hands and knees, this is the kind of woman you die for, this is the kind of woman you live for, hell, this is the kind of woman who could have your baby . . .

Robert's personality filled the boat. He was infuriating, maddening, and incorrigible, but there was something un-deniably attractive about him, a certain unique quality that pushed against the grain. He was always looking for some-thing completely contrary to latch onto and was currently devoted to *One-Upmanship*, Stephen Potter's satire on how to acquire, maintain, and wield power. It was, in other words, a self-help book for assholes. Satire or no satire, Robert figured there was no better place to practice the art of the power play than in Amsterdam, where everyone else was trying to lose the competitive spirit and live in harmony. He learned where to position himself in a room in order to get a psychological edge, seated his guests in wobbly chairs to give them feelings of insecurity, and mastered the power handshake, the power greeting, and the power stare. Robert began to see himself not as the captain of a sinking ship, but as the admiral of a fleet, and as far as I was concerned, all of Amsterdam was in danger of being sacked and pillaged.

With his newfound confidence, Robert started a sideline business to complement his candles. Candles and plane tickets, that's what he was into – a curious choice that went together like, well, candles and plane tickets. I came back one day to find a phone line strung over the canal, a rickety catwalk that led up to the deck, and two customers squeezed into the tiny steering cabin with Robert. 'Okay, sounds fine,' said a guy with an English accent. 'We'll just leave you the money and pick up the tickets tomorrow.'

'Good, good,' said Robert, 'but I just want to show you the train schedules out of New York – you're going to Chicago, right? That's where I'm from. You know anyone there? I got plenty of friends, my parents even, you could give them a call if you need a nice meal, and how about Detroit, nobody goes to Detroit, there's a train out of Chicago every afternoon, gets you in around ten, you might like it there, Motown, Berry Gordy, Marvin Gaye, they're all there. Of course Minneapolis is good, a little safer, let's see, there's an express at eight, gets you there four the next morning, that's not bad, my sister is there but we don't talk, still she might talk to *you*, just don't tell her I sent you, but let's consider some other places, there's Des Moines, Sioux Falls, Fargo, Laramie, Salt Lake – hey, wait, wait, where are you going?'

The door to the cabin swung open and the British couple hurried out. 'We just need to think about it a little longer—'

'Okay, well, I'm here till midnight,' he called after them.

The couple passed me on the side of the canal and never looked back. '*Fuck!*' yelled Robert when they were out of earshot. 'What assholes! You try to help somebody, look what happens.'

'I think maybe you oversold them.'

'What do *you* know about it?'

'I'm just saying. They were handing you the money one minute and diving into the canal the next. They probably figured you were gonna pull up anchor and float off with their money.'

Robert clenched his heart. 'I need a herring.' He left me there to answer the phone and ran down to a fish stand on the corner for a herring and a pickle. Robert loved herrings and pickles. He said the herrings calmed him down and the pickles picked him up. When he got back, I made the mistake of mentioning that I missed Annika. Robert didn't have time to worry about my love life, especially when I mentioned that Annika and I were real equals. '*Equals?*' he bellowed pulling Potter's book off the shelf. 'There's no such thing as equals! Relationships are defined solely by power, and in every couple there's a winner and a loser. Which do you want to be?'

'I don't want to be either. I think you're full of it.'

'Oh, really? Think back to every relationship you've ever been in. Who does the dishes? I'll tell you who – the one who gets dumped in the end.'

'That's ridiculous.'

'Is it? Well, I've never done dishes and I've never been dumped.'

'You've never *had* a relationship, Robert, and you've never *owned* any dishes.'

'What do you call these?' he said, holding up a bag of styrofoam cups and saucers. 'The point is, she needs to know who's in control. Right now, you're in the worst possible position. You left her for a little vacation, that's good. That could have been *very* good. Except for one thing. *She* paid! Do you have any idea how weak that makes you? She fucking pulled a classic on you, and you didn't even realize it!'

'Listen, leave me alone. I've got to write her a letter.'

'You're going to *write* to her?' he said with equal parts disbelief and condescension. 'Are you out of your mind?'

'Oh, God, here we go . . .'

'Ten-to-one she read Potter's book. Oh, she's a master, all right – you're in deepest shit – and *this* is your reaction? You're going to *write* to her? What're you gonna say? "Oh, baby-baby, I miss you so much, I can hardly wait to see you, I think about you every night, I can hardly wait to get back to Stockholm to do the dishes"? No, you're not gonna say that, I won't *let* you say that, not as long as you're staying on my boat.'

'So, what do you think I should say?'

'You should say absolutely nothing. You shouldn't write one word. That's what Potter would do. He'd make her crawl, especially after pulling that ticket stunt. She's a clever one. You have to make her start wondering if you met somebody else, if you're having such a great time, you've completely forgotten about her, or if you're dead – that's better still, she should be so miserable that she's wearing black all the time, planting little flowers in the snowdrifts, crying herself to sleep every night. You've got to teach her a lesson.'

'For what? Sending me to Amsterdam? That's her crime?'

Robert looked at me and just shook his head. 'People like you, when they lock them up, they take away their pens and pencils. You know why? Because you might write some love letter you'll never live down for the rest of your life. You should thank your lucky stars I'm here, my friend, because I'm clearing out every pen on the boat. Consider your writing privileges revoked.'

'I didn't realize I had been officially committed to this institution.'

'You'll thank me for this one day.'

'No, I won't.'

'Of course you will.'

I wasn't listening to Robert, but I knew there was a kernel of truth to what he said. Even though I'd precipitated the whole mess with Annika, I kept thinking she'd overreacted to the situation. Okay, she needed some time apart, fine, then that's what she'll get. Somewhere, in the back of my mind, I felt that if I stayed away long enough, she *would* somehow love me all the more. As for the letter, well, Robert was totally crazy. I'd write to her first thing tomorrow.

There was just one thing: The tiniest, thinnest shred of doubt had entered my mind. I'd been awfully happy in Stockholm, happier than I could ever remember, and that made me uneasy. Happiness isn't really my thing, it's not like God put me here to be in a state of harmony and bliss, no, I was here, I'm pretty sure, to be tortured a little more than most, maybe to make up for something really unspeakable I'd done in a past life, or to be punished for something I was still about to do (God, after all, isn't necessarily subject to the laws of time and space, especially since those laws are all wrong anyway), and wouldn't it be just like God to punish me for something I hadn't even done yet, how's *that* for all-powerful perversity, so this happiness business with Annika – now that I'm a thousand miles away, I really do need to reexamine things, I mean, when you get right down to it, I hardly know her, maybe I was just so happy to get out of that freezing van I would've fallen for anybody that night, hell, maybe I would've even fallen for Eva if I'd met her first, yeah, Eva's not so bad, and one thing I know for sure, she wouldn't have tossed me out for some minor indiscretion, no, I could probably be just as happy with Eva, especially given that my happiness quotient only goes to eight anyway, and that's when it's on full bore, pedal to the metal, whereas I've seen plenty of other people who seem to *idle* quite nicely right around nine, no, nine isn't in the cards for me, and to tell the truth, even eight makes me a little nervous, my dad, after all, hits eight, and he's only warming up, and I sure as hell don't want to follow him down *that* road, no, eight is tops for me, I always make sure of that, I've got this little internal governor that kicks in at eight and caps it off, okay, so this thing with Annika, I have to consider the possibility that I've rushed rather wildly into this whole relationship, a relationship that, when you get right down to it, seems to be based on the fact that she may or may not have a book on hold in a bookstore I may or may not have worked in on a day she may or may not have been there. Yeah, I definitely gotta think this over. This happiness thing is way overrated, anyway.

When Robert became too unbearable, I moved in with Michael and Lois on their Amstel River houseboat. I awoke each morning to Van Morrison's *Astral Weeks* on the record player. *Astral Weeks* played over and over, not because they didn't have other albums, but because there was no point in listening to other albums. *Astral Weeks* was the culmination of music, a dreamworld of slip streams, high-flying clouds, and gardens misty wet with rain, of rainbow ribbons, sweet summertimes, and the click-clacking of high-heeled shoes.

One morning, I awoke to a strange silence. There was no Van Morrison. There was no record player. There was no Lois. She'd packed up and run off with Fantuzzi to Spain. Michael seemed okay with it – the Israeli girl was already there – but I suddenly realized that if Lois could leave Michael, Annika sure as hell could leave me. I walked outside and discovered that the canals had melted, the flowers were in bloom, and the early Dutch spring had settled in over the city. With it, a great fog lifted off my head: What the hell am I doing here, I've been in Holland for five weeks, have I lost my mind, oh, shit, what was I thinking, okay, calm down, maybe it's not too late, she'll still take you back, just get it together, I'll say some quick good-byes, I'll buy her that sexy velveteen skirt I saw in the window on Leidsepleine, I'll get some pot for the trip back, I'll pack my stuff, I'll get on the night train, shit, what about the pot, you never know about borders, especially when they see you're coming from Amsterdam, okay, what am I gonna do, c'mon, the train is leaving pretty soon, think, why don't you, just think for once in your life—

'I've got the perfect thing,' said Robert when I showed up

on his boat on the Oudezijds Achterburgwal. 'How about we put it inside one of these?' He held up a candle that had great bursts of color swirling around like comets.

'That's not a bad idea,' I said. 'Can you, *uh*, make one look professional?'

'What do you think I've been doing here,' he bellowed, 'running a retread factory?'

'No, no, I'm just saying. You know, to put in the wick and everything.'

'I'll put in the wick . . . I'll put in ten wicks, okay?'

'One is fine.'

Robert fired up his burners, threw in a block of wax, and picked out a starburst mold. 'Hey!' he yelled over to me from behind the bubbling paraffin.

'What!'

'Good luck with the chick.'

I looked over at him and we shared a little smile. I was happy to see that the herrings had finally kicked in. 'Thanks, Robert,' I said, 'it was good to see you again.'

'You, too,' he said as the paraffin began to boil out over the pot and onto the floor. 'Glad I could help.'

# 9

## The Downside of Up

The train to Stockholm passed through tulip fields blossoming beneath azure skies, but heading north into Germany was like turning back the calendar. The vegetation dried up, little patches of snow appeared, and low, somber clouds rolled in. By the time we hit Denmark, it was back to the middle of winter. The passengers were all bundled up in thick coats, the windows fogged over in the icy wind, and mounds of snow were piled along the tracks. I slumped back against my seat, watching the Technicolor dissolve to stark black-and-white.

Fourteen hours out of Amsterdam, the train pulled into Helsingør, Denmark, where it was transported by ferry across a tiny stretch of the Baltic Sea to Helsinborg, Sweden. I was surprised when an immigration officer boarded the train – they rarely check within Scandinavia – but he wasted no time making it down the aisle to where I was sitting. He checked my passport, saw that I was coming from Amsterdam, and immediately emptied all of my belongings onto an empty row of seats. The other passengers turned back with morbid curiosity to watch the search as he unwrapped one of my presents and pulled out a velveteen skirt. Then he opened my box of harmonicas and looked carefully at each one. Next he tore apart another present, pulled back the wrapping paper, and stared at a candle wick that poked out. 'You're under arrest,' he said.

'What?' I said, my heart sinking as a hundred thoughts

raced through my mind. Maybe I could pretend I didn't understand him, I mean, there's no law that says I've got to speak English, I speak Russian, that's what I'll tell him, my parents were from the old country and we always spoke Russian at home and I never learned the local lingo, no, that's ridiculous, the guy's gonna get even more suspicious, he'll probably think I'm a spy, what would I be doing with an American passport anyway, yes, definitely a spy, I smell an international incident brewing, the U.S. embassy's gonna take one look at me and say, nope, he's not ours, the Russians are gonna furrow their big bushy eyebrows and pass on the rare opportunity to welcome home one of their own, and I'm gonna be stateless, trapped on a five-mile stretch of the Baltic, neither American nor Russian, Danish nor Swedish, no, I'll have to ride back and forth on this god-damn ferry until somebody decides whose jail to put me in, but, of course, with my luck, it'll be the Swedes, I already know how full of shit they are with the deserters, sure, they'll lock me up nice and tight in one of their oh-so-modern sterile cells, oh, God, I can't do it, it's gonna be as clean as my mother's house, they'll make me pick up my socks and clean the sink, after all what would visitors say if they saw a mess, but I'm not gonna have visitors anyway so what's the difference, no, wait, I've got it, I'll tell them I'm Indian, Potawatomee Indian from up near Rice Lake and these are my sacraments, do you realize how oppressed my people are, screw those deserters, they're a bunch of fucking ingrates, no, it's us Potawatomees who should be given political asylum, it's been two hundred years of abuse, the white man killed our buffaloes, they stole our land, they made us into mascots for their baseball teams, and for what, you might ask. 'For what?'

'For importing harmonicas.'

'*What?*'

The immigration officer pointed to sixteen harmonicas, all neatly packed together. 'What's this?'

'I *play* harmonica. Look at them, they're all in different keys.'

The officer tossed the candle onto the seat and examined the key signatures embossed on the metal plate of each harmonica. I breathed a sigh of relief, but just then a second immigration officer showed up and with him was a sleek black Labrador retriever – what's *with* these people? Do they think I'm Timothy Leary or something? – and the dog goes straight to my stuff and starts sniffing around my pants, my shoes, my shaving cream, and my toothpaste, and then he moves toward the candle. 'Good dog, good dog,' I whispered, hoping he understood Potawatomee. He took a deep sniff, wrinkled up his nose, and looked at me. His tail stopped wagging. I looked into his eyes. 'Wag your tail, wag it,' I said telepathically. 'It's just marijuana, for God's sake. You want me to do three-to-five for some lousy African pot? Wag your tail, I command you!' The Lab opened his mouth and a big, sloppy tongue hung out. He took another whiff of the candle, his eyes mellow and languid, and then, miraculously, he started wagging his tail. The immigration men, greatly disappointed, led him away when the ferry reached shore, but the dog looked back at me and, I'm almost certain, gave me a big wink. He looked totally stoned.

The skies got darker, the snow deeper, and the weather colder as the train headed farther north. Staring out the window, I had an overpowering feeling of going in the wrong direction. I'd left the joyful spring of Holland to return to the depressing winter of Sweden and I felt the life completely draining out of me. When the train pulled into Stockholm, everything seemed even grayer and more dour than when I'd left. People were lined up along the tracks, waiting to jump in front of the next locomotive. The only thing that kept me from joining them were my thoughts of Annika. I couldn't wait to see her.

No one was home when I got to Eva's apartment – no one except Frederick, that is, who was sleeping that sound sleep of smug moral superiority. I thought for a moment about flushing him down the toilet, but gave up on the idea when I realized I could never fit his cage through the pipes – and I sure as hell wasn't going to pick him up with my bare hands. The spare bedroom where I'd been staying looked smaller than I remembered. The apartment looked darker. All of Stockholm, in fact, looked both smaller and darker. I waited half an hour, then called Annika's number, figuring she'd be getting home from work right about then. I was right. She answered on the sixth ring, a little out of breath. '*Godag*.'

'Hi. It's me.'

There was silence on the other end, then a cool voice. 'I'm sorry, who is this?'

I could immediately see I was in trouble. 'I just got back. Can you come over?'

'Oh, yes, of course, now I remember. The harmonica player. You were going on vacation or something.'

'Listen, I'm sorry. I got a little hung up down there.'

'Amsterdam, isn't that where you were going?'

'I was going to write, but you know what happens.' I was sounding lamer by the minute. Annika had managed to pop my five-week-long balloon of illusion in a few quick seconds.

'Of course. Oops, that's the doorbell. Gotta run.'

'C'mon, Annika, don't do this to me. I've got to see you.'

'Well, I'm busy tonight. Maybe some other time.' The phone went dead.

Busy? Who could she be busy with? How could I have left her alone with all those psychotic drunks and deserters and draft dodgers? Who was she fucking? Curt? Per? Tomas? I spent the whole night imagining her in the arms of every guy who had ever ogled her at Magnus Ladulås. Why had I stayed away so long? Why hadn't I written her? What was I *thinking*?

'Well, look who's back!' said Eva when she arrived hours later. We hugged – a very *cursory* hug – and sat opposite each other in the living room. 'We thought you'd gone forever.'

'What, and give up this climate?'

'I was telling Yerry just the other day that you were probably in Spain by now, but Yerry said a broken-down musician like you would never just leave his van up here.'

111

'Good old Yerry,' I said as I pulled a box out of my ruck-sack and handed it to her.

'What? For me?' Eva excitedly unwrapped the paper and held up a bottle of Dutch gin. 'Oooh, *Genever*. How did you know?'

'Wild guess. So . . . have you seen Annika?'

Eva's expression suddenly changed. 'Annika?'

'Dark hair, blue eyes, about five-five . . .'

'Yes, Annika. No, I haven't seen her. Not really.'

'Well, either you have or you haven't.'

'Yes, well, I don't remember exactly.'

'*Uh*, Eva? Is something going on?'

'Going on? What could be going on? No-no, I wouldn't know. Certainly not.'

'Because I just called her—'

'I'm sure it's nothing.'

'—and she—'

'Nothing at all.'

'Okay.'

Leaving Sweden had been a mistake, but coming back was even worse. Annika didn't answer her phone over the next few days. She didn't go to Magnus Ladulås. She didn't show up for work. I walked the streets of Gamla Stan, having dug my own grave and filled it with ice, slush, and freezing rain. Why had I stayed away so long? Why hadn't I written her? Was I crazy? More snow fell and my van was completely buried. Soon, the houses would be buried, then the shops and office buildings, before long the whole country would be buried, everything except for the tip of one radio transmitter, where the last human would weakly broadcast his dying words: 'What was I *thinking*?'

A letter came one day, like a bolt from the blue, like a Midwestern thunderclap, like eight glasses of premium Milwaukee beer. It was from my parents and boy have we got news for you! We're coming to Europe! A five-city tour! We'll meet you in Paris! In three weeks! Or else!

Let's see, it's early spring, it's that time of the year, it can

112

only mean one thing: Dad has completely wigged out, oh, yes, he's really done it this time, he's bringing his mania overseas, I'm *really* smelling international incident this time, do they even give shock treatments in Europe? No, I simply won't go, I'll say I never got the letter, or I'll convince them the exchange rate is prohibitive these days, or how about if I mention strange stirrings from the Eastern Bloc, wait, I've got it, I'll warn them of some deadly Swiss flu, yes, that'll work, the Swiss flu. Shit! Wait a minute! Lemme look at that postmark again! It's too late! They've already left for London! Oh, *God*, is he gonna be wound up . . .

'*Aaaaaaaaaah!*' I screamed as I awoke to the sparse surroundings of Eva's spare room. What the hell *is* a spare room, anyway? Spare change I can understand, spare tires I can understand, spare underwear I can understand, but how can you have a spare room? There are people sleeping in vans in museum parking lots, for God's sake. There are deserters sleeping in subways. There are Potawatomees sleeping in buffalo-skin tents!

'What are you mumbling about in there?'

'Huh? – Nothing . . . nothing.'

'I can't sleep, either. Come, have a Genever.'

I joined Eva in the living room, where she was working on her third glass. 'That picture,' she said, pointing across the room, 'see if you can straighten it.'

I walked over to a stern family portrait of Eva's clan, an unhappy bunch glaring into the camera. It looked perfectly fine to me. 'What's wrong?'

'Down on the right,' she said, lining it up with the hands of a tipsy cinematographer.

I pushed it down a half inch. 'Like this?'

'More.'

'Like this?'

'More.'

I shoved it down a good five inches. 'Like this?'

'Pcrfcct.'

I looked over to see Eva with her head in her hand, at a

forty-five-degree angle to the floor. 'So, how's the Genever?'

Eva giggled like a goose. 'I've barely touched it.'

'Then you'd better pour a couple of stiff ones.'

Eva was only too happy to oblige. She filled two glasses and proposed a toast. '*Skål.*'

I took a sip, then returned a toast. '*Prosit.*'

She knocked back a deep gulp and clinked glasses once again. '*Oogy wawa.*'

Perfect. I had her just where I wanted her. 'So, what were you telling me about Annika?'

'Annika? What about her?'

'You know what.'

'Who ever knows with Annika? Who knows what she is thinking? She's a bit of an enigma, don't you think?'

'She's hard to read sometimes.'

'Exactly . . . *ach*, it was nothing.'

'Then tell me.'

'It was really nothing.'

'Okay, then *don't* tell me.'

'*Ya*, well, why not? She lost the baby.' The words fell out of Eva's mouth like leftover crumbs of a cookie. She immediately wiped her hands on her lips, as if to clean up the mess.

It took me a moment to understand. Did she say – 'What baby?'

'No-no, that's not what I meant.'

'Eva, what baby?'

'No, really—'

'*Whose* baby?'

She sat straight up, suddenly sober. 'Your baby.'

'But . . . how?'

'I don't know. I mean, it wasn't correct for me to ask. Especially not me—'

'When?'

'I – I think only a week ago. Please, don't ask me any more.'

I sat there a moment in dead silence, then got up, returned to my room, and closed the door.

114

*  *  *

I phoned Annika fifty times. I camped out in the hospital parking lot. I pounded on her door. The days passed, and the trip to Paris was suddenly looming. I decided I wouldn't go, I'd simply stay here until Annika showed her face, but wait, I *can't* not go, I can't do that to my mother, she can't handle Dad all by herself for this long, hell, I feel bad enough about ever leaving Milwaukee in the first place, I deserted her, didn't I, yes, I deserted her when she needed me most, when she was getting older and couldn't deal with him as well, why did I leave, I'll tell you why, because I'm selfish, I'm a selfish prick who decided to flee that trap, not me, I decided, I'm not gonna be one of those minks or otters or beavers who gets his feet snatched in the Midwestern wilderness, but even a prick like me has his limits and Paris is the limit, if I don't go to Paris, I could never live with myself again, and that's when I wrote a note, wrapped it around a rock, and tossed it right through Annika's bedroom window. The cold Stockholm morning shattered with the sound of breaking glass – the first noise, I'm pretty sure, anybody had heard in two months. The note said:

> I'm leaving Sweden. Eva told me what happened. I am sad beyond words. My parents arrive in Paris in a few days and I must meet them. I won't be coming back. You have every right to hate me, but please, this one last time, please meet me at the Cattelin Restaurant in Gamla Stan tonight at eight. I have something for you. Love.

Another blizzard hit Stockholm that afternoon and by the time I arrived at the Cattelin, it had already closed for the night. I wondered if Annika had already been there, if she'd try to find me somewhere else. I walked down Västerlånggatan, then turned down some alley whose name was obscured by the snow. There was a woman standing there, under a streetlight, and for a moment I wondered if it was an apparition. 'So, you finally made it,' she said.

I felt my heart pounding as we embraced. Then I stepped

115

back and looked at her. Her eyes penetrated the darkness and her soft skin glowed under the shadows of the lamp. She looked more beautiful than ever. 'Thanks for coming,' I said.

'Thanks for asking.'

'The restaurant—'

'I know, it's closed. There's a little Greek place up the street.'

We trudged through the snow, slipped into the Athena, got a quiet corner table, ordered mousaka and a feta cheese salad, and drank retsina while waiting for dinner. 'I have something for you,' I said, handing her a package.

'Really?' she said, looking genuinely surprised. She tore open the wrapping and pulled out the skirt. 'Oh, my . . . it's beautiful!'

'It's velveteen. From India.'

'Yes, I see. There's a little tag here that says: VELVETEEN, FROM INDIA.'

'Oh, and here's something else.'

'Well, this is quite interesting,' she said, unwrapping the candle.

'Wait till it burns about halfway down . . .'

'So, Paris.'

I took a quick drink, then thought about my parents' imminent arrival. 'Yeah. It's gonna be something.' Annika watched me and smiled just slightly, as if anticipating my plight. We sat there quietly for a moment as the future visions of France succumbed to the past memories of Sweden. Finally, I leaned in a little across the table. 'What happened, Annika?'

Annika hesitated for just an instant, then responded almost offhandedly. 'Well, I rather stupidly got pregnant and then took care of things.'

'Took care of things? You don't mean—'

'It was very simple, really. Sweden's a civilized country. I just went in to work a little early one morning, lay down on a nice white table, and opened my legs.' I leaned back in my seat and tried not to look at her, no, I can't think about this, not here, not now, I can feel the blood pounding in my veins,

116

it was all my fault, I stayed away for five weeks, she kept waiting to hear from me, she figured I was never coming back, she didn't want to raise a child alone, no, no, I'll think about this later, I'll take a long walk somewhere, this will all make sense tomorrow – 'Oh, good,' said Annika, 'the mousaka's coming.' The waiter, sensing the strained atmosphere, quickly put down the dishes and disappeared into the kitchen.

'It was that night in the van, wasn't it?'

Annika stared at her food for a moment. 'So, Paris,' she said, signaling an end to that conversation.

'Yeah,' I finally responded. 'It's gonna be something.'

'Then what?'

'I'm thinking south.'

'Italy? Greece?'

'Maybe a little further.'

'What, Malta? I don't think they have any blues clubs in Malta.'

'Africa.'

'*Africa?*'

'I know, it sounds a little crazy, but I keep thinking about lying under a palm tree on some faraway beach.'

'They've definitely got faraway beaches.'

'There's just one more thing.'

'What's that?'

'I want you to come with me.'

'*What?*'

'Yeah, I think you should quit your job, give up your room, say good-bye to your relatives, and leave with me.'

'Just like that?'

'Just like that.' I leaned over and took her hand. 'Annika, I don't know what happened between us, but I never meant for things to turn out this way.'

'No, I suppose you didn't.'

'Stockholm isn't the place for either of us. I've been thinking about it ever since I got on that train. I kept thinking the two of us should've been heading south.'

Annika took a long look at me, then squeezed my hand.

'It's a very nice offer.' She glanced out at the swirling snow. 'Especially on a night like this.' I felt heartened by her response, by the feel of her skin against my hand, by the look of warmth in her eyes. 'But I can't possibly do that,' she said.

Reality interceded – the stark reality I knew deep down was lying in wait. 'Yeah, I didn't think so.' We sat there for a long moment, staring into our food. Then, as if on cue, we both reached for our wineglasses. 'To you, Annika,' I said, lifting my glass.

'And to you,' she said as the glasses clinked and echoed and reverberated and then fell silent on a cold dark Swedish night.

# 10

# The Bubble

Two things happened to me when I was five years old. The first was that while watching a cartoon on our new black-and-white TV, I saw a big red apple on the screen – a big delicious apple that just radiated redness. The second was seeing a car driving down the road with no driver. When I told my mother about these events, both times she said, 'Honey, it's just your imagination.' It was a dagger to my heart, the first time she'd ever expressed any doubts about me. How could she question what I knew to be true? To this day, I am absolutely certain that the apple I saw on TV was red. The car without the driver, I'm not so sure about.

'Well, look who's here!' my mother cried out upon opening the door of her room at Le Meridien. We hugged for a long moment, then pulled away to look at each other. I thought she looked a bit haggard, as though she'd aged more than the year and a half that I'd been away.

'How are you?' I asked, trying not to sound concerned.

'Well, you know—'

I glanced around the room. 'Where's Dad?'

'He got impatient waiting. He went down to the lobby to look for you, or across the street, or—'

'I understand. How's he been?'

'London and Lucerne weren't too bad. Basel was so-so. Then we got to Rome—'

'Tell me he didn't take you to the opera.'

'Listen, I want you to promise me something,' she said, getting suddenly serious.

'I know, Mom.'

'Promise me you'll never get too happy.'

'Okay, I promise.'

'You won't forget?'

'I won't forget.'

The door swung open and Dad drove in at 112 miles an hour. 'Son!'

'Dad!'

'Hah!'

'Ho!'

'I've been looking everywhere for you!'

'Paris is a big town.'

'Big, shmig, now Rome, *that's* a town.'

'Yeah, Mom was just telling me—'

'God, I wish we could extend this trip. Whattaya say, honey, another three weeks?'

'Well—'

'Hell, you only live once, right, Son?'

'Unless you're Hindu.'

'Hindu, schmindu. Always with the jokes, eh?'

'You know me, Dad.'

'I sure do, Son.'

'Ha.'

'Ho!'

'Ho-ho-ho.'

'I'm thinking we should expand our horizons. What's Europe got that's so great, anyway? I'm thinking the Pyramids, the Great Wall, Easter Island—'

'Now, dear—'

'You see what I've got to put up with? I want to explore a little, head off the beaten path, shoot an elephant or two.'

'Dad, you don't hunt.'

'Figuratively I'm talking about. What, I'm gonna shoot an elephant? Am I crazy?'

'Nobody said you were crazy, honey.'

'I know that, I didn't say you said anything.'

'Okay, honey, I just wanted to make that clear.'

'You see what I've got to put up with, Son?'

'I sure do, Dad.'

'I've got everything planned, don't you worry. Tonight, we relax. Just dinner, drinks, maybe take in a show, a moonlit buggy ride, early to bed. Tomorrow we hit Versailles.'

'Maybe I'll just rest up a little tomorrow, honey.'

'Rest up? Are you kidding?'

'I thought I'd do a little window-shopping. Maybe the two of you can go it alone.'

'You see what I've got to put up with, Son?'

'I sure do, Dad.'

'Ha!'

'Ho!'

'Ho-ho-ho.'

The next four days were a mad marathon as Dad ran us ragged. The Eiffel Tower. The Champs Elysées. The Louvre. The Tuileries. Les Halles. Jardin du Luxembourg. Place Vendôme. Arc de Triomphe. Palais Royale. Place de la Concorde. The Bastille. Ile Saint-Louis. Ile de la Cité. Odéon. Boulevard Saint Germain. Gare du Nord. Porte Saint-Denis. Sacré Coeur. Saint Sulpice. Jardin des Plantes. The Seine. Pont Neuf. The Left Bank. The Right Bank. Pigalle. Montmartre. Rue Fourbourg. The Marais. Notre Dame. The Sorbonne. He was drawn to every place he'd ever read about, heard about, or dreamt of seeing. And through it all, nonstop chatter about London and Lucerne, Rome and Basel. History lessons, geography primers, literary references, political comparisons, economic analyses, health and welfare statistics. Photographs of this, postcards of that, presents for relatives, bric-a-brac for the mantel. It was all becoming a big jumble.

Each night I was glad to get away from Le Meridien, a big, American-style hotel on the outskirts of Paris, to my little Hotel Renoir in Montparnasse. Shortly after I had trudged back from a late-night dinner, my head still spinning from the day's events, there was a knock on the door. Oh, God, no, he followed me here, he couldn't sleep, how about we go out for a drink, maybe a little walk along the Seine, did I ever tell you how many barges per month travel between Paris and Le Havre, or, worse, he's gonna want to just sit here and talk, oh, shit, he's gonna tell me about his childhood, how his mother died and nobody bothered to tell him and how he walked downstairs in the morning to find her lying in a casket in the hallway, and he's gonna tell me how he had to support the family when he was still just a boy and how bad things were, and they *were* bad – I know they were bad, but the thing is, he only talks about this stuff when he's really gonna wig out – and I'll feel so bad for him because I know what's gonna happen next, he'll start crying and my blood will run cold, and he'll be so sorry for everything, for all the pain he's caused me and Ed, but worse, how he's ruined Mom's life, how she never should've married him, how he'll carry that guilt with him to his grave, and I'll try to talk sense to him and say that I understand and I don't hate him and he'll cry some more and before you know it the sun will be rising and we'll both finally collapse on the sofa, and oh, shit, I can't take it, I swear, not tonight, not now, just let me sleep, find somebody else to talk to, a French guy, sure, they love to talk, maybe if I don't breathe, he'll think I'm not here and he'll just go away, no, no such luck, he's knocking again, he'll wake up the whole place and cause a scene, here it comes, the international incident, they're definitely gonna toss me out of here in the morning, okay, here I come, but goddamn it, *please* don't cry.

'It's very late, you know,' I mutter as I open the door.

'Well, should I come back tomorrow?'

'No, no, tonight is fine,' I say, very slowly, very softly, because I'm afraid that if I speak the words too forcefully, this bubble will surely burst.

'Aren't you going to invite me in?' Annika asks.

'Yes. Come in.'

When the first rays of the morning sun peeked through the ruffles of the draperies, I was still awake, running everything through my mind, trying to convince myself this wasn't a dream. Annika and I hadn't spoken another word that night, she simply came into the room, put down her bag, and stood there quietly as I took off her clothes. When we made love, I thought for a moment that I was already in Africa, floating down the Nile or gazing out over Kilimanjaro or swinging on a vine through some jungle, no, it was definitely another world I was in, a world turned magically upside down, a world in which destiny had played its final card, yes, destiny was giving me another chance, and I wouldn't blow it this time. Love has conquered all, it's stronger than both of us, and if love asks me to be quiet, I shall never speak again. Yes, love, I am yours.

'So, this Africa thing,' said Annika as she slowly opened her eyes. 'You've thought it all out?'

'All the way from A to B.'

'I see. So, I assume you have no plans for how we'll survive along the way?'

'No plans.'

'And you have no idea how we'll actually get to any of those places?'

'No idea.'

'And you have no experience traveling at all?'

'Well, not to those kinds of places.'

'*Hmmm.*'

'C'mon, what's the use of going somewhere if we can't be a little spontaneous. It's gonna be fine. It's gonna be finer than fine. Hell, it's gonna even be finer than finer than fine.'

'Let's just shoot for fine, okay?'

'Okay.'

'I'm not making any promises. Just so you understand.'

'I wouldn't want it any other way. It'll be like a trial period, and paid subscriptions, no obligations, money-back guarantee.'

Annika leaned back against the pillow, at least momentarily satisfied. I could see just the hint of a smile at the corners of her mouth. 'So, do they speak Swedish in Africa?'

'In North Africa, I think. Up near the Tunisian fjords.'

'Makes sense.'

'Know what they call the car company there?'

'What?'

'Fjord Motors.'

Annika dug a finger into my ribs. 'One more joke like that, and I'm going home.'

'You *are* home.'

She smiled at the thought of this little room – and of all the little rooms to come – as being her permanently temporary address. 'You know this is completely insane, don't you?'

'Completely.'

She pulled me over on top of her, cradled my head in her hands, then pulled back and looked me straight in the eyes. 'Can I trust you?' she said, with a seriousness in her voice I'd rarely heard before.

I thought about Eva, I thought about Amsterdam, I thought about the hospital, and for a moment I wasn't sure how to answer. 'Yes,' I said.


Dad was won over by Annika the moment she cuffed her hand under his arm as they walked out of Le Meridien the next day. He glanced at her with wide eyes, clasped his palm over her fingers, and expanded his chest like a peacock. My mother followed Annika's lead by taking my arm, and we walked a few steps behind, the four of us on a double date to the Restaurant Orleans. It all seemed innocent enough at the time. Mom ordered a steak, Annika a ratatouille, and I the salmon, but Dad, deciding to be a little daring, a little *français*, a little *je ne sais quoi*, went for the escargots. Out came a steaming platter, six big shells swimming in a savory sauce, a few sprigs of parsley, and a dollop of potato. Dad admired the presentation, recounting for us how some general or other, at one battle or another, said: 'Give me escargots or Brigitte Bardot.' We all laughed at his little joke as he dug into one of the shells and pulled out a plump snail. '*Mmmmm*, absolutely delicious,' he said before even taking a bite, as he was often prone to do. He washed it down with some wine, pretending to savor every smell and taste, then moved on to the next shell, made some other crack, and had more wine. '*C'est magnifique!*' Then, as he went for the third escargot, something happened. There was no plump snail oozing out of the shell. As a matter of fact, there wasn't even a skinny snail. Dad dug around the insides with a tiny little fork and came up empty. 'How do you like that?' he said. 'It's blank.' He inspected the other shells with a suspicious eye. 'Look here, another one. They sent me two blanks.'

'Sometimes things like that happen,' I said, trying to defuse the situation.

'What kind of a place is this? They think they've got some raw tourists?'

'You're only going to get heartburn from those things, anyway,' my mother said, in a soft, even tone. 'Here, have half my steak.'

He looked at her a moment, his eyes growing darker. '*Garçon!*'

A waiter ambled over. '*Monsieur?*'

'You gave me two blanks.'

'*Pardonnez-moi?*'

'Blanks, blanks. Two of them. Look here.'

Dad held up the plate for the waiter to see. The waiter responded with the famous French Shrug. '*C'est la vie.*'

Dad turned to me with an annoyed look. 'He doesn't understand. You tell him. You speak French.'

I turned to the waiter with a pained expression. 'Uh, the *deux escargots*, they're, uh, mis-*sing*.'

My father stared at me. 'This is what I paid four years of college for?'

'Look, Dad, just forget it,' I said, feeling sixteen again.

'Forget it? They're charging twenty-six dollars for this. You know how much that is?'

'Uh—'

'Four-thirty-three each.'

'*Monsieur, s'il vous plaît,*' said Annika, '*est-il possible d'échanger ce plat pour un autre?*'

Dad looked at her with beaming eyes. 'Now we'll get somewhere.'

125

'*Non*,' said the waiter. He turned and walked away.

Uh-oh, here it comes, the *incident internationale*, he's ready to blow, it's been building too long, the continental plates are shifting, the magma is rising, the lava is bubbling, and it's definitely time to evacuate the scene, ladies and gentlemen, no time to bother with possessions, we have a level-four situation here, code red, code red, head for the nearest emergency shelter, oh, shit, I can see it now, they're gonna reopen the Bastille just for us, we'll have our own wing, Mom cleaning from morning to night just in case we get visitors, Dad pacing his cell, not sleeping, recounting the history of the French penal system from Charlemagne to Napoleon to Pompidou, talking about bagging an elephant, about visiting the Galapagos Islands about going to the opera, and me, trapped in my own cell right between them, chained to the wall, my fingernails six inches long, rats nibbling on my toes, a pool of rancid water beneath my feet—

Then something remarkable happened. Just as Dad started to get up to follow the waiter, Annika put a hand on his arm. 'Why don't we just forget it?'

He looked at her, and something in her eyes melted him. 'You're absolutely right, my dear,' he said, sitting back in his seat. My mother and I just stared at each other, wondering if we were seeing right. Dad took a forkful of potato and savored the taste for a moment. 'France,' he finally said, 'whatta place.'

'Your mother's very sweet, isn't she?' Annika said later that night in our blissful bed at the Hotel Renoir.

'She's the sweetest woman in the world.'

'She seems to have a lot of strength.'

'She's the strongest woman in the world.'

'And a sense of humor.'

'She's the funniest woman in the world.'

'And your dad is very sweet, too.'

'*Um-hmm.*'

'I don't know what you were so worried about.'

'Crazy me.' I stared at the ceiling a moment, thinking about how Dad was severely depressed ten months out of the year and wildly manic for a month and a half. Then there were the two other weeks in the year, the two weeks in which his state was in transition between depressed and manic. It was those two weeks that were both the most wonderful and tragic periods of his life. This was the period when he became what I considered his natural self, and for those two weeks he was the most irresistible man I ever encountered. He was even-tempered, kind, and brilliantly insightful. There was a sparkle in his eyes and a warmth in his heart and a goodness in his soul that made people gravitate toward him, for there seemed to be something to be gained by merely being in his presence. Dostoyevsky, who was an epileptic, said that before his seizures there would be one minute of extraordinary clarity – a moment when the world made sense, and that those moments were worth all the horrors unleashed by the illness itself. I wondered if it might not be that way for my father, too. It was almost worth the eleven and a half months of misery to be around him for those two weeks when he became himself. It is that person whom I've always aspired to be.

The next day my parents flew back to America. Five days later, my dad's lid blew off, and he wound up at St Michael's hospital for six weeks. When he came out, he didn't talk much about his trip to Europe. As the years passed, and as his memory receded, he eventually forgot all about ever being in Lucerne or Rome or London or Basel. But as for Paris, no matter how old he got, he never, ever, forgot about the two missing escargots.

It was mid-May, and Paris was unseasonably cold and gray, but the next ten days went by in a dreamlike blur. There were a hundred details to contend with – passport extensions, visa applications, yellow-fever shots, smallpox inoculations, gamma globulin injections, malaria pills, traveler's check purchases, clothes to be sorted out, things to buy, things to get rid of, maps to study, brochures to read, schedules to check, climates to consider, monsoons to ponder, vitamins to ingest, postcards to write. On a bright Monday morning, I returned to the room with matching rucksacks. Annika took one look at them and shuddered. 'What's this?'

'What does it look like?'

'*Uh*, were you planning on discovering a new mountain or something?'

'Look, this is the only sensible way to travel down there.'

'Maybe for you. I'm taking my suitcase.'

'No, you can't do that. You'll get tired carrying it and who do you think will wind up dragging it through the mud?'

'Mud? I thought we were going to the beach.'

'Mud, sand, what's the difference?'

'Next thing you know, I'll have to leave my high heels behind.'

I didn't have the heart to tell her that I'd already given her shoes to a woman down the hall. 'Look, check out all the compartments.'

Annika barely gave it a sidelong glance. 'Did you have to get *matching* rucksacks? What are we, the Bobbsey Twins?'

'I don't know, it just made sense. C'mon, at least look inside.'

Annika begrudgingly pulled back the flap. 'What's this?' she said, holding up an envelope.

'Take a look.' She slit open the envelope to find two airline tickets. I couldn't wait for her to read them. 'They're from Paris to Athens,' I blurted out.

'Yes,' she said, flashing a big smile, 'there's a little tag here that says: PARIS TO ATHENS.'

I figured what the hell, it'll be our last splurge, let's get out of this cold and hit the beach. From there it'll be nothing but boats and trains.'

'When do we leave?'

'In two hours.'

'*What?*' she screamed, checking the tickets to make sure I was kidding.

I wasn't.

# 11

## Happiness

Annika and I held hands as the plane took off from Orly. We snuggled over Switzerland, embraced over Yugoslavia, and kissed as we circled Athens, slowly descending through the clear, bright skies. Ah, Athens, what a place to rekindle romance, the hot days and cool nights, the smell of olive blossoms in the air, a bouzouki serenading us over dinner, and Annika blossoms too, every day she's more relaxed, she's happier, she's more in love, and we can't keep our hands off each other, we're always touching, we're holding each other, we're kissing, we're never apart, not for long, and this is what it's about, this is what I dreamt of, yes, this is it. Sometimes Annika would catch me staring at her. 'What? What is it?' she'd ask. 'Have I told you how much I love the shape of your head?' I'd respond. 'What *do* you mean?' she'd say, her eyes sparkling, and then we'd hug and kiss and hug some more.

We went everywhere – to St George's Chapel atop Lycabettus Hill, to the flea market in Monastiraki, to Ceramicus, Filopappou Hill, Adrianos's Gate, the Roman Market, the Parliament House, Pnyka Hill, Lysikratous Monument, and the Temple of Zeus – but mostly we strayed off the path, leaving Constitution Square for the tourists while we crossed over to Zappion Gardens, where we laughed with the children playing on the grass, petted the animals at the miniature zoo, and watched the women pushing strollers under the shade of giant oak trees.

We even put aside, for the moment at least, our distaste at seeing the endless photos of 'the Colonels,' the right-wing dictators who had taken over Greece. They were everywhere – on billboards coming into town, on government buildings, on the sides of buses, on shop windows, on the trees in the parks, even in the restaurants like the one we were peeking into on one of our first nights on the town. '*Kali spera sas, para kalo,*' an effusive woman called out in greeting as she came running to the outdoor patio. She insisted that we inspect the kitchen, where a half-dozen kettles were boiling away, each smelling better than the next, and it seemed as good a place as any. We ordered mousaka, feta cheese salad, and retsina, just like in Stockholm – not for lack of imagination, but in order to rewrite that evening with a much happier ending.

'I can't believe we're here,' said Annika, looking out from our table over the Plaka. We were halfway up a hill, in the shadows of the Acropolis, and the whole of Athens was spread out beneath us. Annika was wearing the velveteen skirt from India and I couldn't take my eyes off her. The view of Athens, after all, would always be there, but Annika, Annika at this very moment, that's what I always wanted to remember. Spread out next to us were three empty retsina bottles. It's a Greek custom to leave all the 'dead soldiers' on the table as a badge of honor, and we were being nothing if not patriotic. So we laughed and we drank, piling up dead soldiers beneath a photo of the Colonels, while they were piling up plenty of real dead soldiers throughout the rest of the country. Growing tired of their staring down and ogling Annika's breasts, I finally stood on a chair and turned the photo to the wall.

'*Ochi . . . ochi . . .*' a waiter whispered, waving his finger in a warning. He hurried over and turned the photo back around, glancing nervously at the door to make sure no one else had noticed.

'C'mon, let's blow this place,' I said to Annika. We floated out onto the street, thumbing our noses at the Colonels one last time for good measure, then walked along the cobblestone paths of the Plaka, holding each other, tipsy, getting lost in the streets and never once caring, because nothing bad could happen to us, that was for sure. Athens is a movie backdrop, the perfect setting for a romantic comedy in which the sun always shines, the stars twinkle brightly, and the music swells at just the right moment. We stumbled up the stairs of our pensione, kicked the door closed, and fell onto the bed. I thought about the first night we spent together, when we kissed under a mist of perfume, and it felt like that again, right now, as I ran my fingers through her hair and along her neck and reached down to unzip her skirt.

God, I'm happy, happier than I've ever been, this is even better than Stockholm, better than Paris, better than I ever imagined, hell, I'm pushing the happiness quotient right to the edge, I'm at seven and a half for sure, maybe even eight, yes, how do you like that, I'm at eight all right, eight's great, eight rates, meecha at eight don't be late we gotta date, ho-ho, do I hear eight-point-one, c'mon, folks, we're goin' for a record here, who'll give me eight-point-one – yes! The young Swedish lady with the perfectly shaped head! – do I hear eight-point-two, c'mon, somebody's gotta gimme eight-point-two, going once, going twice—

'Are you okay?' said Annika as she cuddled into my arms.
'Sure, why?'
'You look kind of sad.'
'No, it's nothing. I was just thinking about my mother.'
'She's very sweet.'
'Yes, she is.'

It was time to hit the islands. We checked out brochures of the closest chain, the Cyclades, fifteen islands not far from the coast promising fun and sun. We each did our own reading, then had a powwow to compare notes. 'Mykonos,' said Annika, indicating her first choice.
'Too gay,' I responded, using my first challenge.
'Tínos.'
'Too small.'
'Naxos.'

131

'Too big.'

'Syros.'

'Too popular.'

'Ios.'

'Too many Germans.'

'Milos.'

'Too many Italians.'

'Páros.'

'Too many Greeks.'

Annika just stared at me. 'Okay, where do you suggest?'

'Santorini.'

'No, really.'

'I'm serious.'

'*Santorini?*' she said in disbelief. 'It's in the middle of nowhere. They've barely got any beaches there. Why in God's name would you want to go to Santorini?'

'It appeals to my sense of alienation.'

'*Nobody* goes to Greece to be alienated.'

'That's not what I hear from the Colonels.'

Annika slumped back against her chair. 'Fine. We'll go to Santorini.'

'You won't be sorry.'

'I'm already sorry.'

Now the journey truly begins, this is it, we're on a ship, traveling like the locals, yes, deck class on a ship, and it's different from the airplane, on an airplane everybody's buckled into a tiny little space, locked into a straight-back seat, pretending they don't hear the guy who's snoring eighteen inches away, something happens at thirty thousand feet, our brains become slightly displaced from our bodies, both of which are hurtling through space much too quickly, no, planes are a completely unnatural way to travel, either they should slow them way down so that we can adjust to the space-time continuum or, better yet, speed them way up, yes, Paris to Athens in four seconds, that's more like it, and they could do it, too, if it wasn't for Nixon and the oil companies and the military-industrial complex keeping

things artificially slow so they can sock it to the poor traveling class, God, they're bastards – 'Please, do you think we
could talk about something else?' – okay, sure, she's not into
politics, that's fine, I'm not either anymore, she's right, talking about Richard Nixon while cruising the Mediterranean is
a bit ridiculous, well, maybe not *ridiculous*, that's rather
strong, no, at most it's slightly *inappropriate*, Nixon, after
all, would start shooting dolphins from the deck if he were
here, that trigger-happy son of a bitch – 'Did you hear me?'
– okay, okay, I'm sorry, we're on a boat, it's cool, everybody's
smiling, everybody's talking to each other, where you from,
where you going, oh, yeah, we've been on the road forever,
we're heading for Africa, really, no fooling, we're gonna
blaze some trails, oh, yeah, we've got plenty of experience,
the vaccinations alone were an experience, well, nice to meet
you, maybe we'll run into you in Mombasa some day, ah,
yes, this is just what I expected, meeting people, all kinds of
people, French, Germans, Italians, learning about exotic
villages and hidden treasures and continents that pop right
out of the sea, passing a half-dozen islands along the way, all
of them glistening with white, sandy beaches and dappled
with quaint whitewashed villages, and we're eating and
drinking and laughing until the tears come down, and – yes!
– there in the distance, that's it, Santorini, our first port of
call, our first of hundreds, and we're pulling into harbor and,
strange, there seems to be a dramatic change of mood, the
passengers are eerily quiet and the crew is eerily quiet and all
I can hear is the low growl of the turbines in the engine room
as I look out at the sheer cliffs of the island, the black rock
of the beaches, and the jagged peak of an ancient volcano
that juts directly out of the sea, but it's not just any volcano,
at least that's what the first mate is telling us, no, it's the
grand pooh-bah of volcanoes, it blew away two-thirds of the
island 3,500 years ago, sent a monstrous tidal wave across
the Mediterranean, and put an end to the Minoan civilization on Crete, and you know who lives in the volcano these
days, vampires, that's who, vampires, *heh-heh*, and just the
other night some villagers found two bodies down around

the cliffs with fang marks in their necks and all their blood sucked out. God, I love this place. From the desolate harbor to the town at the top of the cliff, there were 576 stone steps heading straight up. 'See, aren't you glad you've got a rucksack?' I said to Annika.

'Thrilled,' she replied, eyeing some donkeys that were carrying up everybody else's suitcases. When we finally got to the village, we checked into a creaky pensione run by three nervous sisters. They had the rather disconcerting habit of wringing their hands whenever they spoke, adding a touch of melodrama to a place that didn't need it. 'Stay away from the beach at night,' warned Maria as we filled out the register. 'Keep the windows locked until sunrise,' said Elena, furtively glancing down the hall. 'Don't go to the west side of the island,' cautioned Angelika, crossing herself. I noticed that every door, window, and entranceway of any kind had a wreath of garlic hanging over it and that convinced me to look at the tourist brochure once more. Ah, yes, I had some-how missed the part about Santorini lying dead center in 'the Vampire Belt,' a swatch of land that ran from Transylvania, down through the Carpathians, across the Balkans, into the Aegean, and ended up right here at the tip of the Cyclades. We weren't just in the belt, we were sitting on the buckle. *Heh-heh.*

Annika was displeased. Maybe it was the wolves howling in the distance. Or the incessant fluttering of bats in the belfry. Or the pounding of shutters against the windows all night long. Who knows what gets into the mind of an in-experienced traveler? Whatever the cause, when I went to kiss her good-night, she dug her teeth into my neck and sucked my blood until I shriveled up like a prune, then she jabbed a stake into my heart and pounded it with a wooden mallet until it pierced me through and through, but then, thank God, I awoke in a cold sweat and realized it was only a dream. I reached over to put my arm around her, but suddenly Annika turned on me, made the sign of the cross, pulled out a gun, and shot me with six silver bullets, *da-da-da-da-da-duh*. Then I awoke again and realized it was a dream *within* a dream, and I laughed and decided to wake Annika to tell her, but she wasn't there, she was in the hallway, pulling a casket into the room, and she pried open the top, and it was filled with black dirt from Romania and white silk from Sweden and purple velveteen from India, and then she flung open the shutters, and a crack of sunlight struck my face, and my skin burst into flames, and I howled like a banshee in the night.

'*Aaaaaaaaaah!*'

'What the *hell* is wrong with you?' said Annika, shaking me awake.

'Why don't you just kill me already?' I screamed.

'Just give me one more reason . . . That's all I ask.'

# 12

## Exile on Crete

The boat to Crete was our chance to put the little mishap of Santorini behind us. We got out of that hellhole as soon as possible, which, unfortunately, wasn't until five days later, when I finally was able to secure tickets. We might've been able to get out a little sooner – like the very next day – had I been a bit more bending about ticket prices, but these are the little things one learns along the way, right? – Right? What, now you're not talking to me? As luck would have it, two hours out of Santorini we wished we'd never left. The southern Aegean can be very rough at times and this just happened to be one of those times. The boat pitched and rolled, rose and fell, and shook side to side. Chairs went flying across the deck, along with suitcases, bags of fruit, and bundles of clothing. When we finally pulled into Iráklion, I even vomited at the shock of feeling solid ground beneath my feet.

'Bed, bed,' we groaned as we checked into the first pensione we found. The manager nodded to us with understanding and put us in a choice room with a balcony overlooking the center of town. He even sent up some warm soup to calm our stomachs. A few hours later, we felt better and Annika even cuddled into my arms as we fell into a dreamy, blissful sleep.

*Da-da-da-da-duh* . . . *da-da-da-da-duh* . . . *da-da-da-da-duh* . . .

The room shook with an incessant racket. I leapt out of bed and saw that a road crew was jackhammering right across the street. It was barely dawn. 'What the hell!' I screamed.

Annika wrapped a pillow around her ears and buried herself under the blanket. 'My head . . . my head . . .'

I closed the window but the jackhammers still pounded straight into our frayed nerves. 'I can't believe this.'

'Do something!' yelled Annika from under the covers. Do something? What was I supposed to do? I yanked on my pants and trounced down to the front desk.

'*Kali mera*,' the manager said, much too brightly. 'You are up nice and early.'

'Yeah, you know, the *mera* would be a whole lot more *kali* if it wasn't for that war going on outside our window.'

'Oh? I forgot to mention? A minor construction. They are certain to be done today.'

'You're sure? It's driving us crazy.'

'You have my word. You will be having breakfast?'

There was another barrage of jackhammering that shook the walls. '*What?*'

'*Breakfast?*' he yelled over the noise.

'*Yeah, yeah . . .*'

By the time I got back to the room, Annika already had her rucksack packed up. 'Let's go.'

'What do you mean?'

'Let's get another hotel. C'mon.'

'No, no, I talked to the manager. He said they'll be done today.'

'Of course he said that. What did you expect him to say?'

'Let's just give it another night, okay?'

'*Why?*'

'Because we're here. It's cheap, it's clean—'

*Da-da-da-da-duh . . . da-da-da-da-duh . . . da-da-da-da-duh . . .*

'It's driving me crazy!'

We bailed out on the free breakfast and went to a quiet restaurant to talk things over. After coffee, juice, and toast,

137

Annika finally agreed to give it one more night if I agreed to spend the day away from the noise. We headed for the old marketplace, where Annika started trying on full-length sheepskin coats – as if *those* were going to make any sense in Africa – but I was glad she'd found something to occupy her time. Still, when she started comparing prices, I thought it wise to step in and remind her of where we were going. Suggesting that she was acting like a raw tourist was perhaps not the best way to phrase it.

'*Tour-ist?*' she replied, stretching out the word.

'Well, that's not exactly what I meant.'

'*You're* calling *me* a tourist?'

'What, you think *I'm* a tourist?'

'At least I've got the sense to get out of a hotel where we're being jackhammered to death.'

'What's that got to do with anything? I'll tell you what matters. *Tourists* carry suitcases. *Travelers* carry rucksacks.'

'Yeah, *matching* rucksacks.'

I ordered an ouzo that night at a small *taverna* not far from the hotel. Ouzo is kind of a watered-down, foul-tasting Pernod, an anise-flavored liqueur I'd grown fond of in Paris. I knocked one back, didn't feel a thing, then ordered another. I watched as the melting ice turned the neon green alcohol into a milky ooze – the *ooze* in *ouzo?* – then finished it off. Still I felt nothing. I ordered a double, which gave me just the slightest buzz, but hardly enough to take the edge off the day. Annika, still sipping her first drink, looked at me like I was crazy when I went back to the bar for another. 'Please, friend,' said the bartender, 'slowly, slowly,' but I kept on drinking, barely feeling a thing, knocking back one glass after another. An hour and a half later, after finishing my eleventh ouzo, I was sitting at the table, minding my own business, when, straight out of nowhere, Muhammad Ali hit me with an enormous uppercut straight to the jaw. Then a freight train came barreling through the door and ran right over me. A second later, some old Greek ruins fell on top of my head and buried me in stone.

138

The next thing I knew, I was being led through the streets, totally blind, one-hundred-proof numb, vaguely hearing Annika telling me when to lift my feet. Back in the room she led me to the balcony, where I sat absolutely rigid. 'Don't move me,' I said, 'not even a quarter of an inch,' certain that if she moved me from that spot, I would surely die.

'I don't know why you have to drink so much.'

'It keeps me from thinking,' I managed to say.

'I don't know why you have to think so much.'

'I keep thinking I wish you'd kept the baby.'

'Well, then, you'd better just keep drinking,' Annika said, angrily snapping off the light.

*Da-da-da-da-duh . . . da-da-da-da-duh . . . da-da-da-da-duh . . .*

Another assault of jackhammers crackled through the dawn, only this time it was ten times worse. Everyone in Iráklion had a jackhammer that morning, every workman and housewife and teacher. They all gathered directly across from our window for a festival of jackhammering, an orgy of jackhammering, a veritable *Who's Who* of jackhammering. Aristotle Onassis was there, Maria Callas was there, Costa-Gavras, Theodorakis, and Papadopoulos were there.

Annika's eyes snapped open and I got out of there before she killed me. I returned a few minutes later with good news. 'It's okay,' I said, in between bursts of jackhammering, 'he says they're definitely done today.'

The next several days didn't go very well. Annika (unreasonably) kept insisting we get a new hotel, while I (wisely) said that no hotel could possibly operate under these conditions and that the noise was certain to stop. She claimed I was being unbelievably stubborn, but I pointed out that it was man's nature to be a creature of habit, to which she inquired how I could possibly have developed this insane hotel habit after only a couple of days, and I responded that I was obviously adapting to the situation much better than she and I certainly hoped this wasn't going to be a sign of things to come since Africa would surely be more challenging than a few little jackhammers, and that shut her up, completely, for fourteen hours and twenty-seven minutes, three hours and sixteen minutes of which, I might add, were absolutely jackhammer-free.

We did agree on one thing, though, which was that Iráklion wasn't really all that great, and it was time to explore the rest of the island.

The journey through Crete went rapidly downhill. Sometimes it was literally downhill, like walking to the bottom of Butterfly Gorge, which turned out to be all gorge and no butterflies, but more often it was figuratively downhill, with a sense of hopelessness, of fate gone awry, of destiny standing there with its big hand held up like a stop sign. We traveled around the island in a daze. We went to Canea in the west and sleepy villages in the south, to the jagged hills of the north and the rock formations in the east. One morning, in some dusty little pensione, I was about to step into the shower when I heard Annika scream. '*What is it?*' I said, rushing into the room.

'Over there! On the wall!' she said, backing away.

I glanced over and saw a giant cockroach. 'Shit!' I said, backing away with her. 'That thing is eight feet long!'

'Kill it!'

'Me?'

'Of course, *you*!'

'Well, now, wait a minute—'

'Are you a *man* or what?' she screamed. As the cockroach crawled toward her bed, Annika completely unraveled. 'Can't you even kill a *bug* for me?'

I heard my voice responding to her, cold and distant, as if it were in some other room. 'Look, you're the one so freaked out, *you* kill it.'

'*Jävla förbannade,*' she said, shaking her head. She glared at me, then slipped off her shoe, tiptoed up to the wall, and smashed the cockroach with the heel. She just kept smashing it and smashing it until there was nothing left but a brown, waxy piece of ooze, and then she smashed it some more.

We came upon Vai, a beach on the northeastern tip of the island, and not a moment too soon. Vai was a stop for seasoned travelers, and we both welcomed the idea of having some other people around. Still, I looked at our new surroundings with mixed emotions. There were no amenities other than a little café, and everyone slept on the beach and shared whatever they had in the way of food and drink. The only Greeks in the vicinity were an old couple who ran the café, and Nikos, a handsome fisherman who went out on his boat every morning, spent long hours on the sea, then returned with his catch.

Annika immediately made friends with the dozen people living on the beach, all of them European, mostly French and German. I didn't feel comfortable around these more experienced travelers and spent most of my time alone, walking the hills and olive groves that dotted the land. One afternoon, I came upon Amélie, a pretty French girl who was reading beneath a tree. She was sitting there topless and immediately covered herself when she heard footsteps, but when she saw it was me, she smiled and uncovered herself. '*Bonjour,*' she said, in a sweet, mellifluous voice.

'*Bonjour,*' I replied. 'You come here often?'

'Isn't that what you call a pick-me-up line?' she said, smiling coyly.

'Yeah, something like that,' I laughed.

'I come here sometimes to get away from everyone.'

'Oh, I didn't mean to—'

'No, it's all right. You can stay. You're the one with the Swedish girl.'

'Yeah, Annika.'

'She's very pretty.'

'I suppose she is.'

'That's what all the guys say.' – Guys? What guys? Those guys on the beach? Who's hitting on her? Jean-Pierre?' Jean-Michel? Jean-Philippe? Sure, it's gotta be Jean-Philippe, I saw the way he looked at her the second we showed up. He's a

141

fast one, that Jean-Philippe, been to India twice already, he's probably regaling her with stories of crossing the desert on his camel, fighting off bandits, saving some girl from Afghani pirates, yeah, he's always squirming closer to her on the sand, well, he's full of shit, Annika, can't you see that, it's so fucking obvious, I wouldn't believe a word he says – Afghani pirates? They don't even have rivers in Afghanistan. What do you see in him exactly, what's he got that I don't have, nothing, I'm telling you, absolutely nothing, and do you know what he does back in Paris, I'll tell you what, he's a fucking *waiter*, that's what. – 'Where are you going?' said Amélie.

'Huh? Oh, I gotta get back to the beach.'

'So soon?'

'Yeah, I, uh, I gotta check on something.'

'Well, then. *Au revoir*.'

Nikos was sitting on the beach with Annika, the three Jeans, and a couple from Hamburg when I got back. Nikos was mysterious, a guy you'd never picture as a fisherman, and people said he had a story. Given that he spoke no English and only a few words of French and German, that story had been coming out in dribs and drabs. Today, though, Nikos was talkative and we began piecing together his tale. He'd been a college professor on the mainland, one of those intellectuals who'd been rounded up by the Colonels and thrown into jail, where he languished for months. Finally, he was released and exiled to Crete, to this corner of the island, where he tried to blend in with the palm trees. He'd been here a few years now, never knowing what the next morning might bring. Nikos drew six squares in the sand, each representing a friend of his. He pointed to the first square with his stick, said 'Yianni,' and drew an X through it. Then he pointed to each successive square and named his other murdered compatriots – Yorgos, Petros, Mihalis, Stavros – drawing Xs through the sand. When he came to the sixth box, he said, 'Nikos,' then dropped the stick to the ground and raised his palms upwards, as if his fate were in God's hands. Annika wiped away some tears and reached out to touch his hand. Nikos smiled stoically, got up, and walked down the beach to the hut where he slept.

The days passed, and I waited. I waited for the chill between me and Annika to end, I waited to recapture the feeling we'd had in Athens, I waited for everything to be the way it was supposed to be. How had everything gone so wrong? I knew that traveling put pressures on a relationship, but, c'mon, we'd barely gotten started. It occurred to me that maybe we didn't really have that much to say to each other, and more than once Eva's words flashed through my mind – '*Who ever knows with Annika? Who knows what she is thinking?*' – maybe that's what attracts me to her, I want to find out what's underneath, I want to explore, I want to dig a bit, but I can be patient, I'll wait for this chill to thaw, that's right, there's no rush, none whatsoever. I'll just learn to adapt to the beach and the travelers, I'll learn to loosen up, I'll learn the sky by night and the ocean by day, I'll learn the natural order of things, I'll learn to fit in.

On the night of the full moon, everyone gathered together for a feast. We brought supplies from the nearest village, built a fire, cooked up a fish stew, and passed around bottles of wine. The owner of the café appeared with his bouzouki, his wife brought retsina, and then, eventually, even Nikos showed up. That's when the party really took off. Nikos guzzled the wine, tore off his shirt, and became Zorba the Greek right before our eyes. He began singing and dancing and everyone cheered him on, this magnificent man, this soulful, remarkable life force who refused to give in, this man who shook his fists at fate, who danced on the bloody soil of his country, leaping higher and singing stronger and laughing louder at the assassins waiting in the trees. I watched him, transfixed, and felt empty inside. Who was I, after all, but some jerk barely out of college. I knew at that moment what I wanted. *I* wanted to be Zorba the Greek. *I* wanted to dance to the bouzouki. *I* wanted to pull in the fisherman's nets with my bare hands. *I* wanted to have a weathered faced and callused hands and be able to drink ouzo until dawn.

It got especially cold that night. When the alcohol wore off, I awoke on the beach, lying on little pellets of freezing sand that sent a chill up my spine. I turned over to hold Annika and pulled the blanket tighter around our naked bodies. I lay there for a long moment, feeling strange, as if I were an intruder into my own life, and it was then that I realized this wasn't my blanket, this wasn't my normal spot on the beach, this wasn't even Annika. I lay there trying to remember how in God's name I wound up with Amélie that night, no, this is impossible, this can't be right, shit, maybe I really *should* drink a little less, yes, that's what I'll tell Annika, I'll promise her that and mean it, I really will, oh *man*, is she gonna be pissed, this just might be the worst thing I've ever done – well, what did you expect ignoring me like that? – no, that's what I *don't* say to her, am I crazy, c'mon, you've got to come up with something better than that—

The sun began to rise over the Aegean and I walked along the beach, past the sleeping bodies, the shuttered café, and Nikos's hut. He was already out on the water, laying nets and pulling in the first catch of the day. I watched from a distance, admiring again his courage, his passion, his will to live. I started down the beach again, expecting to find Annika and then, finally, there she was, yes, there's Annika, a little tired, a little groggy, a little hungover . . . coming out of Nikos's hut.

I walked back behind the beach, in that kind of daze where consciousness just sits in one spot, like an engine revving in neutral, too numb from the cold, too numb to think. I watched the fronds of some palm trees rustling in the breeze and walked through a sandy grove beneath the branches. Then, for a moment, I felt a remarkable lucidity, as if I could remember every single thing that had ever happened in my life. The images flew by, jumbled and out of sequence, and I sensed something important, something I didn't understand, something buried so deep down that I couldn't quite reach it.

I desperately tried to slow down my mind, to make everything stop for just one instant, to capture even one picture that might make sense. But then, just like that, the images retreated and I was left with nothing but an empty churning at the bottom of my stomach.

I circled back around the hills and over the dunes as the sun rose higher in the sky. By the time I returned, I could see that the café was open and everybody was there nursing cups of hot coffee. I pulled a change of clothes out of my rucksack, folded and rearranged a few things, then slung it over my back. I walked down along the edge of the water one more time, cut diagonally over to the café, and headed for the table where Annika was sitting.

# 13

## Ochi

From the upper deck of a ship, I watched the water roiling below and realized how easy it would be to jump, just two little steps, then up and over the railing, a couple of seconds to hit the water, the force of the impact would knock me unconscious and that would be that, but worst case I'd still be alert, by my calculations a 40-foot drop at 32 feet/second/second would send me 22.8 feet beneath the surface of the ocean – of course, since everyone is wrong about everything, that formula too is highly suspect – and then gravity starts pushing me up and it better hurry because, *whoa, I can't breathe*, oh, shit, what was I thinking, my lungs are filling with water, salty, salty saltwater, which strangely enough is making me thirsty, how's that for irony, and, oops, here it comes, I'll bet this is the part where my life passes before my eyes, but nope, guess what, they're wrong about that, too, you know what's on my mind, it's that apple, that goddamn red apple on our old black-and-white TV set, and I'm telling you it's as red as red can be, blood blood bloody red, shit, do they have sharks in this ocean, I hadn't thought about that, wouldn't that be one helluva mess – '*Aaaaaaaaah!*'

'Sir?' asked a ship's mate, who came hurrying over.

'Huh? Oh, I'm fine, I'm fine . . .' Actually, I'm *not* fine, not fine at all, I'm standing on the deck of some broken-down ferry going to, wait a minute, where am I going again, oh, right, Kárpathos, some island I've never even heard of but

146

that's what happens when you roll the dice in the ticket office of Sitia and tell the clerk to get you on the first ship out of there, but how bad can it be, it's just another Greek island, for Chrissakes, and I'm standing there on the dock and Annika says, 'I knew I couldn't trust you,' and I'm thinking, Trust *me*? Wait a minute, trust is a two-way street, I'm not even sure what happened with that girl anyway, maybe we only cuddled a little, and Annika just stares at me and I suggest that we're getting off the point – which is? – which is that trust goes both ways, but she doesn't want to talk about that, no, of course not, that would be much too fair, which pisses me off just enough to say something like, well, what did you expect, ignoring me like that, and she shakes her head and says, 'I think we need a little time,' and I totally agree, a little time is what we need, just enough time for her to marry Nikos, that motherfucker commie prick, and have a whole brood of Swedish-Greek leftist troublemakers, I'll put an X through your name alright, Nikos, and then I'll dance on your grave with a bouzouki, I'll show you who can drink until dawn, and then you'll be sorry, won't you, Annika, you're probably already sorry, you're probably already writing me a letter like you said – 'I'll write' – well, I don't know if I'm gonna be so easy, if I'm just gonna take you back, I mean, that French chick, who knows what happened, I'm thinking nothing at all happened, so what the hell was that, getting even for Eva or something, okay, touché, you got me, I screwed Eva, you screwed Nikos, so we're even, even if you definitely got the better of that deal – 'Yes, I definitely think we need a little time' – well, who knows, maybe she's right, maybe that's exactly what we need, for Annika to sit there all alone on the beach and realize how much she misses me, but of course, she won't be all alone, she'll be with all those hipster travelers, so I ask her what she'll do and she says she's not sure, maybe stay on Crete a while, maybe go to Mykonos, where her friends Rick and Robbie are vacationing on one of the gay beaches, maybe just play it by ear, and okay, that makes sense, that's what we'll both do, play it by ear, you'll go wherever you're going, and I'll go wherever I'm going – 'I'll write,' she says again and yes, I say, I'm going to, uh, Kárpathos, and then probably Rhodes, of course, who knows, since I'm playing it by ear, but, hey, you'll know where to reach me if you want to and she nods and I nod and then they're pulling up the catwalk and the horn is blowing and the ship is pulling out, and Sitia is vanishing and Crete is vanishing and my whole world is vanishing right into the sea.

'Kárpathos is a large island, located midway between Crete and Rhodes,' reads a guidebook I find wedged behind a deck chair. 'Until the 1950s, it was home to some sixty thousand people, mostly farmers working the fields and shepherds roaming the mountains. Today, eight thousand people occupy the fertile island, enjoying its easy pace and fine climate.'

As the ship pulled into the harbor, I mulled over those statistics wondering what happened to all of those other people. War? Famine? More vampires? No, what happened was far worse. They moved to Detroit, Michigan, where they braved the cold winters and built carburetors. Then, when they made it big, they came back to Kárpathos to flaunt their wealth. Kárpathos had exactly one kilometer of paved road, a tiny stretch that went straight through town and up over a hill and ended at an inconsequential grove of olive trees, but on that road were dozens of Buicks and Oldsmobiles, all shipped over from Detroit for the summer. While the men cruised up and down Million Drachma Drive, their wives strolled along the promenade in full-length mink coats, sweating profusely under the Greek sun. The locals watched in envy, dreaming of the day that they, too, could return to this primitive piece of rock in their Rocket 88s.

When I stepped off the boat, the cars screeched to a halt, the women stopped strutting, and the sky cracked in half. I was Icarus falling from the heavens, I was the nightmare, the curse, the plague of locusts, the fly in the ointment, the long-haired hippie freak who had corrupted their children back home. I was the American dream turned inside out, I was the

Anti-Dollar following these poor souls halfway around the world, coming home to bite them in the ass. I turned right around, walked up to the ticket agent, and inquired as to the next boat out. 'One week,' he said. Okay, no reason to panic. I'll get a room somewhere and relax. Four hours later, after being turned down by every pensione in town, I finally found an out-of-the-way dump that gave me a room near the goats. Actually, I think it was a room *for* the goats. I sat in that room for seven days and seven nights, played a sad, sad harmonica, and thought about nothing but Annika.

By the time I got out of Kárpathos, I was half-crazed with anticipation. I paced the deck of the ship as we headed farther east through choppy waters, and when we finally pulled into the harbor of Rhodes, I could barely breathe. I figured maybe, just *maybe*, Annika would be waiting for me on the pier. There were boats directly from Crete to Rhodes, after all, and she could have gotten there already. I looked at all the people milling around the docks and felt disappointed not to see her, then headed straight for the American Express office to collect my mail, going over again in my mind – as I'd done twenty times on the boat – how I'd space out all her letters. The first I'd read over coffee at some outdoor café. The next I'd read in bed that night. The rest I'd save for morning – 'I'm sorry, there is nothing,' said the man behind the counter.

'There must be some mistake,' I said, in disbelief. 'Can you look again?' As he flipped through the mail a second time, I suddenly realized what must have happened. Annika had sent her letters to the post office instead! I headed up the Alexandru Diaku to the main post office, then waited anxiously at the Poste Restante window while the clerk looked through a pile of mail.

'*Ochi*,' she said, shaking her head. I couldn't believe it. There *must* be a mistake.

I walked out into the bright sunshine in a daze, leaned against the wall for support, and stared at the ground. That's when I heard a familiar-sounding greeting. '*Godag!*' My heart leapt with joy. Look how she'd fooled me! She'd been following me all along and was finally putting an end to the charade! Oh, I'll punish you for this, I laughed, as I looked up to see a blond, blue-eyed beach bunny hurrying past me into the arms of her boyfriend. I staggered away, hating her for not being Annika, and headed for the main square. Walking past an outdoor café, I heard Swedish again – a whole family was yammering away – then I heard it again, and then, passing a newsstand, I saw copies of the *Stockholm Aftenbladet* and the *Gothenburg Express* prominently displayed. What the hell is going on here? I checked into a pensione and glanced at the names on the registry. Jenson. Anderson. Johansson. '*Godag*,' said a woman coming down the stairs. '*Godag*,' replied a man coming in. Were they trying to drive me crazy? I soon discovered that this little town, on the tip of Greece's most remote island, was Carlsson Travel's most popular destination. The charter flight was so cheap, the hotels so cheap, the food so cheap, that Swedes couldn't afford *not* to come here. It was cheaper than staying home.

I could have gotten onto a ship to Cyprus that night. From there, it would've been a quick hop to Lebanon, or Israel, or Egypt – any one of which was a good entry point for Africa. If I had one ounce of sense, I would have cut my losses and gotten the hell out of there. Only a total fool would subject himself to this torture. Only a total fool would order Swedish meatballs in Rhodes. Only a total fool would check himself into a room to wait for a letter.

I wasn't a total fool. I was worse. After a few days I got on a bus that wound its way down the east coast of the island to the town of Lindos. Lindos was a spot the Swedes had yet to invade, so it was well worth the fifty miles of potholed roads that rattled the bus the entire way. I looked out over what I think was the Mediterranean – I never got it straight where the Aegean ends and the Mediterranean begins – and decided I'd wait a week before returning to Rhodes. Two days later I found myself back at American Express, where there was nothing, then went to the post office, then got back on the bus. The whole thing took exactly six hours and twenty minutes.

Now I was really getting worried. It didn't seem possible that Annika wouldn't write, no, she must be in some kind of trouble, and here I am, unable to protect her, unable to save her from whatever peril might have befallen her, yes, I've failed her once again, but this time it's worse, this time her life might be at stake – why else wouldn't she write? – my conscience is throbbing with the pain of indecision – should I try to find her or should I wait? – she must be in danger, what else could it be, no, it's the only possibility . . . *unless she lied to me and never planned to write and has run off with some other guy.*

I wandered into a café in Lindos, sat right down next to an attractive woman, and spilled out my full cup of paranoia: 'Okay, you're a woman, right?'

'Uh . . . right.'

'Let me ask you something. Let's say, hypothetically, some guy is crazy in love with you, he worships the ground you walk on, he'll do anything for you, he'll die for you—'

She looked at me suspiciously. 'Yessss . . .'

'And then, all of a sudden, just a couple of days after you start traveling together, you start acting weird, but he's totally cool about it, always there for you—'

The woman leaned back a little in her chair. '*Uh-huuuh* . . .'

'And then you wind up on some island somewhere, and you make his life completely miserable, this guy who loves you, you treat him like dirt, you ignore him, you stop talking, you stop screwing, you stop acting like a human being—'

'Listen, I really—'

'And then you finally get him where you want him, you drive him to the edge, you give him no option but to leave, and *then*, you say you'll write him, that you just need a little time—'

She raised her hand toward the kitchen. 'Waiter.'

151

'But you don't write him, do you? No, this was the little arrow you still had in your quiver, the one thing he didn't see coming, because then he starts thinking that nobody could be that cruel, that nobody could fuck with somebody's head like that, and that's when he starts worrying that something has happened to you, you've been abducted, you need him, you're locked up in some dungeon crying out his name—'

'*Waiter!*'

'Look, I know that guys are assholes, I know we're insensitive and self-centered and total jerks, but when it comes to breaking up, no guy on this planet would even dream of doing to a woman what she'd do to him, because when it comes right down to it, for all the nurturing and kindness and gentleness, when a woman decides it's over, she becomes the worst fucking monster in the world, she'll stop at nothing, she'll stab him in the back, she'll slit his throat . . . *won't* you?' The woman pushed back her chair. 'And why? Because he *loved* you? Because he *cared* about you? Because he *worried* about you? What kind of gratitude is *that*?'

'This really has been lovely—' she said, standing up.

'Wait, wait. You haven't told me what you think.'

The woman turned back and fixed me with a stare. 'I think that if you're her boyfriend, she's in enormously big trouble.'

I watched her leave, wondering what the hell *that* meant, then noticed a clock on the wall. If I really wanted to, I could still catch the bus to Rhodes.

'Nothing,' said the clerk at American Express.

'*Ochi*,' said the woman at Poste Restante.

Pink Floyd had a summer home in Lindos. It was just down from the Acropolis, which is like the one in Athens, only better preserved. The Acropolis is built upon a steep cliff and has a sense of grandeur, scale, and over-the-top exorbitance. The perfect place, in other words, to serve as Pink Floyd's backyard. One night I walked into a restaurant and saw David Gilmour and Roger Waters sitting at opposite ends of a long table. Between them were wives, roadies, groupies, and assorted hangers-on. Probably mistaking me for some-body in their crew, they invited me to join them.

I sat there, glum, distracted, crazy with worry. Why hasn't she written? Is she all right? What now? I couldn't stop thinking about her. I could go back to Crete, yeah, that makes sense, except she won't be there, I know she won't be there – how do I know? – I have no idea how I know, I just know— 'So, what brings you to Lindos?' said a spacey blonde.

'A woman.'

'Oh?' said an intensely alert brunette.

'We were on our way to Africa, but then things went bad.'

'Where is she now?' mumbled a redhead through half-closed eyes.

'Well, that's just the thing, I don't even know for sure. I mean, part of me just wants to get on a boat to Africa, but another part says I need to hear from her first, and another part says I'm crazy to even think of going down there alone, what if something happened to me, nobody would even know, maybe I should carry a gun, who knows what I'll be facing, and I'll need bullets, six at least, maybe a couple dozen, 'cause I figure if I need six, I'll probably need a lot more, but shit, I don't even like *bugs*, what am I even think-ing about, maybe I should just go back to Sweden, where I wouldn't have to worry about shooting anybody.' The three women were so stoned on pot, uppers, and downers that they listened to me as if I were actually making sense.

'Why hasn't she written?' said the blonde.

'Is she all right?' said the brunette.

'What now?' said the redhead.

'That's exactly what *I've* been wondering!' I said, leaping from my seat.

The next morning, sixteen days after arriving in Rhodes, I sent telegrams to Sitia, Iráklion, Canea, and Mykonos:

DEAR ANNIKA. I'M SORRY FOR EVERYTHING THAT HAPPENED. PLEASE TELL ME YOU'RE ALL RIGHT. LOVE.

I knew every curve in the road between Lindos and Rhodes, every bump and dip and pothole. I knew all the villages along the way and could name the storefronts, restaurants, and bars. I knew which hills had sheep and which had goats. I knew if the bus was a little ahead of schedule or a little behind. I knew where we could make up time and where we could get stuck behind the gasoline truck. I knew the lady who got on outside Kolimbia and got off on the third hill past the stone fence. I also got to know the clerk at American Express and the woman at Poste Restante. 'Nothing,' he'd say, shaking his head. '*Ochi*,' she'd say with a sad-eyed glance.

Two weeks after sending the telegrams, there was still no word. I sat beneath the columns of the Acropolis, feeling overwhelmed and insignificant, staring at the jagged rocks far below. I knew this was it, that I couldn't make one more bus trip, but I also knew I'd never forgive myself if I didn't find her.

# 14

## Epiphany on a Park Bench

The ship to Mykonos sailed up through the Dodecanese Islands, coming so close to Turkey several times that I could've jumped off and swum ashore. I considered doing exactly that a few times, but then I reminded myself that the likelihood of finding Annika in some desolate Turkish village was rather slim. The journey lasted forty-five hours, with stops in Kos, Kalimnos, and Samos. As we pulled into each port, I looked out over the docks, wondering if she might be there. By the time we tied up at the harbor in Mykonos, my body was pumping with adrenaline. I ran along the docks, bounded up the stairs of the post office, and pushed to the front of the line. I felt my heart pounding and a strange pressure building in my ears as I explained to the clerk that I needed to know if a telegram had been picked up.

'Sorry,' he said. 'Cannot do that.'

'Why not? I just want to see if it was signed for.'

'*Ochi.*'

'Listen to me. I just spent two days on a boat and I'm not leaving here until you show me your records. Understand?'

He rose up in his chair and called over my shoulder, 'Next.'

I blocked the window with my body, refusing to move. 'Show me the signatures.'

'I will call the police!'

'I don't care if you call the fucking *Colonels*. Show me!'

I must've said the magic words. The clerk glared at me,

pushed away from his chair, walked to a table at the rear, and returned with a tattered notebook. 'What day?' he said coldly.

'July 24.' He opened the book, turned back a few pages, then slid it under the bars of the window. I ran my finger down a list of names. There, near the bottom, Annika's name was printed out, along with the hour the telegram was received. I ran my finger across the page and there it was – unmistakable – her signature. I stared at it a moment, turned away, then looked back. It was signed for on July 25. 'Thank God she's alive,' I said to myself as I walked out of the post office in a daze. 'I'm going to kill her.'

If I'd had an ounce of sense, I would've gotten onto a boat for Cyprus, or Athens, or Istanbul, that very moment, but I'd left my senses, along with my last shred of dignity, on some beach on what may or may not have been the Mediterranean. I dropped off my things at a portside pensione and began searching the town. I looked in every restaurant, shop, and bar. I walked back into the hills, down along the water, and through every alleyway. That night, unable to eat a thing, I checked every corner of every disco, then retraced my steps through the outdoor bars and cafés.

The next morning, before the sun was barely up, I was back at all the breakfast spots, making the rounds from one end of town to the other. Still, I couldn't eat. I felt I was running on some kind of psychic energy that would lead me to the right spot. A hotel clerk suggested I try the outer beaches, where people camped out. I took a motor launch to Paradise Beach, a spot halfway around the island, and forty-five minutes later jumped off the boat onto a long stretch of white sand. There were hills on either side of the beach and mountains in back, where a handful of simple stucco houses dotted the landscape. Paradise had a mixed crowd but was known mostly as a gay beach. Assuming Annika had met up with Rick and Robbie, it seemed as likely a place as any to find her. I walked along the dunes, up into the hills, and back to the little bars and cabanas that dotted the palm groves. She wasn't there.

That night I again searched the discos, bars, and restaurants in town. I kept circling back, around and around, the pop music thumping in my ears, that horrible European beat that never wavers, that just pounds and pounds and pounds. Lying in bed that night, unable to sleep, I couldn't get the sounds of the discos out of my head. 'Hey! Europeans! Listen up! Try it a little *off* the beat once in a while. This isn't Swiss watches you're making, it's *music*.'

The next morning, still unable to eat, I did a quick check of the breakfast cafés, then took a launch to Super Paradise, the next of the outer beaches. As the boatman motored around a jetty and turned for the shore, I saw a beautiful expanse nestled between the hills. He pulled into a little cove and I walked along the edge of the water, then cut up toward some dunes that rolled gently to the base of the hills. A few couples had already declared their pieces of sand for the day, cordoning off territory with towels, shoes, and bottles of coconut oil. Closer to the hills, I noticed a tent pitched just where the ground began to rise, partially sheltered from the sun and wind. A portly Chinese man, his long black hair tied into a topknot, was busy drawing out an astrological chart, while two women watched over his shoulder. A third woman sat up on her elbows in the dunes, consulting her own chart. I watched her a moment from the distance as a million thoughts raced through my mind. Memories of the night we met in Stockholm . . . New Year's Eve at Sten's house . . . the Greek restaurant in Gamla Stan . . . the two missing escargots . . .

'Annika,' I finally said to her, in a bare whisper.

She turned into the sun and shaded her eyes. It took a moment to fully register, but when she realized it was me, she came right over. 'Well, this is a surprise,' she said, giving me a hug.

I stood there like a petrified tree, unable to move a muscle. Finally I choked out a couple of words: 'Can we talk somewhere?' She pointed to a cove just beyond the dunes. I followed her over some jagged rocks to a sheltered inlet, where we sat on a boulder overlooking the sea. My mouth was so dry, I could barely speak: 'Annika . . . I was so worried . . . Why didn't you write?'

'I meant to.'

'You *meant* to? It's been almost five weeks!'

She narrowed her eyes and stared at me. 'Oh, really?'

For a moment I was transported to Robert's houseboat in Amsterdam, where I watched the canals melting in the early Dutch spring. 'Okay, I understand. We're even, we're more than even, you've made your point.'

'What point is that?'

'C'mon, Annika, don't do this to me.'

'I'm not doing anything to you. If you must know, I was actually just about to write.'

'Oh?' I said. A glimmer of hope at last. 'What were you going to say?'

'I was going to say that I thought it was better if we didn't get back together right now.' The days of sleep and food deprivation hit at that instant, and my mouth felt like sandpaper. 'I'm sorry,' she said. 'I don't know what else to say.'

The full extent of the disaster was slowly taking hold. She was leaving me. *No woman had ever left me*. She didn't care about me. *They always cared*. She'd never take me back again. *They always wanted me back*. No, wait, this can't be. I've got to have her. I can't go on like this. I'd give my life for her. 'Annika, listen to me, I've got no idea what to do anymore.'

'Why don't you hang out a few days on the beach and figure it out?'

I thought about it for a moment. Okay, that didn't sound so bad. 'You mean, with you?'

'No . . . we're pretty full up in the tent right now.'

'*We?*'

'There's a bunch of us.'

'But where can—'

'I don't know. There's lots of places. Try one of the other beaches.'

'Annika—'

'Listen, you can't just show up here and expect everything to be the way it was.'

'I don't want it to be the way it was. I want it to be better.'

'Remember what I said in Paris?'

'Yeah, about trust. Listen, I swear—'

'I also said I wasn't promising anything, that we were just giving it a try—'

'What kind of a try was *that*? I mean, hell, so we got way-laid by a couple of fucked-up islands.'

'I don't think it was the islands' fault.'

I felt my mouth going dry again. 'Listen, what happened in Stockholm – I mean – we never really talked about it.'

Annika gave me a cold look and moved away. 'Like I said, try one of the other beaches. I've gotta go. I've got a reading coming up.' And with that, she was gone.

The happiness of Athens had now fully reversed, it had become its mirror image and then some, that's right, I've shot right through the mirror, splintered it into a thousand fragments, and entered some whole new blackness. We're not supposed to be there, behind the mirror, we weren't made for that, it's wholly foreign terrain; I can't get my bearings, I'm being dragged down, I'm gasping for air too thin to breathe, get me out, please, just get me out, because I'm feeling like I did in that palm grove in Crete, I hate this feeling, there's something going on that I don't understand, it's not even about Annika, no, there is something else altogether going on, there *always* was something else going on, the film in my mind, it's slowing down again, it's like that moment on Vai, there's something I can almost touch, it's like a door that's been slammed shut my whole life that wants to open, yes, I can nearly see a tiny crack of light, it's scary, it's like the light in that dream in Santorini when Annika pulled open the blind and my skin burst into flames, but this light is illuminating something too dark, something that's supposed to stay buried, it's like some sarcophagus in an Egyptian crypt about to unleash a horrible curse, no, it's better left untouched, this door needs to remain locked and never be opened.

I moved into a little half-cave on Ilya, the next beach over. Even though there were fewer people staying there, all the good caves were already taken. In a way, though, it didn't really matter. I figured if I cut out my heart and kidneys, I'd just about be able to squeeze my way in. My spine, after all, was already gone. I awoke each morning with Annika on my mind and fell asleep each night thinking about her. I saw her face in the wisps of clouds that floated in from North Africa. I saw her silhouette in the shadows along the pathways. I saw her name spelled out in the little ridges and depressions of the sand. She was in every song, in every painting, in every poem, and destiny told me there was a reason, that this was leading somewhere, that I was being tested, that all of this meant something.

Many of the cave dwellers had been to India, and most of them were going back. They were different from other travelers. They had a look in their eyes, like they knew something, like they were just biding their time. Greece for them was just a way station, a place to escape the monsoon before returning to the source of the magic. I thought back to Berkeley, when I stood in the streets with a brick in my hand, and realized I was now halfway to India, and for an instant I got a glimpse of a cobblestone path, a long windy path that led to a sacred river, but just as quickly it was gone, vanished into thin air, as if it were a road to a kingdom that was being denied me. No, I wasn't ready for India, not even close, India scared the hell out of me, these people scared the hell out of me, I need to go slowly, one step at a time, maybe I'll dip my toes into one of the arcane sciences, sure, maybe astrology, no, that's too obvious, she'll think I'm copying her, I need something of my own, something to prove that I'm not hopelessly tied to Western ways.

I decided to become a palmist.

I found a book by Cheiro – *Language of the Hand* – and learned all about the shape of the palm, the angles of the thumbs, and the Mound of Venus. I studied the palms of saints and sinners, presidents and perverts, geniuses and goofballs. And then I took a look at my own palm. *Shit!* This, quite simply, was the palm of a maniac. There were so many lines going in so many directions that I got dizzy just looking at it. The life line had enough breaks in it to have killed me years ago. The head line was that of an imbecile. The heart line was a twisted mess that had all sorts of curlicues and dead ends. The fate line bothered me the most. I wasn't quite sure if I had one. Add to that a crazy quilt of grids running every which way and it looked like I had enough lines for four or five people. I had lines up the wazoo. I had lines I couldn't use in three lifetimes. I had lines for sale. I started walking around palms down, so nobody would see.

The weeks passed. I adapted to the cave, the hills, and the sky. I got tougher, my skin got darker, and I built up calluses on the bottom of my feet. I rarely left the beach, but whenever I had to go to town, I took the motor launch and watched from the distance as we passed Super Paradise. Somehow, knowing that Annika was just over the dunes made me feel better.

A month after arriving on Ilya, the cave dwellers decided to throw a party. We built a big pit for a fire, got food from the village, and invited everyone from the other beaches. I waited all day, anxious as a kid on Christmas. I had a feeling Annika would show up and I spruced up my cave for her arrival. She would, after all, have to stay the night, and it would only be gentlemanly to offer to share my quarters, such as they were. Sure enough, a launch arrived just before sunset and there she was. She looked incredibly beautiful. Her skin was tanned, her hair hennaed, her eyes a blazing blue. Then I saw she was with some kid, no more than nineteen years old, who had the glassy eyes of someone who'd been in India too long. Annika came over, gave me a hug, and asked how I was doing. The boyfriend hung back a bit, perhaps sensing that I would gnaw off his arm if he so much as reached out to shake. She did introduce me to two other guys, Rick and Robbie. Ah, so they finally arrived. Annika's friends. I'd better be nice to them. It might give me some points.

The sun set, a full moon rose, and the fire crackled against the bright sky. A hundred people gathered around to drink wine, play music, and dance in the sand. I played harmonica and noticed Annika looking at me from across the fire. I wondered if she remembered the night we met in Stockholm, when I stood on the stage of Magnus Ladulås. As the night wore on, everyone got looser. Rick and Robbie wanted to know everything about me – any friend of Annika's was a friend of theirs – and I made a special effort to be friendly. Finally, around two in the morning, the party started breaking up. Even though we'd hardly spoken, I still held out a glimmer of hope that Annika would come spend the night. I stretched out, feeling a little dizzy, my feet as usual hanging halfway out of the cave, when I felt someone approach. There was a rustling in the sand, then the feel of a warm body near my legs. I could hardly believe it. She'd finally come to her senses, just as I always knew she would. I smiled, turned my head, and opened my eyes.

'Hi,' said Rick.

My head nearly went through the jagged rock four feet above. 'Ha-ha-ho-ho-hi.'

'You don't mind if I join you?'

'Uh, well, as you see, it's a little crowded in here—'

'It's very cozy.'

'Uh-huh, well, yes it is—'

'I've been watching you all night.'

'You have?'

'I can see why Annika is so attracted to you.'

'She is?'

'Annika and I always like the same guys.'

'You do?' Then I felt Rick's hand edging up my shoulder. 'Listen, I'm really not into this,' I said.

'Are you sure?'

Am I sure? Of course I'm sure. I'm as sure as anything in the world. I'm as sure as the sureness of my love for Annika.

I'm as sure as the sureness that we're meant to be together. I'm as sure as – that's when I felt his lips on my mouth. They weren't so different from a woman's lips. They were soft, kind of moist. They pressed gently, like a woman's, a little like Annika's in fact, Annika who was lying a stone's throw away cuddled up in the arms of another guy why isn't it you Annika who's here right now why isn't it you whose lips I'm touching why isn't it you whose arms are moving up along my neck why isn't it you whose body is moving toward mine why isn't it you because if it was I might be feeling something other than an overwhelming sense of twisted irony. 'I'm sorry, Rick,' I said, pulling away.

'You're sure?'

'I'm sure. I mean, I'm flattered, you know?'

'Yeah, well, I just figured I'd try,' he replied. 'No hard feelings?'

'Nothing hard at all. Listen, you need a blanket?'

'That would be nice.'

'Here you go,' I said, tossing it to him as he edged out of the cave. I watched for a moment as he headed down the beach. Then I wrapped the cave around me and went to sleep.

I couldn't take it anymore. Everything was always wrong. The wrong place. The wrong time. The wrong person. There was so much I wanted to say to Annika, I felt my insides would explode. Finally, I wrote her a letter. I worked on it all day, all night, and all the next day again. Then I took a boat around the mountain, dropped the letter off in her tent, and was back on Ilya for sunset. This would be it, I figured, it would straighten things out and put all of this nonsense behind us. I told her how much I'd changed, how much I'd learned, how I could forgive everything. Four days passed with no response. Nothing. I went crazy. It was Kárpathos all over again. It was Rhodes and Lindos all over again. I couldn't take it. I jumped back on the boat to Super Paradise and found Annika in a café. '*Did you read my letter?*' I yelled to her from across the room.

'As much as I could,' she said, jerking her head toward me with blazing eyes, '*You're* going to forgive *me*?'

'Okay, forget that part. That wasn't important. What about the rest?'

'There is no rest. I'm going to India.'

'*What?*'

'That's right. As soon as I can get it together. Oh, and by the way, I threw away my rucksack.'

'Annika, you can't do this to me. *I need you!*'

'Listen to me. I don't know what's wrong with you inside. From the day I met you, you've been seething with anger. It's like you're searching for something and you don't know what it is. *I* certainly don't know what it is. All I know is that I can't give you what you need.'

My chest felt like a corroded tin box ready to collapse upon itself. It was a sensation I hadn't experienced since leaving Berkeley, it was a certain taste in my mouth, the taste of an entire nation that had been poisoned. I was suddenly back on Telegraph Avenue and a volcano of bile was pushing up into the streets and gutters, into the rivers and lakes, into the plants and trees, into the air itself, and finally, into each and every one of us, for we were all poisoned, those who went off to war and those who marched in the streets. She was right, there was something wrong with me, and it had nothing to do with her at all. It's that film in my head, if only I could just slow it down, for just one minute, study one frame, just let me think one complete thought through to its conclusion – 'Look, I'm sorry,' said Annika, 'I really am.'

'Me, too,' I said, backing out of the restaurant, 'me, too.'

September arrived and, with it, the first rains of autumn. I might've stayed in Greece forever were it not for nature forcing my hand. My cave was getting soaked and I knew I couldn't stay on the beach much longer. Most of the travelers had already left, but I was more confused than ever. My six weeks in Mykonos hadn't given me a clue about how to proceed with my life. 'Why don't you come to India?' one of the cavemen asked. I didn't want to tell him that I thought

I'd completely lose my mind if I went to India. Still, I had to do *something*.

When the rains became heavy, I moved into town and waited for the first boat out. With everything to the mainland booked for a week, I locked myself up in an out-of-the-way pensione and tried to figure out what to do. I imagined returning to Paris, or to Amsterdam, even to Stockholm, but nothing made sense. Annika also moved into town and got a job at one of the bars. I made a point of never getting near the place. Then, finally, came the night of my departure for Athens, but as I headed for the port, I was suddenly overcome by a need to see her one last time. I found myself sitting across from her at the bar. 'So, you're leaving,' she said, glancing at my rucksack.

'Yeah, time to move on,' I said, with forced nonchalance. I caught a glint in Annika's eyes and wondered if there was still a chance. 'You could still catch the boat with me,' I said.

She seemed to waver a moment, then shook her head. 'No, I don't think so.'

'Yeah, India's probably better.'

Annika touched my hand, then gave me a quick hug. 'Don't get lost out there.'

And that was it. A little glance, a quick hug, and we were done. As climaxes go, it was hardly befitting of Dietrich or Bergman, but why would it be? This was real life, and real life is guaranteed to disappoint all but the hardest hearts among us. I walked out of the club, emptied of all feeling. A chapter of my life was ending that I didn't want to end. I got onto a ship that I didn't want to take. I was facing a journey I didn't want to begin.

The next morning, I found myself lying on a bench in Zappion Gardens, off Constitution Square in Athens. Four months earlier, Annika and I had walked down these same paths, laughing with the children playing on the grass, petting the animals at the miniature zoo, watching the women pushing strollers under the shade of giant oak trees. Now, I was all alone, reliving every painful memory, unable to get her face out of my mind. How could I keep thinking about her? Why couldn't I let go?

The ship from Mykonos had been horribly overcrowded, with barely enough room to stand, much less sleep. Now, I was trying to get one hour's sleep, one minute's sleep, before I completely lost my mind. The heat of the afternoon sun parched my throat and I could feel my shirt and pants clinging to my body. I was fully stretched out on the bench, lying on my back, praying for even the hint of a breeze, my eyes closed, drifting off to sleep, when I heard a sharp crack. My eyes snapped open. I looked around, hoping to find a gunshot wound to the heart, but there was no such luck. There was no blood, no guts, no nothing. Just a mysterious loud crack coming out of nowhere, going nowhere, and leaving no sign of ever having happened. How perfectly Greek.

Oh, God, please let me sleep, just one hour, that's all I ask. Let me forget this miserable place, the toxic blue waters, the horrible beautiful beaches, the terrible quaint villages, the monstrous idyllic islands. I felt myself slipping in and out of consciousness, fading out of the nightmare, falling into a dreamworld . . .

My body jerked awake as a jolt of adrenaline drove up along my spine. I felt myself moving, uncoiling really, like a cobra propelling through the air, and then, for a brief instant, time itself seemed to freeze. I found myself in some space where gravity no longer operated, where there was no up or down, where the laws of physics no longer applied. Then I was on the ground. A twenty-foot limb of the oak tree smashed onto the bench, a jagged branch slashed into my leg, and the earth trembled as the force of impact settled in. I pulled myself up on one arm and looked around in a daze. I saw that I was ten feet from the bench, lying in a cloud of dust, my pants ripped, blood streaming from a deep wound. Then I saw that the main section of the limb had landed exactly where my head had been. Had I not moved – had I been asleep – my skull would have been crushed to pieces. And I began to understand something . . .

I was being given a second chance. I had to pull my life

together. I had to stop thinking about her. I saw ten thousand tiny points of light shining through the broken branches and realized that the last time things made sense I was on my way to Africa. Now I understood that I needed to continue on. Alone.

As I gathered my things together and headed for the airport, I knew I had to change who I was. I had to find something to build upon. I had to become a man.

# 15

## The Heart of Africa

I walked out of Nairobi International Airport and was bitten
by a six-foot-long black mamba. The snake was astonish-
ingly fast. It bolted down from an overhanging tree, zoomed
across some grass, rolled into a tight explosive coil, and
lashed out like a jolt of lightning into the soft flesh above my
stomach. Its fangs dug deep, as if searching for Adam's missing rib, and I felt an extraordinary rush of pain. I prayed it
would let go, but the mamba twisted its jaw deeper into my
skin, shaking and pulling and tearing at the flesh. Its eyes
were unrelenting, piercing rays of anger, its body a throbbing
mass of muscle that jerked hysterically through the air. Just
when the pain became unbearable, I heard a quick hissing
sound, like a valve decompressing, and felt two jets of hot
liquid piercing into my veins. The mamba hung on even
tighter, making sure that not one drop of the venom foaming
in its fangs would miss its mark. At first, it wasn't much
different than receiving a shot of Novocain – a localized
numbness that I almost welcomed with relief – but then the
numbness began to travel up my rib cage and I felt myself
gasping for air. My insides were getting icy cold, like a
steel crypt. I was being buried from the inside out.
The venom raced around the ventricles of my heart, then
shot for my brain. Like an air gun shooting rabbits
at an arcade, it knocked out my hearing, then my sight.
Soon I could smell nothing but fear, and touch nothing
but the innermost traces of my subconscious. Three

minutes to live, two minutes to live, one minute to live . . .

A stewardess gently tapped my arm and pulled me out of my reverie. 'Please fasten your seat belt, sir. We'll be landing in five minutes.' As the plane descended into the heart of Africa, I tried, for a few minutes at least, to put aside my fears.

I walked out of Nairobi International Airport and was met by a tall black man with a friendly face: '*Jambo, bwana,*' he said. 'Do you need taxi?'

'Can you take me to the zoo?' I asked.

'The zoo?' he asked, uncertainly. I showed him a brochure from the tourist desk, and he shuddered. 'Oh, yes-yes, the snake farm. Why would you want to go there, bwana?'

'I want to meet the enemy.' He laughed and picked up my rucksack. I immediately liked this guy. I liked his laugh. I liked that I felt safe with him. I especially liked that he called me bwana. It reminded me of those Tarzan movies, where everybody was bwana-this and bwana-that and now *I* was bwana, a man of respect, and respect was certainly what I had earned, having flown all the way to Nairobi on nothing but my own ingenuity and a severely depleted savings account. At the snake park, the driver – who was even more terrified of snakes than I – waited in the parking lot while my worst fears were confirmed: spitting cobra, number of bites reported in 1971, 18, number of fatalities, 18; puff adder, number of bites, 27, fatalities, 27; gaboon viper, reported bites, 6, fatalities, 6. There were rock pythons, black mambas, mountain adders, ball pythons, night adders, green mambas, reticulated pythons, many-horned adders, boom-slangs, and vine snakes. The boomslang was unique. With a fatality rate of only 96 percent, it hardly seemed dangerous. Mambas, on the other hand, struck you in the midsection, leaving you three minutes to live. The spitting cobra was also interesting. It draped itself in trees, spit blinding venom into the whites of your eyes, then bit the shit out of you.

'Airport!' I yelled to the driver as I leapt into the backseat of his cab. I figured that with any luck I could get back on the plane before it turned around for Athens.

* * *

The driver convinced me that no one ever got bitten in Nairobi, so I decided to give Africa three days. He took me to the outskirts of town, to a campsite where Westerners congregated. It felt a little strange to be in a campsite without a car, but being with Westerners made me feel a bit more comfortable. Not that these were exactly my kind of Westerners. Most of them had driven Land Rovers through the Sahara and were a pretty macho lot. They drank cheap beer, read mountain climbing magazines, and listened to shitty music. Still, as I lay in my sleeping bag between their vans, I was glad to be in familiar company. If I got attacked in the middle of the night by a spitting cobra, at least my dying screams could be in English.

I made my first foray into Nairobi the next day. Even though Kenya had been independent for eight years, Nairobi still had distinct neighborhoods for the British, the Indians, the Arabs, and the Africans. It seemed strange to be in the heart of Africa and hear of a neighborhood referred to as the 'black quarter,' but when I walked through Korogocho, I felt for the first time that I really was in Kenya. The quarter was poorer than the rest of Nairobi but much more alive. Women in brightly colored *kangas* sold fruit at makeshift stands, while men sat along the shell of an abandoned building, fanning themselves against the heat. I walked past a bar and noticed some music equipment set up inside and a hand-painted sign nailed to the door: TONIGHT: ZAIRE ALL-STARS. I'd heard Zairian *sega* music back in the States – the haunting singing of M'bilia Bel and the lilting melodies of Franco and Rochereau – and couldn't resist going in. As luck would have it, a couple of members of the band were sitting at the bar. I tried speaking to them in English but got nowhere. It was French or nothing. '*J'aime beaucoup la musique sega,*' I said.

'*Vraiment? Merci.*'

'*Je joue l'harmonica.*'

'*Oui? Venez ce soir, s'il vous plaît. Apportez vos amis.*'

'*D'accord.*'

They seemed friendly enough. I wasn't sure if they were

170

asking me to come that night or telling me to take my friends to the airport, but then I noticed a Fender Twin Reverb amplifier, my all-time favorite, sitting on the stage, and that pretty much clinched it. Back at the campground, when I mentioned that I was thinking of playing that night, two couples from the Land Rover brigade and two Australian girls decided to come along.

When we arrived in Korogocho, music was blasting out of the club and the place was packed. As we stood at the door, I could see that the stage was jammed with eight musicians, the dance floor was overflowing, and the bar was three-people deep. Realizing there wasn't a white face in the crowd, the two couples and I got cold feet and decided it was foolhardy to go in. The Australian girls wouldn't hear of it, however, and dragged us through the door. The place instantly became like the set of an old Hollywood B movie. The dancing stopped, the music ground to a halt, and everyone just stood there staring at us. It was as quiet as the Christian Science Reading Room in Stockholm on the day of a blizzard. A path cleared as we went to the bar and ordered seven beers. After a few moments of strained silence, I walked over to the stage and examined the Fender Twin. The old tubes glowed behind a beat-up grill and seemed in danger of overheating. When I held open a box of harps, one of the musicians finally recognized me from that afternoon. '*L'harmonica!*' he said, grinning. He pulled one out of the box and held the four-inch, ten-holed instrument up to the audience. The whole place started laughing.

I stood there like Clint Eastwood. You can fuck with my land. You can fuck with my horse. You can even fuck with my boots. But you don't fuck with my harmonica – that you don't do. The band tuned up and I plugged into the amp. Maybe they'd heard some knucklehead noodling around on the street with his fifty-cent harp, but this is the real deal, ladies and gentlemen, and I'm betting nobody in here ever heard it played Chicago-style, through a microphone. The band kicked into a twelve-bar blues – my bread and butter – and I waited for an intro, a chorus, and the turnaround. The

171

Westerners looked at me, wondering if I was ever going to play. In due time, blue eyes, in due time. Because right now, I'm no longer a palmist, I'm no longer a traveler or a seeker or a jilted lover. Because right now, as I take this Marine Band harmonica in the key of D and cup my hands tightly around the microphone, right now I'm a blues musician, and I'm gonna bend this note right down your spine, I'm gonna push it through your stomach and right out your ass, I'm gonna take this tone and bounce it off the walls and reverberate it around the room and blast it so far down inside your soul you'll never know what hit you, I'm going to push deeper and deeper and shake you right to the core because I'm angry, that's right, Annika, you were right all along, I'm as pissed off as they come, and these reeds are vibrating with my anger and throbbing with my anger and I hope you can hear me wherever you are right now, I hope these tones barrel right through your harem tent and knock your astrology books to the floor, I hope the wind blows and the ground shakes and the sky crackles with thunder, and I turn to the guys in the band and they're looking at me in amazement as I bend a note right over the top of a mountain and it comes cascading down in little pieces like fine mist, and the drums start to *chug-chug-a-chug-chug-a-chug-chug-a* and the bass line hits perfectly just off the beat, and the guitars play a lilting counter rhythm, and the horn section blasts in unison, and then the two Australian girls begin dancing to the music and some Africans take the floor and the beer begins to flow. More couples get off their chairs, some women come in from outside, and some guys edge toward the front as the white girls start dancing with the Africans, and now everyone's crowding closer to the stage and a guy is looking up at me trying to figure out where this big big *big* sound is coming from and I hit a note I've been searching for for five years and it nearly blows through my head, an insanely perfect note that comes out of rage and transforms into something I don't understand, something ethereal, something beyond me, something that arises not so much out of me as through me and reaches higher higher

higher higher, and now the place is going nuts; the trumpet player has his arm around me and is blasting some crazy riff, and we all hit the same groove and it's flowing like water, it's raging like a storm, it's pouring sweat and tears and – *what's this?* – the bass player pulls a towel from his bag and I figure it's to wipe his face, but no, he slings that towel around his ass and starts shimmying back and forth while playing bass at the same time, and the audience is hooting and hollering, especially when the towel gets passed over to the sax player, who starts dancing with it while taking a wild solo and never missing a beat, none of us misses a beat, not even me, me who's wondering what the hell I'm gonna do if that damn towel ever comes *my* way and – *uh-oh!* – sure enough, here it is, so now what do I do, I mean, believe me, I'm not that hot of a dancer, but here we go folks, yesiree, I've got the towel around *my* ass, and I'm doing some kind of hippie-hippie shake and ho-*ho*, am I hearing things or is that women screaming in the audience – *yes!* – and the band keeps jammin' and the crowd keeps slammin' and the towel keeps snappin' and the music keeps pushing on and on and I'm thinking maybe this Africa scene isn't so bad, not so bad at all . . .

'Hello, Rajiv?' I said into the phone. 'You probably don't remember me, but we were on a plane together from New York to London – that's right, almost two years ago.'

A few hours later, I was at Rajiv's house having a big Indian spread. I was surprised at the opulence of the place and the number of servants. 'So, how do you like my country?' he asked.

'So far, I like it just fine.'

'It's a good thing you came before it is ruined.'

'How's that?'

'There are changes ahead. This Idi Amin in Uganda, I don't trust him. We hear rumors that he has it in for the Indians.'

Rajiv's cousin Anand leaned over the table. 'Have you seen him? He looks like one of those big mountain gorillas.'

Anand's wife broke off some chapati. 'All the Ugandans look like mountain gorillas.'

'Yes, they're not like our blacks. Our blacks left the trees many years ago,' said Rajiv.

'Oh?' said Anand. 'And when was that?'

'When the Brits shooed them down to polish our boots.' Everyone at the table had a good laugh. I just sat there. Rajiv patted my arm like a dear old friend. 'You'll see,' he said. 'We Indians have become indispensable to the country.'

'Can you even imagine this place without us?' harrumphed Anand's wife. 'The Brits gave us U.K. citizenship to come here. They should've given us medals.'

'So,' said Anand, 'I understand you are headed for the coast.'

'Soon as I get a ticket on the train. They've been sold out for days.'

'The train? Forget the train. You'll come with me.'

'No, no, I couldn't—'

'Of course you could. I'm going to Mombasa anyway to check on some property.'

I searched for a way out. 'But, really—'

'I won't hear of it,' said Anand. 'We'll leave in two days.'


When Anand picked me up bright and early in his new Mercedes, I told the Land Rover brigade that my chauffeur had arrived, and I said my good-byes. 'Watch out for snakes,' I called to them as we pulled out of the campground, 'and please, get some new tapes.' We headed southeast and descended through the tea plantations and dairy farms of the high country. At Machakos, Anand pulled into a gas station. 'Boy,' he yelled to a fully grown man, 'fill it up. Right to the top. Can you do that? *Upesi!*' He watched through the rearview mirror, shaking his head. 'You see what baboons they are? And this is Kikuyu country. Just wait till you see the Samburu!' As the road continued its descent, the terrain changed and the temperature began to rise. I watched as the hills gave way to plains, the lush forests thinned out to savanna, and the moist vegetation turned to the scraggly

174

bush of the Nyiri Desert. By the time we were halfway to Mombasa, about six hours into the journey, Anand had thoroughly gotten on my nerves. For as beautiful as the countryside was, he delighted in pointing out every pothole, every old car abandoned in a ditch, and every destitute tribesman wandering along the road.

We came upon Tsavo, a giant sanctuary, and saw a dozen elephants spraying each other at a watering hole. Anand slowed down to around forty so I could get a glimpse, then resumed speed. 'Mustn't delay,' he said. We stopped at Voi for another refill, Anand made a few more choice slurs, and then we were back on the road, heading toward the coast, watching the terrain change once again. It was no longer as heavily forested as up-country, but there was an endless sea of palm trees, mango trees, and the occasional baobab, a tree that looks like it's growing upside down, with its scrawny limbs shooting out like twisted roots. As the sun began to set, I could see the silhouette of Mombasa on the horizon. The air was thick and heavy, but I could smell the familiar scent of the sea as we crossed over one last range of hills. Moments later it was dark – the sun sets quickly in the tropics – and by the time we crossed a causeway into the city, it felt like midnight. Anand sped through town, turned onto Kilindini Road, and honked at some bicyclists blocking his lane. 'Monkeys!' he muttered as a stoplight turned red.

'Well, that'll do it,' I said, opening the door. 'Thanks for the ride.'

He looked at me in shock. 'But what do you mean? We are not yet at my cousin's house.'

'It's been a real experience,' I said, grabbing my rucksack from the backseat.

'But where will you go? It's a big city. You may get lost.'

'That's what I'm hoping.'

'But . . . but . . .'

'See ya, Anand.'

'Yes, yes, okay, *see ya*.'

\* \* \*

175

Mombasa was immediately more appealing than Nairobi. It's an old city, an ancient Arab sultanate with a hodgepodge of cultural influences that have been absorbed by the local Swahilis. Maybe it was the heat, or the humidity, or the sea air, or the Islamic influence, but the Swahilis seemed mellower than the up-country people and the town more laid-back. Tired from the drive, I checked into a funky hotel and was lulled to sleep by the sound of a harmonium – a kind of Indian accordion – and a man's plaintive singing in the distance. I fell into a semiconscious dreamworld of the sixteenth century, where a sailor sang from the deck of an ancient dhow.

I awoke the next morning to find thirty-four mosquito bites covering my body – a rather bruising welcome to this Sultanate of Swat. With one-in-seven mosquitoes in Kenya said to carry malaria, I prayed that my quinine pills were working overtime. I discovered that most of the shops and restaurants were closed, not for the morning, not for the day, but for the *month*. It was Ramadan, Islam's holiest time of the year, and a time of total fasting from sunrise to sunset. I finally found a Hindu café, had curried vegetables for breakfast, then headed down to the market place. The stalls were lined with dates – huge blocks of dates, dates in storage bins, dates on shelves, dates on the sidewalk, dates in the backs of trucks, dates in barrels, dates in boxes, dates in bags, dates on plates, dates in crates. 'So, what's with the dates?' I asked a shopkeeper.

'It is how we break the fast each night,' he said. The fast became a feast at sundown. Rice, goat, fish, kabobs – on and on it went into the night. Then came the harmonium players and the singers. Then came the mosquitoes. Then came an early waking before sunrise to fill the stomach for the day. And then came the rain.

I had heard plenty about the monsoon. Just the sound of the word made me feel damp. *Monsoon* simply has too many os in it, and I always imagined a deluge slipping right through the letters themselves. I had supposedly arrived at the tail end of the monsoon, but on my second morning in

Mombasa, the tail started flopping around like crazy. The heavens didn't so much explode, it was more as if the hands of God just shoved the sky away so there was nothing left to hold back the water. It rained for thirty-six hours straight, never wavering in intensity – just a massive downpour that kept coming and coming and coming. The sewers backed up by noon, the streets flooded by night, the sidewalks washed away by morning, and then it rained some more.

The mosquitoes stared out the window and just laughed at the rain. They also laughed at me. 'So, who's the white guy?'

'Dunno. He just blew in.'

'You check 'im out?'

'Last night. The shoulder's not bad.'

'Yeah? I tried the ankle.'

'And?'

'I've had worse.'

'Whattaya think? Check out the neck?'

'You're on. Meecha over there.'

When the skies finally cleared for a minute or two, I decided to take advantage of the opportunity to find drier ground. East, west, north, south – it didn't matter. The middle of the ocean would've been drier ground. As no buses were scheduled for that particular direction, however, I chose to go north, because . . . well, there really was no because.

# 16

# Lamu

The road out of Mombasa was well paved, and the bus made good time. It was about forty miles to the town of Kilifi and then another fifty to Malindi. Malindi was the first resort town of East Africa, built up by the British colonials as a spot for their summer homes. Now, a couple of hotels had been constructed and the town was trying to draw tourists as well. Well, sorry, folks, this just isn't for me, I mean these are *tourists*, the kind with suitcases, not rucksacks, not to mention cameras, safari hats, bush jackets, and watches that work in any climate. Me, I don't have a watch, all I've got is a cheap Timex travel clock, the kind you wind up a few dozen times before the spring breaks, and that's only for major emergencies, like getting up in the middle of the night to take my malaria pills, no, not only do I not know what time it is, I don't even know what day it is, and now that I'm slowly acclimating to life in the tropics, I'm not completely sure about the month or year, either. No, I see a guy with a watch and I head the other way, watches and cameras and suitcases are all very bad signs, you know who travels like that, regular people, that's who, and from a quick look at things, Malindi seems to be crawling with them – regular men, regular women, even regular babies, sure, why not, get 'em while they're young, put little watches on their wrists and little suitcases in their hands and little cameras around their necks, and unleash them on the unsuspecting locals. Well, enjoy yourself, folks, but I'll just be heading right back to the station, where I'll catch the next bus to wherever it's going. What's that? Lamu you say? Fine. Lamu.

Wherever that is.

The bus was a poor, broken-down cousin of the one on the Mombasa–Malindi route. A few miles out of town, I realized why. The nice tarmac road ended, and we were on nothing but a dirt track. Because of the monsoon, the road was a series of endless potholes, with whole sections washed away. As we pushed further from Malindi, the Western-style clothing of the city gave way to customary tribal dress, and it seemed like we were traveling back in time. A woman with eight inches of metal rings around her neck sat next to me for a while, then came a man with ochre and beads matted into his hair, and later an old lady with earlobes that stretched to her shoulders. About halfway to Garsen, a hundred miles due north and slightly in from the coast, the driver jumped off the bus, bought a little bundle of what looked like tree bark, and began voraciously chewing it. The old lady sitting next to me giggled when I pointed at the bundle, then opened her eyes wide into a trancelike stare and said: '*Khat*.' The driver shoved a big wad into his mouth, chomped down, and seemed to get energized for the next leg of the journey.

Like *really* energized. As we came barreling around a curve in the road, he saw a family of baboons and did what any red-blooded, amphetamine-crazed guy behind the wheel would do: He tried to run them down. Suddenly we're flying down the road, he's got his pedal to the metal, the baboons are tearing ass ahead of us, turning back with these big red eyes and enormous fangs and shrieking like crazy, and suddenly we're up on the bank of the road trying to nail one of these hundred-pound blurs of fury, and now we're *off* the road, and this guy is nuts – nuts nuts *nuts* – the bus is shaking and creaking, some man with a bone through his nose is stomping on the aisle across from me, a kid is leaning out a window trying to grab a mango off a tree we're about to crash into, and the baboons are *really* getting crazy now, but not as crazy as the driver, who's chewing the khat

179

and having mad ancestral visions as he bears down on the animals and suddenly I hear a *clunk*, and then a *clunkclunkclunk*, and oh, *shit*, he fucking hit one! A cheer goes up among the passengers like they're at a Green Bay Packers game watching Bart Starr connecting with Max McGee in the end zone, and then another *clunkclunkclunk*, oh, God, I can't stand this, and now the baboons are completely freaked out, running up the hills, climbing up the trees, leaping into the bush, and then, all of a sudden, just like that, we're back on the road, the driver's yawning, the guy across the aisle is totally sound asleep, the kid is munching on his mango, and it's like nothing ever happened.

At Garsen a crowd was waiting for the bus, and the moment the doors opened, there was a wild rush to occupy all the empty seats. The fact that there *were* no empty seats didn't seem to matter in the least, not when half the town was hellbent on squeezing in. 'Oh, I get it,' I said to the old lady with the earlobes, 'it's some kind of fraternity prank.' Once every square inch of space was taken, a little kid squeezed between her legs, bent over, and vomited on my shoes.

The bus, nearly tipping over under its weight, pulled out of Garsen and drove about five miles to the Tana River. The river, swelled by the monsoon rains, was raging down the banks so fast, the crocodiles could barely keep up. There was no bridge across the river, just a big barge that the bus had to drive onto, and then an elaborate pulley system to get us across. There was a slight downward grade toward the river, and the bus slowed to about two miles an hour as it approached the barge. That, unfortunately, was still too fast. The road was so muddy, and we were so incredibly overloaded, that the bus started sliding into the water.

'*Ooooooooooooh!*' the women cried.

'*Eeeeeeeeeeeeh!*' the men yelled.

'*Aaaaaaaaaaah!*' I screamed.

The doors swung open, and a bunch of people threw themselves onto the road. Others climbed through the windows. Some tried to squeeze their way down the aisle.

Just as we were about to be engulfed by the river, the driver tossed a wad of khat into his mouth and made a last-ditch effort. He gunned the engine, popped the clutch, spun the steering wheel, and somehow got that damn bus right up onto the barge, where it skidded to within a heartbeat of the water. Everyone piled back on and grabbed a long steel cable that was strung from shore to shore. The boatman called out – '*Umoja!*' – and the passengers started pulling – '*Together!*' – hand over hand, until the barge started creeping across the Tana River. Half an hour later, the barge docked, the bus pushed off, and we were back on the road to Lamu.

When we pulled into McCoy, a two-shack town at the end of the road, the few remaining passengers piled off and headed for a motorboat that served as the ferry to Lamu. We were sixty miles south of Somalia and ten minutes east of nowhere. Lamu is only a mile out in the Indian Ocean, but the main town is on the far side of the island, and the journey took nearly an hour. The boat skimmed along a cove, then crossed to the thick mangrove swamps that engulf the coast. We chugged along into open waters, angled out to avoid a sandbar, then followed the curve of the island. As we came around a bend, the port and town suddenly became visible. A dozen dhows, Arabic-style sailboats with wide bodies and forward-leaning masts, were anchored in the bay. A crew of workers floated heavy mangrove beams out to a barge, while a bunch of naked kids dove off an unsteady pier into the water. When we pulled up to a dock, I jumped off the boat and landed in what could have been the sixteenth century. There were no cars anywhere on the island, no TV antennas, no radio transmitters. The streets were an Arabian maze from medieval times. Thee marketplace looked like it was selling items off the ships of Vasco da Gama.

The people, too, wore clothes that probably hadn't changed in centuries. The men had on *kikoys*, cotton sarongs that wrapped around their waists, and loose-fitting shirts that hung unbuttoned off their shoulders. The women wore full-length black chadors that left nothing visible but their eyes, hands, and feet. The only sartorial concession to the twentieth century was the footwear. Pretty much everyone wore rubber flip-flops, except for some women down around the port who wore colorful plastic shoes with two-inch heels beneath their chadors. I wouldn't learn until much later that they were prostitutes. As I walked through the town, I immediately felt at home. It was small – five thousand of the island's eight thousand inhabitants lived there – but large enough to get lost in the endless alleyways. There was an air of mystery down every turn, a new sight, a different smell, an unusual sound. Night was falling fast, so I checked into a small guest house just across from the port. By the time I came back outside, gas lanterns had lit up the streets and people were strolling along the water's edge. Moments later, I heard an atonal chant from the tower of a mosque and then the clatter of flip-flops against the cobble-stone paths. It was the call to prayer of the muezzin. Lamu is the spiritual center of Islam for eastern Africa. If a Moslem can't make the hajj to Mecca once in his life, then at least he goes to Lamu. I was to learn that Lamu drew all sorts of people. There were sixty-six mosques and twenty-two whorehouses. Or was it the other way around? I could never remember.

Walking along the port, I met Jeff and Barbara, two Westerners who lived on the island. They moved slowly, spoke softly, and said they'd left America years ago to seek out a new truth. I liked them immediately. Barbara mentioned that a room might be available at their friend Pete's house, then looked at me closely and said: 'You're going to be here a while.'

The next day, I walked forty-five minutes to Shela, a village at the tip of the island that was known for having the best beaches around. The village wasn't much more than a few dozen huts and a restaurant, but the beach was worth the trek. The white sand stretched on endlessly, and the water was warm and clear, with waves big enough for bodysurfing.

As the midday sun beat down, I headed back toward town. Following Barbara's directions, I cut inland at the halfway point and walked half a mile to a house that was surrounded by fifteen acres of land, four giant mango trees, one cashew tree, and countless palms. This, apparently, was where Pete lived.

I walked up a sandy path to an open porch and went to knock on the door. Strange. There was no door, just a doorway. I then noticed there was no glass in the windows, no door at the other end of a hall, and no doors to any of the rooms. It was . . . airy. On the front porch was a large grass mat, a kerosene lamp, a little burner, and a couple of utensils. That was it. The place didn't look so much abandoned as bombed out. I hoped I wouldn't find a dead body. '*Uh*, anybody here?' I called out.

I heard some rustling from inside one of the rooms, and a good-looking guy in his thirties poked his head out. 'Good afternoon,' he said with an English accent.

'Hi, Jeff and Barbara suggested I stop by—'

'For a room?'

'*Uh*, yeah.'

'Okay,' he said, pointing to an open doorway at the head of the porch. 'You can have that one.'

'Oh.' That was certainly easy.

'The rent's sixty-five *shillingi*.' I did a quick conversion. Nine dollars a month? For a house with fifteen acres of land? 'Can you pay half?' he asked.

'Does that include utilities?'

'Nice one. Washer and dryer are just down the hall.'

Good, I thought, a Brit with a sense of humor. I looked around at the cracked walls and collapsing ceilings, then walked into my prospective new digs. The room was bizarre. It was a large semicircle with one straight wall, six open windows, and, of course, an open doorway. The heavy ceiling beams were held up by mangrove poles that were jammed into the floor. Other than having a roof over my head – which in this case may or may not be a blessing – it was pretty much like living outdoors.

'I'll take it,' I said as I returned to the porch.

'There's a well out back with questionable water. The loo is the last room on the right.'

'Flush toilet?'

'Nice one. Don't go in there at night.'

'Why not?'

'Just don't go in there at night.'

'Okay, well, I guess I'll just get my things, then. Anything you need from town?'

'Like?'

'I don't know,' I said, looking around. 'Napkins?'

'Nice one. Wake me when you get back.'

Pete gave me detailed instructions, and I took off for town under the sweltering sun. I walked down the path of my new *shamba*, hopped over a bamboo fence, followed a trail over some scraggly dunes, skirted around the back of a deserted house, strolled beneath two enormous mango trees, hurried past the headstones of a Moslem graveyard, climbed a sandy hill, edged down along some jagged rocks, avoided a place Pete called the haunted house, followed a donkey path, and found myself on the outskirts of Lamu thirty minutes later.

As I packed up my things in the guest house, I stopped for a moment and looked at a photo of Annika. 'Am I really going to do this?' I asked her.

I bought a straw mat so that I wouldn't have to sleep on the bare cement floor, then trudged back out to the *shamba*. Pete was meditating when I got there – this really *was* a spiritual island – and I decided not to disturb him. I swept out my room as best I could, then sat on the ledge of the porch watching the sunset. 'Best you not sit there right now,' said Pete, appearing from down the hall a short while later.

'Why's that?'

'Well, what with sunset and all.'

'The . . . sunset?'

He looked a little concerned. 'No, really, you shouldn't—' Something suddenly flew down from the rafters right above me and nearly hit me in the face. 'Shit! What was that?'

'I've been trying to tell you. That was a bat. The scout.'

My skin crawled. 'A *bat*?'

'He's going to do a quick circle and make sure the coast is clear for the rest of them.'

'The *rest* of them?' I said, jumping off the ledge. 'Just exactly how many bats do we have in our belfry?'

'I wouldn't want to venture a guess.'

'Humor me. Two . . . three?' The sun was just about to set when the scout swooped back and disappeared into the rafters. I heard some faint high-pitched rumblings from above, then noticed two feral cats approaching the porch. They checked me out, then jumped up on the ledge and stared straight up. Suddenly there was an enormous whoosh and the entire sky was covered in a cloud of flapping wings – the wings of hundreds and hundreds of bats. 'Holy . . . fucking . . . shit,' I said, diving for cover.

The cats swiped at the departing bats – missing, mercifully – and then, within a few seconds, it was all over. 'They'll be back,' said Pete.

'That's reassuring.'

'They're off to the mango trees. The moms return from time to time to feed the babies.'

'So, all night long there's gonna be bats flying around out here?'

'You'll get used to it. It's only bad when the cats catch one.'

'Christ.' Over the next few nights, I learned more than I ever wanted to know about bats. For example, they're blind as bats. I'd read about their highfalutin radar system, which guides them in for a landing, but what I didn't know is that bat radar sometime fails – like the batteries run down or the wires get crossed or something gets wet – and before you know it – *pow!* – a bat flies smack-dab into a wall, knocks itself silly, and falls to the floor. Bats, being bats, can't just take off like birds or other decent animals, no, they have to crawl up the wall about three feet in order to swoop down and then get airborne. This wouldn't be such a big deal if it weren't for . . . the cats. To a cat, a bat on the floor is like a rat on crutches. Cats, having their own particular insanities, can't just kill the bat and be done with it, no, they need to see how many decibels of shrieking radar they can get going before finishing it off. One night I was sitting on the floor of the porch, and a bat hit me straight in the chest. When the cats saw it fall into my lap, they leapt after it, claws first, and my body became a bloody battleground. Bats suck. Cats suck. The porch sucked.

But, like they say down on the old *shamba*, if the bats don't get you, the ants will. Ants own Africa. They've got the deed and the mortgage and control the banks. Somebody – I think it was me – once said, if you took all the ants out of Africa, you'd have a very nice place. The thing about ants, *safari* ants to be specific, is that they're not all that big. They kind of lull you with their lack of stature. If you put one under a microscope, however, you'd discover an unusual phenomenon: They're all teeth. A safari ant gets his jaws into you and you're screaming bloody murder, you're swatting your arm or your leg or your ass, and the little bastard is just chomping away like there's no tomorrow.

The thing about Africa is that sometimes there *is* no tomorrow.

I figured safari ants were something you encountered on a safari. In fact, they bring the safari to you. They're great movers. You leave something lying around, and half an hour later it's gone. 'Hey, Pete, you eat that roll? No? Oh, guess the ants carted it away.' I saw pieces of bread moving down the porch. I saw loaves of bread heading down the stairs. I saw whole bakeries sliding down into ant holes. One day, we hooked up an intricate rope-and-pulley system and hung food in a bucket from the ceiling. 'Hah!' said the ants an hour later, running up and down the rope. 'Is that the best you can do?' Then we put food in a bowl and floated it in a bucket of water. 'Oooh, tri-*cky*,' smirked the ants as they climbed over a brigade of dead comrades whose suicides formed a perfect bridge. That's when I got mad as hell and decided I wasn't going to take it any more. I went to Haji's Hardware Emporium and bought a gallon of DDT, a pump gun, and a mask. I sprayed the ants on the porch, in the bedrooms, and down the stairs. Then I followed their trail and sprayed all the way to the nest. The next morning, I got out my gear and went after them again. On the third day, I escalated my attack and poured raw DDT down the hole, lit a match, and blew the nest to smithereens. I did this every day, without fail, for two weeks. Then, I awoke one morning, and there wasn't a single ant in the house. I may have done irreparable harm to my respiratory system, but the ants were gone. I had won!

It was a miracle. Pete and I kept food in the house overnight. We left stuff lying around. We had breakfast the next morning without trekking to town to get supplies. We went a whole day without getting bitten. It was one of the happiest times of my life. I had accomplished something through grit, brains, and perseverance. Two days later, I awoke to find the entire house overrun with ants. The walls, the floors, the ceilings – everywhere I looked, there were ants streaming in to fill the void. I followed the trails and discovered at least three new nests had been constructed overnight. I stood there, devastated, my two-day victory turned to crap. I returned to Haji's that morning with the DDT, the pump, and the mask. 'One kilo of sugar,' I said. I returned to the *shamba*, set out two bowls, one on each side of the porch, and filled them with sugar. It took only moments before some ants discovered their version of nirvana, and less than an hour before there were two solid lines snaking up the side of the house, over the ledge, and down to the dishes. The lines were an inch thick with ants – it was a freeway of ants – all on their way to an unbelievable prize. They were giddy with sugar, they were crazed with sugar, they were blinded with sugar. They had absolutely no interest in exploring the rest of the kitchen area, and certainly not the bedrooms or hallway. I had given them exactly what they wanted and, so long as I kept the bowls full, I was never bothered by them again. Sometimes you've got to adapt. Sometimes you've got to compromise. Sometimes you've got to let nature win. I'm not saying always, necessarily. I'm just saying sometimes.

For three months, I sat on the porch of the *shamba* and stared at a palm tree. The fronds unfolded like a lotus as they grew out from the trunk, staggered and irregular, yet somehow perfectly balanced. Perhaps if you stare at anything long enough, you can find the full universe, because everything is made up of everything else.

The first time I saw the universe, it was in the skin of a strawberry. I was in my apartment on Riverside Drive in Manhattan, I had just taken my first hit of acid, and Mary, a girl I'd started seeing, said, 'Here, have this.' I took the strawberry from her hand and was about to put it into my mouth when I was suddenly taken by its remarkable texture. I pulled it back and studied its shape and form and the way it kind of kept curving around into itself. This strawberry could never be photographed or painted or written about in a way that could do it justice, I realized, it could never be improved upon or enhanced or embellished, it was absolutely perfect just as it was, even the slight discoloration near the stem was perfect, it added the *imperfection* that made for an even *greater* perfection. I stared at this strawberry for forty-five minutes, never speaking, never blinking, just going deeper and deeper into the wondrous molecular structure that held it together, watching the electrons spinning around, watching the waves of gravity and the force fields that connected it to every other thing in the cosmos. How could I ingest such a thing of pure beauty? This strawberry deserved to be in a place of honour, on an altar perhaps, for within it were the secrets of the universe.

Mary passed by and walked to the living room window. She paused for a moment, then climbed up to the sill, bent down, and stepped out onto the ledge. She was seven stories up on a six-inch ledge overlooking Ninety-fourth Street, and I wondered what she was doing out there.

The green stem of the strawberry sat like a little hat on the fruit, almost like a jester's hat, with its many corners flapping this way and that. I wondered why hats weren't very popular these days and thought about buying a jester's hat for myself so that I could be just *slightly* as perfect as the strawberry, not to compete of course, but more to remind myself of the oneness of the universe and to never forget the beauty of this night. Maybe Mary can help me pick out my jester's hat, if she doesn't jump, that is, and we can go down to Orchard Street on Sunday and look through all the stalls until we find the one that's just right, a red one hopefully, with just a hint of discoloration near the top, not that it would be so bad if she jumped, of course, because the molecular structure of the street and the force fields of Mary are one and the same and while it might end one form of energy, it would merely transform it into another, equally magnificent manifestation.

I nodded and smiled to myself as Mary stood perfectly still and I thought about all those stories about people taking LSD and jumping to their deaths and I wondered if there was room on the ledge for both of us but thought better of it because I'd feel naked without my hat. 'Mary, do you want to come in?' I said, very calmly.

She turned slightly – what was holding her up, I had no idea – and said, 'Okay.' She bent down on the ledge and gracefully backed into the room. 'I do this every time I take acid—' she said.

'Cool,' I replied.

'—because I used to be suicidal and my parents locked me up in institutions all through high school.'

'Uh-huh, cool,' I said as I got up to close the window.

'Now I do it just to prove to myself that I can.'

And now I'm in Africa just to prove to myself that I can, and I'm staring into a palm tree and watching it sway in the breeze and am overwhelmed by its grace and balance, how it is so delicate and yet holds up to the strongest winds, and I wonder if my roots will ever grow strong enough to allow me to just bend like that and give in to the forces around me.

# 17

# Tropical Meltdown

People moved in and people moved out, sometimes staying a few weeks, sometimes a month, but through it all, Pete and I were the only constants. As I watched them come and go, it was always Annika whom I imagined coming over that path from the edge of the *shamba*. 'I've been looking for you since Mykonos!' she'd say, rushing into my arms. 'We just missed in Athens, and I've been following you ever since Nairobi!' We'd hug and kiss and then I'd help carry her suitcase over the hot sands. 'See, aren't you sorry you don't have your rucksack?' I'd say, and we'd laugh and laugh until the bats came home to roost.

One day, on a rare splurge, I stopped into Petley's Inn for a beer. Petley's was an old mansion that had recently been restored to its original glory and opened as a spot for well-heeled tourists. Sitting at the bar was an attractive woman whom I'd never seen before. I overheard her order some hoity-toity mixed drink in an accent that just dripped of the British upper class, then I watched as she sipped at it, turned up her nose, and said, '*Wellll*, I suppose it will have to do.'

I had gone pretty much native by this time. I wore a *kikoy* around my waist and a loose T-shirt hung off my shoulders. My hair was past my shoulders, and my skin was deeply tanned. I wore a necklace of Guelmim beads and a bracelet made from the hair of an elephant's tail. To a young woman from poshest London, I looked, I should imagine, like an absolute lunatic. When I went over to introduce myself, she looked at me a long moment, then held out a thin hand with impossibly long fingers. 'I'm Katherine Hamilton-Davies,' she said. 'I'm a distant cousin of the royal family.' Okay, that did it. I had to fuck her. And not just anywhere. I had to fuck her on the cement floor of my *shamba* and then make her walk home alone through the Moslem graveyard.

What the hell is wrong with me, I wondered. Do I hate women all of a sudden? Have I gone completely crazy out here? Is this some subconscious desire to get back at Annika? I never thought of women that way before, hell, I love women, most of them anyway, and wouldn't dream of treating anyone like that. No, this is just some aberration, some deep-seated antiroyalist sentiment, I'll bet. I was, after all, an Arab serf in one of my past lives.

When Pete saw Katherine Hamilton-Davies coming up the stairs of the house, he almost fell over backwards. A thousand years of class consciousness kicked in, and it was as if he felt compelled to go trim her hedges or polish her car or wax her banisters. He sputtered around, offered to make tea, then disappeared down the hall to meditate. I took Katherine Hamilton-Davies into my room, fucked her on the cement floor, then made her walk home alone through the Moslem graveyard. Pete came out a little after she left. 'Nice one,' he said.

Barbara and Jeff were devotees of Maharaji, a twelve-year-old Indian guru, and had decided to take a spiritual plunge by shaving their heads. Pete was quite taken with their new look when they stopped by one afternoon; I wasn't so sure. With them was Sultan Athumani, a fisherman who lived over in Shela with his wife and eleven children. Sultan appeared to be in his fifties and had an easy laugh, a broad smile, and remarkable eyes that bespoke a certain wisdom. Barbara, who'd picked up a fair amount of Swahili, listened to everything he said with the utmost respect. 'You can learn a great deal from this man,' she said, taking me aside. He seemed like an intriguing character, but I could only guess, since he didn't speak a word of English.

The next day, I heard someone calling from the pathway and looked out to see Sultan standing there. '*Jambo*,' he said, '*jambo sana*.' I invited him in, honored that he would pay me a visit, and I put on some water for tea. Sultan spoke a few words and I nodded as if I knew what he was talking about. I waited anxiously for the water to boil, feeling increasingly uncomfortable, and finally handed him the tea. '*Asante sana*,' he said.

I had no idea what to say. Finally, I pointed to the air and said, 'Hot.'

Sultan nodded and said, '*Asante sana*.' A few minutes later, he got up to go. '*Kwa heri*,' he said, putting out his hand. I shook hands with him, glad that he was leaving, but he just stood there, waiting. '*Kwa he-ri*,' he repeated, more slowly this time.

'*Kwa heri*,' I said, parroting his words.

Sultan smiled broadly and left.


One evening, Pete went to roll up a joint and realized we were in a crisis situation. 'My *bangi*'s almost gone!' he said. This was the most concerned I'd seen Pete about anything since I'd been there. Pete without pot was like heat without hot.

'Well, that's a bummer,' I said.

'It's more than a bummer! It means a trip to Mombasa!' Pete hadn't been off the island in months and clearly didn't relish the idea of the journey. He replayed the trip over and over. Boat to McCoy. Bus to Garsen. Bus to Malindi. Bus to Mombasa. Taxi to the old slave market. Walk to the third portal. Negotiate a price. Wait thirty minutes. Score. Taxi downtown. Overnight on Kilindini. English breakfast at Spencer's. Bus to Malindi. Bus to Garsen. Bus to McCoy. Boat to Lamu.

Pete left early the next morning for the ferry, and I sat alone on the porch, contemplating what a mess the *shamba* had become. There was garbage piled up, old cans lying all around, and fallen palm branches everywhere. We were living like tropical hillbillies. I found a rake, a shovel, and a panga, an African machete, and set out to work. I raked the junk into piles, dug a big hole, and tried cutting through the spines of the long palm branches to make them more manageable. I saw immediately that one hit wasn't enough to cut through, but I couldn't quite hit the exact spot twice in a row in order to finish it off. After a couple of hours, I crawled to my mat for a siesta.

Too much activity in the tropics isn't advisable, and it took me a while to fully adapt to the pace of the island: *pole-pole*. Slowly-slowly. I realized I'd gotten the hang of it when I awoke one morning and said, 'Shit, I've got to brush my teeth today.' I had arrived. The idea of cleaning up the *shamba* was, therefore, sheer madness, and therein lay its appeal. By the time Pete got back, I'd already cleared the whole area around the porch and was trying out the panga again on the palms. I'd yet to split my first branch, but I was getting closer. The days wore on, and I was out there every morning, clearing, digging, and, eventually, cutting. Maybe this was my own meditation, a way of clearing my mind and not thinking about what had led me to this place.

Every few days, Sultan would show up and just watch me from the distance. '*Pole-pole, bwana, pole-pole*,' he'd call out.

'*Asante sana, bwana*,' I'd call back. '*Kwa heri.*'

After a while, some of the other Swahilis got wind of what was going on and came out to watch the crazy white man working under the blazing sun. But then Big Ali and Little Ali showed up with their own pangas and the three of us had at the palms together. Big Ali had his own *shamba* on the other side of town and lived off whatever coconuts he could harvest from the trees. He was Pete's friend, sharing with him a love of *bangi*, and was not the most motivated person I'd ever met. The perfect day for Big Ali was to get high, watch the coconuts grow, and maybe go down to the ocean and catch a crab or two for dinner. Little Ali was the sweetest guy on the island. He had a beautiful voice and played harmonium with a group of traditional musicians, but was too small to lift the heavy mangroves in the harbor and had difficulty finding work. It was perhaps divine intervention that Jeff and Barbara had met Little Ali and given him enough money to open a stall in the market. He, his wife, and their two infants had been getting by ever since.

Maybe we were all nuts, the three of us swinging our pangas under the midday sun, but two weeks after raking up that first pile, I had the cleanest *shamba* on the island. I became one with the panga. I became one with the branches. I became a Zen panga banger.

'*Jambo, bwana, habari yako?*' called Sultan from the porch. He was coming by pretty much every day now and I was both happy and irritated to see him. I was happy because I saw more and more the goodness and wisdom of this man and felt he had something important to offer me. I was irritated because he was forcing me to learn Swahili in order to find out what it was.

'*Mzuri sana, bwana, habari yako?*' I replied.

'*Mzuri. Habari rafiki yako?*'

'*Rafiki yangu ni mzuri. Habari mama?*'

'*Mama mzuri. Asante sana.*' The traditional greeting went on and on. How's it going, how's the house, how's the wife, how's the friends, how's the harvest, how's the weather, how's the well, how's the ceiling, how's the backache, how's the tooth ... No wonder nothing ever got done on this island.

I found a book on Swahili grammar and discovered a certain blurring of the past, present, and future tenses. To me, this had the effect of breaking down the barriers of time. This seemed perfectly reasonable since in the tropics – where the days and weeks and months all blend together – the sense of time is altogether different. Who's to say what time is, anyway? Einstein says the only reason for time to exist is so that everything doesn't happen all at once. In Lamu, where not much of anything ever happened, I'm not sure we needed time at all.

'*Kuja, kuja,*' Sultan said, motioning for me to follow him. He led me to one of the mango trees and pointed to a

194

hundred pieces of fruit hanging low off the branches. I'd been waiting two months for the harvest and now it was time. Lamu was famous throughout Africa for having the best mangoes in the world. On this tiny island, there were twenty-six varieties, ranging from deep green delicacies that were sprinkled with spices and eaten before they were ripe, to orange-red beauties that grew ten inches long. Sultan pulled one off the tree, then pointed to the stem. A small drop of sap formed at the top and ran an inch or so down the side. It looked exactly like a tear. Sultan looked at it a little sadly, then wrapped the mango in a piece of newspaper as if it were a precious jewel. We gathered a dozen more, then headed back to the house, where he stashed the mangoes inside a dark room. '*Siku nne*,' he said. Four days.

I started getting more interested in the plant life around me. Cashews are a big deal on the coast and are surprisingly expensive. As I examined the lone cashew tree on the *shamba*, I began to understand why. The cashew is actually the nut of a pepper-shaped fruit and grows in its own separate shell. I was curious what the fruit itself tasted like and bit into one. I felt something sizzle on my tongue, spat it out, raced to the well, and washed out what was left of the inside of my mouth. Cashews are extremely acidic; if harvested too early, they can be toxic even after being roasted. People in Africa have died from eating too many unripe cashews.

The next day, I went to town and ate too many unripe cashews. I didn't die, but I felt pretty lousy by the time I got home that night and headed for the loo. The loo wasn't much more than a cement room with crisscrossing mangrove beams and a narrow hole in the floor. The hole appeared to be extremely deep and, even by daylight, I could never quite make out the bottom. Occasionally, I saw the feelers of cockroaches on the sides – always an inducement to get my business done quickly – and figured there must be more farther down. When I put down a kerosene lamp and squatted over the hole, my eyes adjusted to the light, and I saw an enormous cockroach on the wall across from me.

Not including its feelers and spindly legs, it was a good four inches long, its dark brown body encased in armor that made me think of the medieval knights. I watched those creepy feelers moving around independently of each other, angling this way and that, twisting back on themselves as if they would snap, and then I happened to look down. *Christ!* There were cockroaches all around the hole, at least six of them, and one was crawling over my foot! I kicked it away, then looked at the wall behind me. There were more cockroaches and more still on the floor in front of me. Then I looked up at the ceiling beams and saw dozens and dozens of feelers and spindly legs dancing in the shadows. They were covering every square inch of the room. '*Aaaaaaaaaah!*' I screamed, rushing into the hallway.

'What? What is it?' Pete called from his room.

'*Cooooockroaches!*'

'Oh, God, you didn't go into the loo, did you?'

'Yes! I went into the loo!'

'Didn't I tell you never to go into the loo at night?'

'What the hell are they *doing* in there?'

'Keeping things tidy.'

'What's *that* supposed to mean?'

'You ever notice how it doesn't smell in there? That's because the roaches get, shall we say, nourishment from us.'

'*The cockroaches are eating our shit?*'

'I wasn't referring to spiritual nourishment.'

'That's disgusting!'

'Think about it. It's better than the alternative.'

'I'm thinking of all sorts of alternatives.'

'It's really no big deal. You simply don't go into the loo at night.'

I thought about it for a while, thought about the ants and the DDT fiasco, then walked to the door of the loo. 'Hey! You in there! Cockroaches! Listen up! I'm gonna forget about what happened tonight, I'm gonna forget I was ever in there. From now on here's the deal. Sunrise to sunset, it's our turf. You stay clear, understand? Then, sunset to sunrise, it's all yours. Do whatever you want – feasts, picnics, I don't give a shit. Even-steven, twelve-twelve, *nusu-nusu*, get it? But I'm warning you, you so much as take one step into the hall-way, and I'm coming in there with grenades, you hear me? Gre-*nades*.'

A retired fisherman had given Sultan his dhow to use and Sultan relished the opportunity to be his own boss. He took me out one day and smoothly maneuvered the forward-slanting mast and sails as we crossed from Lamu to Manda, a smaller island just up the coast. When I leaned over to help pull in a sail, I noticed two wooden disks on either side of the prow that were painted like eyes. Sultan said they were there to help steer the dhow through fog and that made total sense to me – more sense, in fact, than gyroscopes, radar, or sonar. Out on the ocean, Sultan was truly in his element and he became more effusive with each passing hour. Even though my Swahili was still primitive, he regaled me with tales of his forty years as a fisherman. He told me about his days in Mombasa and his nights in Zanzibar, the 'pearl of the Indian Ocean.' He explained how these three former sultanates comprised the three dialects of Swahili, and how Lamu's was the most poetic and beautiful to the ear. As we glided over the water, Sultan seemed to be part ocean and part sky. I felt that if a squall were to suddenly blow in, we would be untouched by the wind.

That night, after docking at Shela, I joined Sultan and Mama and their eleven children for dinner in their two-room hut. There was a large platter of rice and one piece of fish to go around. We ate with our hands from the same plate and when Mama finally dropped her chador to join in, I realized I was looking at a Swahili woman's face for the very first time. Glancing around at the surroundings, I was struck by the level of poverty. There were four beds crammed against the walls, a couple of pots and pans, a smattering of clothing. Yet, as the tiny pieces of fish were mashed into balls of rice, this family of thirteen laughed and kidded each other, ate slowly, and managed to stretch out the meager dinner into its own kind of feast.

After we ate, one of Sultan's sons pulled out a harmonium, another a tabla, and Sultan sang a song about a beautiful young woman who waited along the docks for her lover to come in from the sea. I glanced over and saw Mama blushing beneath her chador. Sultan looked at her as he sang, at his children, his two rooms, his beds, and his fireplace, then leaned over to me and smiled. 'God has blessed me,' he said.

Four days after Sultan picked the mangoes, Pete unwrapped one and squeezed the skin. It gave just a little and he deemed it ready. He sliced the fruit vertically along the pit into two halves and cut a grid of a dozen squares into each piece. Then, he turned the mango inside out and the little squares unfolded like a lush flower. He bit off a piece and savored it a moment. It was both tart and sweet, without even a hint of pulpiness. 'Nice one,' he said.

With Christmas only a week away, and with four ripe mango trees, a replenished supply of *bangi*, and a showplace of a *shamba*, Pete and I decided to throw a party. Lamu was a gathering place for Westerners during the holidays, and travelers were already showing up from all over East Africa. Pete got a bunch of supplies from town and set to work on making cream cheese, his *spécialité de la maison*. I tidied up the grounds and planted a dozen flowering shrubs in front of the porch for the final touch. On the morning of the party, I awoke to the strange sound of gnashing teeth. I looked around to make sure nothing was gnawing at my legs, then walked out onto the porch. There, just outside, four wild donkeys were eating my flowers. 'Bastards!' I screamed as I ran down the stairs. I saw that the tops of all the shrubs were gone except for one lone plant. Determined to save it, I swung at the donkey who was moving in that direction. My fist bounced off the side of his mouth just as he chomped down on the flower. He looked at me, a little stunned, with a big blue iris hanging between his teeth. 'Drop it!' I yelled. The donkey stared at me, swallowed the flower whole, turned his big ass toward me, then slowly walked away.

Okay, this is Africa, nothing is going to go quite perfectly. I looked around and decided to count my blessings. The porch was clean. The *shamba* was tidy. The ant freeway was moving with no bottlenecks. The bats were back in their belfry. The cockroaches had relinquished the loo at sunrise. The ceiling had made it through another night. Life was good. People started showing up around noon. Jeff and Barbara baked banana bread. Little Ali climbed a palm tree and knocked down some coconuts for fresh milk. A crew of Englishmen lugged a cooler filled with beer all the way from town. Big Ali came with a tub full of live crabs. On and on, people arrived throughout the day. A guy with a guitar, a drummer, Ali's band of Swahili musicians. Then Jesse Allen showed up. Jesse was a well-known painter in San Francisco whose work I'd seen at the Vorpal Gallery. He'd grown up in Kenya and his paintings drew on fantastical images of surreal plants and mystical animals, all executed with outlandish colors and psychedelic swirls. Now he was back to visit his family for the first time in fifteen years, and there he was, a box of chalk in his hand, painting the inner wall of the porch. I pulled Pete away and showed him Jesse's work. 'Do you realize we now have a nine-dollar house and a twenty-five-thousand-dollar wall?'

Pete sliced mangoes, I played harmonica, Jesse painted, and the party continued on into the night. In fact, it never ended that night. People passed out on the porch and started right up the next morning. There was a continuous flow of people, perhaps a hundred in all, travelers, locals, whoever happened to come by, and the food kept coming and the beer kept flowing and the music kept playing and I thought it would never stop. It didn't stop – not for three days and three nights, and as we counted our way into the New Year, I thought about being in New York two years ago in a snowstorm and getting ready to leave, and being in Stockholm one year ago in a snowstorm and getting ready to leave, and being here right now in this tropical paradise and getting ready to stay.

\* \* \*

On New Year's Day, 1973, I awoke feeling a little dizzy. Around noon I felt hotter than usual and my muscles began to ache. At dinnertime I had no appetite and felt nauseous. By late evening, I thought I was dying. I was lying in a pool of sweat, a fever was raging through my body, and I could barely move. The air was absolutely still and the only sound I could hear was the buzz of mosquitoes. All night I lay there, unable to sleep, just sweating, then shivering, then sweating some more. Pete had left to spend a week on the other side of the island and Sultan was off on a fishing trip, so I was there all alone. When morning came, I decided to go to the hospital but by the time I got my *kikoy* wrapped around my waist, I was too weak to even think of walking thirty minutes to town. I collapsed back onto my grass mat, which was still soaked with sweat, and just lay there. The heat kept building through the day and, with it, my fever. I sprinkled a few drops of water over my face to try to cool down, but then even the water ran out.

I forced myself down the hall, out the back doorway, and down a pathway that led to the well. I felt myself stumbling along and a few times nearly fell in the sand. Finally, I got to the well. I threaded a rope over a pulley, made sure the bucket was securely tied on, then dropped it into the water below. I yanked at the rope over and over until I finally got the bucket to take on water. Once it was full, I pulled it up, feeling weaker than I could ever remember, barely having the strength to get the bucket over the top of the well. I carried it back up the sandy path, slipping more often now under the weight of the load. The water sloshed around and I could feel big splashes of it on my legs and feet. Finally, I got back to the house, made it up the stairs, and pulled the bucket, only half-full now, to the porch. Every muscle in my body felt like it was on fire. Everything was throbbing – my head, my nerve endings, my internal organs, my eyes, my lips, the tips of my fingers. I brushed some water onto my face, but it was like squirting kerosene onto burning coals. As it slowly dripped away, I thought I could actually hear it sizzling.

As night came, the fever got worse. The mat was thoroughly soaked and barely separated me from the cement. I longed not so much for a bed as for a simple wood floor. Cement doesn't give at all, it just stubbornly sits there, refusing to bend to your body. It makes cold nights colder, hot days hotter, and wet skin wetter. I stared up at the ceiling and was certain I saw it move. The mangrove poles seemed thinner than before and I wondered how they could possibly hold up the weight. Everything seemed to be creaking – the ceiling, the poles, the walls, even the palm trees outside my glassless windows. I stumbled onto the porch for more water, saw a few bats whoosh by, and dipped a coconut shell into the bucket. I took a few sips, then glanced down the hallway, where, in the shadows of the kerosene lantern, I saw a cockroach crawling my way. 'Oh, God, no!' I cried out as I collapsed back onto the mat. 'We had a deal!' Then a new thought struck me: I hadn't been in the loo in days . . . Pete was gone . . . They were getting hungry . . .

I slept fitfully that night, waking every few minutes to sweat pouring down my face, over my chest, and into the small of my back. The walls of the room didn't quite intersect anymore, the ceiling angled in strange ways, and the floor had unusual dips that I didn't remember being there. The light refracted oddly off the semicircular walls and cast little dancing figures all over my body. I imagined tiny medieval knights from the sweltering plains of Italy, sweating under their armor as the sun beat down on their dark brown shells, valiantly holding their lances up against the enemy, their spindly legs and feelers bravely warding off the onslaught of heavy swords . . .

Spindly legs and feelers? My eyes popped open to see a dozen cockroaches crawling over my arms, legs, and chest. I leapt up and madly brushed them off me, screaming now so that my voice reverberated down the hallway: '*We had a deal!*' I grabbed my rubber flip-flops and swung at the first cockroach that crossed my path. I smashed at it again and again, harder and harder, until it stopped moving. I turned to the next one. I smashed and screamed and yelled as I worked my way down the hallway toward the loo, swinging wildly as my skin crawled and my sweat flowed and my fever grew, and then I went into the loo itself, focused and zeroed in with the precision of my panga, and I smashed the cockroaches – *fwap-fwap* – until pieces of their guts oozed out through their broken shells, until their legs and feelers broke and glued themselves to the walls with their sticky hairs, until their eyes and mouths and noses were flattened into a putrid mess, and suddenly I was transported to the pensione in Crete where Annika recoiled from the bug on the wall and I stood there and smashed it and smashed it good – is this what you want, Annika? Now am I a man? Now do you feel safe? Now will you follow me to Africa? – and I smashed it and clobbered it and killed it until I fell into a heap lying on the bathroom floor.

# 18

# Nietzsche's Brain

The Lamu hospital consisted of one large, dirty room where the sick were on one side and the dying on the other. There was only one nurse and she subsidized her salary by tending to a flock of chickens that had the run of the place. Under her black chador, it was difficult to determine if she was young or old, pretty or plain, but I'm almost certain that she'd never had a day's medical training in her life. The doctor was an Indian intern from the not-so-illustrious University of Dar Es Salaam, and Lamu was his testing ground. When I described my symptoms, he screwed up his forehead and said, 'It sounds like malaria, except for one thing.'

'What's that?'

'You complain of a sore throat. That is not typically malarial. Please, say *aaaah*.'

'*Aaaah*.'

He put a tongue depressor into my mouth and looked around. '*Um-hmm*, just as I suspected. You have tonsillitis.'

'Really?'

'Quite definitely.'

'Strange—'

'Not really. Adults often get tonsillitis.'

'Would you mind taking just one more look?'

'But why?'

'Because then you might notice that I don't *have* my tonsils. They were taken out when I was seven!'

'Say *aaaah*.'

'*Aaaaaaaaaaah!*'

'Aha! Quite right! A very commendable job, I might add.'

'You have no idea what's wrong with me, do you?'

'It's a highly unusual case. I think I should consult with the nurse.'

'I think you should give me some penicillin.'

'Yes-yes. My thoughts exactly. How many would you like?'

'Five days' worth.'

'Excellent.'

I never found out exactly what I had, if it was malaria or dengue fever or cholera or typhoid. All I know is, five days later, I felt fine again.

Once I regained my appetite, I went to an African restaurant near the port and saw an attractive young Western woman sitting there munching on *matoke*, *irio*, and *ugali*. 'How's the food?' I asked, staring at the green plantains, peas and potatoes, and maize meal.

'Quite good, actually,' she said, in the clipped tones of an English colonial.

'Would you like some company?'

'My pleasure. I'm Sigrid Shaffer,' she said. 'I'm the illegitimate great-granddaughter of Friedrich Nietzsche.' Okay, that did it. I had to fuck her. And not just anywhere. I had to fuck her in the middle of the jungle with a hundred wild animals looking on.

All right, it didn't exactly happen that way. I didn't find out about the Nietzsche connection until a week later, when Sigrid and I drove toward Mount Kenya, loaded down with a tent, cooking gear, and enough supplies for a six-week safari. We'd hit it off immediately in Lamu, and when she offered to take me through the bush country, I jumped at the chance. We headed for Nairobi, cut up through Thika and Embu, then angled off toward Meru, where we were going to camp out for the first time. We both felt a certain uneasiness as we got closer to our destination, given that our relationship was still being defined. We would, after all, be sharing very small quarters.

I'd been hearing bits and pieces about her family since we left Lamu and now, as we approached the foothills of Mount Kenya, right on the Equator, Sigrid finished the tale: In 1876, a beautiful young Dutch piano student named Mathilde showed up in Geneva, where she met the most eligible bachelor in town, the dashing Ernst Shaffer, noted composer and head of the Conservatory of Music. She also met Ernst's best friend, the moody German philosopher Friedrich Nietzsche. Mathilde began dating Ernst, but was also drawn to Friedrich, and before long both of them proposed to her. Mathilde sat in her room, trying to decide between Ernst – tall, dark, and handsome, the heartthrob of every woman in Geneva – and Friedrich – homely, intense, big bushy eyebrows, nothing much going for him at all except for having perhaps the greatest mind of the nineteenth century. How could she choose? Finally, Mathilde's girlfriends came by to talk some sense into her. 'Are you *nuts*?' they asked. 'Is your mind a big *Gouda*? You can't fuck Nietzsche's *brain*!'

So Mathilde accepted Ernst's proposal, but oddly enough, just four months after the wedding, she had a baby. As the years passed, everyone began to wonder why baby Hubert had no musical abilities but wrote like the wind. Or why he had such a high forehead and dark, piercing eyes. Or why he had such big bushy eyebrows. No one said anything, but everyone knew, of course, that the boy was Friedrich's – Friedrich, who never married and supposedly left no heir, whose story to this day has never been fully told. Hubert became an early fascist, one of the writers from whom the Nazis drew their inspiration. In an act of great irony, he even had a hand in perverting his own father's words into something the Nazis could claim as their own. Hubert had a son, Karl, who was quite the opposite. Hoping to get away from the rising tide of fascism, Karl went to school in England, where he met a young woman named Elizabeth and fell in love. With war about to separate them, they fled to what was then called German East Africa. They cut their way through the bush until they wound up at eight thousand feet on Mount Kilimanjaro, where they settled and eked out a living by growing coffee.

Sigrid, who was born on that coffee plantation, seemed especially attractive as I fucked her in the middle of the jungle with a hundred wild animals looking on. True, all that the animals could really see was our tent, but what I saw was a hundred years of history, and, in my mind, I was fucking a Dutch piano student, I was fucking Swiss high society, I was fucking the Geneva Conservatory of Music, I was fucking the Nazi party, I was fucking the brain of Friedrich Nietzsche.

Outside, it sounded like every animal in the bush was following our cue. There were shrieks and howls and thumps and grunts, and suddenly we were all fucking on the floor of the jungle, hundreds of crazed animals going at it, all with our own fantasies and delusions and daydreams – gazelles, water buffaloes, giraffes, peacocks, zebras, rhinos, leopards, lions, all of us were humping away until the earth shook and the trees bent and the sky expanded and finally the whole jungle joined together in one huge enormous insane orgasm, and then, when it was all over, we all exhaled and the forest fell into a long, slow, unhurried slumber.

'I have to pee,' I said, turning to Sigrid in the tent.

'Be my guest.'

'But, wait, what happens if I go out there?'

'If the lions don't get you, the leopards probably will. Then the hyenas and the vultures will fight over whatever scraps are left.'

'C'mon, don't fuck around. You said we're safe so long as we don't leave the tent. Am I supposed to just pee in bed?'

'Well, the chances are at least fifty-fifty of your making it back alive if you go out there. If you pee in bed, your chances of surviving are zero.' I hated that Sigrid took pleasure in torturing me. Everything was a big game to her, and I could never tell when she was being serious. Jokes or not, I began to realize that if animals don't sense trouble from humans, they pretty much stay away. There are exceptions, of course. If you walk between a mother and her nest, you could be in danger. Or if you step on a snake, you could really be in trouble. This is rare because snakes sense you coming long before you see them, and they get out of the way. You can walk through areas just crawling with snakes and never know it. One of the few exceptions is the night adder, a very lazy snake that ignores the rumblings in the ground as footsteps approach. If you are unlucky enough to step on a lazy night adder, your ass is grass.

My ass was mostly just sore as we bounced along one dirt track after another. For six weeks, Sigrid and I traveled throughout Kenya and Tanzania, through territory she knew like the back of her hand, camping far off the beaten track, going to places where tourists weren't allowed. We saw colobus monkeys in the trees of Nanyuki and elephants stampeding outside Nyeri, we saw a sea of flamingos at Lake Naivasha and angry rhinos in Amboseli, we saw 400,000 wildebeests migrating through Serengeti and three lazy lions sleeping in the trees of Lake Manyara. Then we saw the Masai of the Ngorongoro Crater.

The Masai, a tribe of fierce nomadic warriors, live in isolated areas of northern Tanzania and move with their cows to wherever there is land to graze and water to drink. They set up temporary *mauyattas* for a month or two, then move on to the next watering hole. Their hair is matted with red ochre, their faces and chests are a tableau of tribal scarification, and they carry spears just in case anybody wants to mess with them. But nobody messes with the Masai. The other tribes looked upon the Masai with absolute dread. I watched a lone Masai warrior walk into a Wachaga village and saw ten men run into the bush.

For the Masai, the cow is everything. They mix its milk, blood, and urine into a high-protein cocktail. They eat its meat. They wear its skin. The Masai believe that many years ago they owned all the cows in the world. One fateful day, they lent one of their cows to another tribe as a gesture of friendship. This turned out to be a terrible mistake because the other tribe had evil intentions and stole off with the cow into the bush. After searching high and low in the vast wilderness for their beloved cow, the Masai returned in great sadness, but one thing was certain: Should they ever come upon another cow, it would clearly be the offspring of the one that had been stolen, and it was their sacred duty to bring it back into the fold. The Masai have been known ever since as the most fearless cattle rustlers of Africa. To them, they're only taking back what's rightfully theirs. If you flew a Masai in a helicopter over a cattle ranch in Texas, he'd look down and say, 'Hey! Those are my cows!' Then he'd probably try to figure out a way to rustle them the hell out of that godforsaken place. I would love to drop off a hundred Masai warriors onto Main Street in Amarillo, Texas, just to see what would happen.

The Masai have another tradition. They believe, like some relatives of mine, that they are the Chosen People. Sigrid steered the car deeper into the Ngorongoro Crater, and we pulled up to a *mauyatta* in the middle of nowhere. Five Masai warriors picked up their spears and, looking rather excited, glided over to the car – the Masai don't walk, they glide. I immediately decided that if they gave us any trouble, I'd trade them Sigrid for a cow. 'Ho-ho, the joke's on you!' I'd yell, getting back at her for all of her practical jokes. Little did I realize that the Masai wouldn't make that trade, Friedrich Nietzsche's great-granddaughter or not. As the warriors approached, I couldn't imagine what they wanted. They went to Sigrid's side of the car – so far, so good; better her than me, after all – and then, one after another, they bent down to look into the side mirror. The first guy stared at himself, preened, grinned, and stuck out his jaw like Clark Gable. The next warrior pulled him away and went through his own routine. Warrior after warrior admired himself and when the fifth guy was done, the first one started in again.

'Well, what do you think?' said Sigrid.

'I think they're a bunch of raving egomaniacs!'

'You didn't expect to see this in the bush, did you?'

'I wouldn't expect to see this backstage at the Grammies.'

The warriors began twisting the mirror around, fighting to get the next look. 'Okay,' said Sigrid, 'we'd better go before they yank it off.'

'Aw, c'mon, Sigrid, give 'em the damn mirror. We can get another.'

'Not on your life.' She turned on the engine and slowly backed up the road. The warriors ran alongside the car, trying to get one last look at themselves. I don't think they even noticed the two of us were there.

'Sigrid?'

'No!'

Karl's plantation was a broad expanse of rolling fields sculpted out of the midsection of Mount Kilimanjaro. His house, set on four hundred acres of land, was comfortable but not overbearing like so many of the other colonial estates. Behind it, the mountain disappeared into the clouds, below was a deep valley, and across was Mount Meru, the continent's third-tallest mountain. Both mountains rose straight up from the plains and were visible from foot to peak.

Karl had been growing coffee for forty years, and for most of that time he'd struggled to make a go of it. Even though the land yielded more and better coffee, transportation had been nearly nonexistent, and Karl watched helplessly as his beans withered on the vine. Now eight years after independence, he was finally doing well, but a new problem arose. The government was nationalizing all the plantations and it was only a matter of time before his family would have to leave. Sigrid, who'd grown accustomed to the vagaries of life in Africa, looked at their uncertain future as just another bump in the road. Karl and Elizabeth, not wanting to uproot their lives all over again, were considerably more apprehensive.

One night, a Polish hunter named Smolinski arrived for dinner. Smolinski was a tough old codger who'd fled Warsaw at the beginning of World War II and walked right through the minefields and trenches of Europe. When he couldn't walk any farther, he stowed away on a ship and wound up in the jungles of East Africa. There he became the proto-typical Great White Hunter. Smolinski wasn't interested in namby-pamby photographic safaris, no, he went out and dug into the ground and shot charging elephants between the eyes and prayed they wouldn't land on his head. He walked with a limp, had an arm that bent backwards, and was a mass of scar tissue running up and down his body. He'd been gored by water buffaloes, clawed by lions, bitten by snakes, stung by scorpions, and cornered by leopards. It was a miracle he was alive. Smolinski passed me a platter of meat. 'No thanks,' I said, 'I'm a vegetarian.'

He stared at me a moment: 'Good, I like someone with principles.'

'I think killing animals is criminal,' I went on, pushing my luck.

Sigrid buried her head in her hands, Elizabeth pretended she was needed in the kitchen, and Karl just sat there. 'I must agree,' said Smolinski, bemused, but eager for discourse. 'I take hunters out into the bush, many of them from your own country, just so they can add a trophy to their dens. And do you know who many of them are? Doctors. Men who spend their lives curing diseases and mending broken bones, and then they come here and try to kill as much as they can. They sit in their big chairs and blast away at the animals running past, but when a real trophy approaches, a lion or an elephant, an animal that could do *them* harm, almost always they freeze. They're unable to shoot or, worse, they shoot wildly and wound the animal, and then it's up to me to track the beast into the bush, where it is dying and enraged, where it has nothing left to lose and wants nothing more than to take another piece out of this old Polish body of mine.'

'So, why do you do it?' I asked.

'It's a terrible thing, but in the bush I still feel alive. And it's not always I carry my big gun. When I walk unarmed, I feel safe.' I wasn't sure what he meant by that. Smolinski went on: 'Animals smell guns as clear as they smell a rotting corpse. They smell guns and fear. If you are unafraid and walk unarmed in the bush, you will have no trouble. The animals wish you no harm. Take my advice, never carry a weapon.'

'A couple of months ago, I was actually thinking of buying a gun to bring down here.'

'And now look,' said Sigrid. 'You can nearly pee in the jungle without holding my hand.'

'The people who get killed are the ones with guns,' said Smolinski. 'The same is true in the cities. The robbers and burglars sense them just like the animals. It brings out their predatory instinct. People without guns in their houses rarely get killed.'

'Look what is happening to my plantation,' Karl groaned. 'I am surrounded by long-haired vegetarians, recalcitrant hunters, and a daughter as flighty as the wind.' He called out to Elizabeth in the kitchen. 'It's a good thing we're finally getting the hell out of here, my dear.'

As Sigrid and I explored farther into the bush, I found my fears evaporating. One day, while driving through an endless savanna, we came upon a pride of lions. They were snoozing, as lions like to do twenty hours a day, and a number of easy prey were within reach. Finally, a lioness yawned, stretched, and moseyed down to a watering hole. The animals around her seemed completely unconcerned until her thirst was sated and she stretched her neck and looked around. At that moment everything changed. The bush became dead quiet, and all eyes focused on the lion. Wildebeest and gazelles and zebras all stared at her and then, as she moved, they moved, as she walked, they walked, as she ran, they ran. There was an unmistakable feeling in the air – a feeling shared by the biggest animals and the smallest birds – that something was going to die, there was no way around it, some animal was going to fulfil nature's demands.

I watched with a sense of horror as the lion trained her eyes on a gazelle. She stalked and chased it, and no matter if the gazelle skirted over the savanna or circled around the stream or leapt over bush, the lion was always right behind.

Then, finally, the gazelle turned left when it should've turned right, and charged straight into the jaws of its pursuer. The lion dug deeply into its neck and pulled the gazelle to the ground. A great cloud of dust arose amid kicking feet and pounding bodies. Then, just as quickly, it was all over. In the end, it didn't really seem so bad. It didn't seem cruel. It was finished with as cleanly as possible. A few seconds later, the sounds of birds and monkeys and jackals returned to the bush, and the animals went about their business. They didn't move when the rest of the pride passed by to join in for dinner. They knew there was enough to go around.

Animals aren't gluttons. They don't kill for pleasure. They're not like doctors.

We passed through a Wachaga village and saw a woman with Nestle's Cocoa cans in her earlobes. Another woman had stretched her lobes so far that she was able to tie them together at the top of her head. I kind of liked that look. I stared at Sigrid's ears. 'Forget it,' she said. We drove to a spot where a friend of her family operated a tiny zoo for tourists. To cage animals right in the middle of the bush seemed particularly cruel, but I couldn't help being drawn to a large chimpanzee that sat quietly, nibbling a banana that his African master fed him through the bars. The man motioned for us to watch, then squatted down in front of the cage so that the chimp could no longer see him. Suddenly, he thrust out his arm and began yelling for help. The chimp jumped up and grabbed the bars in panic while the man flailed around as if he'd been attacked. The chimp went absolutely crazy. His master was in trouble, and he couldn't do a thing. He pounded the side of the cage, tore at the bars, and leapt up and down, until the man stood up and showed the chimp he was all right. The animal collapsed with relief, staring upon his master with the purest show of love I'd ever witnessed. His eyes softened to moist brown pools of adoration, and he gently poked his fingers through the bars, hoping for just the slightest touch.

As we returned to the car, I felt in awe of a raw emotion I

could only begin to imagine. I envied the chimp, and I envied his master. Neither Sigrid nor I said anything as we drove off, each of us wondering if we would ever feel that strongly about anything in our lives.

We drove through Moshe and Arusha, headed east through the Blue Mountains, then went north to Kenya. After passing through Tsavo, we arrived in Mombasa and checked into an old colonial-era hotel. For Sigrid and me, this was the end of the road. In our six weeks in the bush together, I think we developed a true fondness for each other. When we made love, the ground never moved again the way it did that first night beneath Mount Kenya, but as friends we were, as Sigrid would say, top-drawer. In a way, I think we both regretted that it couldn't have been more.

The next morning Sigrid came into the hotel dining room with a newspaper. 'Aha!' she said with a wicked grin. 'This explains everything!' She handed over the front page of the *Daily Nation* and pointed to the headline: MOI SAYS KENYA INVADED BY HIPPIE CIA AGENTS.

I stared at the headline and reread it a few times. 'You've really outdone yourself, Sigrid. Where'd you get this printed up?'

'Oh, that it were so, my dear. I'm afraid that's beyond even my capacities.'

I wasn't sure whether to believe her or not. Sigrid was always bullshitting me – I even began to wonder if the Nietzsche story was true – but who makes up something like that? As for the article, it went on to say that Daniel arap Moi, the vice president of Kenya, had determined that the poor performance of the country's economy was due to the subversion of long-haired CIA agents and that citizens needed to be vigilant during this time of crisis. 'This guy is crazy! Who's gonna believe him?'

'You really had me fooled there for a while,' said Sigrid. 'I didn't think anybody could be that naïve in the jungle, but now I see it was only a ruse. Good try, Mr. Bond, a very good try.'

'Sigrid!'

'Okay, okay. Listen, everybody knows that Moi is a lunatic. Jomo Kenyatta just plugged him in there for tribal balance. It's not like he's going to become president or anything.'

'Uh-huh, well, in the meantime, there's probably not more than eight people in all of East Africa who could be called hippies.'

'*Hmm.* Good point. It's probably not all that safe to be around you.'

'Sigrid, for just one minute, can you stop fucking around?'

'Listen, you're going to be perfectly fine. This will pass over in no time.'

'And you're just going to leave me like this?'

'Like what? Sitting in a luxurious hotel drinking mimosas?'

'You know what I mean.'

'No, my dear, I'm afraid this is it. My bags are packed, the tank is full, and Kilimanjaro calls.'

I could see there was no point arguing. I followed Sigrid to the parking lot and helped pack up her car. 'I hope you know how much I appreciate the last six weeks,' I said.

'My pleasure.'

'You know, that's what you said in Lamu when I asked if I could sit with you.'

'Well, that'll teach you a lesson.'

We stood in the shade of a palm tree and hugged for a long moment. Sigrid then slipped out of my arms and walked to the car. 'Hey, Sigrid?' I said, calling after her.

'*Um-hmm?*' she said, turning around.

'Happy trails.'

She looked at me a little sadly, then smiled. 'You, too.'

# 19

## The Big Hit

It was time to renew my visa and I stood at the desk of the immigration officer in Mombasa, wondering if he'd pop for another month. The I.O., like all government officials on the coast, was an up-country Kikuyu. The Kikuyus were the dominant tribe in Kenya and pretty much ran everything. The I.O. took my passport, went to a back room, then returned with two other bureaucrats and a copy of the *Daily Nation*. 'Excuse me,' he said, 'but, are you a hippie?'

'Oh, no, certainly not,' I quickly responded.

'We wondered because of—'

'The long hair?'

'Yes, and—'

'The mustache?'

'Yes, and—'

'The beads? *Um-hmm*, I can understand the confusion.'

The I.O. glanced at the newspaper again, then looked up. 'But, you are not a hippie?'

'No, no . . . that's another tribe.'

'Ah,' he said, glancing at the other guys, still a little unsure.

'I'm mostly Potawatomee, from up near Rice Lake.'

'*Aaaah*,' they said, nodding to each other, fully satisfied. The I.O. smiled and stamped my passport for another month. I went straight to the bus station and got on an old clunker to Lamu.

\* \* \*

When I stepped off the ferry, I felt like I was home. Everything seemed to be moving in slow motion as I made my way up from the port and through town. I waved to all the familiar faces, stopped to chat with Haji at the hardware store, then headed out for the *shamba*. When I saw the open doorways and glassless windows from the pathway, my heart raced a little. I hurried my pace up through the sand and arrived at the porch. Pete was sitting there smoking a joint. 'Well, look who's back!' he said, getting up to greet me.

'Did you miss me?'

'Day and night.'

I looked around the old homestead, and everything seemed to be in order. The ant freeway was chugging along, the bats were snoozing in the belfry, the ceiling was still about to collapse, Jesse Allen's painting hadn't even faded from the wall. I reached into my rucksack, pulled out a paper bag, and handed it to Pete. 'Here, I've got something for you.'

Pete opened it, and his eyes lit up. There were a half-dozen English scones from the hotel in Mombasa. 'Nice one,' he said.

'So, how's the gang?'

'Everybody's fine. Sultan comes by every day or two to see if I heard from you. The Alis are cool. Jeff and Barbara said to say good-bye.'

'Good-*bye*?'

'Oh, right, you didn't know. They left for India a couple weeks ago. Packed up everything to move to their guru's ashram.'

'India? Just like that?'

'Who knows? I might be next,' said Pete.

'*You?*'

'I've thought about it. Next ship leaves in a month.' I was pretty sure it was just the *bangi* talking. Pete leave Lamu? No way.

I adjusted to my old routine in no time: get up, think about brushing my teeth, stare at the palm tree, go to town, eat a little something, walk home, pass out. I saw Sultan almost every day and now had a few stories of my own to tell. He

216

especially got a big kick out of my being afraid to pee in the jungle. He said he thought that the journey was good for me, that I seemed more at ease than when I left. Maybe so. Maybe I wasn't fighting things quite so much anymore. If nothing else, Africa had taught me the futility of fighting nature.

Pete and I decided to visit Big Ali's *shamba* on the other side of town. We rolled up a bunch of joints and headed off down the path under the hot sun. Halfway there, I noticed a man walking behind us who wasn't wearing the traditional Swahili *kikoy*. It was funny in a way: I'd become so acclimated to the local style that even an African in shirt and pants seemed like a foreigner. Big Ali was thrilled to see us. He gave us a tour of his land, pointing out which palm trees were big coconut producers and which were laggards. The moment Pete lit up a joint, the man from the path suddenly appeared on the porch. I tried to make out what he was saying to Ali, but couldn't quite get a grasp of it. Pete just stood there, toking on the joint. I didn't like the look of things when the guy came over to us. 'I am Joseph Mzingi,' he said.

'*Jambo, bwana*,' I replied. '*Habari yako?*'

'That is unnecessary. I am capable of speaking English.' His response told me more than I wanted to know. First, he was a Kikuyu. I had met plenty of Kenyans who spoke perfect English, but only the Kikuyus seemed irritated when I spoke Swahili. Everyone else seemed honored that I was making an attempt. Second, since he was a Kikuyu on Lamu, he was certain to be some kind of government official. Third, since he was a Kikuyu official who had followed us all the way out here, he must be a cop.

'What's the problem?' said Pete, looking annoyed.

'The problem is that you are breaking the law of the Republic of Kenya.'

Pete looked at the joint in his hand. 'What, this?'

'Yes, I believe you are smoking *bangi*.'

'So what?'

'You are not aware that smoking *bangi* is illegal?'

'Sure, sure, maybe technically, but everybody smokes *bangi*.'

'That is not true. *I* do not smoke *bangi*,' said Joseph, a little too seriously.

'Well, maybe you should,' said Pete.

I cringed. 'I think what my friend is saying is that we were not aware that it was illegal to smoke *bangi* on private property. We'll just throw it away.'

Pete looked at me like I was crazy. 'Throw it away?'

'*Will you shut the fuck up?*' I whispered between gritted teeth.

'You are an American?' said Joseph, turning my way.

'Yes, sir, I am.'

'My cousin went to a university in America. Florida State University.'

'Really? Why, that's the finest university in the country.'

'Now he lives in the city of Oakland.'

'Oakland! What a very lucky man!'

Joseph smiled proudly, then turned away. 'It is unfortunate that I must place an American under arrest.'

'Under ar-*rest*?'

'If it were up to me, I would just let you go, but the government of the Republic of Kenya would then lose ten thousand shillings in fines.'

'Ten *thousand* shillings?' I said, feeling faint.

'Each.'

'Well, Mr Mzingi, I don't think any of us have that kind of money—'

'You may call me Joseph.'

'Thank you, Joseph, you see, we are just poor students on holiday—'

'But you have been here for many months.'

'Yes, yes, it is a very *long* holiday. Pete here is studying Third World economics, and I—'

'If it were not for the loss the government would incur, I could perhaps turn a blind eye.'

'What *loss*?' fumed Pete. '*We're* not asking for money—'

I glared at Pete and cut him off. 'I understand, Joseph. You

218

are, very wisely, looking at it from the angle of *potentiality*, and from that angle it is a terrible loss indeed.'

'Yes, that is the problem.'

'If only there was a way for you to forget you saw us smoking *bangi*, then, in a sense—'

'—then there would be no loss,' he said, after thinking it over for a long moment. I made sure Pete didn't say anything else stupid, while Joseph further considered the issue. 'You are my very best friend,' he said. 'I could not sleep at night thinking of you in jail.'

'Thank you, Joseph, that is very kind.'

'I will somehow forget this ever happened. Please, give me your bag.'

'My bag?'

'I must make certain you have no more *bangi*.'

'No, no, of course we don't—' Joseph turned the bag upside down and three fat joints rolled out. 'Except for those, that is.'

'So, there are three more cigarettes.'

'I'm not sure where those came from,' I said, as visions of spending the rest of my life in a Kenyan jail passed before my eyes. The visions were not pretty. 'I'll just throw them away.'

'No, no, I know you need them.'

'I wouldn't say we *need* them.'

'Smoke them right now. Each of you take one.'

'Now? *Uh*, how about later?'

'I am sorry. I cannot let you leave here with *bangi*. You must smoke it now.'

So Pete, Ali, and I lit up three joints and smoked them right down to their tips. It was one of the strangest highs I ever experienced. Joseph, my new best friend, explained that he was head of the Criminal Investigation Division, and he said how lucky we were that some lower CID agent hadn't caught us instead. 'Uh-huh,' I said, getting more and more blasted, looking at Joseph's orange polyester pants and wondering if he really liked those creases down the middle, I mean, what the hell *is* a crease, after all, but a mind-set, a statement to the world that you're serious, you've got an agenda, you can be trusted, you know right from wrong, you're a guy who can walk the straight and narrow, you can take orders, you understand hierarchy and position, you can march in formation or hit the ground running, and then I thought how my *kikoy* had no creases whatsoever, how nothing I owned had creases, and I wondered if maybe a crease or two wouldn't be such a bad thing, I'd get an iron and some starch and put a nice vertical crease along the side of the *kikoy*, right where the edge tucks under and maybe another two in front along the legs, and then, of course, two more in the back for balance and—

'It is getting late,' said Joseph, 'shall we walk to town?'

I blinked a few times, said good-bye to Ali, and floated off the *shamba* as Joseph kept going on and on about the CID. 'The guy's crazy, you know,' said Pete under his breath.

'No shit,' I whispered back. 'Let's split up in town. See if you can get out to the *shamba* and bury the rest of the *bangi* before the whole force shows up.' That's what we did. I diverted Joseph long enough for Pete to disappear, then managed to lose Joseph myself in the marketplace. I split through some side streets, slipped into a guest house, and snuck into a shower at the end of the hall. I definitely needed to cool off. I stood under a stream of water and splashed it onto my face, trying to come down from my high. I had a strong feeling that I wasn't quite done with Joseph, and I wanted to be reasonably alert if I encountered him again. I encountered him sooner than I expected. He was standing right outside the shower the moment I stepped into the hallway. 'Joseph!' I said. 'I've been looking everywhere for you!'

'You know that you are my very best friend,' he said.

'Yes, and I feel exactly the same way.'

'That is why I am troubled.'

'Oh?'

'I know how much you love *bangi*, that you cannot stop smoking *bangi*, that your body craves *bangi* from morning to night.'

'No, no, it's not really like that.'

'Of course it is. Do not be embarrassed. As you know, I

would never do anything to harm you, but I am concerned what might happen if one of my twenty agents were to catch you breaking the law.'

'*Uh* . . . I see.'

'I believe that if you were to give them a small donation, you would no longer have anything to fear.'

This, of course, was exactly what I was afraid of. The big hit. 'The thing is, Joseph, I really am very poor, and I couldn't possibly come up with—'

'Twenty shillings.'

I was certain I hadn't heard correctly. Was he asking for twenty thousand shillings? Sure, that sounded about right. Before, he wanted thirty thousand for the three of us, now he was giving me the best-friend discount. I was dead. Okay, I'll just play dumb – '*Uh*, how much?'

'Twenty shillings.'

'Twenty shillings?' I repeated, just to make sure. Wait a minute, he's asking for $2.50? To bribe twenty CID agents? 'Well, that's a lot of money,' I said, trying not to jump up and click my heels, 'but I suppose if it would show my appreciation . . .' I reached into my bag and pulled out some money. I couldn't believe it. A fifty-shilling note was the smallest thing I had.

Joseph didn't react. 'Come, we'll get change.' I followed him to a bar down at the port. The bar, patronized by up-country Christians, was never entered by nondrinking Moslems, and I had avoided it, too, knowing it was popular with cops, undercover agents, and other unsavory types. Joseph handed the fifty shillings to the bartender, got change, and handed me the balance. He then walked me down the bar and introduced me to the CID agents. 'James, this is my very best friend. You are never to bother him for any reason.' James shook hands, studied my face, and nodded. 'Matthew, this is my very best friend. You are never to bother him—' On and on it went, right down to the end of the bar. When it was all over, I had the entire secret service of Lamu in my pocket for two and a half dollars. It would have been a bargain at twice the price.

* * *

By the time I left the bar, night had fallen. I walked along the docks, then cut up toward town. As I neared Petley's Inn, I heard something that sent shivers down my spine. Disco music! I looked up at Petley's roof garden and saw colored lights, a big sound system, and a couple of tourists dancing. I stood there a moment in culture shock – shock at my own culture, that is – then quickly moved on. This, I was certain, was a very, very bad development. When I got back to the *shamba*, I was in for another surprise. Pete's bags were packed and lined up on the porch. 'What's this?' I asked.

'I'm going to India.'

'*What?*'

'This was the final straw. It's time to move on.'

'Pete, listen to me, you're overreacting. We're cool with the cops. I took care of everything.'

'No, I've been thinking about it anyway. The ship leaves in a couple of days. I'll be in Bombay in two weeks.' I knew there was no point in arguing with Pete. He hardly ever made up his mind about anything, but when he did, that was it.

So, the very next morning, I found myself at the edge of a dock watching as the ferry pulled away from the harbor. 'Don't go joining any ashrams,' I called to him.

Pete gave me a thumbs-up, then turned, looked out at Lamu, and bowed his head in reverence. 'Nice one,' he said.

I watched as the boat chugged out of view, then nodded one last time. 'Nice one,' I said, missing him already.

# 20

# Bwana Mkubwa

Okay, so now I'm all alone. Just me. Just me and my shadow.
First Jeff and Barbara left, now Pete. What's the big deal with
India, anyway? What's India got that Lamu doesn't? Let's
see, lots of gods, that's all I can really think of. Oh, and
curried peas. And a five-thousand-year-old culture that was
once the flower of civilization. And hashish. That's it. God,
curry, culture, and hash. Well, big deal. Jeff, Barbara, and
Pete can smoke all the hash they want, I'll just sit here with
all the extra *bangi* I'll be able to buy by staying put.

'Okay, stop bullshitting yourself,' came a voice from somewhere in the attic.

'Huh?' I said, looking up at the ceiling.

'You know that India is pulling you, too, it's like gravity,
it keeps pulling you closer, it's like you're in a far orbit that
isn't quite enough to suck you in, but is strong enough to
keep you spinning ever closer.'

'Says you.'

'Oh, yeah? Where do you think Annika is right now?'

'Annika? What's Annika got to do with anything? Why'd
you have to bring Annika into this?' I said in a huff.
'Anyway, ten-to-one she got no farther than Istanbul. I'm
sure she came to her senses and turned around. She's probably back in Sweden by now, knee-deep in snow, sitting
at the bar of Magnus Ladulås, waiting for me to come
through the door.'

'That's what you think? That she's in Stockholm, waiting

223

for you? Would you like to know what *I* think?'

'I don't really care what you think.'

'Fine. I'll just go back to the attic.'

'Yeah, you do that. There's just one thing.'

'What's that?'

'We don't *have* an attic,' I hooted.

As a matter of fact, we barely had a ceiling. What was holding it up, anyway? Those little mangrove poles? Maybe the whole thing would collapse on my head in the middle of the night and then I wouldn't have to think about it anymore. Yeah, that wouldn't be so bad, because this gravity stuff is making my head spin.

I wasn't really prepared to be out on the *shamba* all alone. It was one thing to live in an open-air wind tunnel of a house – where anything could show up in the middle of the night, open its jaws, and chomp off my head – but before, at least, there was someone else down the hall. Now, it was just me against the elements – a stacked deck if there ever was one. I started hearing strange sounds, things rustling and creaking, weird shrieks, the pitter-patter of hundreds of tiny feet. I'm not sure which was more haunted, me or the house, but it was getting spookier by the night. Okay, just stay calm, I told myself as I tried to take stock of the situation. I'm in a nine-dollar house on fifteen acres of land thirty minutes from town a mile off the coast of nowhere. I'm all alone, with nothing to do, nowhere to go, and no one to talk to. I've been in Africa for six months, have gone more native than the natives, and am telling myself jokes in Swahili.

Did you hear the one about the Masai tribesman who flew over a cattle ranch in Texas? He looked down and said, '*Hatari! Mifugo mile ni mangu!*' Oh, God, wait . . . let me catch my breath . . . I'm gonna split a gut here.

What, exactly, was I trying to prove? Did I have a plan? Was I going to stay in Lamu for the rest of my life? Was I even going to make it through the night alive? I thought back to Greece, where I barely knew the difference between the sea and the shore. I wondered if this was what it's all about,

learning the natural pattern of things, learning my relationship to the stars, the tides, and the seasons. When will I
know enough? Will I ever know enough? How many seasons
will it take? One full cycle? Is that what I need? A full year
in Africa?

I wondered if there was a way I could attach two wooden
eyes to the side of my head to help me see through the fog.
Perhaps they wouldn't have to be as large as the ones on the
sides of Sultan's dhow, and maybe I could even rig up some
kind of metal strap, like the ones on earmuffs, so that I could
just slip them on and off when I really needed them. They'd
be kind of like eyemuffs. Yeah, I'll start on that tomorrow.
Eyemuffs will be cool. And they'll go nicely with my *kikoy*
especially after I get those creases ironed in.

As the weeks passed, I found myself spending more and more
time in town. One day I ran into Little Ali. He looked down-
cast and could barely flash his beautiful smile. 'Ali? You
okay?'

'I miss Jeff and Barbara,' he said.

'Yeah, me too.'

'And I have lost my stall at the market.' He turned away,
ashamed. 'The baby needed clothes. I didn't have money to
restock the shelves.'

'Oh, man, I'm sorry. Listen, maybe I can help a little—'

'I would only lose it,' he said, staring at the ground. 'I am
terrible at business.'

'Well, something will work out. It always does.'

'By the grace of God,' he said, trying to put a brave face
on things.

I walked around town that day, trying to imagine what Ali
could do. Lamu, after all, wasn't exactly the land of opportunity. Down at the port, big, strapping guys loaded
mangroves onto dhows for a couple of shillings a day. Those
who owned property barely eked out a living on their
*shambas*. The few shopkeepers huddled over their accounts,
trying to make things add up. It all seemed pretty hopeless. I
was about to head for home when I heard Petley's Disco

225

cranking up and actually felt ill. I stood on the outskirts of town for a moment, then turned back for the inn.

Roger, a red-faced English colonial, was knocking back whiskeys at the downstairs bar when I arrived. His father had set him up as manager of Petley's, and Roger was desperately trying to make a go of it. He'd done a nice-enough job restoring the old building, but business was far from booming. 'How's the disco going, Roger?' I said, sliding up next to him at the bar.

'A little slow so far, but it'll catch on. It's quite smashing, don't you think?'

'Absolutely. You did a great job.'

'It's just what Lamu needs, bring the place into the twentieth century.'

'You're right. Look at Malindi. The discos down there are full every night.'

'My point exactly.'

'Yeah, I think you're doing a smart thing. I mean, you take away the discos from Malindi, what've you got?'

'You've got nothing,' said Roger, nodding and pouring another drink. 'I'm thinking maybe of acquiring a grander sound system, like they have in Nairobi. What do you think?'

'Sure, why not? I mean, Lamu's beautiful and all, but I don't think anybody's coming here to see your restored hotel, right? I mean, how much culture can anyone stand in one day?'

'Not that we should completely diminish that attraction, I should think—'

'No, no, of course not, I'm just saying people want to be entertained. They need to unwind, hear a little music, dance a little. You're providing a real service.'

'Well, yes, quite. With just the *hint* of tradition, of course.'

'Hey, I'm with you. I'm not saying the hotel isn't beautiful. I'm not saying the local music isn't beautiful.'

'*Hmm?*'

'You know, the harmoniums and all. But tourists want something to feel familiar with. I mean, let's face it, they'd probably rather be in a Holiday Inn watching TV.'

'Well, I don't know precisely about a *Holiday* Inn.'

'What are you saying?' I asked, pouring him another drink. 'That tourists might want to hear traditional music in a traditional hotel?'

'Well, I, *uh*—'

'Yeah, I see what you mean. Instead of all the colored lights on the rooftop, there could be grass mats and over-stuffed pillows and big urns of Arabian tea. The tourists could listen to harmoniums and tablas while looking out over the old town.'

'It's . . . it's just an idea.'

'Well, it's very interesting. I'm sure it wouldn't cost much of anything and you could probably transform the whole upstairs in a couple of days.'

'I recall seeing some old urns in storage, if memory serves me right,' said Roger, uncorking a new bottle and warming to the idea.

'I wonder if that group is still available.'

'What group?'

'Weren't you telling me about them once before? Some guy named Ali who sings and—'

'Yes, yes, of course. We'd have to get the best group on the island.'

'I'll bet you could get them for peanuts.'

'How much do you think?'

'I don't know, a hundred shillings a night?'

'*Hmm*, that's a little steep.'

'Okay, let's call it eighty. That's only twenty shillings each.'

Roger laughed. 'It's a damn sight cheaper than a new sound system, I should say.'

'Knowing you, Roger, I'll bet you'll have the whole thing together in a week.'

'It's possible. Certainly, why not?'

'Let's say . . . Wednesday?'

'Absolutely. Wednesday it is!'

'That's great,' I said, clinking glasses. 'I'll tell everyone I know.'

* * *

A week later, Petley's Disco had been transformed into an exotic harem room from the eighteenth century. Every dignitary on the island was there for opening night, along with more tourists than Roger had ever imagined. Little Ali and his band played for hours, and Ali just kept shaking his head in wonder: 'They're *paying* us to play?' Even the Kikuyus were happy for the local guys and felt proud, perhaps, that something from their country's heritage had stood up to the cultural onslaught from the West. At one point during the concert, the chief of police leaned over to me and said: 'You can stay in Lamu forever, *bwana mkubwa*, I will fix your visa.'

Stay in Lamu forever? Was that such a bad idea? After all, now I was *bwana mkubwa*, a man of *big* respect. I lit up a joint outside the CID office, thought things over, then headed for home. I passed the old haunted house outside town, where, rumor had it, the one-armed ghost of an old Portuguese fisherman still roamed the land, his bloody stump leaving trails along the sand. The wind whistled through an open window, and I hurried along as I felt a chill down my spine. I crossed over some dunes, glad for a large moon that night, and headed for the Moslem graveyard. By now, after months on the beach, desert, bush, and coast, I knew the phases of the moon right down to the minute. I knew that each night a waning moon rose fifty-two minutes later and gave off one-fourteenth less light than the night before. I could look at the sky and tell almost exactly what time it was. For a city kid, I wasn't doing so bad, but city kids – this one, at least – aren't all that crazy about Moslem graveyards. Maybe it was all those tombstones jutting this way and that out of the sandy ground. Maybe it was the weird Arabic writing with the exaggerated curls and swooshes. Maybe it was the intermittent sound of footsteps and breaking twigs.

On this particular night, as I turned a bend in the middle of the cemetery, I was startled to come upon a bird sitting right in the middle of the path. The bird just stared at me and didn't move a feather as I came closer. What kind of crazy bird is this, I wondered, as I gingerly walked around it. Is it trying to tell me something? Is it warning me of danger up ahead? '*Aaaaaaaaaaah!*' I screamed as a bevy of bats swooped down just inches from my head. I realized, finally, that I was near their feeding ground, and I got the hell out of there as fast as my legs would carry me.

The next night, I returned to Petley's, got blasted on *bangi*, checked out the moon in the sky, zipped past the Portuguese sailor's pad, and turned the bend in the graveyard. I couldn't believe it. There was that damn bird again! What was it trying to tell me? '*Aaaaaaaaaaah!*' I screamed as a coconut fell from a tree, hit a branch, bounced off a headstone, and rolled just inches from my foot. My heart pounding, I fled for home.

The third night, I finished off a joint, timed the waning moon, scurried past the bloody ghost, and hightailed it through the cemetery. Shit! That madman of a bird was waiting for me! What do you want from me? Shoo! '*Aaaaaaaaaaah!*' I screamed as the wind howled through the trees, the shadows played upon the graves, and some brush blew across the path. This goddamn bird had it in for me, I realized as I turned and ran.

The fourth night, I was determined not to get stoned, which meant, of course, that I smoked twice as much. The moon was receding, the sailor was clanking around, and I was heading for the bend in the path when I took a deep breath, walked gingerly, and turned. '*Aaaaaaaaaaah!*' It was the worst thing ever! The bird wasn't there! Oh, crap, now I'm really in for it. Maybe I was wrong about the bird all along. Maybe the bird was my ally. Now it was gone! Come back, little bird, come back! Save my sorry ass!

Somehow or other, I got home, thankful to be among the bats, the cats, and the shrieks that awoke me each night. As I lay there on my grass mat, it occurred to me that maybe, just maybe, I had completely lost my mind.

# 21

## Showtime

It seemed like a good time to make another foray outside Lamu. My hair had grown lighter from the sun, my face was dark and weather-beaten, my hands were callused from working on the *shamba*, and the bottom of my feet were tough as nails. Even inside, I felt a little tougher and more confident. I'd heard about a fishing boat that left from Mombasa for the Comoro Islands, and from there it was a quick shot to Mauritius. Why Mauritius? I had no idea, other than that I always liked their stamps.

I had a stamp collection when I was twelve and I remember just staring at a map of the world hour after hour. Certain places stuck out. Spain was my favorite country because they had a Goya nude on one of their stamps, a big rectangular stamp of a woman with big round breasts. God, how I wanted to go to Spain. Every afternoon I'd run home from school and just stare at that stamp, dreaming of all the naked women of Madrid and Barcelona I would meet, how I'd stand at some post office in Catalonia and offer to lick their stamps for them and then paste them carefully onto their pink, perfumed envelopes, and gently, oh so gently, insert them into the mail slot and then slip off like a cat in the night.

You could tell a lot about a country from its stamps. Take Argentina, for example. I was especially intrigued by the Eva Perón airmails, the ones where she's wearing a low-cut dress that, when held beneath a magnifying glass, created magically heaving breasts. Then there was Timor (more breasts), Senegal (still more breasts), Cameroon (unbelievable breasts), and, of course, any stamp at all from the Virgin Islands. The world was a wonderful magical place of endless possibilities.

At first my parents liked the idea of a stamp collection, thinking it would keep me out of trouble. Years later, after my endless travels to places like Mauritius, they became convinced it was the stamps that had ruined my life.

The Hotel Rafiki in Mombasa wasn't much more than a glorified hostel, and it wasn't really glorified, at that. There were six rooms, six beds to a room, and six guests in all, so we each had plenty of room. The boat to the Comoro Islands, a dinky little tub, was scheduled to leave any time now, and each morning I gathered my stuff together, checked out of the hotel, and headed for the port, only to be told to come back the next day. After the fifth morning of this, I got tired of the routine. Meanwhile, I heard about a local band that was playing at the Hotel Dolphin, a big, Western-style resort that was part of a chain between Mombasa and Malindi. It was run by a Swiss-German-Kenyan consortium that shuttled tour groups back and forth every two weeks. The band, made up of local Swahilis, a Seychellois, and two up-country Kenyans, wasn't half-bad. They invited me to sit in with them for a blues jam and, as luck would have it, the manager of the Dolphin heard the crowd cheering me on. The next thing I knew he was offering me a gig as a featured performer during *Showtime*, a nightly twenty-minute interlude. At a thousand shillings a week – a small fortune in Kenya – I could hardly say no.

*Showtime* consisted of African drummers, a fearless fire-eater, and Wendy the Snake Dancer. Wendy, a mad Englishwoman, wrapped a twenty-foot python around her body and jumped up and down in ecstasy until the snake couldn't take it anymore. The show usually ended with the python taking a big dump on the stage. The audiences, meanwhile, seemed to include an unusual mix of interracial couples on the dance floor. I learned why later, when *Der Stern* blew the lid off things with a cover story entitled 'African Sex Safaris.' It turned out that right beneath my amazingly naïve eyes, all those pink-cheeked Europeans weren't just dancing with the Africans, they were screwing them right and left. Husbands and wives split up at the airport, went off on a two-week binge, then met back at the plane for what I'm sure was a very interesting flight back to Europe. This was who I was entertaining each night? I had a whole new musical outlook.

All right, you crazy German sex fiends, this is the *blues*, you understand? This isn't Der Beatles or Tangerine Dream or Kraftwerk, this is down and dirty, just the way you like it, this is torn panties and ripped shirts and bare flesh, this is late nights with too much whiskey, this is James Cotton and Big Walter Horton and Paul Butterfield on an all-night binge, this is 'Good Morning, Little Schoolgirl,' this is 'Another Mule Kicking in Your Stall,' this is *Shooooowtime*.

I awoke one morning to find fourteen Indians sharing my six-bed room at the Hotel Rafiki. Idi Amin had gone on a rampage and thrown all of the Asians out of Uganda – just as Rajiv and Anand had warned – and now, thousands of Indians, many of them third-generation Ugandans, were in Nairobi and Mombasa, looking for a way out. Kenya couldn't support them and India, their ancestral homeland, didn't want them back, so England, through an intriguing twist of fate, became the default destination. Those British passports that had been issued years ago to induce the Indians to come to East Africa were now the only citizenship they could claim, so the xenophobic English had to open their arms to thousands of their fellow 'countrymen.' And just like that, almost overnight, all the Indians were gone and I had my room back.

While all this was going on in Uganda, the Indians in Kenya and Tanzania were growing uneasy about their own status, as were the English colonials. The result was a sudden upsurge in the value of dollars on the black market. Since

232

local shillings were worthless on the international exchange, black marketeers were trading for dollars at highly inflated prices. Overnight, my money was worth 50 percent more and life in Mombasa, already dirt cheap, became ludicrously inexpensive. There was an item I had my eye on, something I'd been putting off for years, and I decided now was the time to take the plunge. I bought my first guitar.

I sat in the hotel room every afternoon and played until my fingers bled. The steel strings were like little knives cutting into my fingertips as I learned chords and scales. After a while, I got a neck brace for my harmonica and began playing along with the guitar. This was the real goal. If I could learn to accompany the harp, I'd no longer have to rely on other musicians to supply the background. I was quite proud of myself. I actually had something approaching a schedule for the first time since I'd left the States. Every morning, right around ten or eleven, I'd get out of bed and have breakfast. Every afternoon, I'd play guitar. Every night, I'd perform in one of the hotels for twenty minutes. Life was good. Awfully busy, but good.

I learned to play basic twelve-bar blues on the guitar, but I couldn't keep the chord changes straight when playing harmonica at the same time. What worked better was simple two-chord progressions where I didn't have to think about what my hands were doing. I decided that if I was going to play only two chords, I'd better at least make them interesting, so I tried out major sevenths, minor ninths, augmented elevenths, and diminished thirteenths. These chords were associated more with jazz than with blues, but I found they opened up a whole new range of scales for the harmonica.

By night I played blues standards – songs about pimps, hustlers, drunks, and hookers. It was absurd, of course, this white guy playing black blues with an African band for a bunch of German swingers. Especially when right outside was a moonlit sky that engulfed a long expanse of white sand and a sea that stretched to the horizon. That's where I really wanted to be, I wanted my music to breathe with the sky, to illuminate the shore, to roll like the waves in the sea.

Each day was a contradiction as I progressed musically in my room, then backtracked in the club. Soon I started coughing – that familiar cough of flat beer and stale cigarettes – and then, one night, when the hotel was particularly crowded, I was reminded of a blues club in Berkeley, where everyone was drinking and smoking and groping each other. I played a jagged solo and realized something was wrong. I was playing the wrong music. I'd made a wrong turn. I was moving backwards. I wondered what Pete was doing right now – was he walking down some cobblestone path toward a sacred river? – and I suddenly realized that I'd been in that club for two months, that I'd gotten completely sidetracked, and that I'd had enough. Mauritius still called, yes, Mauritius, which, after all, was more than just a stamp from my childhood, no, Mauritius was halfway to India, and that's when I quit, right then and there I quit, I quit playing with the band and I quit playing the blues, and the day after that, I left for the Comoro Islands.

The Indian Ocean is the calmest water in the world nine months of the year, the roughest the other three. With all the boats now tied up in harbor, I instead caught an ancient DC-3, the sole plane that made up Air Comores. A stewardess informed me that I was in the president's seat and I sat down gingerly, duly impressed. When I pushed the button to make the seat recline, nothing happened. I pushed it again and leaned back harder in the seat. Still it wouldn't budge. Then I pushed it again and really gave it a good jerk backwards. I heard something snap, then felt the seat flopping back. *All* the way back. Shit! I'd broken the president's seat! Thankfully, the flight was only half an hour long. When we landed in Moroni, the capital, I heard a military band playing. 'For me? Really, you shouldn't have,' I joked to an attendant. He looked at me gravely, then pointed to an entourage waiting to board the plane. It was the president of the Comoro Islands. I fled for the hills.

There were no hills. The Comoros, four little windswept

islands, didn't have much of anything except for the coelacanth, a fish from 400,000,000 years ago that paleontologists thought had been extinct for eons. Its discovery was one of the most important zoological finds of the century – equivalent to finding a living dinosaur – for it provided a missing evolutionary link. Its prehistoric mouth was all wrong, its primitive scales seemed screwy, and its fins had weird lobes jutting out all over the place, but deep beneath the seas of the Comoros were caves where hundreds of coelacanths still lived, and now everyone was trying to capture one.

I met a biologist from the Vancouver Aquarium who wanted to build a decompression chamber, snag a coelacanth deep in its habitat, and somehow get the thing out of there alive. I listened to his various plans and concluded he was out of his mind. Over the years, Jacques Cousteau and many others would try to capture a coelacanth. No one would succeed. Well, of course not. If the coelacanth hadn't been captured alive in 400,000,000 years, it was pretty obvious to me that it wanted no part of the modern world. What, it was going to swim around somebody's tank in Canada and do tricks for the tourists?

The world is made up of knuckleheads.

Mauritius, fifteen hundred miles out into the Indian Ocean, was something altogether different. Mauritius had been home to a goofy, flightless bird that took a liking to the first Dutch settlers when they arrived four hundred years ago. 'Look at it,' the Dutch said, 'look how it walks right up to us, look how it trusts us, look how sweet it is, look how we can blast it to kingdom come for no good reason at all, look what a dodo it is.' After the Dutch got rid of all the dodo birds, the French got rid of the Dutch, then the English got rid of the French, and now it was a big hodgepodge of people from all over the place – Indians, Pakistanis, Chinese, Creoles, they all shared this little island and somehow got along. I wondered how long it would be before someone came along and decided they were a bunch of dodos, too.

Now that I was in the middle of the Indian Ocean, I found myself looking farther east. I wasn't sure if I was done with Africa – something still felt unfinished – but I felt India calling me, yes, the pull was getting stronger, gravity was sucking me in. After a few days in Port Louis, the capital, I learned that a freighter, the *Vishva Vinay*, was due in from Calcutta within the week and would be turning around and heading for Bombay. As luck would have it, the shipping clerk knew the captain and figured he could arrange passage. He was expecting a cable from the *Vishva Vinay* any day now and suggested I check out the island while awaiting the ship's arrival. Okay, that made sense. Things were lining up. I'd just let it all unfold naturally. That's what Africa taught me. Let nature decide.

Mauritius is a pristine paradise of white sand, rolling hills, and endless sugarcane fields. When I arrived at Tamarin, I found a cove that reminded me of Mykonos, and I decided to sleep on the beach. Shortly after sunset, I felt some raindrops and saw a big patch of dark clouds moving in. I noticed a little cabana at the edge of the beach, a run-down shack that looked long abandoned. As more rain began to fall, I went over to check it out. Even though there was a lock on the door, the place seemed flimsy enough to break into. Sure enough, after I gave the door a couple of good yanks, the lock pulled right off its hinges. I aimed my flashlight inside, saw a bunch of junk piled all over the place, and had second thoughts about going in. Then a big gust of wind kicked up and I decided to clear enough space for my sleeping bag. I stretched out on the floor, lit a candle, propped my head against my guitar case, and looked around the primitive shack. The dancing flame of the candle made it hard to see what exactly was there, but the roof seemed reasonably intact and only a few drops of rain were leaking in.

That's when I noticed something on the wall across from me. At first I thought it was just a shadow from the candle, but I decided to pull out my flashlight and shine it over there just in case. '*Holy . . . fucking . . . shit,*' I whispered as I stared at an enormous hairy hideous spider that had been coughed up from the depths of hell. The spider was the size of my fist, not including the legs, and the legs – *aaaaaaaaaah!* – the legs were some kind of Darwinian bad joke. Nothing would survive the clench of those legs, nothingnothing-*nothing*. How many legs does a spider have? Six? Eight? Thirty-two? Who remembers? All I knew was that each leg was overgrown with hundreds of sharp, pointy hairs – hairs that I'm pretty sure had poison dripping off them, oozy sticky gummy poison, the kind I hate the most, the kind that gets on your skin and makes your fingers stick together and the more you try to get it off the more it seeps inside your pores, and now this spider is staring at me like he's planning to suck out my eyeballs and deliver his insidious glutinousness right inside the orb sockets so that I won't even be able to see where he's attacking next, okay, that's it, I'll just be leaving, I'll just gather my things and slip over here to the door . . . *where there's another spider! With even more legs! And triple the poison!* I dove back into my sleeping bag and waited to die. Just exactly how many spiders were in that shack? Fifty? A hundred? How many of them were crawling into my sleeping bag at that very minute?

Now are you happy, Annika?

All night, I watched the spiders and they watched me. When the candle burned down, I flicked the flashlight on and off periodically, just so they knew I was still awake. The next thing I remember is the sun shining through a crack in the wall, the dead flashlight lying on the floor, and me getting the hell out of there as fast as possible. I inspected my body in the light and found, amazingly, no bites. I spent the day on the beach, swimming, eating fruit, and resting up. That night, just as I was getting comfortable in my sleeping bag, I felt raindrops on my face. Shit! Now what? A few minutes later, I found myself back in the cabana watching the shadows on the wall from my flickering candle. It was at that moment I realized three things: first, that Smolinski the hunter had better be right about animals in the wild not being aggressive; second, that my flashlight was still dead; and third, that I was, without any doubt, a hopeless creature of habit.

It didn't rain the third night at Tamarin, but I decided to sleep in the cabana anyway. The spiders and I had reached a nice détente: I wouldn't people them if they wouldn't bug me. The next day I returned to Port Louis to check in with the shipping clerk. 'No,' he said, rubbing his chin, 'still no word from the *Vishva Vinay*.' Okay, no problem. I headed for the beach at La Gaulette, slept out overnight, and awoke to a dozen families setting up a picnic. I tried to slip away, but they'd have none of that antisocial behavior. The Mauritians are probably the friendliest people on the planet, and the idea of someone going off by himself to ponder the horizon was simply beyond them. I was pulled into the family circle and taught the proper way to cut a pineapple. Once the outer skin has been pared, there are dozens of spiky little eyes still in the fruit, which are mildly toxic. If you look at them closely enough, you see that the eyes form a spiral pattern and if you cut a half-inch groove along that spiral, you wind up with a beautiful twisting flower of a pineapple. Some women insisted that I practice until I got it just right. Then a cheer went up: 'Hooray! Hooray for lonely white man!' I was to be lonely no more, not if the Mauritians had anything to do with it. When they packed up to leave, the family insisted that I not sleep on the beach and, the next thing I knew, I was on a bus with sixty people who were singing and dancing in the aisles. As we careened down the road, a buxom mama grabbed my arm and showed me a few steps. Another cheer went up: 'Hooray! Hooray for dancing white man!'

'Any word yet?' I asked the shipping clerk in Port Louis.

'No,' he said, furrowing his brow. 'I'm sure there's a good explanation. Come back in a few days.' I came back in a few days, then in a few more days, then in a few weeks, until finally, three weeks after arriving in Mauritius, I began suspecting the *Vishva Vinay* simply wasn't going to show. With no other ships scheduled for India, I wondered if I'd be sitting there forever. Not that Mauritius was a bad place to wait for a phantom boat – I was having a great time on the beaches of Baie du Cap, Bois des Amourettes, and Pointe aux Piments – but I felt it was time to take action. I decided to throw the *I Ching*.

The *I Ching* is a book of pre-Confucian oracles meant to guide one through life's difficult moments. By casting three Chinese coins, a hexagram is formed, within which a coded answer can be found. I believed in the *I Ching* but used it sparingly, as I didn't want to take advantage of its powers. After casting the coins, I drew out the hexagram and consulted the book. It said: 'You will cross the great water, but not in a boat.' *Hmm*. Usually, the hexagram was oblique and required a good deal of interpretation, but this was so clear, even I could understand it. The *Vishva Vinay*, just like the tub to the Comoros, simply wasn't in the cards for me.

Nature had decided. For maybe the first time, I knew not to question it. I knew not to argue. That afternoon, I went to the airline office and booked a flight back to East Africa. I could've flown directly from Mauritius to India, but that didn't feel right. A place as old as India demands something a little more traditional. Better to walk to India. Or, at least, sneak in through the back door on a boat. Maybe even the one that Pete, Jeff, and Barbara had taken. Any boat but the *Vishva Vinay*.

# 22

# Martine

There's a story they tell in the restaurants of Mombasa, that they can tell how long you've been in Africa by the way you drink a glass of water. If you find a bug in the water and ask the waiter to bring you a new glass, they know you've just arrived. If you find a bug and merely remove it before drinking the water, they know you've been there a while. But if you see a bug in the water and don't even bother digging it out, then they know you've fully acclimated to life in the tropics. I drank down a big glass of bug water at a restaurant on Kilindini Road, then headed for the port. When I found out the ship to India wasn't scheduled to leave for another five weeks, I wondered if I'd made the right decision in coming back. The idea of spending another month in Lamu far outweighed any inconvenience, however, and I left on the first bus north. Deep down, I always knew I wasn't finished with Lamu. I'd never properly said good-bye to Sultan and I looked forward to returning. After another typically harrowing bus ride up the coast, I could feel my heart pounding as we pulled up to the ferry at McCoy.

There was a commotion near the dock when we arrived. Some foreigner had left his Land Rover in the village and hired a boy to keep an eye on it while he was in Lamu. He tore a ten-shilling note down the middle, gave the boy half, and said he could have the other half when he returned. Now he'd just come back and found a contingent of soldiers waiting for him. They pointed out that the ten-shilling note bore the likeness of Jomo Kenyatta, and said the man's ripping that likeness in half was a grave insult to the father of the nation. The guy was tossed into jail for three months, which, as far as I was concerned, was just about right. Not for defacing old Jomo – who cared about that? – no, for the way he treated that kid.

When the ferry pulled into the port, I stared out over the town and realized that Lamu was still the most beautiful and exotic spot in Africa. There was an allure, a magic, that was unique to the island. The *shamba*, unfortunately, was another story. While I'd been gone heavy rains had wreaked havoc on the house and left it in a shambles. It's a shame to leave a *shamba* in shambles, but I had neither the time nor the energy to undertake major repairs. So, regretfully, I returned to town. I ran into Haji at the hardware store and learned that he had a house available about fifteen minutes away. I jumped at the chance not to have to spend a month in a hotel and headed straight out there. When I arrived, I couldn't believe what I saw. Doors! Windows! A bed! It was a little steep at fifteen dollars a month but, hey, you only live once.

Across the path, an old lady was sweeping the dirt in front of her porch and I realized she must be the woman Haji had told me about. She was the oldest person on the island, 110, he claimed, and I went over to greet her. '*Jambo, memsahib.*'

'*Jambo, mzee,*' she replied as she backed up and bent her head.

I wasn't sure if I'd heard right. She called me *mzee*? *Mzee* means great old man and is reserved for village elders and leaders. Jomo Kenyatta is called *mzee*. I knew the woman was a little batty, but did she really think I was an old man? '*Habari yako, memsahib?*'

'*Mzuri kabisa. Habari yako, mzee?*' Christ! She did it again! Me, a *mzee*. I had enough trouble keeping a straight face when they called me *bwana mkubwa*. To this woman, I should be *mtoto midogo*, a little kid. When I offered to sweep the dirt for her, she looked at me in fear and backed up even further. It was then that I realized what this was all

241

about. This woman had spent almost her entire life living under the colonials and to her I was still the great white man. So many decades of deference had been ingrained into her that, even now, she was unable to let go. I don't remember ever feeling as embarrassed to be white as I did at that moment, or ever feeling so conscious of what it must have been like for generations of Africans under the British. As I turned to walk away, she bowed once more and called after me, 'Asante sana, mzee, asante sana.'

I found Sultan sitting outside his hut in Shela. He seemed glad to see me, but I sensed that something was troubling him. He finally told me that the man who owned his dhow had reclaimed it, and he was now back to hiring out on other boats, where the work was sporadic and the pay poor. Sultan, who just barely had been able to support his family, was worried how he would make up the difference. A fisherman in his mid-fifties, after all, had few options in Lamu but to go to sea. When I left to return to town, I saw that the usual glow was missing from his eyes.

'How much would it cost to buy a small dhow?' I asked Haji when I got back to Lamu.

'Maybe twenty-five hundred shillings,' he said.

Even on the black market, that came out to $250. 'And to build one?'

'Well,' he said, leaning back and thinking, 'there's teak for the hull, mangrove for the mast, sealant, rope and pulleys, cloth for the sails, steel fittings . . . perhaps seventeen hundred.'

'And if it was for a *very* close friend?'

Haji smiled. 'All right, maybe it could be arranged for fifteen hundred.'

'Good,' I said, shaking Haji's hand. The next day I was on the bus to Mombasa to change money on the black market.

'No, no, no!' protested Sultan when I placed the money in his hand.

'Yes, yes, yes!' I insisted as I forced his fingers around the

242

bills. We were sitting in a local café in town where I had invited him for *ugali* and *matoke*.

'*Aieeeee!*' he shrieked in disbelief. 'Our own dhow! We will sail to Zanzibar!'

'Well, we'll see,' I said.

Sultan looked deeply into my eyes and understood. 'You are leaving . . .'

'Yes. In one month.'

He ate quietly for a few moments. 'You will come back after the dhow is built?'

'I don't know . . .' Sultan sat there a moment, then reached over for a pencil and began drawing on a piece of paper. The pencil sat awkwardly between his fingers – he had never learned to write – but soon the shape of a boat began to appear. He drew the hull, the mast and the sails, then took special care to put in the two painted eyes on the prow. He looked up at me.

'To help see through the fog,' I said. Sultan nodded, pleased that I remembered. I decided not to tell him about my idea for attaching the eyes to the side of my head. There was no word in Swahili for eyemuffs.

A few days later Sultan showed his completed plans to Haji and the necessary fittings were ordered. After he picked out a few tools and paid with his first hundred-shilling note, the process had officially begun. We went out to celebrate at a restaurant. On the way home we passed Petley's and saw that a party was in full swing. Roger was throwing himself a birthday bash and, when he saw us, he insisted we come in. The bar was jammed, the dance floor packed, and the liquor flowing as we squeezed our way through the throng of tourists and travelers.

I got separated from Sultan and was drawn to a young woman on the dance floor. There was something about the way she moved – so natural and unaffected – that I couldn't take my eyes off her. She danced to the music with a kind of joy and just floated along with the melody. It took me a while to even notice that she was dancing with another woman, and a while longer to notice that the other woman had switched partners and was now dancing with ... Sultan! I couldn't believe it. There he was, in his *kikoy*, flip-flops, and skullcap, kicking it up on the dance floor, taking the woman by her waist, twirling her around, leaning her over, pulling her back, then snuggling in a little closer. If ever I was sorry not to own a camera, this was the time. When the song ended, Sultan dragged his partner over and I found myself acting as translator. She was French, it turned out, and I wondered how much I could possibly screw up a conversation in two foreign languages. '*Bwana, yeye ni kuitwa Odette*,' I said to Sultan. '*Mademoiselle, il s'appelle Sultan*,' I said to Odette.

'And I am Martine,' came a voice from behind. I turned to see the woman I'd been watching on the dance floor, now standing next to me and speaking nearly perfect English.

'Thank God,' I said. 'I was afraid you'd be speaking Spanish or Portuguese.'

'Yes, that would give you quite a job, wouldn't it?' Up close, Martine was even prettier than on the dance floor. Her hair was long and jet black, her eyes a softer brown. I couldn't stop looking at those eyes. 'Do you live here on the island?' she asked.

'I've spent about six months here.'

'It seems like a very magical place ... and *very* open-minded,' she said, gesturing to Sultan.

I looked over and saw that Sultan had a beer in his hand. 'Oh, Christ,' I said to Martine, 'excuse me a minute.' I turned to Sultan and asked him what in Allah's name he was doing.

'I will go twice to the mosque tomorrow,' he said.

'Not with that alcohol on your breath, you won't.'

He shrugged, then pointed to Martine. 'This woman you are with, I like her.'

'Yes, so do I.'

'The woman I am with, I like even better,' he said, with a devilish glint in his eyes.

'*Uh* ... Sultan? Have you forgotten about Mama?'

He looked at me innocently and took a swig on his beer. 'Who?'

A song started up and Sultan pulled Odette back onto the dance floor. Martine called to me over the music. 'He seems like a great character.'

'I'm just finding out *how* great,' I laughed.

'Would you like a drink?' she asked. I reached for some money, but Martine wouldn't hear of it. 'You can buy the next round, if you'd like,' she said as she edged toward the bar. Her hand slightly brushed my arm as she passed by and I felt a tingling sensation along my spine. It was strange, I hadn't felt that sensation since—

I told her about Lamu, and she told me about the little town in France where she taught English, to grade-schoolers. Sultan caught my eye a few times and nodded his approval. '*Mzuri*,' he called over. '*Mzuri kabisa!*'

Later in the evening I looked around the bar and dance floor, but couldn't locate him. Martine likewise couldn't find Odette. 'Well,' she said.

'Yes, well,' I replied, feeling a little nervous. 'Would . . . would you like to see where I live?'

'I'd love to.'

As we walked along the moonlit path to Haji's house, Martine glanced around at all the moving shadows. 'Are there wild animals out here?'

'Here? In the middle of the jungle? Nah.'

'Okay, well, that's good then.'

'You're not afraid, are you?'

'Maybe just a little.'

I put my arm around her and could feel her body lean into mine. 'I'll protect you.'

'Yes, I feel much safer now.' We walked a little farther, turned down another path, then stopped outside the old lady's house. I saw Martine's eyes glistening in the moonlight and could no longer help myself. I bent down and kissed her.

Sometimes, something sets itself in stone. It can be the smallest gesture or the slightest glance or the mere hint of a scent, but it will never be forgotten. When I kissed Martine, I knew I would remember the feeling forever. Whatever else was transitory in life, I knew this was real – the taste of her tongue, the touch of her skin, the flush in her cheeks, the look in her eyes. I felt her hand rise up around my neck and I wanted to stand there forever, to freeze this moment in time, to just hold on. That's when I heard a slight giggle from behind the old lady's window and a lilting, if slightly cracked, voice: '*Asante sana, mzee, asante sana.*'

Martine and I laughed and ran the rest of the way home. When I awoke with her in my arms the next morning, I could feel her breath against my chest, cool and gentle and regular, like a soft breeze wafting through the branches of a palm tree. We were planted there in bed most of that day, and that night, and the next day too, as if rooted in rich fertile soil. We spent every moment together in a kind of magical haze, but then the magician's time was up, it was time to leave the stage, and in the snap of a finger, *shazaam*, the prestidigitator made her disappear, now you see her, ladies and gentlemen, now you don't.

I stood alone on my front porch a few days later, and already our time had blended together into one long breath and all I could really remember was that moment on the path. I wondered if Martine would even remember that. For her, after all, it was a two-week trip to Africa during school holidays, the trip of a lifetime, and there was a lot more to see than some white guy wearing a *kikoy* on a remote island.

I found a new palm tree on Haji's *shamba* to stare into and thought about a religious fanatic I'd met who'd tossed away his passport and traveled through Africa on nothing but his bible. If you paged through his copy of the Old Testament, it now read: 'In the beginning there was [an entry visa to Egypt] and Adam begat [a stamp to Sudan] and Cain begat [an entry to Ethiopia],' on and on, right down the coast – the bible had visas and extensions all over the place. I wondered if I could get through Asia that way on the *I Ching*.

I wasn't all that crazy about borders, myself. What exactly

was a border but some arbitrary line drawn in the sand to create artificial differences between people? Hell, I never could even understand the concept of land ownership, much less nationhood. How could you *own* a piece of land? Who could possibly *sell* you a piece of the earth? How did *they* ever get hold of it? No, in my country – which, of course, would have no borders – nobody would own land. You could maybe hang out for a while, but ownership would be out of the question.

The first piece of land that my family bought was on Sherman Boulevard, in Milwaukee. That itself was somewhat ironic because my ancient uncle Harry had years earlier walked down that very street, liked what he saw, and decided to change his name to whatever it was called. He looked up at the street sign and forever after was known as Harry Sherman. I always regretted that this epiphany hadn't occurred just one block over. In that case, he would have been known as Harry Forty-fourth Street, which would have suited him just perfectly. In another era, I'm quite sure that Uncle Harry would have been a horse thief.

Sherman Boulevard had lost a bit of its luster by the time my dad decided to move the family to Milwaukee. Still, it was one of the finer streets in town and, more to the point, he had found a little section of three nearly brand-new houses, one of which was for sale. These weren't just any houses, they were *ranch* houses, a new style that was turning plenty of heads. I felt proud of our ranch-style house, which was set among all those older, clunky estates. To me it felt like we were connected to the Ponderosa, the Prairie, and the Marlboro Man. It wasn't until much later that I realized how ungodly ugly that house was. It also wasn't until later that I found out how happy the neighborhood was to get *anything* built there, because it turned out that the land had for years been nothing but a dump. Considering it was the 1950s, I'm guessing it was a toxic dump. That's how I grew up. Over a toxic dump. Next door to a member of the American Nazi party, and to Dr. Merton, who never smiled. No wonder the place was for sale.

For my mother, the main attraction was the central heating and air-conditioning. This meant that we would never have to open the windows again and had to rush in and out of the doors lest we let in some *air*. Air, for my mother, was the enemy. Air carried all sorts of invisible things that were probably up to no good, and she decided we'd have none of that in *our* house. Whatever the stuff was that we were breathing had been cycled and recycled through a central compressor that drew its supply from the toxic dump beneath the house. Some years later, my mother became convinced that my stamp collection, a Dodge Dart convertible, and going away to college had ruined my life. It never occurred to her that a profound lack of oxygen was actually to blame.

A voice floated through the palm leaves and pulled me out of my reverie. '*Bonjour, mon cher.*' I looked up to see Martine standing there with a big smile.

'I don't believe it! I thought you'd be in Serengeti by now!'

'Well, exactly how many more elephants does a young woman need to see?' she said as she rushed into my arms. I don't think I'd ever been as happy as when Martine and I fell into bed that day. I never imagined she'd come back to Lamu, but now here she was, the magician had been called back on stage by an audience insisting on more, encore, encore, we screamed, but no weird stuff, okay, no cutting the young lady in half or throwing knives at her head or turning her into a cute little bunny rabbit, no, the magic of her return is quite enough, thank you, and if only you could hypnotize her to stay, well, I'd be awfully grateful, we'd all be grateful, me and Sultan and Mama, who just sat there smiling at us, and the kids on the beach, who knew enough to leave us alone, and the people in town, who nodded and whispered, yes, we'd all be grateful if by some sleight of hand you could stop the calendar or change the year or move time back just a bit at least, so that we could stretch these few days a little further.

'What do you see in your future?' Martine asked as we lay beneath a palm tree.

248

'Well, mango season isn't too far off.'

'*Um-hmm—*'

'I guess that's not what you meant.'

'I'm being serious. How long will you keep on traveling?'

I thought for a moment. 'I'm not so sure I'll ever stop.'

'No home? No family? No career?'

'I don't know. It's a little hard to imagine.'

'Yes, I already have a home and a career and it's hard for me to imagine.' Martine turned her palm up and cupped it in my hand. 'Read my palm,' she said.

'You don't want me to do that.'

'Yes, I do.'

'You have to understand something. I'm a crappy palmist.'

'Then give me a *crappy* reading,' she said, giving the word such a lovely French intonation, I couldn't resist.

'Okay, well, you have a very long and well-defined head line swooping down right into the Mound of Venus.'

'And what does that mean?'

'You're very intelligent and have a vivid imagination. Of course, I already knew that.'

'Go on.'

'Your heart line is very solid and curves up between your first two fingers.'

'Yes?'

'That means you're very well-adjusted emotionally, are very romantic and very loyal in your affairs. Of course, I already knew that, too.'

'Oh? *Did* you?' she laughed. 'Go on.'

'You have a strong, deeply etched, unbroken life line with very few crossing lines.'

'Is that good?'

'Very. Not only will you live a long life, you will be very healthy.'

'Tell me more.'

'I see a long trip in the near future. Crossing the great water. I hear sitars and smell incense.'

Martine suddenly pulled away her hand. 'Don't be cruel,' she said. 'You know how badly I want to go with you.'

I was surprised at her reaction. 'I'm sorry, Martine, I didn't mean anything. I wish you could come.'

'Well, I can't,' she said as she got up and walked alone to the house.

The days passed much too quickly and, before I knew it, Martine was gathering her things together again. 'You know, I must leave for Nairobi tomorrow,' she said.

'Yes, I know.'

'And soon you'll be going to India.'

'Martine, I've been thinking—'

'It's impossible. I have a contract at the school—'

'Break it.'

'Break it?'

'Why not? Just simply don't go back.'

Martine giggled at the possibility, then sat back with a serious look. 'I could not do that. And anyway, who knows if you would still like me with all of those beautiful women around?'

For the first time since Martine's return, I thought of Annika. 'Well, I—'

'You see?' she laughed. 'Already you are cheating on me.'

Her laugh concealed a concern I couldn't deny. I realized at that moment that Martine *could* break the contract, she *would* break the contract, she'd come with me on that ship if only I asked her one more time, we'd lie on the deck crossing the Indian Ocean, we'd hold each other as we approached a new continent, we'd discover it together, we'd be a good team, she and I, we'd talk about important things and laugh a lot and have fun together, we'd make love in perfumed gardens and hold hands under waterfalls and walk barefoot down the beach and feed each other passion fruit beneath moonlit skies, yes, Annika already is fading a bit from my memory – did I even really know her? – it would be better with Martine, Martine whose eyes glisten in the sun, whose hand fits perfectly into my palm, whose legs wrap perfectly around my waist, Martine who would be the most perfect companion I could ever dream of, yes, ask her, that's all it will take, ask her one more time and it will be the right thing and it will make you happy and it will make her happy, and then I turned to her and the words came out of my mouth and they said: 'I want to stay in touch with you, Martine. Who knows what the future will bring?'

'Do you promise to write?' she said, with just the hint of disappointment in her voice.

'I promise.'

'All right, then,' she said, squeezing my hand. 'We shall write.'

The next day, I said good-bye again to Martine. '*Kama Mungu akupenda, tutaonana alafu,*' I said as she stepped onto the ferry.

'That sounds so beautiful. What does it mean?'

'If God wishes, we shall meet again later.'

'I'm going to miss you,' she said. 'I can't tell you how much.'

We kissed one last time and I watched the ferry take Martine Galland across the sea, wanting so very desperately to call out to her and tell her to wait for me on the other side, I'll be on the next boat, just wait for me, Martine, just wait for me.

Two weeks later, it was my turn to leave Lamu. The days had gone quickly and I tried to savor every experience, every sight, and every smell, knowing I might never be back again. I went out one last time to the old *shamba* and looked around. The ceiling in my bedroom was teetering on the mangrove poles, ready to finally collapse. The ant freeway was gone, the bats were gone, and the cockroaches had moved on as well. There were a couple of grass mats still there, and Pete's old kerosene burner. I thought about the first time I walked onto that porch, and I lit up a joint in Pete's honor. What was he doing now? Was he still in India? Was he in some ashram with Jeff and Barbara? I looked at Jesse Allen's drawing on the wall, which by now had almost completely faded away, then finally pulled myself away and set off for town. It was particularly hot that day, and I was particularly stoned, thinking about mangoes and cashews, when I reached for the top rung of a bamboo fence that circled the property. I'd climbed that fence so many times, I didn't even need to look where I was going and, in fact, I wasn't looking when something caught the corner of my eye. There, three feet away, curled around the bamboo pole I was about to grab, was a long black snake with a narrow stripe down its back.

It was a black mamba. I had just come within one second of grabbing a black mamba. Three minutes to live . . . two minutes to live . . .

I instinctively stepped back and just stood there a moment, watching as the snake slept under the beating sun. Then, for reasons I will never understand, I decided to get a closer look. I stepped to within a few feet of the mamba, examining its beautiful black scales, when it suddenly awoke, looked at me, and flew off that pole so fast it left a little jet stream in the air. It was incredible. The mamba didn't lunge for the soft skin above my stomach. It didn't shoot hot liquid into my veins. It didn't bury me from the inside out. How peculiar, I thought, that only days before my departure I would wind up confronting my greatest fear of Africa. I climbed over the fence and continued on down the path, feeling strangely unafraid.

Sultan surprised me the next day by insisting he accompany me to Mombasa. I was grateful beyond words and then that was it, I said good-bye to the house, the beach, and the town. I said good-bye to Big Ali, Little Ali, and a couple of medium-sized Alis. I smoked a joint on the steps of the CID office and said good-bye to Joseph Mzingi and the chief of police. I watched the outline of sixty-six mosques and twenty-two whorehouses – or was it the other way around? – as the ferry pulled away from the harbor and I said good-bye to Lamu.

When we pulled up at the port, the *Star of India* looked bigger than I expected. There was a tremendous bustle as crewmen loaded luggage and crates onto the decks. Dozens of passengers were already climbing up and down the catwalks, getting themselves situated in first-class cabins, second-class decks, or, as in my case, third-class steerage. Steerage was like a big dormitory on the sea, with a double layer of bunk beds from port to starboard. About two hundred people were crammed into that space, most of them Indians, along with a few Africans and a handful of Westerners. Although we were still tied to the dock, a couple of Indians already were vomiting – Indians the world over, I would learn, have amazingly weak stomachs – so I quickly found my assigned bunk, stashed my rucksack underneath, and headed back up to the deck with Sultan.

Sultan slipped into a men's room along the way, and I waited for him outside. A few minutes later, he poked his head out, looking embarrassed, and asked where the water was. I went into the large bathroom and saw at least ten faucets along the wall. I couldn't understand how he could have missed them. I pointed to one, and Sultan just looked at me blankly. It was then that I realized he had never used a faucet in his life. I was absolutely astonished. This wise man, this worldly man, was like an innocent child in the not-so-modern world of Mombasa. I understood more clearly than ever just how primitive life in Lamu had been.

A deep, bellowing horn sounded, announcing our imminent departure. Sultan asked me for the twentieth time how long the journey would be. 'Nine days to Karachi,' I said, 'then two days to Bombay.' He whistled, then nodded. We stood there a moment, then clasped hands and hugged. 'Thank you, Sultan,' I said. 'Thank you for everything.'

'*Kama Mungu akupenda, tutaonana alafu,*' he said. And then he was gone.

After another blast from the horn, the catwalk was pulled up, the giant steam engines engaged, and the lines from the tugboats tightened. As we slowly pulled away from the pier, we passed other ships on the docks and I read their names and countries of registry. There were freighters from Panama, Liberia, and Taiwan. There were old dhows from Abu Dhabi and oil tankers from Great Britain. One freighter especially caught my eye. It was an old rust bucket, a miserable piece of junk with an Indian registry. As we passed by, I caught a glimpse of its name. It was the *Vishva Vinay*! I could still be waiting in Mauritius for this wayward scrap of crap! Watching as it listed along the pier, I thanked my lucky stars that it had never shown up.

I stood on the deck of the *Star of India*, watching as Mombasa receded in the distance. I thought back to a year earlier, when I first arrived in Nairobi and tried to remember who I was at that time. I remembered a person consumed with anger and fear, a person whose emotions were raw and fueled by obsession. I didn't feel quite so afraid anymore, and probably wasn't half as angry. I still thought about Annika, but now there were other things to ponder as well. I had come to Africa because I was too weak to make any other decision. Now, I was leaving because I was strong enough to go on. As the mango trees and palms and baobabs blended into the horizon, I felt tears in my eyes for the first time since I was a child. I thanked Africa for embracing and nurturing me. I had thrown myself upon its mercy, and Africa had shown me its heart.

# 23

# The Sea

Hemingway and Meville notwithstanding, the sea is not a place for deep contemplation. The whole thing is altogether too watery, the air especially, and water is the great obfuscator, it blurs the lens, it submerges the brain, it liquefies thought. The sea is mellow and placid and engulfing, it puts its arms around you, and you're back in the womb, everything is nice and warm and secure, no thoughts about war or starvation, no, it's just pure love, the love of doing nothing, just being there, no cares in the world, ah, why can't it go on forever, this womb, this is exactly perfect, I'm at one with the universe, I'm a happy little electron in this postnuclear family, I'm just spinning around and around, doing my cosmic job, whatever that is, but I don't question it, I don't even care what it is, I just spin, that's what I do, and if anybody asks, that's what I'll tell them, I'm a spinner. This is the sea, after all, it's all part of the flow, and the sea, as we know, is not a place for deep contemplation.

There was a sense of excitement in the air. It was the ninth day out of Mombasa, and there, off in the distance, was our first glimpse of land since leaving Africa. Yes, there, just where the mouth of the Indus flowed into the Arabian Sea, was Pakistan. I was so transfixed that I didn't hear the lunch bell ringing from the dining hall below, but then Krishnan poked his head up from the stairwell and said 'Come, come, mustn't miss your *thali*.' Krishnan was fourteen and, like me, was making his first visit to Asia. His family decided it was time for the children to see their ancestral homeland, so they packed up the whole gang, from Krishnan and his four brothers and sisters to various grandmothers, aunts, and cousins. I'd somehow been adopted into the clan at mealtimes and shared their corner of a table. I think they'd seen me struggling with my food and decided I might make for an interesting diversion on the journey. I'm pretty sure, in fact, that Grandma had a side bet with Auntie that I'd never master the art of eating with my hands before we got to Bombay, and so, Auntie took me under her wing: 'Well, of course, you must never use the left hand,' she said to me in hushed tones as I broke off a piece of nan with both hands.

'Oh, right, of course,' I said. 'Because . . .'

'Because the right hand is the clean hand.' Auntie, like most Indians, was good at euphemisms. She managed to avoid saying that since the right hand is the clean hand, then the left hand must be, well, the hand you clean your ass with. Enough said. I noticed how she hid her left hand under the table and I decided not only to hide my hand, but to sit on it, just to make sure I didn't forget. So, with my left hand properly immobilized, if not numb, I learned how to break off pieces of chapati without their landing on the floor, how to mush rice together into manageable balls, how to mix in curried vegetables, and how to flick the whole thing into my mouth with my thumb so that it didn't all dribble down my chin.

I looked to Auntie for approval, hoping I wasn't disgusting her with my manners, but no matter what I did, she always shook her head. I was getting pretty discouraged until I discovered that those shakes didn't always mean no. In fact, I began to realize that while sometimes no meant no, other times no meant yes, and occasionally no meant maybe. It all has to do with a bobbing action of the head and neck, where a particular twist gives the intended meaning. For me, these subtle distinctions between yes, no, and maybe went straight to the heart of the Indian view of life. Life was ambiguous, if not downright tenuous, and to make clear distinctions was futile. Indians don't live in a black-and-white world of absolutes, they live in that huge gray middle zone where nothing is quite real or unreal, true or untrue.

*Thali*, the national meal of India, is served in large, circular aluminum plates that are separated into compartments for rice, vegetables, *raita*, and nan. The only real difference between one *thali* and another is that instead of, say, potato-and-cauliflower curry, you might have potato-and-pea curry. Other than that, every *thali* is exactly the same. We'd had *thali* for lunch and *thali* for dinner every day since we'd left and now, as I sat down to my seventeenth straight *thali*, Auntie and Grandma and Krishnan chatted, their heads bobbing and twisting as the ship steamed toward port. 'Why must we stop in Pakistan?' asked Grandma. 'There is nothing in Pakistan.'

'Sure there is, Gran,' said Krishnan.

'Oh?' she said, raising one eyebrow. 'And what might that be?'

'They've got Pakistanis in Pakistan.'

'Yes, and that is exactly why you are not to leave the boat.'

'*Graaaaan*,' he moaned.

'Enough! They will slit your throat! Is that what you want?'

'Please,' said Auntie, 'don't put such thoughts into the boy's mind.'

'Why not? Is it not true?'

Krishnan looked at me for support. 'Yes, well, I'd like to believe that people are just people,' I said, 'that we're all pretty much the same underneath . . .'

'And that is exactly why *you* are not to leave the boat, either,' Gran replied.


As we neared the port, we passed dozens of ships that were anchored far out to sea. The docks had been hit by a strike, but, luckily for us, passenger ships were still allowed at the piers. So we steamed right past all the tankers and freighters, waving to the frustrated crewmen who were stranded on the water. Approaching the dock, I could see hundreds of porters, all pushing and shoving as they jockeyed for position to service the one ship that was allowed to land. The porters looked like they'd been stamped out of some kind of medieval cookie cutter. Each of them had black stringy hair, long drooping moustaches, billowing pajama pants, and big iron hooks that were slung over their shoulders for lifting crates and bags. I stared into this sea of faces as the *Star of India* tied up at the dock, and I was overcome by an uncontrollable impulse. 'Hashish!' I called from the deck. 'Who's got hashish?' The porters looked around with furtive glances, as if a squad of secret police were about to descend upon them. 'C'mon, guys,' I yelled to them, 'let's get loaded! Screw the formalities. Is this Pakistan or not, for God's sake?'

I waited impatiently for the catwalk to be lowered, but absolutely nothing happened. It was my first dose of the painful lack of urgency that I was to learn defined Asia. We waited and waited, hundreds of passengers desperate to get onto solid ground after nine days at sea, but nothing stirred. Finally, a pack of self-important-looking immigration officials, festooned in braids, turbans, and sashes, appeared at the side of the ship, and the catwalk slowly creaked down to meet them. After an endless conversation with the first mate, the dignitaries meandered onto the deck, fussed around behind a long table, then painstakingly checked each and every passport. Okay, this is getting ridiculous. I'm in Asia, I've dreamt about this moment forever, and now, here I am, I'm ready to explode, I've been smoking nothing but *bangi* for nine days, hell, I've been smoking nothing but *bangi* for eleven months, and I desperately need a new high, and there it is, I can almost touch it, there in the distance I can see mosques and minarets and whole hillsides, and all of them surely are carved out of hash, just chip some off, that's all I ask, just chip off a block or two and we'll load up a pipe and get blasted like never before, because I'm in Asia, I'm actually here, and it's only right that I enter under a cloud, I've got thousands of years of catching up to do and there's no time to waste, I'm here with the pros, whole nations of higher beings whom I wish to embrace in the hope that by some kind of hashified osmosis I might experience just a fraction of their enlightenment, and then, just like that, the porters are allowed up onto the catwalk and here they come, there's a mad rush of them charging onto the ship, and I'm welcoming them like long-lost brothers while the other passengers are wondering who the hell *are* all these guys with the greasy hair and drooping moustaches and jagged hooks slung over their shoulders and then, yes, it happens, a big block of hashish magically appears out of nowhere and then a match and a pipe and a wonderful sweet pungent smell begins to waft over steerage and suddenly I'm smoking with twenty-five Pakistanis, just like I'd always imagined, okay, maybe I didn't imagine quite such a *large* group, but what the hell, this is Asia, they've got lots of people, and more pipes are firing up, and now Auntie and Grandma are desperately holding onto their suitcases and more passengers are coming down to find porters sprawled out on their bunks, and God, I'm happy, this has got to be the best hash in the world, and then somebody passes me my guitar and suddenly twenty-five porters with greasy hair and drooping moustaches and jagged hooks slung over their shoulders are singing along and ogling the women and leaning back like they're here for the long haul, and okay, sure, I'll play a little harmonica, and I'm adjusting the neck brace and wondering if there might be a way to slip the pipe right alongside the harp so that I can be totally musical, totally stoned, and totally hands-free at the same time, and then I play a quick tune, and okay, well, guys, maybe it's time to leave, I'm sure your families will be worried about you and – no? – you don't *have* families, well, still, it's getting dark and hey, you with the suitcases, are you sure somebody asked you to take those, okay, well, just one more pipe, but then it's *definitely* time to call it a day, and suddenly there are quick footsteps and the captain and first mate are rushing in and policemen are charging down from the upper deck and the porters are leaping through the portals, and I'm playing some of those jazzy major-ninth chords, trying to mellow everybody out, but the cops are swinging bamboo-stave *lathis* and the porters are swinging back with their hooks and it's all becoming absolute pandemonium as I take another hit from a pipe and think about all of my dreams of Asia and realize, as I duck under my bunk, that this place is even cooler than I had ever imagined.

Outside the port, I jumped onto a mule cart and clippety-clopped into downtown Karachi, where I was immediately surrounded by a dozen beggar children. 'No mama, no papa,' said a little girl with the biggest, brownest, saddest eyes I'd ever seen. She held out her hand and I immediately dug for some change. Then the chant went up from all around. 'No mama, no papa . . . no mama, no papa,' and whether it was true or not, whether these kids were truly orphans or were working for some kind of street syndicate, really didn't matter. They looked hungry and sick and emaciated and the least I could do was give them a few paisa each. The more coin I handed out, the larger the group became. Suddenly, it seemed as if all of Karachi had ground to a halt and the whole city was lining up for spare change. The president of the university was there. The president of the bank was there. The president of the *country* was there. I escaped into a restaurant, but a sea of faces pressed up against the window while I studied the menu. I wasn't really hungry anymore, not with a dozen pairs of eyes staring at me. I'd dreamt of anything other than the same meal I'd had for nine straight days, but now, faced with a hundred choices, my imagination completely eluded me. 'Twelve *thalis*,' I said to the waiter as I glanced outside. 'To go.'

No, the sea is not a place for deep contemplation, it's a place of simple fantasy, of primordial connection, of assessing one's place in the natural order of things. But now, as I stood on the deck while Karachi faded in the distance, a host of old fears began to surface. Pakistan was one thing, but soon we'd be arriving in India, the place I'd felt equally drawn to and terrified of for as long as I could remember. India with its chaos and perpetual unrest. India with its promise of spiritual awakening and threat of mental meltdown. India with its endless juxtaposition of contrary images – of love and war, joy and pain, beauty and desolation.

As we sailed southeast for Bombay, the mix of elation and trepidation was almost too much to bear. Couldn't I just stay on the ship a little longer? This, after all, was where I really felt comfortable, right here on this deck, watching the dolphins surfing the waves left in the wake of the ship, gazing out at the endless horizon. The ocean was so calm that night, I could barely feel a slight sway as we steamed ahead. I lay on my bunk, wishing the voyage could just go on a bit longer, just another week or two, so that I could pre- pare myself. Eleven days on the sea weren't enough and I hadn't really thought at all about what I was heading into, what I would do when I got there, where I would stay, no, I'm not ready yet, I'll stay on the boat, hell, I'll stow away back to Africa, why did I ever leave, it was ridiculous to leave, no, I'm definitely going back, it'll just be twenty-two more *thalis* and I'll be there, maybe I could live with Sultan, they've got plenty of room, I was nuts to leave, I'm not even close to being ready for India, not even close, as I drifted off to sleep, not even close, and then, when I awoke the next morning – we were there.

# 24

## Gateway to India

Freighters and yachts, tankers and dhows, tugboats and junks – there were thousands of them, all jammed together as we sailed into port. Ten million people awakened to the blasts from the ship's horn and, from the look of things, a good many of them were on their way down to the piers to greet us. Despite the sea of faces I was reminded, inexplicably, of Rhodes and its tiny port. As we neared the docks, I leaned out over the railing and a wild thought suddenly hit me. What if she was here? What if this time Annika was actually here awaiting my arrival? At the moment it seemed entirely plausible, for isn't India, after all, the land of miracles?

I headed down the catwalk and found myself replaying the whole scene again: taxi to American Express, where there was nothing, then to the post office, where I anxiously stood in line. The post office was enormous, with dozens of windows and endless lines snaking every which way. Along the walls, up the staircases, and down the hallways were masses of people who appeared not to be waiting in line at all, but rather were camped out with all their possessions, and then, as I looked more closely, I realized they were actually *living* there, right there in the post office, hundreds and hundreds of people, whole families, old ladies wrapped in saris and children running naked and babies sucking their mothers' breasts. It was as if the building itself were alive. 'Yes, there is something,' said a clerk from behind a partition

– *I knew it!* – as he slid my passport under the bars with a letter folded inside. I felt my heart pounding in my ears when I saw my name written out in a beautiful, feminine script. The swirls of the lines angled just slightly, like two people leaning against a wall, and the letters were close together, as if embracing. My eyes finally moved to the upper corner of the envelope and, for a moment, I felt confused. I thought I saw a French stamp and wondered what Annika would be doing in France, of all places, and then, as I looked at the cancellation mark, my confusion deepened because it said Marolles, in the postal zone of Vitry-le-Francois, and I couldn't, for the life of me, figure out what she'd be doing in some tiny village in the middle of nowhere.

The letter read:

> Dearest, today you are leaving for India. I hope it will be a discovery, a fulfilment, a way to genuine happiness.
>
> It's hard to live without you here, very hard, the thought of you is in me all the time, happiness when remembering, sadness in the present, obscure fears which drive me crazy sometimes. Do write and tell me how you are, how you feel, how it is where you are, how are the people & how is the sky.
>
> I can't stick to this reality. I want to get rid of my contract as soon as possible but after writing all the people & authorities I could think of, I realized what I knew before. I am reduced to waiting for an appointment as an 'auxiliary teacher,' the same job as a qualified teacher, but underpaid & a prey for the administration. Will begin next week & will fight fiercely in the union!
>
> Life here is dull & gray, rain & cold, agitation & indifference. Am feeling strange & loose in the head & miss you terribly. Never felt as strongly as when we parted that I wanted to know you better, & all the more now. Fondest kisses & love.

I found myself in the Colaba district of central Bombay and, as I reread the letter, I felt not quite so all alone anymore. I pictured Martine dancing at Petley's, how she moved so gracefully to the music, how we met that night. I pictured her lying next to me as we made love in the sand. I pictured her as she got on the ferry to the mainland, and I wondered again why I hadn't tried harder to convince her not to leave. How could I think for even one minute about Annika? Annika didn't care if I was in Africa or India or back in New York at the East Side Bookstore. No, it's Martine who cares, Martine is the one—

I heard the pounding of a drum and the beating of tambourines and I put down the letter to see a troupe of wildly dressed women dancing along the side of the street. They wore red saris and orange veils and yellow scarves and twirled to the rhythms of a ragtag band that marched behind them playing their instruments. A couple of street children ran out and danced along for a while, then fled back to a woman who was cooking up a pot of vegetables right on the street. Next to her, a man sat at a flimsy table with an ancient typewriter and a weather-beaten sign that read: WRITE LETTERS. BEST PRICE. A young boy raced past him with three cups of tea balanced in his tiny hands and delivered them to a tailor's shop, where a lady examined some fabric, stepped into the street, and was almost run over by a bicycle rickshaw that came barreling down the road. A torrent of angry words spewed forth as a crowd gathered around, and then, just as quickly, it was all over and the cyclist pedaled away. A barber returned to cutting a man's hair beneath a tree while his partner sharpened a straight-edge razor on a leather strop. Under the next branch, a man in a dirty lab coat maneuvered a pair of rusty pliers into the mouth of a dental patient, who held his jaw in pain. A few feet away, a six-foot-high machine gurgled and shook as a vendor inserted stalks of sugarcane, turned a giant lever, and squeezed out every last drop of juice until there was nothing left but dry pulp. A little girl handed him a coin, ran off with the glass, and almost tripped over a Gujarati tribeswoman who was selling tattered pillows with tiny mirrors sewn into the fabric. The woman's admonitions were drowned out by a blind man who played a flute and a legless boy who click-clacked around on a piece of wood with rollers. He nearly toppled over the tin cup of a sadhu, who had three stripes painted across his forehead, sat perfectly motionless, and held a six-foot trident in the air without ever flinching. A woman dropped a coin into the cup, then swept a broom along the sidewalk so as not to step on an innocent bug. She passed a holy man wearing saffron robes who dabbed red *holi* powder onto the head of a cow as it sauntered across an intersection, sat down, and brought all traffic to a halt. A thick cloud of incense wafted over the cow from a stall where five hundred bottles of spice were stacked to the ceiling, while a man with red lips and red teeth chopped up betel nut, cardamom, and cloves into little leaves and spat out a long stream of red saliva into a puddle on the street. A horse-and-cart trotted by and splashed the puddle onto a billboard, where the red spittle dripped from the lips of a pudgy Indian film star who was bending over to kiss his bride. A little ragamuffin pointed at the poster and mockingly reenacted the love scene for a tiny girl who squealed with delight, while pop music blared from the megaphone of a passing truck.

There were more people and more smells and more music, and wherever I looked I saw yogis and snake charmers, fire walkers and dancing girls, street performers and laughing children. I felt like I'd gotten off a boat and stepped right into the middle of a carnival. I was under the big top, all right, a nonstop, twenty-four-hour circus called India, and when I wrote Martine later that night, I told her that the sky was purple with great swatches of turquoise and amber, that the people were warm and welcoming, and that I wished she were here.

Bombay is the most international city in Asia, home not only to hundreds of sects of Indians, but also to Iranis, Iraqis, Yemenis, and Afghanis. Then, scratch beneath the surface, and the truly unusual can be found, because Bombay is where borders blur, where passports disappear, where Interpol washes its hands. Bombay is the home of the aberrant, the fugitive, the outsider. Bombay is the Polish concert pianist who fled the Nazis thirty years ago and has lived underground ever since with neither passport nor nationality. Bombay is the hawk-nosed Austrian and his twelve-year-old niece whom he ties to his bed every night. Bombay is the Peruvian revolutionary wanted for the assassination of eighteen hostages. Bombay is the Saudi emir getting cancer treatment at Breech Candy hospital and his harem of twenty wives camped out at the Hilton Hotel. Bombay is the Russian technocrat who slipped out from the embassy one night and disappeared into an opium den on Sukalachi Street. Bombay is the Jewish exile from Shanghai who prays at the Indian synagogue every Friday night for her long-lost family. Bombay is the Tibetan refugee monk counting beads on his *mala* while trying to cross Carnac Road. Bombay is the Belgian antiquities dealer hiding a thousand-year-old bronze in his shaving kit, the Dutch banker living high off purloined funds in Malabar Point, the German religious fanatic doing an ecstatic dance to Lord Chaitanya in the hallway of his hotel.

I paged through the *Times of India* and noticed a strange headline – TWO LAKH LEPERS CROSSING INTO MAHARASHTRA – which I didn't understand at all. What is this lakh thing? I checked a phrase book and discovered that lakh actually is a number, 100,000 to be precise, and that 100 lakh equal a crore. A crore is 10 million, a mindboggling sum, but India, with its unimaginably large numbers of people, needed extra words to count them all. So now it all made perfect sense. The headline simply meant that 200,000 lepers were arriving in Maharashtra State, the capital of which is Bombay. *Uh-huh* . . .

'*Aaaaaaaaaaaaaah!*'

The story on page two was about 280 people who died from using adulterated cooking oil after a merchant mixed in motor oil to save a few rupees. At the bottom of page three was an article about 5,000 deaths in Bihar State due to heat prostration. The good news on page four was that the cholera epidemic in Uttar Pradesh was abating. The bad news on page five was that the typhoid epidemic in Madhya

Pradesh was completely out of control. Indira Gandhi said on page six that India's holy men were fleecing the nation, and she decreed that a slogan be put up on billboards throughout the land: HARD WORK IS THE ONLY MIRACLE. A sidebar noticed that 26 of those holy men were found lying along the train tracks in the northern states with their skulls smashed in. The economic forecast on page seven was for continued no-growth, while the population statistics on page eight indicated nothing *but* growth. Food supplies were down, foreign debt was up, and prices were unstable.

As I continued reading, I came up with ten lakh reasons for getting the hell out of there. But then I looked out at the Colaba from the tiny balcony of my room at the Hotel Rex, and the feeling of wonder I'd experienced upon arriving overwhelmed me once again. There were a hundred colors and a thousand sounds, there were horses and buses, rickshaws and trucks, kites and airplanes, and they all mixed together, pushing and pulling and straining at the seams as the city teetered on the cusp between the ancient past and the not-so-modern future.

There were beggars everywhere. They stood with their palms out, beseeching passersby for a few paisa. I'd heard stories of parents intentionally deforming their children to make them into better beggars, but seeing them firsthand, these beautiful little kids with horribly mutilated arms and legs, it seemed all the more incomprehensible. I was standing there, feeling helpless, my stomach clenching up, when an Italian woman appeared on the street. She was dressed in the religious robes of an ashram and looked like she'd been there a while. She smiled at me, then held out her hands as if to encompass the whole scene. 'Isn't life perfect?' she said.

I stared at her, wondering if I'd heard right. 'Yeah, *real* perfect,' I finally responded, but her smile never wavered, not even for a second. She cupped her hands to her head in a blessing and continued on her way while I stood there, half-angry and half-intrigued, wondering how anyone could have gotten to such an amazing level of self-delusion. Yet, as

I looked into the eyes of the children, I saw a sparkle and a sense of playfulness and wondered what the hell *I* was so angry about. There was something going on here that I didn't completely understand.

I walked through Bindi Bazaar, changed money on the black market, and bought a bottle of shampoo. I noticed how thin the liquid was, thought about the story of the adulterated cooking oil, and realized that someone had undone the cap, removed half the shampoo, and replaced it with who-knows-what. I soon learned that anything with a twist-off cap was sure to have been tampered with, whether it was a tube of toothpaste, a jar of jam, or a bottle of detergent. Even canned goods had been drilled, drained, refilled, and sealed up with metal plugs. Nothing in India is exactly what it seems to be.

Merchants waved to me, but even the wave took some getting used to. Just like the head-and-neck gestures, hand-waving in India leaves much to interpretation. The fingers beckon, but the palm is held down rather than up, so I was never sure if I was being encouraged in or shooed away. All these gestures seemed odd to me. I'd always thought that humanity had its own particular body language, that wherever you went a wave was a wave, a nod a nod, and a shrug a shrug. Now, I wasn't so sure. Was it possible that Indians were wired differently?

I slipped into Dipti's Fruit Bar for a mango *lassi*. 'You new here, then?' asked an Englishman, who was wearing purple pajama pants, an embroidered vest, and a wool skullcap.

'Is it that obvious?'

'Just a wild guess. What do you think so far?'

'I don't know. It's a lot to take in.'

'Well, don't forget, first impressions and all . . .'

'I'm trying not to jump to any conclusions.'

'Yeah, the first days in India, it's hard to figure out what to make of it. It took me six months before I thought I had it down. Then, a year later, I realized I knew less than before. I've been here for five years and I'm just now getting back to where I was the first five days.'

I looked at him incredulously. 'You've been here five *years*?'

'Give or take. If you're interested in trying to figure out this place, I'd say get out right now, before you get all muddled up.'

'Thanks, that's probably very good advice.'

'But you won't take it.'

'Probably not.'

'I didn't think so. You've got that look. You're going to have to go through the whole cycle. Just like me.'

I took a sip of *lassi* and laughed. 'Well, I'm pretty sure I won't be out here for five years.'

The Englishman just smiled. 'You never know what's going to happen. Nothing in India is what it seems to be.'

# 25

# Track 32

I decided to head for the Himalayas before winter set in. I was presented a bewildering array of possibilities for getting to New Delhi at the ticket counter of Victoria train station. There was the first-class overnight sleeper, which made the trip in about ten hours, the express, which took twice as long, and the various locals, which took as long as they took. This being my first train ride in India, I decided to splurge for first-class. 'Very good, sir,' said a clerk in flawless English. 'Next available is October 18.'

I stared at him a moment. 'But that's five weeks from now.'

'Were you wishing to depart at a sooner time?'

'I'd like to depart in the next twenty minutes.'

'Very good, sir. How about second-class on the express?'

'Fine.'

'Next available is October 14.'

'No, you don't understand. I want to go *today*.'

'Today? Ah, then how about third-class sleeper?'

'*Uh* . . . okay.'

'Very good, sir. Next available is October 3.'

'Listen, I don't think I'm explaining myself clearly. I need to leave for New Delhi immediately.'

'Ah,' he said, twisting his head in a manner that either meant yes, no, or maybe, 'then you must be taking third-class, sans sleeper.'

'All right, whatever you've got.'

'Very good, sir. Next available is September 30.'

'Excuse me . . .' I said, taking a long look at him, 'do you speak English?'

'You are wishing passage for New Delhi, isn't it?'

'Yes,' I said, very slowly. 'I wish . . . to go . . . to Delhi . . . to . . . day.'

'Ah. Then you must be going to second floor. Unreserved ticket.'

'Why didn't you tell me that in the first place?'

'Third room.'

'Wait, what's that? Second floor, third room?'

'Section six.'

'Section . . . six?'

'First counter.'

'You're kidding, right? Let me guess. Aisle three?'

'Aisle five.' He gave me another twist of the head that could have meant pretty much anything and I headed for the second floor. Along the way, I passed rooms that were stacked floor to ceiling with an unbelievable number of documents. India had managed to incorporate 350 years of British bureaucracy into its own particular love of red tape, and the result was a paper trail the likes of which I'd never imagined possible. Forget duplicates and triplicates, India deals in ten-plicates.

On the second floor, third room, sixth section, first counter, fifth aisle, I encountered a line that curled, snaked, wobbled, and gyrated around the room. People were coming and going, cutting in and checking out, as I slowly inched my way toward the window. Three hours and twenty minutes later, I was there. 'I'd like a third-class unreserved ticket.'

'Madras or Calcutta?'

'New Delhi.'

'Next window.'

'*What?*'

'This window Madras and Calcutta. Next window New Delhi and Agra. Third window Amritsar—'

'No, wait,' I pleaded with him. 'The guy downstairs screwed me up. I've been standing here for hours. Can't you just sell me a ticket?'

'Madras or Calcutta?' For a moment, I considered going to Madras or Calcutta, but decided I wasn't going to let one mistake compound into some total disaster, like winding up in the Black Hole of Calcutta. Instead, I went to the end of the next line. Two hours and fifty-five minutes later, I had my ticket.

Standing along Track 32, I heard a whistle blow and the click-clacking of metal against metal. Then, appearing through great bursts of white steam, a train roared straight out of the annals of railroad history. The engine was a big, black monster of moving parts – the turbines were pumping, the furnace was belching, the wheels were screeching, the headlight was shaking, and the hulking steel body was pulsating like an overworked heart. As the engine crawled into the terminal, the steam cleared and I saw dozens of passenger cars, each with enough people to fill a small town. There were people in the seats and in the aisles, in the luggage compartments and in the bathrooms, hanging out the windows and jammed between the doors. Outside, there were whole contingents on the roof, as well as a few brave souls who rode the couplings between the cars or squeezed into little crawl spaces beneath the carriage.

When the train came to a halt, there was an absolutely mad rush of humanity. It was unclear to me who was getting on and who was getting off, but, before I knew what happened, the car in front of me had been emptied, filled, and sealed tight. I hurried down to the next car, the next, and the next one still, but each of them, all the way down the track, was bursting at the seams. By the time I reached the end of the train, the engine was blowing its whistle, and, in a great cloud of steam, it began to pull away. Thousands of people were crammed into every possible square inch, and a few inches that weren't possible. Not only had I missed my train, I hadn't even come close to getting on. I was left standing there, holding a puff of steam in my hands.

I checked back into the Hotel Rex.

The next day I made a few discreet inquiries and

discovered that by going to an office on the third floor of Victoria Station, one could, for a 'fee,' procure specially reserved tickets for the train. As much as I was philosophically opposed to baksheesh, I was able to overcome my qualms and was back on track by afternoon. Track 32, that is, and this time with a guaranteed ticket. I had the window seat in a third-class berth for six people. I was irritated when the seventh and eighth passengers squeezed in, but decided not to say anything. Two more people joined us, then the whistle blew and six more shoved through the doors. I noticed that the guy in the facing seat was staring at me. I smiled. He continued staring.

The train finally pulled out of the station, built up to about ten miles an hour, then slowed to stop at the first station. There was a burst of activity along the tracks as food vendors descended upon the train. '*Garam chai!*' yelled a man selling hot tea. '*Garam chai!*' Others had Indian sweets, oranges, and deep-fried vegetable *pakoras*. I couldn't imagine how anyone could be hungry so soon. We'd barely gone three miles. The whistle blew, the steam puffed, the wheels engaged, and we were off again. The train wobbled a little as we rounded a curve, straightened out, and gradually built up speed. Two men vomited in the aisle. Four minutes later we slowed to a stop. '*Garam chai!*' intoned a man carrying a metal thermos. '*Pakora!*' bellowed a woman holding a tray of greasy homemade fritters. The whistle blew, more steam was released, a vibration shook the train, and we pulled out once again. I noticed that the guy across from me was still staring. I smiled at him as we coasted toward the next village, where a few people got off, a few people got on, and another man vomited. About two hours later, and still barely out of Bombay, I realized that I was on a local mail train and that we'd be stopping at pretty much every village all the way to Delhi. I started wondering if I couldn't get there faster by walking and, at one point, I was sure that I kept seeing the same guy, village after village, walking along the tracks. Walking along the tracks, or on the roads, or in the fields, seemed to be a major preoccupation in India.

Wherever I looked, there was a swarm of humanity crossing from one place to another, from the cities to the villages to the deserts to the plains.

The hours slowly passed as we crept our way up through Maharashtra and into the state of Gujarat. By the time we hit the Rajasthan Desert that night, the temperature had risen to well over a hundred. All the doors of the train were thrown open and those passengers lucky enough to be near an exit leaned out and tried to catch whatever breeze they could. I dozed off a few times but was awakened by the constant jerking of the train, the intense heat, and the guy sitting across from me. His gaze was searing right into my flesh. 'Hey, knucklehead, what're you staring at?' I finally demanded. He blinked twice, glanced at the ceiling, then resumed staring at me.

By the first light of morning, I was covered in a layer of desert sand. The heat was increasing and everyone around me was coughing, sweating, and trying to clear the dust from their noses and throats. When we pulled into what was probably the five-hundredth village, I called to one of the tea vendors. I was suspicious of whether the water had really been boiled properly but I figured if I didn't drink something soon, I'd pass out. '*Garam chai?*' he asked, as he hurried over.

'*Garam chai,*' I nodded.

'*Garam chai?*' he repeated, as if to make sure.

'Yes, yes, *garam chai.*'

He stood there for a moment, staring at his thermos, staring at the ground, and staring at the tracks. Finally, he looked up. '*Garam chai?*'

'Listen, you guys have been screaming in my ears for twenty hours. Now, do you actually sell *chai* or not? Because if you do, you'd better give it to me right now, before the damn train pulls out again, understand? I want *chai*, it better be *garam*, and I want it now!'

The vendor looked frightened by my reaction and quickly poured some tea. '*Garam chai,*' he said, handing it to me.

'Thank you,' I said, drinking it down. I then turned to the

guy across from me. 'And you, stop staring at me before I pick you up and throw you right through that window.'

He stared at me as I finished my tea, he stared at me as I paid the vendor, and he stared at me as I returned the glass. He stared at me as the whistle blew and then he stared at me as the train pulled out of the station. He stared at me through all the little villages and all the big towns. He stared at me through Vapi, Valsad, Surai, Ankleshwar, Bharuch, Vadodara, Godhra, Himatnagar, Udaipur, Mavli, Marwar, Ajmer, Phulera, Jaipur and Alwar.

Then, just before New Delhi, he gathered his bags as the train pulled into yet another village. He walked toward the door, then turned back and looked at me one last time. 'President Richard M. Nixon,' he said, for no particular reason other than that it was probably the only English he knew. He climbed down the steps, walked along the train, and disappeared into the station.

A short while later – forty-six hours after leaving Bombay – we arrived in New Delhi. I felt like I'd accomplished something. I'd made it across the Rajasthan Desert more or less in one piece. I'd gotten a little taste of the real India. I'd helped deliver the mail. I had the feeling, standing in the train station, that maybe I could deal with this place after all, that Africa had prepared me for anything India might throw my way. Later, as I stood under a cold shower trying to wash the layers of dirt and grime off my body, I thought about the guy on the train and his piercing stare. What the hell was he looking at? What was in his mind? Was that some kind of secret code? *I'll* give you President Richard M. Nixon . . .

# 26

## The Twist

Delhi is two cities, Old and New, and nothing better defines India than what they each represent. Old Delhi is swarms of people, abject poverty, and centuries of unbreakable tradition. New Delhi is orderly crowds, manicured gardens, and the face of modern India. Old Delhi is religious fanatics, the caste system, and reactionary politics. New Delhi is Indira Gandhi, scientific socialism, and central planning. Old Delhi is open sewers, collapsed houses, and endless rubble. New Delhi is government office buildings, foreign embassies, and new construction.

Needless to say, I got out of New Delhi as fast as possible. I'd come to India, after all, to experience an ancient culture and its eternal truths, not to look at a bunch of soulless socialist architecture. Still, something about the old city made me uneasy, a sense of something bubbling beneath the surface, ready to explode. After hours of walking around, I took a bicycle rickshaw back to my hotel. I didn't much like rickshaws because they made me feel like some kind of white pasha, even if they were the cheapest mode of travel. As my driver pedaled through a particularly poor area, someone stepped out onto the road and nearly got clipped by a wheel. Had there been an Indian in the seat, that probably would have been the end of it, but when he saw a Westerner, something clicked. He started screaming, a bunch of people darted into the street, and we were suddenly surrounded. Feeling vulnerable in the open rickshaw, I jumped off, which only caused more pushing and shoving as everyone strained harder to see what was going on. And what *was* going on? Absolutely nothing was going on. But that didn't matter. I felt like I was in a theater where someone yelled fire, and *I* was the fire. I felt a jolt of adrenaline, pulled out my harmonica, and somehow transformed the tremor rushing through my body into the loudest, harshest, most insane note I ever played. It hung in the air for a fractured second, then clanged to the ground like a loose hubcap. Once I had everyone's attention – and the silence was so dead, it could've been embalmed – I figured an old jazz standard might mellow things out. Sure enough, as I played the first few bars of 'Summertime,' the crowd backed up to give me room and the mood completely changed. Once I got them clapping along, I climbed back onto the rickshaw, motioned for the driver to pedal, and rode off playing the chorus – always the pro, leaving them wanting more.

The train north from Delhi crossed the sweltering Gangetic Plain to Chandigarh, a city designed by the French architect Le Corbusier. With its planned streets and blocks of buildings and open parks, it stands in stark contrast to the haphazard sprawl throughout the rest of India. Chandigarh is like a science-fiction outpost plopped down in the unlikeliest spot on the planet. It's cold and alienating and to have built such a city amidst the warmth and vibrancy of India was so thoroughly ill conceived that I couldn't help having a certain begrudging respect for Le Corbusier for pulling it off. I caught a bus and continued north through the plains. The temperature rose as the day wore on, and by the time we stopped at a little way station, I was half-dead from thirst. There were a dozen varieties of soft drinks, none of which I'd ever heard of, with names like Binki, Noop, Zum, and Lali. I grabbed a Binki, popped it open, and took a big gulp. *What?* It was curried! Burning, stinging, curried cola! It occurred to me – and not for the first time – that India, quite possibly, was a nation of screwballs.

The bus crossed a corner of the Punjab, then headed up

into the foothills of Himachal Pradesh. As we rose a hundred feet and rounded a curve, three women across the aisle, a boy two rows back, and the man sitting next to me all simultaneously vomited. We climbed gradually into the lower Himalayas, pushing farther north into the Kulu Valley along a treacherous road that unconvincingly hugged the side of a mountain. The curves became sharper, often with no more than a foot to spare, and I realized that the slightest miscue would send us careening thousands of feet to the jagged rocks below. A spinout would kill us. A flat tire would kill us. A rock slide would kill us. I looked at the driver, who was hunched over the steering wheel, and wondered if his childhood had been happy. 'Life is good,' I told him in little telepathic messages as the bus wobbled along the edge of the road, 'don't despair.' We skirted along the Parvati range on one side and the Barabhangals on the other, going higher and higher, the snowcapped Himalayas jutting into an infinite sky. 'Whatever you do, don't despair . . .'

That night we pulled into Manali, a town famous throughout India for its hashish. It was late September, the harvest was in, and the moment I walked into a *chai* shop, I was handed a chillum. A chillum is about six inches long and is shaped like an ice-cream cone, only it's not quite so flared and is open at both ends. It's usually made of clay, but occasionally is carved from agate, soapstone, or marble. Clay chillums are the cheapest, and by far the best, as they allow for the optimum burning temperature of hashish. Stone chillums burn too cold and marble chillums, which are a bit too fancy-schmancy anyway, burn too hot.

The *chai* shop was lit by a few candles and a single kerosene lamp, which was barely visible through the heavy cloud of smoke. A Dutch guy took the last blast from his pipe, then turned it upside down and tapped out the residue. He pushed a thin rope through the bottom of the chillum and handed one end to a Sikh who sat across from him. Without either of them saying a word, the Sikh pulled the rope taut while the Dutchman briskly rubbed the inside of the chillum against the fibers to remove any sediment. I noticed that his palms were all black and sticky, from the base of his fingers down to his wrists and right across the whole width of his hand. The Sikh's palms were just as black and that's when I realized who they were. They were the ganja rubbers.

The ganja rubbers worked the pot fields of Manali, rubbing countless buds of ganja into their palms until only a thick, sticky, oily residue was left. It was hard work, requiring hours of rubbing to get all the leaves, seeds, and twigs out of the mix, and, by the end of the day, so much cannabis was ingrained into the pores of their hands that washing it off was impossible. Manali sits in the center of the hashish belt, which runs through Iran, Afghanistan, Pakistan, India, and Nepal, and Manali *charas* is the best in India. The Dutchman wasted no time preparing the next chillum. He took a chunk of hash, held a match beneath it for a few seconds, then crumbled off a gram or two into his hand. Next, he split open a cigarette and rubbed the tobacco into his palm until the consistency was as fine as the hash. He added a little ganja for flavor, then placed a small stone inside the chillum before pouring it all in. He then took the outer leaf from a *bidi*, an Indian cigarette, and crumbled it on top of the mound to help it burn.

A German guy took a small piece of cloth, known as a *safi*, dipped it into a glass of water, wrung it out, and wrapped it around the bottom of the chillum. *Safis*, sad to say, are the bastard stepchildren of chillum smoking and, frankly, are more often than not a total disgrace. They usually have frayed edges and an ambiguous shape, and they're rarely chosen with any regard for color or design. While most *safis* are cut from thin cotton, there are also silk, velvet, rayon, and, almost unthinkably, polyester *safis*. The worst thing about *safis*, however, is that they tend to be used over and over, accumulating not only the tar from the tobacco, the oils from the *charas*, and the residue from the ganja, but also the various germs and diseases of countless previous users.

The chillum was finally ready to be lit. The Dutchman

placed the chillum between the first three fingers and thumb of his right hand. With his left hand, he cupped the fingers around the stem to make an airtight chamber. The little finger of the right hand slipped around the outside, basically just staying out of the way. The maneuvering of the fingers, chillum, and palms is critical for the creation of the chamber, for if anything is out of place, air will escape, and if air escapes, the chillum will not light. To be in Manali and not know how to smoke a chillum would be a disgrace almost beyond description. The Dutch guy signaled that he was ready by touching the chillum to his forehead, thereby invoking the proper spirits. The Sikh took three wooden matches and struck them against the side of the box. The first two attempts were failures – Indian matches are notoriously ineffective – but when they finally lit, the rest of us all unconsciously leaned back, knowing the tendency of Indian matches to occasionally blast off like rockets. The Sikh held the three matches – and for some reason, it's always three – approximately two inches over the mound of the chillum. Since the Dutchman, who was holding the chillum at a forty-five-degree angle, couldn't exactly see what was happening, he needed to rely on doper's intuition to inhale at just the right moment. Otherwise, the Sikh, whose fingers would be in danger of burning off, would have had to say something like, 'All right, already.'

As the Dutchman drew a long, deep breath, the hash flamed up, a great blast of smoke appeared, and an Englishwoman yelled out, '*Bom, Shankar*,' invoking one of the names of Lord Shiva, the god of intoxication. He passed her the chillum in a clockwise direction – with the right hand, of course – and, as an added Hindu gesture of respect, held the fingers of his left hand beneath his right elbow. A good chillum can last for fifteen or twenty tokes, depending on the hash, the smokers, and the phase of the moon. An exception to this might be if you're smoking with French morphine junkies, like the ones who were sitting at the next table, in which case your chillum might disappear after just one round, along with the stone, the *safi*, and your passport.

French morphine junkies were the bane of travelers throughout the world – a lying, thieving bunch of parasites who caused no end of trouble. Having had my fill of them in Amsterdam and Paris, I left the *chai* shop, checked into a guest house, collapsed onto a lumpy straw mattress, and fell into a deep, deep sleep.

I awoke late the next morning to the coldest weather I'd experienced since leaving Sweden. Manali lies between two steep mountain ranges, and the sun doesn't rise until ten and sets around four. By the time I forced myself out of bed and had a bowl of porridge, the sun appeared and the temperature quickly rose into the seventies. I decided to walk higher into the mountains while I had the chance. I came upon a little village whose inhabitants looked very much like Greek peasants. Their skin was light, their hair black and wavy, and they wore a style of clothing and jewelry that reminded me of the Mediterranean. I knew that Alexander the Great had conquered these parts two thousand years earlier. Were these his descendants?

I climbed higher and looked back over the terraced wheat fields and golden fruit orchards. There was something magical in the air. The sky was crystal clear, the snowcapped mountains loomed majestically above, and a path seemed to beckon me into the woods. I thought I heard flutes in the distance and was certain my mind was playing tricks on me, but as I continued on, the sounds became clearer. They were flutes, all right, and sprightly flutes at that. I wandered off the path, came upon a clearing in the woods, and stood there a moment, unsure of myself. Finally, I pulled back a branch and saw, sitting in a large circle, twenty Tibetans. I'd heard there were Tibetan refugees in the area and now, finally, I was actually seeing them. The first thing I noticed about Tibetans was that they didn't sit in very orderly circles. In fact, to call it a circle at all was stretching a bit; it was more of an unruly squiggle that vaguely connected as it curved around. The next thing I noticed about Tibetans was that they didn't really sit in the classic meditation position; in fact, their posture was much closer to what I'd call a sprawl. The third thing I noticed about Tibetans was that they seemed to have a fondness for a milky white liquid that was being ladled out by the only woman in the group, and as they sipped from large bowls, I began to get the suspicion that – *hey, wait a minute here* – they were dead drunk!

Not just drunk. No, these, my first Tibetans – the most spiritual of all people – were knocking back one shot of *chung* after another and were rip-roaring, three-sheets-to-the-wind fucked-up. I couldn't remember reading about this in my Buddhism course back at the University of Wisconsin. Then they noticed me. 'Come, come, sit here in the honored spot next to our patriarch,' they seemed to be saying. So I followed their welcoming waves, crossed the clearing, and approached the old wise man. He smiled at me, motioned for me to sit, and then, as I began to kneel down, he grabbed my balls. 'Whoa, *kemo sabe*, this *definitely* wasn't in that Buddhism course! Or was it? I remembered how I didn't really understand a lot of the terminology.

'*Twiss! Twiss!*' someone started chanting, while pointing my way.

'Hey, who do you think you're calling a *twiss*?' I was about to say, but then I began wondering, what exactly is a *twiss*? Maybe it's not so bad. Maybe it's their greatest honor, like 'great white man from across the many oceans.'

They all started yelling, '*Twiss! Twiss!*' until some red-faced guy pulled me right to the center of the clearing. In a way, that wasn't so bad – I was glad to be away from the ball-grabbing wise man – but just what the hell was I supposed to do now? Then the guy started moving his arms back and forth, real stiff-like, and shaking his hips and moving his feet and he's like . . . oh, no, a Tibetan *Chubby Checker*!

'You want me to *twist*?' I asked incredulously.

A big roar of approval erupted. '*Twiss! Twiss!*' they kept yelling, and suddenly we're all on our feet and we're doing some insane dance to a happy flute, they're pouring *chung* down my throat – the vilest, most potent hooch this side of the Ozarks – and we're all floating around the dance floor like drunken egrets. Everyone's arms were out-stretched and, almost imperceptibly, the Tibetans began flapping them like wings. Their heads bobbed up and down, their knees bent slightly, and then the flapping increased a little, me right along with them, me and twenty Tibetans and a woman whose father had just died, and we're flapping his spirit away, we're drinking to his memory, we're dancing to the good old days, we're flapping and floating and flying at ten thousand feet, and I'm starting to really like my first Tibetans, they've got a certain style, and I'm warming up to the idea that come what may, we're gonna twist again, like we did last summer.

# 27

# Ticket to Ride

What is travel? Why am I doing this, month after month, year after year, why am I taking broken-down lorries through the plains of Africa, decommissioned DC-3s over uncharted waters, wayward ships across the Indian Ocean, ancient trains into the baking desert, suicidal buses over the Himalayas? Why am I living in vans, caves, collapsing *shambas*, spider-infested cabanas, and freezing guest houses? Because travel is putting yourself in impossible situations to find out who you are. And everybody you meet along the way, whether they know it or not, is doing exactly the same thing. That's why people meet so easily on the road. Deep down we're all after some answer and we figure that maybe, just maybe, someone might be able to help us find it. Getting to an exotic destination is only part of it – the struggle of getting there is just as important. All over the world, people are making pilgrimages by foot and bus and train to places that are holy to them, places that might shed some light. It might be a palace in Versailles or an acropolis in Athens or a mosque in Lamu or a ganja field in Manali, but that's what we're all doing, we're all trying to connect to something sacred.

When I first arrived in Europe, I always knew exactly how many days I'd been away, how many countries I'd been to, and how many entries I had in my passport. Now I was beginning to realize that I'd been completely missing the point. Travel has nothing to do with time and, in fact, not much to do with place. Travel is about discovering something within. I no longer owned a map or an almanac or a guidebook and had fought off any impulse to carry a camera. While others were relying on film to spark their memories, I was forced to create photographs in my mind. I had to capture everything right down to the tiniest detail and imprint it for posterity. Ultimately that mental image means much more, it lasts longer and grows stronger. Photographs take one's experiences, reduce them to two dimensions, and remove all depth. Cameras are artificial trappings of the journey.

The bus ride back down the Kulu Valley was even more treacherous than the way up. There'd been a rockslide and hundreds of villagers were building up the side of the mountain. Their techniques were ancient, but what India lacked in machinery, it made up for in manpower. The workers broke boulders into smaller stones with unimaginably primitive tools, loaded them into huge bags, and tied them around their foreheads like a yoke to an ox. They carried the load up a steep path, struggling with the weight until they reached the top, then dumped the contents onto a pile. Keeping a watchful eye over the proceedings was the quarry manager, an enormously fat man who made sure that each load was properly broken up and of sufficient weight. Once satisfied, he handed over a five-paisa coin – equivalent to about half a cent – and each laborer tied it into his *lungi* before climbing back down the hill to start his next pile. What really struck me, beyond the backbreaking work and the pit boss's resemblance to Ali Baba, was the immediate connection between work and pay. I wasn't sure who was more suspicious of whom, but it was clear that trust – and one's job – lasted only as long as that trip up the hill.

I thought about how this system had been ingrained into the culture for thousands of years and how I could, right now, be in virtually any period of history. Time had stopped in these mountains; maybe it never even got started. I awoke each morning with the feeling that anything could happen and went to sleep each night wondering what exactly *did* happen. It felt sometimes as if this journey had a deeper meaning, but I could never quite place what it was. Everything around me harkened back to centuries ago, when this civilization was at its height, and I felt a sense of loss, as if modern India were trying to recapture some of its past greatness, trying to uncover its lost teachings, lost medicines, and lost nobility. I didn't understand much of anything yet, and – like the Englishman in Bombay had warned – maybe I knew less today than when I first arrived. I just hoped that I hadn't gotten to India five thousand years too late.

You need to enter India in a rickety bus or on a slow-moving train or on a ship from some faraway port. You need to kind of sneak up on India; otherwise, India will sneak up on you. After a daylong journey, I found myself back in the Chandigarh train station. The platform was packed and I got flashes of Victoria Station in Bombay. Sure enough, when the train pulled in, there was the same mad rush and chaos. This time, however, I decided I wouldn't be left behind. I could shove, too, I could crawl through a window, or push through a door, or climb over somebody's back. Once the doors flew open, I made my move. I felt myself bobbing along like a cork in the sea, sometimes fighting the tide, other times going with the flow. I'd nearly made it into one car when the wave pushed me farther down along the platform. I regrouped for another assault, paddling now, as if on a surfboard, and suddenly I felt a big whoosh, like a giant vacuum cleaner sucking me in. The whistle blew, there was a burst of steam, and there I was, securely situated in third-class. A guy sitting across from me stared at me as we entered a tunnel, he stared at me around a bend, and he stared at me as we hit the plains. 'Indira Gandhi,' I said, in the only Hindi I knew. He thought it over a moment and nodded. And then he stared at me some more.

Delhi was stifling hot. I'd been back for three days and was thinking about where to go next when I noticed that my travel clock was running slow. In the bazaar I found a watch-repair stall, where four men studied my Timex Traveler – a six-dollar job with real fake leatherette case and windup spring – as if they were doctors about to perform the most delicate brain surgery. 'What do you think?' I asked.

They looked at each other, conferred, then gave little twists of the head that either meant yes, no, or maybe. 'Not to worry,' the chief of staff said.

'Not to worry, chicken curry,' I responded, having no idea what that meant, but it sounded cool. 'When will it be ready?'

'One hour ready.'

I decided to hang out in the market, even though the stultifying dead air made me feel like I was roasting inside a slow-cooking tandoori oven. When I came upon a food stall, I asked for something cold to drink. 'Cold not good,' said the man behind the counter. 'Hot weather coming, hot *chai* drinking.'

'Yeah, right,' I mumbled, but then I noticed how much this guy looked like an Indian version of Willard Schultz, my junior-high-school science teacher. I figured anybody who looked like Willard Schultz must know something. 'What do you mean?' I asked.

'Must balance system. When weather overheating, must bring body up to outside temperature.' He sipped some tea, then pointed to his own body. 'I very comfortable feeling.' I had to admit that he did look pretty comfortable. I was dripping with sweat, while he looked cool as a cucumber. I thought about how *cucumber*, in fact, was an Indian word, and how maybe this guy had special insights. I drank down a cup of scorching hot tea and was certain I'd melt. My lips burned, my tongue stung, and my throat sizzled. Then, a few moments later, I actually did feel cooler and wondered if the guy was maybe on to something. I looked at him more closely and for a moment I thought it actually was Willard Schultz. What the hell was Willard Schultz doing here in India selling tea? Had we finally driven him crazy in eighth-grade chemistry?

I returned to the watch stall an hour later, only to find they were closed for lunch. Two hours later, the stall was open, but my clock wasn't ready. Three hours later, the stall was closed for dinner. Four hours later, the stall was open, but there was a new shift at work and they couldn't find my Timex. Five hours later, the stall was closed just for the hell of it. Six hours later, the stall was open, but was now selling oranges and cigarettes. The next morning, I headed over to the bazaar expecting to find a used rickshaw lot, but there they were, the original four guys sitting in their usual spots. I felt more irritated than relieved to see them. 'So, have you got my clock or *what*?'

'Why not?' said the crew chief, as if there shouldn't be the slightest doubt. He ceremoniously dug under the counter and produced my Timex.

I looked at the dial and saw that it had the perfect time. 'Hey, good job,' I said, feeling guilty for having been suspicious.

'Takes a licking, keeps on ticking,' he said, quoting the Timex motto.

'Just like India . . .' I said, nodding to him.

'Yes,' he said, smiling slyly, 'just like India . . .'

I headed for the train station, hoping to catch something going east, but just outside the terminal I noticed a VW van with a sign attached: VAN TO KATHMANDU – SHARE RIDE. Intrigued by the possibility, I waited around until a guy with long, reddish blond hair showed up. He looked like Wild Bill Hickok. When I inquired about the ride, he took a long look at me. 'You're not crazy or anything, are you?' he said, with a thick Australian accent. I thought that was a rather odd question, but who knows with Australians? They're disarmingly blunt.

'Not completely.'

'Because we've already got one madman,' chimed in another voice. I looked over to see a wiry Englishwoman headed our way. 'The bonkers quotient is all filled up, thank you very much.'

'No problem, it's all yours.'

'It's not *me* I was referring to. It's one of your countrymen we seem to have inherited. Crazy as a loon, he is.'

The Australian saw that I had my rucksack and was ready to go. 'I'm Guy' he said, putting out his hand. 'That's Sarah. We've been looking for one more.' As Guy and I worked out the details and discussed the itinerary, Sarah jumped into the front seat.

'Yanks in the rear, them's the rules.'

'*Uh* . . . aren't we missing someone?' I asked.

'Oh, gawd, you would have to remind us. Where is he then, Guy?'

'He'll be along, luv, he'll be along.'

'Bonkers,' she said, shaking her head, 'frightfully bonkers . . .' Guy studied some maps, Sarah escaped into a novel, and I got situated in the back, getting used to the idea that, just like that, I was going to Nepal. Images of Mount Everest, Buddhist temples, and mysterious hidden valleys spun through my mind: Was I actually doing this? Was I ready? A few minutes later, Sarah looked up from her book. 'Blimey, what time is it?'

I dug into my rucksack, pulled out the Timex, flipped open the case, and discovered that the hour hand and minute hand were just flopping around at the bottom of the dial. I stared at it in disbelief, turned it over, and saw that the screws weren't even mounted. Then I pried open the back to find that the original parts had been replaced by cheap Indian substitutes. The spring wasn't really a spring at all, but something that looked suspiciously like a wet noodle. They had adulterated my Timex! 'Those *bastards*—'

The sun suddenly disappeared and I looked up to see a guy standing in front of the double doors of the van. His girth filled the whole space. 'I'm Albie,' he said, sticking out a big, beefy paw. 'I didn't always look like this.' Sarah rolled her eyes and leaned back in the front seat as Guy turned on the ignition. Albie wedged his way through the doors and plopped down. There was just barely room for the two of us. 'Kathmandu?' he asked.

I nodded. 'You?'

'Benares.' I felt the seat shift as Albie dug into his back pocket. He pulled out his wallet and produced a photo of a thin, handsome, hip-looking guy. 'This is me two years ago.'

Sarah turned back with alarm and mouthed the words: 'Don't ask him what happened.'

'Want to know what happened?' asked Albie.

'*Uh* . . . maybe later.'

'To really understand, I probably need to start at the beginning. It's hard for me to say this, but in some ways I don't think my mother really liked me.'

'Oh, *gawwwwwwd* . . .' moaned Sarah as Guy pulled into traffic. 'Not the *whole* flipping story!'

'As for my father, well, he wasn't really around all that much . . .'

The road through Uttar Pradesh reminded me of driving through the wildebeest migration in Serengeti, except that these were *people* on the move – people in cars, people in trucks, people in buses, but mostly people on foot, thousands and thousands of people on an endless march to nowhere. The highway was essentially one big pothole with a little tarmac thrown here and there to help create the illusion of motion. We bounced along, going fifteen or twenty miles an hour, swerving around water buffaloes, cows, mules, and hundreds of carts. It reminded me of newsreels of people escaping wars or natural disasters, but there was no particular disaster at hand, just the basic disaster of life in central India.

Albie laid down the soundtrack for the journey, supplying all the details of his life – the troubles at home, the affronts at school, the minor successes and major disappointments. It was all pretty much the normal stuff, but for Albie everything took on monumental significance. Guy essentially tuned out and Sarah desperately tried to, while I kind of faded in and out, picking up snippets of a story that seemed, finally, to be getting around to the point – 'So there I am, in Bangkok, on Patpong Road, strippers to the right, hookers to the left, and they're *fighting* over me, you know what I mean? Me, a guy from Brooklyn, I'm like a god to them, maybe it was the hair, or maybe the eyes, or the sound of my voice, I dunno, the point is, this, of all times in my life, this is *no* time to be broke – hell, I'm in a sexual Disneyland without a ticket to ride – so I'm looking for some quick cash and who should I meet but Sergeant Wacks from the U.S. Army. Wacky – that's what they called him – was stationed up in Japan and he's telling me, sitting in the dark corner of some bar, how he could move as many hits of acid as I could deliver and how there's a guy he knows down here with the goods and they just need somebody trustworthy enough to make the run. 'Well,' I told Wacky, 'ask any of the girls in here, *I* can deliver,' and he takes a close look at me and says, 'Yes, my friend, I believe you could—'

'Watch out!' yelled Sarah as a cow suddenly darted onto the road. Guy jammed on the brakes, swerved, and skidded across the tarmac. The van finally came to a stop just inches from the cow, which was now staring right at us through the front windshield. 'Buggering cows!' Sarah screamed. 'We hit one of those and it's up the river for all of us.'

'You okay back there?' asked Guy, who looked shaken from the close call.

'Yeah,' I said, pushing back into the seat, 'I think so.'

Albie was unaware that anything had happened. He simply went on, never missing a beat. 'So, a couple of days pass, Wacky goes back to Japan, I meet the Man, he checks me out, I check him out, and, before you know it, I've got a plane ticket to Tokyo, a hotel reservation in Ginza, and six hundred tabs of Owsley acid taped inside my camera case' – Albie's story kept wafting in and out of my consciousness while Guy cautiously pulled back onto the road. As the sun set over the endless flat plains, I tried to imagine how people could eke out a living on such desolate land. Little scrubs of brush seemed to be the only vegetation for miles around. What if these people were in Wisconsin? It would be pure heaven for them – a heaven of real dirt, real plants, and real rivers, yes, we need to shake things up a bit, why not move ten million Indians to Wisconsin, not too far north, of course, the dhotis could be a problem in winter, no, maybe around Milwaukee, Milwaukee could definitely use ten million Indians, *real* Indians, not the Potawatomee kind, Indians from India, give the place a little color yes, Milwaukee would become quite cool, cool as a *cucumber* – 'So I'm in the Bangkok airport and it's bing-bang-boom, right through customs, but it turns out the plane is delayed and I'm sitting there, not even a book to read, and I'm getting bored as hell in the departure lounge, they're saying it's gonna be another two hours, and I figure well, okay, so I'll drop a hit of acid. Perfectly reasonable, don't you think?'

'Perfectly,' said Sarah.

'Now, let me just tell you, some people, they take acid in a foreign airport, all those people talking gobbledygook around them, it's not the most conducive place. But me? Piece of cake. I'm groovin' on the runways, goofin' on the stewardesses, it's a maximum gas. And I'll tell you, today, tomorrow, anytime, anyplace, you name it, you dose me ground level at any airport and I'm totally cool.'

'Note the subtle stipulation,' Sarah chimed in.

'That's right, ground level, because even with planes flying in, with all the hustle and bustle, people getting off, people getting on, friends, relatives, balloons, all sorts of nonsense, *still* I'm cool. Why? Because I've staked out my territory, exactly two paces in any direction from my seat in the lounge is sacrosanct, there's an invisible shield I've erected, nothing comes in, nothing gets out. But then – and to this day I don't know how it happened – an attendant somehow reaches right through, it's like she found the one weak spot in the zone, and she grabs my arm and leads me to the gate. Next thing I know, I'm sitting in the plane, they've got me strapped into the seat, this big chunk of metal is going a million miles an hour down the runway, and I look around and discover that my invisible shield is not only gone, it's around some *other* guy six rows up. Now, I ask you, what would *you* do in a situation like that?'

'Why, go stark raving loony,' said Sarah. 'Threaten the

stewardess. Hit the man next to me. Try to eat through my seat belt. Isn't that what we'd *all* do?'

'Exactly. Fortunately, once we're up around 10,000 feet, everything is cool again, even 20,000 . . . 25,000 I'm feeling loose, but *30,000*, that's a whole new ball game, I'm telling you the roof is gonna cave in. I yelled to the pilot – '*Dive! Dive!*' – but when I realized he was gonna John Wayne it all the way to Japan at that altitude I said, '*Nuh-uh*,' and tore ass up there to explain the danger we were in. Well, talk about gratitude. Not only does he not listen, not only do they tie me up in the back, not only do they stuff a shirt in my mouth, they fucking have half the cops in Tokyo waiting for me when the plane lands!'

'This is my favorite part of the story,' said Sarah.

'So I'm standing naked in some room, one guy's looking up my ass, one guy's looking down my throat, and another guy is holding up a bag, screaming: "*What's this? What's this? What's this?*" Never one to bullshit, I look him straight in the eye and say, "LSD, made in the U.S.A., none of those cheap Japanese knockoffs," and now he's really pissed and says: "You bring drugs to sell to Japan!" Then I said, "Not at all, it's for personal use."'

'Six hundred hits,' said Sarah.

'Five ninety-nine,' said Albie.

'For personal use,' sniffed Sarah.

'The judge didn't buy it either. He gave me six years. Way up north somewhere. And they're taking it real serious, like I'm some kind of criminal, for God's sake. No books, no music, no TV, no exercise, no nothing. I'm feeling as bummed out as I could ever remember. I'm thinking about what got me here. I'm thinking about my childhood, my mom, my dad—'

'Go on!' Sarah screamed.

'Fact is, I probably would've offed myself if given the chance, but even that, those bastards, even that they thought of – no belts, no razors , no shoelaces, like I said, no nothing. Except for one thing . . .' There was a long pause. 'Rice.'

'Rice?'

'Rice. That was the one thing prisoners could have. As much rice as you wanted, un*limited* rice, big *pots* of rice, whole *mountains* of rice. That's how I passed the time. I ate rice all day long. I figured, why not? Rice is good for you. Nobody gets sick from rice, nobody dies from rice, nobody gets *fat* from rice.'

'You mean—'

'That's right. How do you think sumo wrestlers get so fat? Turns out if you eat enough rice, it's the most fattening thing in the world. I put on two hundred pounds in two years.'

We all sat there for a moment in dead silence. The traffic had thinned out a bit and we were making better time. 'But . . . you said they gave you six years.'

'That's where Wacky comes in. He found out what happened and contacted my parents. It took forever, but he had some ins with the law and managed to work out a deal. So, two years later, my parents, who'd never been off the East Coast of the States, hop on a twenty-hour flight to Japan, take a train to the prison, and are led to my cell. My dad was the first one in. He takes a look at me and was so shocked, I thought he was going to faint. He just leaned against the bars and said: "*Albie?*" That's all he could say. Then I hear my mother's high-heeled shoes clicking down the corridor. She walks in, takes a look at me, smiles with relief, and says, "Well, at least you look healthy!" Sarah and I tried not to laugh, but when we caught each other's eyes in the rearview mirror, we couldn't contain ourselves. 'Mothers,' said Albie, shaking his head. 'Anyway, I have to admit, my parents came through. They paid off the cops and sprung me. Got me out of there a couple of months ago.'

'So, what are you doing here? You didn't go back with them?'

'What, and let all my old friends see me like this? Hell, no. I came straight to India. It was the obvious choice.'

'Uh-huh. Because . . . ?'

'Look around out there, man. Don't you see where we are?'

'Well, yeah, I guess it's a good place to get your head together.'

'Get my *head* together? I didn't come to India to get my *head* together.'

'Well, why *did* you come?'

'I came to India to diet.'

# 28

# The Bone Man of Benares

We pulled into Benares at 3.00 A.M. It was the dark of the moon, everything was shut tight, and the city was pitch-black. Guy, who'd been there before, drove toward the Ganges River – or the Ganga, as it's called in India – got as close as he could, and parked the van. Albie and Sarah were sound asleep, and Guy and I couldn't see a thing, but when we got out to stretch, I felt a surge of excitement. We were in India's holiest city – in recent times called Varanasi, but more often referred to by its ancient name – and were within walking distance of its holiest river. 'What do you think?' I said, 'should we check it out?'

'Not me,' said Guy, yawning. 'I've got to get some sleep.'

I pulled out a flashlight and saw what appeared to be an entrance to the marketplace. The maze of narrow alleyways and twisting paths reminded me of Lamu. 'It must be that way.'

'Yeah, it's down there somewhere. I don't know exactly.'

'Okay, I'll see you in a bit.'

'Don't get lost,' Guy called to me as I headed for the market. I stepped over a sleeping cow, passed some people huddled in a doorway, turned right, angled down another alley, avoided an enormous river rat, turned left, slipped around a corner, hooked back, and was totally lost. Just as my flashlight began to fade – someone had probably sucked half the acid out of my Indian batteries – I noticed a bonfire in the distance. Using it as kind of a North Star, I stayed along a path until it dipped down and eventually leveled off onto a stone promenade. It was still almost impossible to see anything but as I got closer, the light from the fire burned brighter and I thought I could smell smoke. It was strangely sweet and acrid.

I walked down a few steps and saw the reflection of a half-dozen fires in a broad expanse of water. This was it – the Ganges. As I stood there, a slight breeze kicked up and the smoke from the fires blew directly into my face. Again, that sweet and acrid smell. As my eyes began to focus on the dancing light, I heard the sound of shuffling feet and turned to see two men carrying a simple bamboo stretcher. I saw something that looked like a package lying between the poles, wrapped in a plain white cloth, then noticed the outline of a foot underneath. It was then that I realized I was at the burning ghats – the Hindu cremation grounds – that each of these fires was fueled by human flesh, and that the smoke blowing up my nose was the putrid stench of death.

I saw more stretchers on their way to the river and imagined a whole trail of them, dozens, maybe hundreds, all lined up and ready to go. More smoke blew into my face. I shuddered and was turning away from the fires, feeling a little ill, when I heard a familiar call: '*Bom Shankar!*' I looked over toward one of the ghats and saw a group of sadhus lighting up a chillum. I wasn't sure, but it looked as if one of them was waving for me to join them. I instinctively backed away, but then he waved again and it occurred to me how perfectly insane this would be, to smoke with sadhus for the very first time right on the burning ghats of Benares. They were there, I assumed, as part of some religious discipline to overcome the fear of death, and to honor Shiva in his twin roles as the god of destruction and the god of intoxication. To get high is to have a religious experience, to come closer to God, and Shiva sadhus are the consummate hash smokers of India. They are immediately recognizable by their huge mounds of matted hair, the three broad stripes painted across their foreheads, and their naked, ash-covered bodies. As I walked toward the *dhuni*, their ritual fire, I felt my stomach clench up. Six sadhus were gathered around, and they made room for me to sit cross-legged in the circle. The chillum came my way almost instantly, and they all watched as I took it with my right hand, held my left hand under my elbow, and touched the chillum to my forehead. I took a long, deep hit, managed not to cough, then handed it clockwise to the sadhu on my left and tried not to fall over into the fire.

The sadhus nodded almost imperceptibly. They were way too cool to congratulate me for knowing how to smoke a chillum, so I took their non-reaction as a sign of acceptance. As the chillum went around the circle, I slowly exhaled and became aware again of the body burning on the ghat just a few feet away. I glanced over and saw a charred leg sticking out between the pieces of wood and a hand pointing straight up. Then I heard a magnificent voice, a deep tone that was both comforting and compelling, and I turned to see the oldest sadhu in the group, speaking to me from across the *dhuni*. He looked at me with penetrating eyes, and I felt myself being drawn into some other world. He was speaking Hindi and I didn't have any idea what he was saying, but I sensed that something important was being communicated, some piece of wisdom that – if only I could grasp it – would change my life. I nodded to him, not to pretend that I understood, but to indicate that I appreciated his efforts, that his words meant something to me even if I didn't know what they were, that I would try to live up to his message, whatever it might be. The smoke from the chillum, the smoke from the *dhuni*, and the smoke from the body all blended together, and something, I'm not quite sure what, made perfect sense.

Another Indian was invited into the circle, and he squatted next to me while the old sadhu, a beautiful man with a mile of hair and a flowing white beard and orange stripes painted across his forehead, took such a massive hit from the chillum that a flame briefly burst forth from the hash. I glanced at the guy sitting next to me and we smiled at the sadhu's prowess. I was really getting into it now, grooving with the holy men, feeling like I somehow knew more than I did an hour ago, even getting used to the idea that there's a dead body being cremated a few feet away, and the smoke is furling all around, and the chillum is coming my way, and the guy next to me takes a big hit and hands it to me, and my fingers clasp around the stem of the pipe – my hands and the guy's hands and the chillum and the smoke all mixing into some kind of moody Impressionist painting – and I notice something, and then I look again, and I'm not sure if I'm really seeing right, but this guy doesn't actually seem to have all of his fingers, they're more like stumps, and then I look once more – *shit! He's a leper!* – and I try to be cool – I'm smoking with sadhus, after all – and okay, so I'm touching his stumps, maybe that's not so bad, but then I'm wondering how he even got his hands around the chillum and I'm thinking he must've had his lips right against the *safi* – this rotten, filthy, piece-of-shit *safi* – and then it all starts making sense, this must be some kind of a test from the sadhus to see if I can take it, well, of *course* I can take it, and I grab that chillum and put it right up to my lips and take a big hit and hold it in, the hash, the germs, the smoke from the dead body, the leprosy, and then I feel something fall to the ground, and I glance down and I can't really see because it's nearly pitch-black, but as my eyes begin to focus, I'm a good 90 percent sure that – *it's his finger!* – I fucking pulled off the poor leper's last finger when I grabbed that chillum! – *oh man, I'm sorry* – and he's looking up at me like, don't worry, it's okay, and I want to say to him, no man, it's *not* okay, I feel like shit, I don't know why I grabbed it like that, and then the ghat attendant comes by and turns the body, and the old sadhu adds some more wood to the *dhuni*, and a stretcher passes by with yet another corpse, and, even though I feel absolutely terrible about what happened, it just seems like it's too late to do anything about it, it's too late for the leper, it's too late for the corpse, it's too late for India, and, as I take another hit off the chillum, it more than likely is too late for me.

\* \* \*

I hurried up from the river, my flashlight nearly burned out, when a voice called from a doorway: 'Friend? You are needing bone?' I shone the light onto a strange-looking guy who peered out from the shadows. Something about him looked oddly familiar.

'No, thanks,' I said, figuring he was trying to unload some stolen buffalo bone, the kind they carve into elaborate knick-knacks and sell in the marketplace.

'Only looking. No charge looking,' he said as he stepped forward, opened a dirty old satchel, and dug around inside. I heard a clinking sound, took a look, and felt my skin crawl. There, in his hand, was an assortment of human fingers, knuckles, wrists, and probably an ankle or two. 'Finger 50 rupee,' he said, then quickly added, 'okay, for you, 40 rupee.'

I thought about the leper whose finger I may or may not have pulled off and wondered if there was any way this would be of use to him. 'Where did you get these, anyway?' I said, trying to remember if it was his forefinger or ring finger I had so clumsily dismembered.

The man smiled and I could see a twinkle in his eyes. 'Come, come,' he said, giving me that upside-down motion with his hand. There was, of course, no way I was going anywhere with this guy, but the next thing I knew I was following him through the back alleys of the marketplace and down a shortcut to the banks of the Ganges. 'There,' he said, pointing out over the water.

'There?' I said, having no idea what he was pointing to. 'Where?'

'India is having many poor people,' he said. I nodded, waiting for him to go on. 'Many family not having 3 rupees for ghats. Some family having only 2 rupees . . . 1 rupee . . .' I nodded again. 'Body taking four hours to burn. Two rupees wood lasting maybe two hours.' I nodded once more. '*Bas*,' he said, wiping his hands like a clean slate.

'What do you mean, *bas*?'

He looked at me impatiently. '*Bas*. Finish. Body going into Ganga.'

'*What*? They don't finish the job? They just throw what's

left into the river?' He gave me that little twist of the head that either meant yes, no, or maybe. 'And you actually go swimming in there . . . looking for *bones*?'

'Very difficult. Ganga very dirty. Very hard to see.'

'Okay, that's it,' I said, moving away from him.

'No sale?'

'No sale.'

'I taking special order. Skull, hip, toe—'

'No sale!'

He shrugged and pointed to the river. 'In Ganga are many blind dolphin.' I sat on the banks of the river and wondered what the hell *that* meant. Did he fight the dolphins for the bodies? Were these dolphin bones? Was *he* a dolphin? More importantly, I wondered what the hell I had even been thinking about. What was the poor leper going to do with one of these fingers? What was *anybody* going to do with these fingers? How did this guy make a living?

The first hint of sunlight appeared on the horizon and I began to see the outlines of a thousand temples along the Ganges. They were built nearly on top of each other, their walls leaning together for support. It seemed as if one building fell, the whole city would collapse. Just down from the pyres, people waded into the river to bathe. They kept their dhotis discreetly wrapped around as they soaped up and washed off, while boatmen rowed farther out into the river with cups full of ashes. The first sounds of early morning carried down from the ghats and I heard the tones of a tabla and tambura welcoming the dawn. The drummer counted out the beat – *teen tal, dah, dah, tiki-tiki dah* – while the simple drone of the strings rose and fell with the breeze. The sounds blended into a long deep tone, so rich and full and all-encompassing that it reminded me of nothing so much as absolute, total silence.

That's when I felt a hand on my arm and turned to see the Bone Man looking right at me. 'Love is not the answer,' he said, fixing me with a stare. Huh? Love is *not* the answer? Sure, that figures, doesn't it, what else would I expect a guy like this to say? Well, thanks, pal, I'll remember that, I'll enter it into my book of pithy sayings, of all the people in Benares to latch onto me, why him, why this guy who redefines bottom of the barrel, this bloodsucking creep from the Hindu netherworlds, this guy who lives off death itself, this guy who is worse than a parasite – parasites at least feed off the living – I wish he'd just pack up his bones and get lost, go find somebody else to bother, how about Albie, the two of you could probably have a very interesting conversation, yeah, go see Albie, who knows, maybe he'll buy your whole supply, but, you know what, I think it's really time for you and me to part ways, I'll just take the high road, and you, needless to say, can take the low road, yeah, don't trip over yourself leaving, the sun's just about to come up and you wouldn't want to get caught in the daylight, no, my friend, you're much better off in the shadows, or in a cave somewhere, just you and your bones, I'll bet you've got some real interesting furniture – *skull* cups and *foot* stools and *finger* bowls and *hand* bags and *arm* chairs and *head* phones – yeah, I'll bet it's real cozy, but you won't just leave, will you, no, you're gonna sit here ruining this perfectly fine sunrise, maybe if I just turn my back on you you'll get the hint, no, wait a minute, that's probably not so smart, maybe business is slow, you could be selling my body parts in the market by noon, get 'em while they're fresh, ladies and gentlemen, they're going fast, only two toes and one ankle left, okay, fair enough, but I swear, you better at least get fair market value, these bones been to college, buddy, no, wait a minute, to hell with him, I'm not turning my back on this guy, in fact I'm not letting him out of my sight, I'll look him straight in the eye, let him see who he's dealing with, okay, here we go, here's the first rays of the sun, I'll just glance at him, *hmm*, he looks kind of familiar again, like when I saw him with the flashlight, he's tall, long hair, kind of light skinned for an Indian, hazel eyes, long, thin nose, I swear, I've seen this guy somewhere, maybe it was in Bombay, or was it in Delhi, it could've been in Manali, no, wait, maybe it was that guy walking from village to village along the train tracks, I don't know, maybe not, it's still too dark to see, even now with the sun coming up he's hiding so that my body blocks the rays, well, let's see how you like this, I'll just do a quick little maneuver and fake you right out of your sleazy skin, that's right, a little basketball move, fake right, turn left, and there you are, totally exposed, man, I could dunk on you big-time right now, in your face, yes, in your face, which now I'm finally seeing in the full light and ho, ho-ho-ho, now I know who you are, how could I have missed it, it was so obvious, you know who you look like, I'll tell you who, you're an absolute spitting image, that's right, the whole package, it's really uncanny, isn't it, Mister Bone Man indeed, you had me fooled for a while, but now I've got you in my sights and guess what, the jig is up, the game is over, and now I'm running, I'm running as fast as I can, I'm running up along the river, and past the burning bodies, and over the promenade and through the twisting alleys and up into the marketplace and I'm not gonna stop running, not even for a second, because I just found out that I am one crazy motherfucker, that I am my own worst enemy, that I have just met my doppelgänger, and I am the Bone Man of Benares.

# 29

# The Essence of Time

The road through Bihar was so crowded, it seemed we were
barely moving. How anyone could survive on this parched
land was completely beyond me. As India's poorest and most
populous state, Bihar serves as a testament to human
perseverance, if nothing else, for to live there stretches the
bounds of human endurance. Still, now that Albie was gone,
the journey seemed more relaxed. Guy had left him at some
dump of a hotel on the outskirts of Benares, where he was
last seen stocking up on fried *pakoras* and *samosas*. He
was sure to have dysentery by morning, and then his diet
could begin in earnest.

I stared out the window of the van, watching India go by.
Is this all just a dream? Am I really here? Am I really in
India? I glanced at Guy's map and discovered that if I were
to travel as far away as possible from this spot, I'd wind up
in . . . Milwaukee! Yes, I'd done it, I'd gotten as far away
from Milwaukee as I could go, and you know what? I like it!
A lot! I wondered what my friends from high school were
doing now, these were important years, after all, the years to
start a family or go to medical school or start a business.
Even my friends in Amsterdam had something going, not
that a light show was exactly the stablest career one
might choose, but from this vantage point a light show
sounded downright pragmatic. I mean, what's the worst
thing that can happen to you doing a light show –
somebody boos your slides? Hell, here, they don't like

the way you sit around a *dhuni*, they sic a leper on you.

But lepers don't scare me. India doesn't scare me. The Bone Man scares me. I mean, what the hell was *that* all about? Love is not the answer? Of *course*, love is the answer. Only a truly twisted mind could think otherwise. I figured God was testing me just when I'd started to feel a little too comfortable. Well, God, if I might be so bold, you really didn't need to go that far, I mean, I know all about looking into the face of madness and all, but that was completely unnecessary. I'm sure you're up there having a real good laugh, but really, let's go a little easy here, I'm from Wisconsin – remember? – we're a little slower than most, so next time maybe you could just ease up a bit, maybe a light-ning bolt or a flood or a plague of locusts, because if you're trying to completely freak me out, you're doing way too good a job of it. So let's make a deal: How about I don't take your name in vain anymore, and you cool it with the Bone Man? We'll just forget that ever happened, okay? We'll just never mention him again. Not a word. Deal?

At Patna, we headed north for Muzaffarpur, then continued up through the Gangetic Plain to Raxaul, a sweltering border town that reminded me of the Old West. Border towns exist in their own little worlds, it's where bribery and corruption become high art, where no demand is too outrageous, where smugglers, gunrunners, dope dealers, and money launderers huddle over tea and bullets. We lined up in a caravan of cars, buses, and trucks and waited to cross into Nepal. After a lengthy inspection at the immigration post, payment of an entry fee, and another 'gratuity' just to get things moving along, we passed with surprising ease through the border.

The Terrai District, the southernmost province of Nepal, was nearly indistinguishable from Bihar, except for one thing: There were no people. Not like India, anyway, where everyone was lined up shoulder to shoulder, coast to coast. We headed due north, making reasonably good time on the broken-down, two-lane road, then we slowly began climbing the foothills of the Himalayas. At first, it reminded me of the approach to the Kulu Valley, but as we climbed higher, I realized that Kulu had given me only a taste of what was to come. The gradual ascent gave way to an abrupt rise in elevation. Up, up, up we went, the van struggling against the steep incline and the thin air. Snowcapped mountains surrounded us on all sides as the road curved precipitously along the sheer escarpments. Then we reached the ridge of a mountain pass that looked out over a broad valley. It stretched thirty miles across and was nestled between lush forests that rose up along the hills. Perhaps it was the high elevation or the angle of the setting sun or the sparkling clarity of the sky, but there was something about the view that was so welcoming I could hardly wait to make it down the long and winding road that still lay ahead of us.

I thought back to Europe, where this journey began, then to Berkeley and even Madison, where the plans were first hatched. I thought about how the road led through Amsterdam, Paris, and Greece, how for Guy and Sarah it continued through Central Asia, and how for me it detoured through East Africa. I thought about how many people had started off on this same journey, and how few had made it this far. I thought about how, of all the possible destinations, this was the farthest outpost, the most remote spot of all. Kathmandu was the end of the road.

We pulled up at Durbar Square, the central plaza of Kathmandu, and just stared out the window. I wasn't quite sure if we were in a Hindu country or a Buddhist country, in some ancient backwater or some futuristic time zone. There were temples everywhere, built almost on top of each other, some pagoda-shaped and Eastern in influence, some similar to the shrines of India, and some, well, some looking very much like spaceships pointing to the heavens. That, I wasn't prepared for. No, nothing in my journey through Asia had made me think of space travel, but here, as close to outer space as one can get on the planet, here I'm suddenly thinking of wider orbits, yes, cosmological orbits, the air is thin, after all, maybe we could just kind of float away, yes, that's what we'll do, we'll float right into the heavens.

'Let Us Take Higher'
EDEN HASHISH CENTRE
Oldest & Favourite Shop In Town Serving You the Best
Nepalese Hash & Ganja
(Available Wholesale & Retail)
COME VISIT US ANYTIME FOR ALL YOUR
HASHISH NEEDS
51 Bashantpur
Kathmandu, Nepal

I walked the streets of Kathmandu, through Durbar Square to Hanuman Dhoka, past the White Machendranath Temple to Indra Choke, down Asan Tole, across Kanti Path, and up Durbar Marg. The city was an endless marketplace of fabrics, gemstones, weavings, rugs, jewelry, beads, and incense. At the edge of town, an ancient metal footbridge swung precariously over the Bishnumati River, looking as if it were about to collapse at any moment. I stepped over a missing slat and hung onto a rope as the bridge squeaked, groaned, and swayed in every direction. The Bishnumati, which feeds into the Ganges far downstream, is a holy river and the burning ghats of Kathmandu were just below. Across from a cremation pyre, people were washing clothes, vegetables, and dishes in water that looked so polluted, I wondered if even the bacteria could survive. When I finally arrived at the other end, I felt dizzy and stood along the banks of the river, looking at the skyline of the city. The buildings were all tightly packed together with intricately carved window frames that opened up onto the sky. A tree with a thousand hanging bats swayed in the breeze. A lone kite flew in the air. The puff of a cloud hung over a Buddhist temple in the distance. It seemed not to be entirely real, no, it was like walking through an elaborate Hollywood sound stage, a big-budget production of *Lost Horizon*.

The bridge opened onto a muddy square where a couple of smelly water buffaloes stood amidst swarms of flies and mounds of excrement. From there, a path known as Pig Alley wound its way up toward the center of town. I walked past some dilapidated buildings and saw a bunch of naked kids running around with filthy faces and snotty noses. Nearby, a half-dozen pigs lolled about in muddy stink holes along the cobblestone path. I nearly gagged from the smell of their filth, but that was nothing compared to the odours wafting out of an open latrine right next to the path. There was shit everywhere – along the path, in the little crevices of the cobblestones, and everywhere in between. It was the filthiest, foulest, smelliest street in the world, and right in the middle of it, right where the buffalo, pig, and human excrement all mixed together into a big soufflé of shit, right there, was Bishnu's Pie & Chai Palace.

It was too bizarre to pass up. I pulled open a creaky screen door and stepped into a small, dark space where a couple of tables and chairs were scattered around. I'd been trying not to breathe, but now I inhaled and was amazed by the sweet scent of cooked fruit and fresh-baked dough. For a moment I thought I was in my mother's kitchen. When I glanced over to see a counter filled with apple pies, lemon-meringue pies, and chocolate-mousse pies, I was quite certain that I'd lost my mind. 'Apple pie,' I whispered to the man behind the counter.

'Will that be plain or with whipped cream?'

'Yes! Whipped cream!' I laughed, thinking how insanity was definitely underrated. That's when I heard a thump at the door. I looked over to see one of the pigs trying to nuzzle its way in, noticed a swarm of flies buzzing around the meringue, and then got a whiff of the great outdoors. Suddenly, insanity wasn't so much fun and I realized I wasn't crazy at all, at least not completely, that all of this was actually real. 'Where in God's name did you get all these pies?' I asked.

Bishnu explained that he'd been a chef for the American ambassador. The ambassador's wife, probably bored out of her mind, taught him how to make pie crusts that soon became the hit of embassy dinners. Then the ambassador got transferred and Bishnu was left with nothing but twelve pie tins – and a grand vision. 'Pie is good?' he said, offering me a taste.

'Very good, but there's just one thing,' I said as I heard a thump at the door and saw another pig pushing its way in. I nearly gagged at the smell. 'The ambassador didn't tell you the cardinal rule of embassies.'

'No?'

'Location, location, location . . .'

The Nepalese, relying on their centuries-old commercial instincts, had opened a number of establishments that catered to Western tastes. Some of the shops were so Western, they displayed photographs of Peter Sellers, which I thought was very funny. There were portraits of him everywhere – in *chai* shops, fruit stands, even government buildings. What a country this is! A nation of great comedians! 'He's a funny guy, isn't he?' I said to the manager of the Century Hotel, the small lodge where I was staying.

'That is King Birendra,' he said in hushed tones.

'Ah,' I said, 'of course.' I guess that made more sense. Birendra may have looked like Peter Sellers but he was richer than the Rockefellers. He'd inherited half the country and had shares in all of its businesses. He sold off government positions to the highest bidders, opened casinos, and, as if that weren't enough, he was also considered to be the living incarnation of Vishnu. He was God, for God's sake, and God, as any Nepali will tell you, doesn't pay taxes.

There were almost no cars in Kathmandu and the whole city moved at an unhurried pace. I, however, was moving quickly, as I wanted to get to the post office before it closed. I stopped to ask someone the time. 'Is right now 4:35,' a man said, looking at his watch.

'Good, then the post office is still open,' I said, continuing on my way.

'No, is just now 5:10,' called another man.

'So . . . the post office is closed,' I said, stopping again.

A third man checked his watch. 'Plenty time, is only 4:05.' I started.

'Not to dally,' countered a fourth guy. 'Is coming 4:55.' I stopped.

I noticed they were all wearing Indian wristwatches, which meant that somebody had probably replaced the springs with rubber bands. 'So . . . does anybody know what time it is?'

'Mine is correct time,' the first guy said with absolute certainty.

'Yes, mine too,' proclaimed the second man.

'Me, too,' said the third man.

'So is mine,' asserted the fourth man.

'You mean, each of you has the correct time?' They all nodded. 'Even though they're all different?' They each gave that little twist of the head that either meant yes, no, or maybe. Was it possible that each man believed he had the correct time, since to argue with a watch seemed to defeat the very essence of wearing a watch? It almost made sense. That it almost made sense worried me. I promised myself that if it ever *really* made sense, I would leave Nepal immediately.

The post office was still open when I got there. Judging by the three clocks on the wall, it would be closing in either five minutes, thirty minutes, or four and a half hours. The lines moved slowly, but I decided to wait. I was glad I did. There was a letter from Martine.

She wrote:

Dearest, your letter from Bombay made me very happy. It's good to know that you feel enthusiastic about India – puzzled & interested, drifted & loose maybe – in the heart of something where perhaps you can't decide yet if it's chaos or spiritual enlightenment.

Tell me how India smells & tastes, how it sings, how the music flows, how people love, laugh & live. I am dying to hear from you again, to know how you are, to share for a while this journey which, figuratively, I might have believed would be our journey . . .

Autumn is looming, a time to think & to dream, a time of maturation. Red are the leaves, mist in the morning, water on the windscreens, grapes picked up in the vineyards, kids back at school, memories sweet in the hearts, hope getting stronger, fearing the passing of time . . .

Am very busy at the moment . . . a very busy life, but not full yet. The oppression of the French administration is stronger & stronger – the machine swallows our time – but I won't be a puppet in their hands much longer.

Separation before unity, the continuing theme . . . still I find time to think of you a lot. You can't forget somebody who is always at the back of your mind & in your heart. One can be the smiling spectator of one's own busy life & actually live in one's dreams . . .

Did I tell you that I still very often wake up in Lamu among the coconut trees? Life is confusing . . . My fondest thoughts & love to you.

I wondered how long it had taken Martine to write that letter, how many times she'd checked her dictionary and grammar books, in order to try and make it perfect. I loved the little inversions and twists of language and thought about how terrible my French was, how I could never even attempt to write her in her own language. I'd been thinking a lot about Martine lately and, checking the postmark, I saw she'd responded immediately to my letter. It felt unfair, her being trapped in France and me being here, and I tried to remember once again why I hadn't tried harder to convince her to come with me. I reread the letter and stopped at the line 'to share for a while this journey which, figuratively, I might have believed would be our journey . . .'

I thought about how I'd held her in my arms and run my hand through her hair, along her cheeks, and down her neck, how her lower lip opened just slightly when I brushed my fingers against her breasts – 'Your move,' said Fedor, breaking my reverie.

'*Hmmm?*'

'Please, pay attention.' Fedor was staying in a room just

across the hall in the Century Hotel and couldn't have cared less about Martine. Fedor was either a Hungarian from Romania or a Romanian from Hungary – I could never get it straight which – who had a heart of stone, was interested only in chess, and didn't want to talk about anything unless it could be empirically proven. Why I had agreed to look for a house to rent with him was beyond me.

'You know, I really like her. She's smart, she's beautiful, she's poetic, and mostly, she has this indefinable—'

'—quality. Yes, I know. Your move.'

'I mean, it's funny, we weren't really together very long, but I feel this—'

'—closeness—'

'Yes, and a kind of—'

'—connectedness—'

'And a particular—'

'—bond—'

'Yes, and—'

'Your move!'

'Okay, sorry. Here.'

Fedor looked at the board and rolled his eyes. 'You are moving the bishop to king four? Is that the move or have I suddenly developed cataracts?'

'You know, Fedor, about that house . . .'

'Please, I cannot bear this move. I will pretend it never happened.'

'Fine.' I put the piece back and moved the knight instead. 'Check.'

'That is much better. Now I shall win in four moves instead of two.'

'Listen, it's very dark in here and I can't—'

'—think—'

'Yes, because it's late and I'm—'

'—preoccupied—'

'Yes, and I think it's better to just—'

'—surrender—'

'Yeah, that's what I'll do.'

'You have capitulated?'

'I don't know about *capitulated*. I think surrender is sufficient.'

'Surrender implies honor. Capitulation connotes weakness. Because of this letter, your mind is weak and your will is impeded. This is woman's effect upon man.'

'Listen, about that house . . .'

# 30

# The Eternal Knot

I barely had the heart to negotiate with the landlord in Swayambhu. He was wearing pants that were baggy at the top, then tapered sharply at the knee and continued down, skintight, to his ankles. His shirt had a big flap that tied with little bows beneath his armpits and down the side. He wore a Western-style sport coat that was too long at the waist and too short in the arms. His shoes had little points at the ends and on his head was a topi, a cross between a boy scout's cap and a Daniel Boone coonskin hat, only without the tail. It was a bit difficult to take him – or any of the Nepalese, for that matter – completely seriously. They looked exactly like Hobbits. In fact, rumor had it that J. R. R. Tolkien once lived in these parts and modeled Middle Earth after Nepal and the Hobbits after the Nepalese.

We agreed on 250 rupees a month – about $20 – for three small rooms stacked one above another atop Kimdol Hill. Other than a flickering of electricity that made the room seem darker whenever the bulb lit up, it had no amenities whatsoever. There was neither running water nor bathroom facilities, and I realized I'd have to use the tiny backyard as my toilet, in full view of the neighbors.

Swayambhu, a village three miles outside town, is famous for its two-thousand-year-old Buddhist temple, the oldest Tibetan temple in the world. It's perched atop a hill just behind Kimdol and was visible from the back window of the house. The front window looked out over rice paddies and then, just past the Bishnumati River, to a panoramic view of Kathmandu. Since Fedor didn't care about views, I took the top floor. I bought a straw mattress, a quilt, a couple of mats, and some candles and moved in. The first night, I noticed how the floor rippled across the room, how the walls curved, how the windows didn't really fit, and how the ceiling drooped at odd angles. It made me feel strangely comfortable to know I was living in a house that had pretty much been eyeballed together. Precision isn't particularly important to the Nepalese and I found that to be one of their more endearing qualities. Something I had noticed throughout Africa and Asia was the lack of sharp corners. In the villages there were often no corners at all, since people lived in rounded huts with curved doorways and circular window openings. It is possible to be born, live, and die in certain places without ever once encountering a ninety-degree angle. In the West, of course, most everything is square and precise and interlocks exactly into place. I began to think that sharp corners might not be so good for you.

As a candle burned down, I thought about how I'd write to Martine and tell her I imagined the two of us beneath a thatched roof somewhere, lying on a straw mattress on an uneven floor, the walls curving around us, my hands on her soft, round breasts . . .

After three nights in Swayambhu, Fedor and I decided to have dinner in town. We went to the Mandarin, a Nepalese restaurant that served Chinese food unlike anything one would find in China. Still, the restaurant was full of Westerners, most of whom were happy just to have anything that wasn't curried. 'I'm thinking of trekking up to Jomsom,' said Fedor.

'Uh-huh, sounds good.'

'They say this is the perfect time, before it gets too cold. You'll come?'

'I don't know. You think I can take my guitar?'

'What, to Jomsom?'

'Yeah. I mean, you're talking about two, three weeks, right?'

'Right.'

'No way I can leave my guitar that long.'

'I suppose you could always hire a porter to carry it for you.'

'Sure, how much could a Sherpa cost, anyway?'

'You'll probably need two Sherpas, what with all the harmonicas.'

'If I got three Sherpas, I could have backup singers.'

Fedor took a long look at me. 'You're not going to go, are you?'

'Not a chance.'

Fedor sipped some tea, then pulled out a chess book and disappeared into a study of famous openings. A waiter sauntered by, followed by a woman on her way to the cashier. I glanced around and noticed that on every table there were lamp shades made from rice paper and embossed with woodblock prints. On the walls were Tibetan *thankas* – ritualistic paintings of Buddhist deities – and on the floors were thick carpets. The cashier tallied up the woman's bill and, as she glanced at it, I noticed how she angled her head slightly to the side. I looked down at a carpet again and saw Tibetan eternal knots in each corner and borders of swirling clouds. The woman brushed her hair back and I saw how perfectly shaped her head was, like the perfect geometric form of the mandala at the center of the carpet.

I felt my mouth getting dry as I gazed into the mandala. It seemed to collapse into itself, deeper and deeper, the shapes and colors interlocking as if into a whole other dimension. I felt a strange sense of disconnectedness, as if I weren't completely there anymore, as if time and space had blended and I was in some kind of strange orbit. Visual images bombarded me as I stared into the mandala – images of snow and sand, pines and palms, canals and rivers. I saw beaches and caves and dunes, people dancing around bonfires, boats pulling into harbors, twisting alleyways leading up into hills, then more trees, a giant branch blotting out the sun, falling, falling . . .

I felt myself pushing back in my chair and getting up.

Fedor's voice slipped into my consciousness for a fleeting second, but just as quickly it was gone. I stepped into the center of the mandala, then continued walking, past the tables, past the cashier, and out the door. I found myself in the middle of Jhochen Tole, my pace quickening past the hotels and hash shops and restaurants, and then I felt a sound rising from the bottom of my stomach, right up my spine, and into my larynx. 'Annika . . .' said the sound as it pushed into the cool night air.

The woman from the restaurant turned around and looked at me for a long moment in the half-darkness of the street. 'Is it you?' she asked, a slight smile slowly forming on her lips.

I felt myself hovering just slightly outside my body, as if I were watching what was going on. 'Yes,' I said, stumbling over the words, 'it's me.'

Annika looked more beautiful than ever. Her hair had a tinge of red henna and her eyes seemed even bluer than before. She looked thinner – her cheekbones were more prominent than I remembered – but not unhealthy. 'So? So?' she said, her eyes flashing. 'Tell me everything!'

'Well, let's see,' I said, having no idea where to begin. 'I peed in the jungle.'

'Damn,' she said with a mock-serious tone, 'I can't believe I missed that.'

We looked at each other and had a good laugh. Then, finally, we hugged. I was surprised how easily it came. It felt good. 'I always wondered if I'd run into you out here,' I said.

'Lots of paths cross in Kathmandu.'

'Yeah, I suppose they do.' There seemed to be a certain neutrality in her response and I decided not to push it. 'You look good.'

'You, too. You look darker.'

'Africa does that to you.'

'Was it okay?'

'More than okay. Except for one thing. They can't speak Swedish worth shit.'

'I was afraid of that.'

'And the car company—'

'No, don't tell me it's not Fjord Motors?'

'Not even close.' Annika laughed again. I hadn't heard that laugh since Greece. 'What about you?' I asked.

'This and that . . . here and there. You know.'

This and that? Here and there? What did that mean? She was as enigmatic as ever. 'So . . . Kathmandu . . .'

'It's a real trip.'

'Yeah, it seems like. I just rented a house in Swayambhu.'

'Really? I'm visiting somebody over there tomorrow.'

'Oh? Well, maybe we could—'

'We could meet.'

'Sure, we could meet—'

'You know the big tree next to Brothers' Chai Shop?'

'Sure, sure, the big tree—'

'Say around three?'

I nodded and Annika turned to leave. 'I've thought about you a lot,' I called to her. She looked back, stared at me a moment, then turned down a side street and was gone.

'Annika?' said Fedor, furrowing his brows, 'who's this Annika? I thought you were talking about Martine.'

'That was before. This is something different. This is some mysterious force at work. This is fate. This is destiny.'

'Destiny?' said Fedor with a look of disbelief. 'Please, tell me you don't believe in destiny.'

'Listen, I'm telling you, there was a reason for all of this. What were the chances of the two of us being in the same restaurant on the same night in Kathmandu, Nepal, for God's sake?'

'I don't know. Fifty-fifty?'

'No, Fedor, the chances were not fifty-fifty. The chances were just about zero. Just like they were that we would both have been in—'

'—New York—'

'Yes, that's right, and—'

'—Stockholm—'

'Right, not to mention—'

318

'—the little club in Old Town. How many times must we discuss this?'

'I don't know. You don't seem to fully grasp the situation.'

'There *is* no situation. You met a woman, you had a fling, she dumped you, you ran into her in some restaurant a year later, and you've got a hard-on for her. That's it.'

'Okay, listen, I'm bringing her over here tomorrow. You think maybe you could—'

'—disappear for a few hours—'

'Yes, and take your laundry—'

'—off the line outside—'

'Yes, and maybe just—'

'—tidy up my room a bit? You'd like maybe some nice cut flowers?'

'That would be nice.' Fedor looked at me like I was crazy, then blew out his candle. I climbed up to my room and looked around. She'll like it here, I thought. It's big enough for us not to get in each other's way, but still cozy enough to be a nice love nest. I'll have to get a bigger mattress, maybe one stuffed with cotton instead of straw. There's room for her things in the corner, hell, she can have the whole side of the room if she wants. Maybe we'll paint the place, that should be fun, me and Annika painting side by side, me wiping a little speck of paint off her forehead, then kissing her, painting a bit more, then both of us dropping our brushes and falling onto the mattress and making love.

'I don't know what I was thinking,' she'll say.

'Listen, it doesn't matter. It's history.'

'But it does matter. I feel so stupid. A whole year that we should've been together.'

'You don't need to apologize, Annika. All I care about is that we're together again.'

' "Together again for the first time." Isn't that what some crazy movie ad said?'

'Something like that.'

'That's how I feel, like everything is new and wonderful, and yet we know each other so completely.'

'It's a great feeling, isn't it?'

319

'Promise me that we'll always be like this.'
'I promise.'
'Me, too. I don't know what I was thinking . . .'

I awoke to a beautiful day. I swept out my room, headed for the Century Hotel, paid the manager a rupee, and entered a small square room that was lit by a bare bulb swinging in a stiff breeze. The floor was wet, the walls moldy, and the room completely empty except for a shower nozzle that hung precariously from the ceiling. I stared at that nozzle and envisioned a river that started somewhere high in the Himalayas, coursed down along the frozen mountains, and stretched its icy fingers into the valley. The water came blasting out in the form of little ice pellets that shot against my chest and I understood why Tibetans never bathed. While they were busy meditating and expanding their consciousness, I was freezing my brain into some cryogenic state from which it might never recover. I quickly lathered up with Chandrika soap, rubbed in some adulterated Indian shampoo, then darted back and forth beneath the nozzle until I was rinsed off. I was back in Swayambhu by noon. By one, it had gotten surprisingly hot. By two, I'd changed my clothes. By three, I was standing under the tree outside Brothers' Chai Shop. By four, Annika finally showed up. 'Sorry I'm late,' she said.

'It's okay, you've never been on time in your life.'

'Yeah, I guess not. Especially out here. You ever notice the clocks?' I smiled and we started up the back side of Kimdol Hill. At the top of the path, Annika pointed somewhere out past Kathmandu. 'That's where I live,' she said.

'Oh? Where?'

'There,' she said, her arm sweeping out indiscriminately. It could've been Burma, for all I knew. I fumbled with the lock on the door, then led her up to the third floor. She looked around the room. 'I see you still have your rucksack.'

'It's really just getting broken in.'

Annika smiled slyly, then noticed the guitar leaning up

320

against the wall. 'Well, *that's* something new.'

'Yeah, I finally broke down and bought one.'

'Are you going to play me something?'

'I was thinking of putting on some tea.'

'C'mon, I've never known you to shy away from an audience.'

'This is different. I've only been at it a few months. It's embarrassing.'

'I'm *waiting* . . .'

'Okay, but you've been warned.' There was no way in the world, of course, that I would have let her out of there without serenading her. I played a progression on the guitar, then closed my eyes and took an extended harmonica solo. For a moment, I thought I was back on stage in Stockholm, and I could almost hear myself gigging with Per and Sten and Jan. I played some more and wondered if Annika remembered the night we met, when I carried her in my arms through Eva's apartment. Then I sang to her – a song of love and loss, hope and regret – and ended with an overtone from the guitar ringing in the air.

'Wow,' she said.

'Wow?'

'Wow.'

'You really liked it?'

'It's great. The guitar, the singing, the whole thing.'

'C'mon. The guitar's a joke and the singing—'

'I like it. That's all I can say.'

'Well . . . I'm glad.'

Annika looked around the room again and out through the window. 'It's nice here.' I could feel her relaxing.

'Let me put on some water,' I said.

'I'm afraid I don't have the time. I've got to get across the valley.'

'But . . . you just got here.'

'I know. I lost track of time over at my friend's. Can I take a rain check?'

'Yeah . . . okay . . . I just . . .' I hated that she could read the disappointment on my face. All I wanted to do was grab

321

her and pull her onto the mattress. 'I was just hoping we could talk.'

'Well, like I said—'

'I mean, shit, after all this time,' I heard myself saying.

'Was there something in particular?'

'I don't know exactly, I just thought—'

'Things change.'

'Yeah, I know. I think that's good. You've changed. I've changed.'

'Uh-huh.'

I felt myself getting weaker by the syllable. It was as if I'd been transported back to Mykonos and that nothing at all had happened in the year in between, that my life in Africa had meant nothing, that I'd learned nothing. No, it was Annika who had progressed, the gulf between us was wider than ever, she'd left me in the dust, that's what I was to her, a speck of dust – 'I just thought maybe we could spend some time—'

Annika looked at me coldly. 'What did you think, that you could just show up here and everything would be the same?'

'No, of course not.'

'I've been through a lot since Greece. This is a heavy place. It's like all the old stuff doesn't matter anymore.'

'What old stuff?'

'Listen, I can't explain. It's something you have to go through on your own. There's a lot of people out here, some of them for years, they've learned things, put a lot together. Not everybody can take it. You've got to be strong.'

'Okay, that's fine, but what about you and me?'

'I don't think you understand.'

'Maybe I don't. Do you have a boyfriend? Is that what you're trying to tell me?'

'Listen, I've really got to go,' she said, suddenly getting up. 'I'll see you in town.'

'Okay, I'm sorry. I didn't mean—'

'It's okay. The music sounds good. The harmonica is amazing. Keep playing.'

I watched as she disappeared down the stairs. I grabbed

322

the guitar and banged out a chord as jarring as a Swedish ambulance siren. It was all wrong. I wanted to erase everything that had just happened. It was all, totally, deliriously wrong.

# 31

# A Moment of Clarity

Have I mentioned that everyone is wrong about everything? When I was in junior high school, I got interested in the Pythagorean theorem. There were 16 different ways to prove that $a^2 + b^2 = c^2$ and I thought that was strange, it seemed excessive, 16 proofs, what, they weren't satisfied with 9 or 10? 'No,' some guy says, 'those are nice proofs but here's mine, it's a better proof.' What the hell does *that* mean, isn't a proof a proof, I don't know, to me the whole thing started smelling fishy, and, believe me, it *really* started smelling fishy, as in major mackerel, when *I* came up with the Seventeenth Proof of the Pythagorean theorem. Don't ask me to explain it, at this point it's way over my head, but I remember something about different lengths of colored threads that you stretched from here to there and added this or subtracted that and then, voilà, there it was, absolute, irrevocable, unequivocal proof, so much so that my teachers looked at my presentation and said, 'Yikes, he's done it, we'll make him famous, or better yet, he'll make *us* famous,' and the next thing I knew Willard Schultz had entered me into the Marquette University Science Fair, a national competition of minor note, and there I was, up against high-school juniors and seniors, unbelievable dweebs who'd constructed briefcase bombs, sonar systems, and germ warheads, and the judges look over my exhibit, 'Uh-huh, very interesting,' they say, 'the young man seems to have indeed come up with the Seventeenth Proof of the Pythagorean theorem, there's just one problem, he's awfully young, he's *too* young, we don't allow eighth-graders to compete, it's unbecoming, so listen, kid, about that prize money, the five hundred smackers, sorry but no can do, it's for the older guys, the ones going off to college, but here, have this ribbon, it's blue with gold lettering that says HONORABLE MENTION' – *honorable mention?* You don't understand, I need that money for an oxygen tank, my mother is killing me at home, and I'm starting to feel just a little pissed off about the whole deal, but I probably would have felt a whole lot worse if it weren't for one thing: Under certain strict conditions, the proof was a teensy bit flawed, okay, maybe the conditions didn't even have to be all that strict, but the thing with all those colored threads was that they didn't completely, well, add up, and in geometry, whether it be plane or solid, adding up still counted for something, but the more important thing is that I'm the *only one* who realized that possibly, just possibly, my proof was totally full of shit, and suddenly I'm beginning to wonder if the Sixteenth Proof of the Pythagorean theorem is as bogus as mine, hell, it's probably *flimsier* than mine, and what about the Fifteenth and Fourteenth Proofs, I'm getting a bit suspicious, hell, I'm getting very suspicious, that when you get right down to it, five will get you ten that $a^2 + b^2$ *does not* equal $c^2$ at all, and you know what, while we're at it, e does not equal $mc^2$, speed does not equal distance times time, and there's no such thing as id, or ego, or superego. Even if those theories aren't total hogwash, they're only half-truths at best, they're enough to get electricity flowing and atoms smashing, but they'll all be overthrown in due time as the childish fumblings of an infantile civilization.

Nepal's civilization was anything but infantile. It was old, plenty old, and like anything old, it tends to get cranky from time to time. Durga Puja was one of those times. On the ninth day of Durga Puja, the streets flowed with the blood of sheep, goats, and chickens whose heads had been lopped off to sate the appetite of goddess Durga. There was blood everywhere – poured onto the front of buses for good luck, dripped over the entrances of buildings, and smeared onto thousands of Hindu statues. Meanwhile, a hundred Buddhist monks sat high up in the temple of Swayambhu, praying for the departed animal spirits whose souls were transmigrating into the ether. Still, better that than virgins, who not so long ago were sacrificed on this day. If you were a virgin in nineteenth-century Nepal, it was a good idea to call in sick on the ninth day of Durga Puja.

Dewali, the Festival of Light, followed Durga Puja, and every doorway, window, and alcove was filled with tiny mustard-oil lamps. The festival honored Laxmi, the goddess of prosperity, and for a few days the city *did* look prosperous as it became transformed into a fantasy-land of shimmering light. It was fall, it was the season of festivals, and for most of the Westerners it was the perfect time to leave. The cold winter lay ahead and each day more of them departed for Europe, the Far East, or the beaches of Goa. As for me, I decided to cast my lot with the crazies of Kathmandu, the hard core who braved the winters and were permanent residents of the scene. One night I heard music coming from inside a courtyard and pushed open a half-hidden gate to find a subterranean dive called the Eclipse. At the far end of a crowded bar, an archway opened onto a larger room where platforms were built into the walls, then covered with carpets and pillows. No sooner did I find a spot than a little girl, no more than five years old, peeked out from behind a big pillow. 'So, do elephants have good memories or not?' she asked.

'Well, that depends,' I replied, looking into her enormous blue eyes.

'On what?'

'On whether anything interesting ever happened to them.'

'What d'you mean?'

'Well, some elephants have very exciting lives so, of course, they want to remember all the good stuff. Other elephants, sad to say, lead very boring lives, so there's really nothing much for them to remember.'

'See!' she called to another girl, who was maybe two years older. 'I told you so!' She then turned back to me. 'Lucinda says elephants can't remember anything.'

'And Jillian believes anything anyone tells her,' said Lucinda, looking at me with suspicion.

'Oh, no, it's true,' I said. 'I used to live with elephants.'

'*Really?*' said Jillian, her eyes almost popping out of her head.'

'Where?' asked Lucinda, still suspicious.

'In Africa. That's where the really big elephants are. Why, I used to know one family of elephants that had especially good memories because they had so many adventures.'

'*Really?*' said Jillian.

'Sure, there was Elmer the Elephant and Ella the Elephant, and they had two kids named Elton and Elfinetza-letza-metza.'

'*What?*' they both said, giggling.

'Well, they usually just called her Elfie.'

'Do you want a chillum?' asked Lucinda.

'*Uh* . . . sure.'

'They're not bothering you, are they?' came a voice in a soft Southern accent. I looked behind us, where a woman was chipping hash into a pile on her lap. She wore an embroidered Afghani blouse, a pair of intricately carved tribal bracelets, and a matching carnelian necklace.

'Not at all. Are they yours?'

'They most certainly are,' she smiled as she glanced up and brushed her long hair off a pretty face. 'I'm Delia.'

'Elfie's my favorite,' said Jillian. 'Did she have any adventures?'

'Are you kidding? Elfie had so many adventures, she could've written a book.'

'Careful,' whispered Delia, 'you don't know what you're getting yourself into.'

'Like what?' asked Jillian.

'Well? there was the time that Elfie met the famous Masai warriors of the Ngorongoro Crater, or the time she helped free a chimpanzee from a cage, or the time she climbed a tree to save a baby bird—'

'Elephants can't climb trees!' exclaimed Lucinda.

'Wanna bet?'

Delia pushed a rope through the chillum and handed me one end. I pulled it tight as she rubbed out the inside residue. 'You new around here?'

'Pretty much so. I've been over in Swayambhu the last couple of weeks.'

'That's where we live. In Bir Singh's Garden.'

'Really? I'm just up the hill.'

'I want to hear about the baby bird,' said Jillian, pulling on my arm.

'Me, too,' said Lucinda.

'Well, maybe one day—'

'Can he come over sometime, Mommy?' said Jillian.

'Well, of course, if he wants to.'

'That settles it, then,' I said. 'I owe you each a bedtime story.'

'Mommy's got a boyfriend, you know,' said Lucinda, narrowing her eyes.

'Yeah, but he's in Afghanistan,' said Jillian, optimistic as could be.

Delia blushed slightly, then prepared the chillum and handed it to me to light. 'You probably don't know anyone here,' she said, pointing to the bar. 'Well, down there, that's Paul. The Eclipse is his place.' Paul looked to be in his mid-thirties, with long hair, a beard, and piercing blue eyes that lit up with laughter. 'Paul's kind of the grandfather of the scene. Been here forever.' Delia pointed out some other people in the room. There was Angus MacLise, a Beat poet and musician from New York who had a wife and child living up in the monastery. Angus roamed around most of the time looking for his next fix, but back in his Greenwich Village days, he'd been Lou Reed's first drummer for the Velvet Underground. There was Ira Cohen, a poet, film-maker, and photographer who looked like a sage from sixteenth-century Japan, with his balding pate, long beard, black-velvet cape, purple shirt, and silver scarf. Ira had directed an underground classic called *Thunderbolt Pagoda*, a surrealistic interpretation of an opium dream. There was Petra Vogt, Ira's consort, her black hair sweeping to a severe widow's peak, her eyes and lips painted purple and outlined in silver. Petra had trained as a classical actress in Berlin but had run off with the legendary Living Theater and now looked strikingly like Kali, the goddess of death and destruction. There was Jasper, a dapper Londoner who couldn't decide between the life of a holy man and the life of an alcoholic, so simply combined the two. There was Keith, an Oxford scholar who translated ancient Buddhist texts, and beautiful Kiran the Nepalese girl with track marks up her arms. There was Italian Carlotta, who looked like she'd just stepped off the set of a Fellini film, and several members of the Hog Farm, who'd come out of Ken Kesey's acid tests and driven a bus to Kathmandu. There was English Graham, Austrian Wolfe, and oh, yes, that's Swedish Annika, pretty, isn't she, she came across with the Hog Farm from Greece and lives on the other side of the valley.

There was Eric the poet, Dana the woodblock artist, Stefano the jeweler, German Henry, Greek George, Tent Tom, John Chick, Dharma Dan, Bodha Lynn, Charles the tabla player, Andrea the dancer, and Leigh the *thanka* painter, and as I walked out onto the street later that night, my head buzzing with names and faces and endless stories, I wondered why Annika had whispered into Wolfe's ear and left the Eclipse before I even had a chance to say hello.

Swayambhu and Bodha were the two main villages where Westerners lived. They're on opposite sides of the valley, perhaps fifteen miles apart, with Kathmandu itself lying directly between them. While the villages have many similarities – both are home to important Buddhist temples, both are populated by large numbers of Tibetan refugees – the Western populations couldn't have been more different.

The Westerners in Bodha wore jeans and lumberjack shirts. The Westerners in Swayambhu wore pajama pants and Indian vests. The Westerners in Bodha lived in concrete houses with electricity, running water, and indoor toilets.

The Westerners in Swayambhu lived in houses with thatched roofs and no chimneys. The Westerners in Bodha rode motorcycles and horses. The Westerners in Swayambhu piled eight to a taxi or, more frequently, walked.

The Westerners in Bodha drank alcohol and snorted cocaine. The Westerners in Swayambhu smoked hash and sniffed heroin. The Westerners in Bodha exported carpets to friends in the West to support their lifestyle. The Westerners in Swayambhu no longer knew anyone in the West. The Westerners in Bodha listened to the Eagles. The Westerners in Swayambhu listened to Van Morrison. The Westerners in Bodha were tough guys who climbed mountains and trekked to the middle of nowhere. The Westerners in Swayambhu had lungs so shot, they could barely make it up the hills to their houses.

It was a little like the Hatfields and McCoys, except that the Westerners in Bodha were too drunk and the Westerners in Swayambhu too stoned to ever do anything about it.

I lived in Swayambhu.

Annika lived in Bodha.


A letter arrived from Little Ali, who said that his group, now the toast of Lamu, was looking for a harmonica player. Sultan sent his regards, asked about Martine, and hoped that someday we'd return so that we could all sail together to Zanzibar on . . . his new dhow! Inside was a photo of the boat being readied for its maiden voyage. Sultan was pointing to the wooden eyes at the front of the dhow and, although I couldn't be certain, I'm pretty sure he was winking at me. '*Barua ni nusu kuona*,' he wrote, '*nataka kusikia*.' Yes, 'a letter is half as good as seeing someone,' and I wanted to tell them everything that had happened since I left Lamu. I wrote back about the ship to Bombay, the train to Delhi, and the bus to Kulu. I wrote about the beggars of Karachi, the Tibetans of Manali, and the holy men of Benares. Most of all, I said how much I missed them, how much I missed Lamu, and how much I missed Martine.

It had been a month since I'd gotten her letter, and I still hadn't responded. What could I say to her? That she could be here right now? That we'd walk through the marketplace and find the perfect piece of red velvet to wrap around her waist? That we'd sip tea in some dark smoky restaurant and touch fingers beneath the table? That we'd lie together in the cold evening under a cotton quilt and awaken in each other's arms? That if only I had asked—

I suddenly wished I was back in Africa, on the shores of the Indian Ocean, at the place where we met, yes, we'd sail to Zanzibar, we'd secretly slip into port late one night and get lost in the old city, we'd drink palm wine in some seedy bar, dance to a harmonium under the sliver of a moon, and make love in a hotel room with the scent of cloves wafting in on the cool sea breeze.

I crossed Durbar Square and saw Annika in the distance. It was strange how inextricably she and Martine were linked together. If I thought about Annika, I'd get a letter from Martine. If I thought about Martine, I'd see Annika. It had been two weeks since that night at the Eclipse, and now she was walking right towards me – Annika, whose image was ingrained into the back of my mind like an undeveloped snapshot, Annika, whose memory always hung over me, unresolved. She'd have some explanation for avoiding me that night, that's for sure, and I'd be understanding, yes, of course I would, but then, just as she caught sight of me, just like that, she veered away. There hadn't been a second's hesitation, not even the slightest breaking of stride, as she moved across the square and disappeared into the market-place. I stood there and felt a chill at the base of my spine. For a moment, I imagined myself some prehistoric fish, a coelacanth perhaps, that had swallowed a hook and was being yanked up from the depths of the ocean. My lungs were about to explode, my fins were limp, and my gills were pounding in my brain. Yes, don't you see what's happening? You've been cast aside. Thrown overboard. Boned and gutted. How much proof do you need?

That night, sitting alone in my house atop Kimdol Hill, I

thought about what a fool I was, what a spectacular, magnificent, stupendous fool of a fool. Fedor was right, I was holding onto some fantasy that had gone stale months ago. All it took was the tiniest gesture in the marketplace to finally deliver the message. What the hell was wrong with me? It had been obvious for over a year now. Annika couldn't care less about me. It's Martine who cares. Annika is some twisted fantasy figure. Martine is my soul mate. Annika is the past. Martine is the future.

I found myself writing Martine's name across the top of a letter and immediately felt a weight lifting. I told her how much I missed her, how I could almost feel her sitting next to me right now, how the sounds of Tibetan horns were pulsating down from Swayambhu Temple, how the first rays of the sun were peeking over the snowcapped mountains, how the pagoda-shaped roofs of the city were just coming into view. And then I told her how much I wanted to see her, how I would go to France in the spring and how we'd sit in the cafés of her village and walk through the vineyards of the countryside and make love until late into the night. As the sun rose on the icy early morning, I sealed the letter and fell into a deep, warm sleep.

The Bakery, an old bread factory that had been boarded up for months, was suddenly bustling with activity. As I watched some workmen sprucing it up, two Americans came out to greet me. They were wearing saffron robes and had shaved heads, except for little squiggles of hair growing out the back. When I realized who they were – *Hare Krishnas!* – I tried to escape, but it was too late. I was surrounded. That I could be surrounded by only two people was a little scary. Where did they think we were, at some airport? 'I'm Rajaram,' said the taller of the two.

'I'm Devagiri,' said his frail partner, putting out a hand to shake.

'*Soooo* . . . moving in?' I said, hoping against hope.

'We're opening the 103rd international Hare Krishna temple,' Rajaram said. 'We'll have meditation rooms, lecture halls, and living quarters. You should stop by.'

'Uh-huh,' I said, looking for a way out.

'Swami Bhaktivedanta sent us to be the vanguard,' said Devagiri.

'It's a big job, opening a temple. Swami doesn't trust it to just anyone.'

'A *very* big job,' said Rajaram, eyeing me a little too closely. 'We'll need help.'

'Yeah, well, good luck,' I said, finally breaking free.

Another voice called from down the path. 'Ho-*ho*!!!' I looked over to see Paul, the owner of the Eclipse, bounding up the hill. 'The Bakery . . . back in action!'

'Yes,' said Devagiri, 'we're opening the one hundred and—'

'You've got to have a full-moon party!' said Paul.

'Well, I don't know . . .'

'Of course you will. These are sacred grounds. We used to party like crazy up here.'

'Yes, but that's not really the purpose—'

'You see that field over there? We had a big sound system set up, drew people from all over town.'

Rajaram's eyes widened in anticipation of all the potential converts. 'It could be interesting . . .'

'Interesting? Staring into my soup is interesting. I'm talking about a true, transcendental experience. You guys swing that way, don't you?'

'Well . . . of course.'

'All right, then. You've got ten days to get it together. That's plenty of time.'

'I suppose it would be possible . . .' said Devagiri.

'*Jeldi! Jeldi!*' Paul yelled to the workmen, urging them on. He then turned back to Rajaram and Devagiri. 'I'll tell everyone to be here.'

'Good,' said Rajaram, 'it'll give us something to shoot for.'

'Beautiful, babe,' said Paul, putting his arms around the Krishnas. He then looked at me, smiled slyly, and hurried up the hill.

\* \* \*

333

It was approaching two months since I'd arrived in Nepal and with that came the end of my free ride with the Department of Immigration. Visitors were allowed one month on their visa and a one-month extension, but then had to leave the country for a few months before applying for reentry. Fortunately, there was a way out of this – in Asia, there is *always* a way out – that involved high bribery to low places, otherwise known as baksheesh. If you wanted to send a package out of the country, baksheesh made sure it left the post office. If you wanted to fill that package with priceless antiquities, baksheesh guaranteed it would never get opened. If you wanted to ship the whole damn country to the south of France, baksheesh was your answer. Baksheesh got your electricity turned on, your taxi meter turned off, and your harmonicas out of customs. When I first arrived in Nepal, I saw baksheesh as some kind of evil. Now, with my visa magically extended, I had a whole new perspective: Baksheesh, baby, don't leave home without it.

On the night of the full moon, I was surprised to find the Bakery actually up and running. Rajaram and Devagiri had painted the rooms with motifs from the Bhagavad Gita and had books and tapes of Swami Bhaktivedanta at every turn. It was a sedate affair when I arrived, with a dozen people milling around as an evening raga droned on and the sweet smell of incense filled the air. Then, as the moon rose halfway up the sky, Paul showed up with a ragtag bunch of Kathmandu old-timers and everything changed. The raga was popped out of the tape recorder and the Rolling Stones jammed in. The displays of books were shoved against the wall to make room for a dance floor. The door to the kitchen, where Devagiri was cooking up traditional Indian sweets, was closed to improve the ambience. Then a dozen chillums appeared and the room was covered in a giant mushroom cloud of hash smoke. When Rajaram, who'd been giving a tour of the inner meditation rooms, came out to see what the ruckus was all about, his Hare Krishna ponytail nearly spun around in circles. He located

Paul in the middle of the room and hurried over. 'Please, please,' he said breathlessly.

'Hey, babe,' said Paul, offering him a chillum, 'great party.'

'I've got to ask you not to smoke in here. This is a holy place.'

'I know, man, it's the old Bakery, bigger and better than ever. I love what you did with the walls.'

Crazy Helen, a wild woman from the north of England, came by looking like a demented fairy princess. 'Acid . . . acid . . . who wants acid?' she said, holding a magic wand in one hand and a jar of LSD in the other.

'Acid?' said Rajaram. 'Oh, my God, what's going on here?'

'You've been away a long time, babe. Have a hit. It won't kill you.'

The party raged on as more and more people showed up. Helen kept tapping everyone with her magic wand until we were all stoned. The entire building began throbbing and swaying, while on the next hill over Swayambhu Temple glowed like a golden spaceship, ready to blast off from its Himalayan launching pad. Italian Carlotta showed up with plastic Hindu gods tied into her hair, Helen stripped naked, Ira wrote on a scrap of paper, Petra played violin, Angus beat against an Ethiopian kettledrum, Delia danced with abandon, and Jasper sipped from his flask. Paul looked happier than any man has a right to be, his eyes glistening as he looked out over the reborn Bakery.

I don't know what happened with the Hare Krishnas, if somebody dosed them or if they took acid voluntarily, but they were reintroduced to Western culture with a bang. Rajaram discovered Jimi Hendrix and was flying around the room as if he'd finally found nirvana. Devagiri never got out of the kitchen, but the last time I saw him, he had the most insane look in his eyes, stirring and stirring and stirring the sweets until there were huge blocks of candy overflowing from the pots, down along the counters, and onto the floor. Around four in the morning, when the party seemed in danger of breaking up, Paul walked to the center of the room, surveyed the scene, and began quietly chanting. After several moments a few people joined him, then a few more and then the entire room was standing and chanting – a deep, beautiful, transcendent sound that resonated throughout the building and broke down along the hillside like a fine morning mist.

'*Hare Krishna, Hare Krishna, Krishna Krishna, Hare Hare . . .*'

At first I thought it was a joke, but then I realized that Paul was dead-serious; I stood off to the side, watching and listening as everyone grabbed a drum or a cymbal or anything else that was at hand and the whole room began to rumble as the chanting grew louder and louder.

'*Hare Rama, Hare Rama, Rama Rama, Hare Hare . . .*'

I felt a jolt of energy coursing up my spine. I'm in Kathmandu, I kept telling myself, as the sounds began to permeate every pore of my body, it's a full moon, I'm in a glorious valley on the top of the world, I'm actually here, surrounded by the most extraordinary group of people, yes, I'm actually here, and the chanting is building and building until it becomes one great shout of ecstasy, and suddenly I'm chanting too, I've moved into the circle, I'm pounding on a drum, and I'm looking into the eyes of the people around me and I'm feeling part of something big and glorious and magnificently insane.

'*Hare Krishna, Hare Krishna, Krishna Krishna, Hare Hare . . .*'

# 32

## The Hands of Chance

The days passed, the end of December approached, and I settled into a pattern of living in Swayambhu. I played guitar by day, read by night, and woke up every morning to little clouds of condensation hanging in the air. At first, I tried not to breathe quite so much, but then I figured, not to worry, chicken curry, it's too cold to rain anyway. A few days before Christmas, I journeyed to Nagarcote, a village on the rim of the valley, to take in the view of Everest. Despite the spectacular panorama, I felt uncomfortable staring out at the world's tallest mountain. It was like looking through a telescope at another planet, for it seemed as if nothing should really be that high, or that austere, or that remote. The mountain looked like some strange cutout pasted onto the sky. As I gazed out over the Himalayas, I kept thinking about Martine. A month had passed since I'd written her, but there'd been no response. Had the mail gotten through? Had something changed? Was she having second thoughts? I stared into the mountains, imagining Martine's face in the cliffs, feeling strangely disconnected.

Thirteen days into the New Year, two letters arrived from France. One was mailed directly, the other sent to my parents' address and forwarded. I figured Martine wanted to make sure she reached me. The minute I got outside the post office, I ripped open the first letter. It was dated December 22, 1973. Three *weeks* to get to Nepal. Martine wrote:

Dearest, I am very sorry for this delayed answer. Never before in my life has time been so swallowing, pulling me behind because of so much work & pushing me forward because it's all so empty . . .

I kept postponing writing to you because I just wanted to find a relaxed moment, a moment to forget what is going around, the pressures & stress. Today I finally am writing in a train, on my way to Paris, and then to Marrakesh for Christmas holiday. A long-awaited departure . . . a break and a renewal.

I spent the past few months – because I can't escape it now – in a very little village on the river Seine. I work in the local secondary school, very difficult kids & a hopeless direction. Am exhausted & far from feeling this job as a passion. One way or another, next year will see me somewhere else in the world. . .

Yes, I am going to Marrakesh just now. Will I tell you how life is confusing? Sometime, perhaps. Confusing . . . confusing . . . the demands of life . . . and the eternal 'Who knows?' I think of you very often with much love & nice memories, wondering how life will mix it up for us.

I stared at the letter, not sure what to think. The handwriting was irregular and had almost a frantic quality to it. Martine kept talking about the future, but why no mention of my plans to visit her? Had she even gotten my letter? Then again, she was writing from a train on her way to the airport and was a bit scattered. Surely the other letter would explain it all. I went to open it.

'Hey, babe, want a lift?' called a voice from the road. I looked up to see Paul jammed into a taxi with Leigh, Jasper, and Andrea.

'Is there room?'

'Are you kidding? We haven't even started on the roof yet.' I put the letters into my pocket and squeezed into the backseat. The taxi drove toward Tamil, crossed the Bishnumati, nearly hit a goat, swung around the old museum, tore down a straightaway, and screeched to a halt on the main drag of

Swayambhu. I slipped into Lobsang's Chai Shop and pulled out Martine's letters just as Angus walked in and headed straight for my table. 'You busy?' he said.

'Actually, I was just about to—'

'Good,' he said, sitting down. 'I want you to look at something.' He unrolled a long parchment and stretched it out on the table. Etched across the rice paper was an exotic musical notation that he'd transliterated from ancient Tibetan texts. 'It's the score for the Mahakala Puja,' he said, referring to the daily prayers to one of Buddhism's most important deities. I looked at a series of long, swooping symbols, a beautiful calligraphy that rose and fell like a jazz improvisation. 'It's for the *radongs*,' he said, referring to the eight-foot-long Tibetan horns whose tones shook the valley every evening. 'As the line thickens, the music becomes louder; as it rises, the pitch rises; the breaks and swirls indicate tone and tempo; those little curls represent tremolo; the dashes are for vibrato.' Then he read from an accompanying poem:

Great dark Mahakala
Terrible one
Destroyer of the Enemy
Guardian of Cosmic Laws
Unflagging and unrelenting in the defense of Dharma.

I climbed the path up Kimdol Hill, passed Bir Singh's Garden, and heard a voice calling out, '*Yoo-hooo*.' I glanced inside the gates to see Delia sitting on her porch, chipping away at a block of hash and looking for all the world as if she were back on her parents' estate in Alabama. By the time we got inside, Lucinda and Jillian, who'd spent almost their entire lives in the East, were getting ready for bed. The moment they saw me, they started squealing, 'Elfie! Elfie!'

'Uh-oh,' said Delia.

'It's okay,' I said.

'*Yay!!!*' said the girls as they snuggled under their quilts.

'Well, one day, Elfie, who of course was just about the

sweetest little elephant you could ever hope to meet, was walking in the jungle when who should she meet but a little boy who was just sitting there, all alone,' I said, making it up as I went along. '"Who are you?" asked Elfie, and the boy, who was so afraid that he could hardly speak, said "I'm lost . . ."' By the time Delia got the chillum prepared, Elfie not only wound up taking the boy back to his village, but saved a giraffe who had a terrible crick in her neck, got a goofy-looking warthog to think better of himself, and helped stomp out a forest fire. With the kids falling asleep, Delia looking especially pretty, and Van Morrison playing in the background, I didn't want to leave. Then I thought about her boyfriend in Afghanistan and Martine in France and pulled myself away.

'*Mmmmmwwwaaaaaaaaa.*'

I heard the deep tones of Tibetan horns from high in the stupa as I headed up the hill. The sounds cut through the cold, misty night as I made my way along the dark path with just the sliver of a waning moon to guide me. Closer to my house, a pack of wild dogs, unused to the scent of foreigners, lunged at a rickety fence, straining to get through.

'*Mmmmmwwwaaaaaaaaa.*'

I quickened my pace, slipping a little on some damp cobblestones, then turned onto the path that led to my front door. Inside the house, the wind whistled through a crack in the window and it took three matches before I could get a candle to stay lit. Cold and tired, I got undressed, wrapped the quilt around me, and collapsed onto my mattress.

'*Mmmmmwwwaaaaaaaaa.*'

The horns sent a shiver down my back and I pulled the quilt tighter around me. I began fading off into sleep when a thought jolted me awake. I hadn't read Martine's second letter . . .

I fumbled around for my coat, pulled the letters out of the pocket, and reread the first one in the flickering light. Again, I thought about how strange and ambiguous it seemed. It was almost as if, between the lines, something was fading out. I picked up the second letter and noticed that the hand-writing looked unfamiliar. It was dated December 26 and postmarked Charleville, France. I slit open the envelope. The letter read:

> Please excuse me, but I really do not know how to start this letter, for it is a painful duty for me to have to write to you and yet I feel I must do it. It is because I am one of Martine's dearest friends that I take pen and paper and sit down to write to you today.
>
> We went camping together in September in the forest of the Ardennes and had a marvellous week. We talked a lot, cycled, rambled in the woods, ate blackberries, dreamt about Africa . . .
>
> We also exchanged the addresses of our best friends with a promise that if anything happened to either of us, the other would tell it immediately. I'd rather never have written to you because my sorrow is so deep now. Martine is dead. Her plane of last Saturday, 22 December, left Paris on Saturday night and crashed in the surroundings of Tangier in Morocco in the mountains of the Rif. There were no survivors. I heard the news yesterday, on Christmas Day.
>
> I just fulfilled Martine's wish in informing you. She has told me so much about you and about her trip last summer in Tanzania and Kenya that I thought you would much more appreciate to be informed of her death by a friend of hers than by any official source. If I hear of more precise details about her tragic end, I'll keep you duly informed. Best regards.

It took a while before a light snapped on inside Delia's house. Finally, the door opened and she took a long look at me. 'Are you okay?' I heard her say.

I just stood there, unable to make the words come out. All I could think about was how the world takes our innocence and turns it against us, it turns us on each other and maims and mutilates us, it rips our insides out and dulls us to our pains, it beats and stabs and slashes at us until we become as hateful as the gods who manipulate us as their perverse play-things, and then, for those special few who don't succumb to its evils, it saves its special horrors, because in the end, it murders them most cruelly of all.

Delia's jaw quivered. 'You'd better come in,' she said.

A dozen monkeys scampered among the stone Buddhas that lined the steps to Swayambhu Temple. I'd been there many times, to study the *thankas*, or spin the prayer wheels, or sometimes just to look at the view of Kathmandu and the surrounding mountains. This time was different. I was there because I couldn't think of anywhere else to go. I felt a strange sense of calm once I was ushered in to see the *rinpoche*, the head of the temple. A monk whispered into his ear – telling him, no doubt, why I was there – and the *rinpoche* looked at me for a long moment. Then he nodded and tied a white scarf around my neck. I put a hundred-rupee note into a basket, then was led to the main room of the temple, where monks were chanting their daily prayers. I was told to place money in front of each monk, in order for them to pray for Martine. It felt strange, so blatant, like I was buying them off, but I forgot about it once they began intoning the prayers.

Their voices rose and fell like Tibetan horns, and I pictured the long, sweeping calligraphy of the music scores. Then a deep rumble arose from their throats and rever-berated into a prolonged whisper, like tiny helicopter blades cutting through the air. I wondered what they were saying, if they really understood, if they could imagine Martine lying beneath a coconut palm in Lamu. 'How long since she died?' I heard a voice saying.

I turned to see a black-haired woman in a Tibetan dress, wearing a *mala* and a string of coral and turquoise. It took me a moment, as I looked at her more closely, to realize she wasn't Tibetan at all. 'Twenty-four days,' I said.

'It's good that you're here, then,' she said in a Scottish accent. 'This is a difficult day on the *bardo*.' She explained how the *Tibetan Book of the Dead* teaches that in the forty-nine-day passage from death to rebirth, the soul needs assistance in the transition and that the monks could be of help. 'She will confront many things on her journey, some beautiful beyond belief, some more terrifying than we can imagine. The prayers will give her strength.' The woman stood with me as the prayers continued. I looked into the faces of the monks and saw that some were no more than children. One of them had blond hair. 'That's Ossian,' she said, 'and I'm Hettie.' I recognized the names. Hettie was Angus's wife and Ossian was their son. He was five years old.

When the prayers ended, I walked outside and stood under the all-seeing eyes of the Buddha, which were painted on the side of the stupa. I stared into the range of hills just beyond Swayambhu and wondered if this was what the Rif mountains looked like. A cold breeze kicked up and the hundreds of white prayer flags hanging from the temple began flapping in the wind. I buttoned my jacket up around my neck, spun one of the prayer wheels, and walked home.

Odette, Martine's friend from the Africa trip, wrote a few days later:

> I can't admit the reality. The revolt is in my heart when I think about this terrible thing. Martine was so a nice girl, so a good friend for many people.
>
> I know how Martine enjoyed your company. We have often spoken about you for long times in Africa, then in France – it's because I write you. She was so happy by your future arrival in France. How Martine has loved you! It was a short time in Africa but it was a big happiness for her and it was marvelous for her that you come in spring.
>
> Yesterday I have seen her parents. Poor people. Martine was their single child. She was their reason to life. Now they have nothing. Mrs Galland, the mother of Martine, has said to me I write you that you stop to travel in order that it does not happened the same accident for you. These were her own words.

Can I ask to you something? I do not want to be indiscreet but I should like to know something. Martine told me that you looked at her hand's lines and predicted to her a long life. What do you think about it?

I wish you much courage. Live with Martine's memory, and think of how she so felt life, by her eyes, by her ears, by her hands, by her impulses, by her smile, by her breath. We must somehow go on and still gather some roses of Life. It is Life against Death. We are between the hands of Chance.

I threw away Cheiro's *Language of the Hand* that day. Perhaps palmistry could unlock a thousand secrets, but I was not the person to do it, that much I knew. I tried to find some kind of meaning in Martine's death, but I too felt a 'revolt in the heart.' If there wasn't a place on this planet for a soul as pure as Martine's, then in what kind of world were we trapped? Perhaps there was an answer for me at Swayambhu Temple, or maybe with the Hindus down at the river, or with Rajaram and Devagiri, or up in some cave in the mountains. I was surrounded by monks, lamas, sadhus, and gurus – surely someone could explain to me why Martine had vanished into a mountain of burning sand in the desert.

I was haunted by images of her last moments. What was she thinking as the plane spun out of control, what terror flashed through her mind? Tell me it wasn't me, Martine, to whom you'd written only hours before, tell me it wasn't me whose picture appeared, because I cannot bear the weight of your life culminating in this way, of meeting on the dance floor at Petley's Inn, walking through the crooked alleyways of Lamu, making love in Haji's *shamba*, no, I cannot bear the thought of your final memories, of strolling along the beach in Shela, imagining India beneath a swaying palm tree, feeling the fingertips of warm white sand, no, I cannot bear the crush of memories now, flying flying flying by in a tailspin, soundless images speeding through the low African sky, of mango blossoms and harmoniums and the smile of childhood and the scent of a soft midnight breeze, of a ferryboat pulling out to sea, of a final glance, the glance that only lovers make when everyone else has turned away, the wave of long thin fingers kissing the sky, no, I cannot bear the responsibility of keeping these images alive, for I am hollow inside, I am twisted, I want at this very moment, in this deep and sickening sorrow, to rip off your clothes and fuck & fuck & fuck until there is nothing left anymore, nothing left of our bodies, nothing left of our future, nothing left of our memories—

There was a knock on the door. I didn't answer it at first, but when the rapping continued, I finally climbed down from the third floor and opened the door a crack. It was Annika. 'I heard what happened,' she said. 'I'm sorry.' I stood there a moment, trying to put together what was happening. 'Can I . . . come in?' My mind felt dull as I pulled open the door and followed her upstairs. What was she doing here, now of all times? 'Do you want to talk about it?' she said.

'I don't know what I would say.'

'Okay. It's up to you. Should I make some tea?'

I felt my face flushing as Annika went to put on the water. Something clenched me from inside, grabbing and twisting my intestines like an iron glove, as I realized I was counting the seconds for her return. Annika – the very reason I hadn't convinced Martine to come with me to India – was downstairs at this very moment. Would I tell her how we were complicit in her death, how it could be Martine right now making tea and putting biscuits on a plate and closing the door against the icy afternoon wind? Forgive me, Martine, I wanted to scream, please, expunge my face from your memories, for even now, in my deepest sadness, even now, thoughts of Annika crash into my consciousness despite my every effort to quiet them, even now, I want her, and I am so terribly ashamed of myself, more than I can ever remember.

I felt the guitar in my hands for the first time in days. The chords hung in the air as I played and played, and when I opened my eyes, the sun was going down, Annika was gone; there was a cold cup of tea next to me, and a sprig of white rhododendrons in a pot on the floor.

Asia is a mass of contradictions. Nothing is real except for one's conception of reality and, in the end, that's the most unreal thing of all. Asia is compassion and detachment, renunciation and greed, nonviolence and slaughter, all rolled into one. Asia is Indian gurus wearing watches, Tibetan monks eating beef, Nepalese holy men drunk on wine, and all of it makes perfect sense, for Asia, with all of its ancient teachings, is the most malleable land of all. It will accommodate any viewpoint into its pantheon of ideas and throw it back at you to contemplate for an eternity.

My own contradictions rose to the surface as if my subconscious had vomited them up. I wanted to both empty my mind and fill it at the same time, to forget Martine and hold on to her, to escape Annika and chase after her. Most of all, I wanted to just stop thinking. The winter went by in a blur. I stayed home most of the time, reading, playing guitar, feeling both solitary and overly conspicuous within the village. I experimented with more chords and discovered I could get a drone sound by leaving one string unfretted. It reminded me of the tamburas in Benares, but mostly I just hoped that the music could block out the pain, that the wail of the harmonica and the growl of the Tibetan horns would intermix into oblivion.

As spring approached, I escaped to Pokhara, a small village nestled into the foothills of Mount Annapurna, a hulking mass that rose straight up and disappeared into the clouds. In the shadows of the mountain, my problems seemed dwarfed for a few days, but the quiet left me too alone with my thoughts and I returned to Kathmandu a week later.

A letter was waiting for me when I arrived. It was from Martine's mother, who finally had the strength to write. She spoke of sadness and loneliness and memories of Martine:

> After her return from Africa, she confided in me her love and every time she came to visit, she spoke of you and of her hope to see you in the spring. She even drew me your portrait on a

little piece of paper as she knew how to do so well. In our mutual sadness, my husband joins with me to embrace you like a son, which you might have been.

Her pain and emptiness bled through the paper as she ended with the starkest finality:

We brought Martine back to the little cemetery in Marolles.

What more, really, could ever be said?

Eventually, the letters stopped. It was early spring. The long, dead winter was ending.

# 33

## Journey into Night

With spring came Shivaratri, the 'night of Shiva.' Pashupati, a small village on the other side of the valley, was home to an important Shiva temple and was now the destination for sadhus and pilgrims from all over India and Nepal. On the first day of the festival, I saw a man buried alive who was able to slow down his heartbeat so that he didn't need to breathe. Then I saw a sadhu with his arm atrophied into the air and his fingernails curled around his hand. I saw a beggar girl with a six-inch Shiva trident pierced through her tongue. I saw a woman kiss a cobra. I saw a man eat glass. Then I saw a crowd of people who were staring at a good-sized boulder, perhaps sixty or seventy pounds, with a rope attached. I followed the rope and saw that it was tied around a sadhu's penis. My first thought was that he was tied up, like a horse to a hitching post, so that he wouldn't wander off. Then I began to wonder exactly who would have tied him up and why couldn't they have just tied his *foot* to the stone? Hell, that's what I would have done. If I was going to tie someone up, the penis would be way way *way* down the list of places I'd sling that noose. But then I started thinking that tying a sadhu to a rock was downright ridiculous – even in Nepal – and that's when things got really strange. Somebody yelled something, the crowd backed up to give him room, and Prick Baba, as he was known, suddenly lifted the boulder off the ground with his penis and started swinging it back and forth like a pendulum. *Aaaaaaaaaaah!*

When I arrived at the grounds of the temple, I saw an endless procession moving across a narrow bridge of the Bagmati River toward the main gate. The line snaked along slowly, but every once in a while there was a mad rush of people and, with it, the threat of being trampled. King Birendra was inside the temple, handing out hashish to the sadhus as a personal offering. It was on this day that I became a monarchist. Long live Birendra, the living incarnation of Vishnu.

Across from the temple were the burning ghats, where thousands of sadhus were camped out. I walked past the *dhunis* until I came upon a fire where Paul was smoking with the holy men. An old man waved for me to join them as Paul made up a chillum with his best hash. He handed it to the *baba* to light and I struck three matches against a box, but before I got within a foot of the chillum, the *baba* took an enormous toke and the hash exploded in flame. '*Bom Shankar!*'

Paul and I just stared at each other – did you see *that*? The *baba* lit the chillum without matches! I glanced around and realized we were surrounded by sadhus of every possible stripe, each getting blasted outside this holiest of temples. To smoke hash is to honor Shiva and to be in Shiva's hands and now we were all in Shiva's hands, all of us united in some massive high that had the power to levitate the temple, the village, and quite possibly the whole country. I could feel the entire kingdom straining against gravity and then gently lifting into the clouds. Sitting there with an orange stripe painted across his forehead, Paul looked wise beyond his years. 'The journey isn't one straight line,' he said, his stare boring right into my brain.

I looked into the *dhuni* and thought about all the ups and downs, the missteps and sidetracks, the dead ends and wrong paths. 'No, I guess it isn't,' I said.

'It's important at all times to act like a sadhu,' said Paul.

'And how's that?'

'A sadhu does what's right.'

I glanced into the face of the old man sitting next to Paul

and thought about how perfectly this sadhu fit the surroundings. Yes, his every breath, his every glance, his every gesture, seemed exactly right. He was on an incredible journey, that was for sure. So were the other sadhus. So was Paul.

It felt warm sitting around the *dhuni*. I felt connected to the sadhus, to the temple, and even to Shiva. Is this it? Am I on the precipice of something? Is this what I've been looking for? It feels so close, I can nearly reach out and grab it, the answer to all of my questions could be right in this circle, I could follow this path, I could grow my hair six feet long, I could stand in one spot for six years with my arm in the air, I could cover myself in ash, I could smoke chillums all day and chant all night, yes, this is what it's all been leading to, already I feel my mind emptying out, it's slowing down just like in Greece, but this time the filmstrip is coming into focus, this time I can almost make it out, this time things are making sense, yes, of course, Paul is right, I must act like a sadhu, I must do what's right, and now the film stops for one brief second and I take a look, and there it is, my journey, yes, it's anything but a straight line, it's more like a spiral that twists all over the place, just like the lines in my palm, it's a spiral that at any moment could point up or down, in or out, and now, sitting at the feet of the holy men, looking into the warm pools of the sadhu's eyes, I suddenly realize what this is all about. Each person's journey is different, and this spiral of mine isn't finished spinning. At least not here, not now, not in this magical arcade. It's as I always suspected. I don't want a guru. I don't want an ashram. I need to find my own way.

Shivaratri passed, then came Buddha's birthday, and before I knew it, the clouds began to build. It was the middle of April, I'd been in Asia for over seven months, and I'd heard enough about the torrential rains to know I didn't want to be anywhere near Nepal when the monsoon hit. I needed to make a decision, and soon. Going north wasn't an option, since the Chinese had sealed the border with Tibet years ago.

To the south, India would soon be a sweltering torture chamber. To the west – well, Europe was now out of the question. No, the logical thing seemed to be to continue in the direction that had been pulling me ever since leaving America – farther east.

Annika was smart. She'd already gotten out. Vanished without a word. What did I expect, that she'd say good-bye? Of course not. This was the perfect way for her to leave, enigmatic to the very end. Others were leaving, too, and I found myself trying to imagine what Southeast Asia might be like. Not many travelers had been there and the idea of a smaller scene appealed to me.

It all seemed to happen overnight, as if one day I was looking out the window of my house and the next day I was saying good-bye to Rajaram and Devagiri, to Ira and Petra, to Delia, Lucinda, and Jillian, to Angus and Jasper, to Leigh and Andrea, to the guy in the pie shop and the manager of the hotel. It happened so abruptly, I wasn't completely sure it was real.

Then I went to see Hettie at the temple and stood with her as the monks chanted their morning prayers. I looked out over the Kathmandu Valley, at the clouds gathering in the Himalayas, at Durbar Square, the Bishnumati, the rice paddies, the little road into Swayambhu, and my house atop Kimdol Hill. I listened one last time to the deep tones of the horns inside the temple, spun a prayer wheel for Martine, and watched as it turned & turned & turned . . .

# 34

# The Road to Oblivion

Stepping off the plane in Calcutta was like stepping into a Swedish sauna. I sank half an inch into the tarmac and slogged my way over to the terminal, where the immigration authorities were passed out on the counters. I kept thinking about what Paul said – 'The journey isn't one straight line' – and already I wondered if I'd made a wrong turn. Why was I in Calcutta? Because the plane to Bangkok stopped there? Is that a reason? No, there was something else. I had entered India in a state of near oblivion, and it seemed only right that I leave it that way, too. Yes, oblivion, that's what I need, I want to forget everything that's happened, because the more I think the worse it gets, I have to move on, yes, keep moving, don't stay in any one place too long, don't look back, don't think about it. The journey, after all, isn't one straight line.

A customs officer finally rustled up enough energy to stamp my passport, then pointed me toward a bus to town. To call Calcutta a town is like calling India a county. Calcutta is more like a universe, or the underbelly of a universe, a place so unimaginably large that it has no clear beginning and no definite end. You don't really go to Calcutta, it's more like you get Calcutted. I got a cheap room in the New Market District, where the hotel manager informed me that since the city had only seven hours of electricity a day, the lights would be off, the fans wouldn't be working, and there'd be nothing cold to drink. I plopped down on a creaky iron cot, sweat pouring down my face, and wondered how I'd ever get through the night. Then I remembered—

I walked outside and was accosted by a bunch of guys wearing nothing but tattered *lungis*. 'Rickshaw? Rickshaw?' they yelled. I glanced over and saw neither the motorized rickshaws of Delhi nor the bicycle rickshaws of Kathmandu, but *running* rickshaws. I could hardly believe my eyes when I looked at the contraptions. There were two wheels, a padded seat, and two long poles extending forward for the 'driver' to hold on to. Looking at the barefoot runners and this crude mode of transportation, I realized they were about a thousand years on the wrong side of medieval. I don't know when they figured out the wheel in India, but the rickshaw couldn't have come far behind. I looked around for alternatives, but there was nothing else in sight. 'I want to go to Mr Fong's,' I said. The runners just stared at me. 'You know, *Mis-ter Fong's*.'

'Fong! Fong!' one of them cried out.

'Yes, Mr Fong's. You know the place?' The runner gave me a little twist of the head that either meant yes, no, or maybe, then swung the rickshaw over for me to board. I was just about to climb on when I decided I'd better negotiate the fare. 'How much?'

'Hundred rupee.'

'Uh . . . that's a little steep. How about one rupee?'

'Fifty rupee.'

'A rupee and a half.'

'Twenty rupee.'

'Two rupees.'

'Five rupee.'

'Two and a half.'

'Three rupee.'

'All right, all right,' I said. I knew he was screwing me, but it was too hot to argue. I climbed up, slid onto the seat, and felt myself pushing back as he lifted the poles off the ground. We were off and running. At first glance, Calcutta looked almost elegant. The streets were wide, the buildings ornate, and the views impressive. Calcutta had been the British colonial capital and, as such, was laid out much like London or Manchester, but just behind the facade of Edwardian estates and formal gardens, one could see cracks and fissures running up, down, across, and through the walls. It wasn't just the buildings that were cracked, Calcutta itself was cracked. Everything that had ever gone wrong with the British Empire had combined and multiplied in this city until the cracks were pretty much all that was left.

I stared at the rubble behind the walls as the rickshaw runner turned onto a wide street where thousands of people were living, all with little areas carved out, whole families living side by side. I'd seen the homeless of Bombay, Delhi, and Benares, but this was something different, this was *massive*. There were ten or twenty or thirty million people in Calcutta – nobody knew for sure – and it seemed as if half of them were on the road to Mr Fong's. Assuming this was the road leading to Mr Fong's. 'Mr Fong's, right?' I yelled to the driver.

'Fong! Fong!' he yelled back.

Staring into the faces along the road and thinking back to the first time I'd seen beggars in Karachi, I wondered if my time in Asia had inured me to their plight. It was strange how the streets were often the places of the greatest humor, energy, and laughter, how the beggars of India, unlike the impoverished of the West, had their own place in society and carried themselves with a certain dignity. It was another of the contradictions that blanketed India, that the poorest and most miserable people of all seemed to be the happiest.

In colonial times, the British sent their young men to the Orient to get some experience – to become 'oriented' – but now, watching the streets pass by, I was getting downright *dis*oriented and quite possibly in danger of being Calcutted. When the runner turned onto yet another street, I had the distinct feeling we were headed in the wrong direction. Not that I knew where we were going, but I was beginning to worry that we were not on the road to oblivion. 'Mr Fong's, right? Chinatown?' I yelled.

'Fong! Fong!' he yelled back.

The whole of India, of course, is disorienting. Living in India can drive you nuts. The religion alone can drive you nuts. There are a hundred versions of every story, and, depending on whom you talk to, you'll even get a completely different explanation of the basics of Hinduism. There are, in fact, 3,333,333 gods in the Hindu pantheon which at first might seem like an awful lot, but given the population of Calcutta alone, there were more than enough people to keep them busy. Of course, I'm convinced that every story of each of these gods is completely contradictory to every other story, because nothing, after all, is real in India. India is not the place for people to come looking for answers. India is better for people who already think they have the answers. India will kick their asses out of complacency and right through the goalposts of befuddlement.

The heat got more intense. Where was this guy taking me? Watching the muscles twitch in his legs, it occurred to me that I'd never seen an Indian win an Olympic medal. Come to think of it, I wasn't sure if I'd ever seen an Indian even entered into the Olympics. India, the second-largest country in the world, had never won a medal? Why? I'll tell you why. Because the rest of the world was running all the wrong events. There *were* no Indian broad jumpers, swimmers, skiers, shooters, pole-vaulters, volleyball players, weight lifters, or wrestlers. What the Olympics needed was rickshaw races – then we'd see how the Indians would measure up. Or marathon chillum smoking. Or tag-team self-mortification. Until then, I decided to boycott the Olympics for being culturally biased. I'd boycott them until I heard an announcer on ABC Sports say: 'And now, placing the gold medal around his neck for stone lift and twirl, Mr Prick Baba . . .'

I was getting delirious from the heat. 'Stop!' I finally screamed, and the rickshaw came to an abrupt halt. 'You don't know where you're going, do you?' The runner stared at his feet. 'You've never heard of Mr Fong, have you?' The runner kicked a rock. 'You don't know where Chinatown is, do you?' The runner looked at me with sad eyes. 'What the hell were you thinking – that if you ran far enough I'd just get off anywhere? Does that actually make any sense to you? Take me back to New Market, damn it, before we both die out here!'

'New Market?' he said. 'Hundred rupee.'

'One rupee.'

'Fifty rupee.'

'A rupee and a half . . .'

Back at the guest house, I was in danger of a total meltdown when the manager miraculously produced a taxi driver who knew Mr Fong's. The taxi, unfortunately, was in danger of overheating, so the driver decided to turn on the heater, thereby releasing the hot air from the engine straight into the backseat. I was just about to bail out through the window when we pulled up at the dilapidated remains of Chinatown. 'Up there,' he said, pointing to a rickety building. 'Top floor.'

I made my way across a desolate street, pushed open a creaky door, and was immediately engulfed in blackness. I felt my way down a windowless hallway, found a handrail, and began climbing flight after flight of stairs. Finally, at the top, a thin sliver of light shone from beneath a door and I followed it to the end of the hall. I knocked, waited a moment, then knocked again. Eventually, the door opened a crack and two suspicious eyes peered out at me in the near-darkness. 'What want?' a woman asked.

'I'm here to see Mr Fong.'

There was a brief pause, then the door opened just wide enough for me to slip through. The woman, who wore the conspicuous dress and jewelry of Tibet, led me to a waiting room. 'Wait here,' she said.

'*Tashi deleg*,' I said, in the only Tibetan I knew. She turned, surprised to hear her own language, then disappeared down the hallway. A moment later, a tall, thin Chinese man shuffled into the room. He took a long look at me, then motioned for me to follow. We passed a couple of closed doors, then entered an atelier that opened onto a larger room. The space was sectioned off by low-lying benches and rows of thick mats that crisscrossed the floor. There were four or five elderly Chinese men in the room, but, it was so quiet, I felt as if we were alone. I followed Mr Fong to a corner of the room, where he pulled over a wood block with a well-worn, slightly concave top. He motioned for me to lie my head on it, and I was surprised to find the wooden pillow to be quite comfortable. He then opened the drawer of an old lacquer chest and pulled out three bottles, which he placed in front of me. 'Four . . . eight . . . twelve,' he said, as he pointed to each successively larger bottle.

'I . . . *uh* . . . I don't know,' I said, having no idea which to choose. 'Twelve?'

Mr Fong raised an eyebrow, then unscrewed the top of the container. He pulled out a metal prong, dipped it into the bottle, and rolled it around the inside edge until a gummy, amber-colored sap adhered to its sides. He then reached for a bamboo pipe that had ivory tips at the ends and a damper that screwed into the stem. The damper was made of ceramic and rimmed in silver, and had a small hole in the middle. Mr Fong rolled the molasseslike substance over its rounded surface until it formed a cylinder, then inserted it into the hole, pulled out the prong, and handed me the pipe.

He turned it upside down so that the damper was directly above a small oil lamp, two inches over the flame. 'Okay . . . okay . . .' he said impatiently, as I slowly inhaled. I couldn't get any smoke to come out and two seconds later, Mr Fong swore under his breath and pulled the pipe away. 'This no way to smoke opium,' he said, pointing to the hole. I was embarrassed to see that the opium had all dribbled out onto the glass bezel of the lamp. He ran the prong inside the bottle again, rolled it along the damper, and inserted it once more. This time I was ready when he tipped the pipe over the flame. I took a deep blast that would have made any chillum-smoking sadhu proud, but, again, no smoke escaped. Mr Fong swore even louder, grabbed the pipe, and showed me that I'd drawn so hard, the whole mechanism had clogged up. He dug the opium out of the hole, rolled a fresh batch on the damper, and began again. This time, however, instead of handing it to me, he turned the pipe over the flame, brought it to his own lips, and said, 'You watch.'

He inhaled slowly and steadily, modulating his breathing so that the opium stayed perfectly balanced at the tip of the hole. The ball expanded and contracted, hovering between the pull of gravity and Mr Fong's lungs. He reminded me of a glassblower as the opium pulsated and danced to the rhythms of his breath. He finished the bowl, then looked to see if I was ready. I nodded. He dipped into the bottle, rolled more opium along the damper, inserted it into the hole, and turned the pipe upside down over the flame. I inhaled carefully, sucking on the pipe like it was a harmonica, and that's when I tasted the smoke entering my lungs. I kept playing it like an extended blues solo, bending the air slightly, controlling my breathing, increasing and decreasing the tempo until the smoke drifted up into my brain. I continued drawing on the pipe until there was nothing left to inhale, held my breath as long as I could, then exhaled a pungent cloud of smoke. 'Okay,' said Mr Fong. He prepared the next bowl and we went through the process until all twelve balls were used up. I lay back against the wood pillow, staring up at the ceiling, and felt myself floating as the room began to dissolve. I felt my skin tingling and became aware of the sound of my breathing, and then of the breath itself, how it went in and out, building and dissipating into the air, rising and falling, curving slightly, like the path of a comet through some faraway galaxy, and it seemed as if the tiny particles of breath were no different really than the dust particles of a comet's tail, floating through some endless orbit, millions of light years into the void, floating, floating, floating—

There was a cough, a door opening, four Chinese men shuffling through, another man, as obese as obese can get, snoring away in the corner in his own dream, his snore so regular and rhythmic that he could have inhaled his next bowl right in his sleep, another cough, another opening door, two more men approaching now, more quickly than the others, stumbling a little, inept, like foreigners, out of place, what were they doing here in my dream?

'I am Kabir,' a young Indian man called over from the next mat.

'And I am Sitaram,' giggled his friend.

'It is his first time in an opium den,' said Kabir, motioning for Sitaram to sit down.

'But not my last,' Sitaram giggled.

I immediately recognized the two of them as being part of that small, but frightening, phenomenon known as the Indian Middle Class. I tried to turn away.

'You are enjoying yourself?' asked Kabir.

'You are from America?' giggled Sitaram.

'You are coming here often?' asked Kabir.

'You are Calcutta liking?' giggled Sitaram.

Indians can be a very spiritual people, a very brilliant people, inventive and gifted and artistic, they can be great scholars and philosophers, renowned teachers and pundits, but the one thing that Indians can almost never be, is cool. There's something in the genetic makeup, something handed down for tens of thousands of years, that absolutely prevents Indians from knowing that you just simply shut up when somebody is on an opium high, you stop giggling and you stop asking stupid questions, you just lean back and relax. But these guys weren't going to leave me alone, not here, not now, not in a million reincarnations. I got up and left.

When I came out of the dark building and into the bright sunshine the heat was pounding down and the air was vibrating off the pavement in shimmering energy patterns. I felt dizzy and nauseous. I went over to the side of the building, climbed over a pile of rubble, and saw a big hole in the ground – a giant festering hole that seemed to go on forever. I leaned over, my head swimming, my stomach churning, and was sickened to see a hundred snakes slithering out of an underground nest, their tongues darting in and out between fangs that dripped with venom. Deeper down, I saw the reflection of purple light in the eyes of a thousand rats and I knew there was something terribly incongruous about it, it was altogether the wrong color, everybody knows that rats eyes are piss yellow, not vibrant purple, purple is the color of the Catholic Church, for God's sake, of the vestments of the pope, purple is the color of the occult, of Madame Blavatsky and Aleister Crowley, purple is the color of the surreal, of Ira Cohen and Petra Vogt, and then, still deeper down in the pit, I saw maggots and cockroaches, slime and ooze, it just kept going, deeper and deeper, all-encompassing, and it was growing, this putrescent pit, even as I was staring into it, it was growing, like some monstrous toxic dump it kept radiating and regenerating itself, it sucked in entire buildings, expanding and slurping in whole neighborhoods, sucking helpless babies and wide-eyed puppies into the lurch, arms, legs, intestines, everything was mixing up into some stinking steaming stew, and that's when I realized where I was, I'd actually found it, it wasn't some figurative expression but an actual place, and I was standing at it right now, right on the edge of the Black Hole of Calcutta, and as I stared inside, I saw my life swirling around, an endless strip of yellow photographs with the edges all singed and curled up, my life was flying by in this roiling primordial soup with only the barest thread connecting it, this disconnected life that made no sense – I didn't understand Calcutta, I didn't understand India, I didn't understand palmistry or astrology, I didn't understand Buddhism or Hinduism, I didn't understand the people in the trains or the Tibetans in Manali or the sadhus in Benares or the monks in Kathmandu, I didn't understand why Martine was dead, I didn't understand why Annika had left without saying good-bye, I didn't understand even what I had understood the day I landed in Bombay – and then I knelt down on my hands and knees and I vomited, I vomited out my guts, I vomited out my entire insides until there was nothing left, and then I vomited some more.

# 35

# Lido Redux

And then I vomited one last time. The film on the wall flickered, flickered some more, then finally faded to black. A door slammed from somewhere downstairs, a baby cried, and a prostitute led someone up the back staircase. The noise didn't bother me so much this time, now that I had finally kicked heroin. Now I remembered why I was here, and in remembering I felt somehow purged. My muscles no longer ached so much, my stomach felt relaxed, I even had a bit of an appetite. I'd been at the Lido for almost a week and when I went outside again, I realized just how crazy it was to be here. The shops were shuttered, convoys of cars and trucks were heading for the border, and most of the embassies had been closed down. The last attempt at a coalition government had just failed and now the Pathet Lao was massing troops to finally overrun the rest of the country. For a minute I thought about staying. Maybe I'd run into those same soldiers again, the ones I met in the Buddha Garden, hell, maybe I'd even join up with them, I'd learn to shoot a gun and march through the jungle and live off beetle larvae, once we'd freed the villages in the central highlands and liberated the capital, they'd see I could be trusted, they'd even see I had leadership qualities, yes, I could be a leader of men, I'd rise through the ranks, all the way from foot soldier to an important figure in the central government, I'd be indispensible, why, they'll probably want to make me chairman of the party, well, I'm honored, brothers and sisters, I really am, but I'm just a humble boy from Wisconsin and I really must go, please, no bronze statues or cities named after me, okay, maybe a stamp, just to show my parents, but a small-denomination stamp, definitely nothing over 200,000 kip, and if you can fit a large-breasted woman somewhere on there, all the better, well, good-bye everyone, maybe we'll meet again one day, we'll reunite for one last battle, we'll march to the far north one last time, right up near the Canadian border, and we'll liberate the Potawatomees once and for all, but for now, dear friends, be well, think of me sometimes, but be well.

The Mekong flowed a little faster at Vientiane than up around Ban Houayxay or Luang Prabang. I watched the raging currents from the deck of a ferry, still on the lookout for any headless bodies that might go zooming by. The German junkie and his girlfriend, whom I'd met on the street, were also on the ferry. We stood at the railing together, watching Vientiane recede in the distance. About halfway across, they pulled syringes from their bags, along with their stash of heroin. Great, I thought, they're going to shoot up right here. I was wrong. The couple held each other's hands, clinked the syringes as if in a toast, then tossed the works overboard.

We shared a compartment on the train to Bangkok and I watched tiny beads of sweat forming on the guy's forehead. There were thousands of them, glistening little toxic diamonds that he would towel off, only for them to magically reappear seconds later. As we slowly traveled south, it got even hotter and muggier than on the plains. Then, as we neared the city, the sky filled with a cloud of soot and smog that seemed to crackle with electricity. We got into a taxi, sped up Rama IV, turned onto Soi Ngam Du Phli and barreled into the parking lot of the Hotel Malaysia. Inside the lobby, the German guy looked like he was about to lose it. He leaned against the counter as his girlfriend did the paperwork. 'You gonna be okay?' I called to them as they headed for the elevator. They nodded back uncertainly.

'How many day?' the clerk asked from behind the counter as he checked my passport.

'Two, maybe three,' I responded.

'Destination?'

Okay, let's see, destination, right, I've got to go somewhere, don't I, unless I stay here and that's out of the question, what, am I gonna camp out in one of these rooms and order 7-Ups with ice all day long, no, that might not be such a good idea, I'm thinking maybe it's time to head to – where? – oh, good, there's a map on the wall, let's see, ah, of course, Borneo, that's where I'll go, Borneo has always held a certain fascination, what with the headhunters and all, no, that's ridiculous, what am I gonna have in common with headhunters, I don't even eat meat anymore, okay, how about some of those other islands, let's see there's Vanuatu, Tuvalu, Kiribati, Nauru, *hmm*, never heard of any of them, what do you do at night on Kiribati anyway, watch reruns of *I Love Lucaluca*, no, c'mon, let's make a decision, it's not such a big deal, you just go somewhere, spin the wheel, it's a game of chance – 'Indonesia.'

The clerk nodded, filled out a form, and handed me the registry. I signed in, then glanced through some names. 'You have someone named Zed Habib?' The clerk shrugged. 'He must be here, medium height, black hair, looks kind of—' It was funny. I couldn't remember his face.

The clerk suddenly looked up. 'You mean Turkish guy?'

'Yeah, that's him.'

'He go! Everything still in room! He just go! No pay!'

'What do you mean, he just disappeared?'

'Couple week ago, just go. Fuckin' guy.'

Zed must've really done it this time, I figured. He was probably about to burn the place down and decided to get the hell out of here before they charged him for the furniture. Either that or he found some other hotel with faster room service or colder ice. Still, it seemed a bit strange, even for Zed. 'Yeah,' I said, nodding to the clerk, 'fuckin' guy.'

The elevator cage rattled as it began to rise and the film noir soundtrack leaked out of the speakers. I was again assaulted by that creepy feeling of Bangkok. It wasn't like any other place I'd been and I was glad to be leaving in a few days. I got out on the fifth floor – the soundtrack still insinuated in my ears – and headed down the hallway for my old room. I couldn't get the image out of my head of some wicked femme fatale, some tough-guy hood, or some cop on the take just waiting for me to turn the wrong way. For me, London might be a musical comedy, Nairobi an action adventure, and Paris a romance, but Bangkok, scratching just beneath the surface, Bangkok would always be film noir.

An hour or so later I glanced out the window of my room to the fountain in the parking lot. The German guy was standing there shoving some money into the hands of a Thai dealer whose face was hidden behind a pair of dark aviator sunglasses. A few minutes later, the elevator door opened and I heard footsteps coming down the hallway.

There was a knock on the door. I got up to answer it, then stopped near the bed. I remembered the last time someone knocked on my door in this hotel. It had a similar sound, urgent and weak at the same time. I wondered if it was Zed, if maybe he'd been hiding out in the linen closet until I got back, nah, it's not Zed, it's not Zed at all, it's the German guy, I'll just count to three and what do you wanna bet he'll knock again, one . . . two . . .

# 36

## Entranced

A thousand years ago, I might've been a Brahmin priest. I think I would've been a good priest since I'm a good listener and am very comfortable with the concept of guilt. I probably would've been an even better priest were it not for a somewhat excessive devotion to Lord Shiva, god of intoxication. Still, life would've been good, until—

'Master, we have a problem!'

'Go away!'

'I'm sorry, Master, it is very serious.'

'Didn't I tell you never to bother me when the lovely Sita is rubbing my back?'

'Forgive me, Master, but the Moslem hordes are at the gate.'

'*What?*'

'They have slain the Sikh armies that were sworn to protect the Brahmin priests. You must make like a tree.'

'And *leave*? Damn!'

'I have packed your harmonium and six-stringed lute into a large sack with adjustable straps to be slung over your back. You must flee, Master, flee like the wind.'

'Prepare a chillum whilst I consider where to go.'

'There is nary time, Master—'

'For a *chillum*? How speak thee?'

'The Moslems are throwing the priests into great pits of hungry snakes, then cutting out their kidneys and making kabobs for the feast.'

'*Aaaaaaaaaaaaah!*'

And so, I fled. I fled east through India, until there was no more of India left to flee, and then I fled into Burma, the Moslems nipping at my heels, and I settled a while in Thailand, and then I fled down through the Malay Peninsula, meeting up with my brethren who had taken great ships from the southern ports of India, and we continued on, for countless years, until finally we settled in the central plains of Java, in the town of Jogjakarta, and there we advanced our Hindu civilization and things were good, they were very good, until the nosy Moslem hordes picked up the scent of our curry, and once again we fled, we fled east through Java until there was no more of Java left to flee, and then our backs were against the wall, for the land had ended and the waters were too turbulent to pass, and we stood there, trapped against the sea, waiting to die, when a great bird descended from the skies, Garuda his name, and he commanded us to board his back and we did, the many thousands of us, and the great Garuda swooped into the sky, the Moslems waving their scimitars at us in fury, and the Garuda dropped a scent into the water to forever remind them of this day, and there a small village was born, Banguwangi – 'scented waters' – and then the Garuda flew over the roiling sea and gently dropped us onto a lush island where the rice was plentiful and the rivers flowed and the mangoes grew and he said to us, 'This is paradise, build a great civilization of dancers and sculptors and poets and musicians, make great paintings and weavings and hold your past dear,' and this we did, we created a society of religion and devotion and cooperation, and for a thousand years it thrived, and now, reincarnated as a wanderer and seeker, I retrace my steps, I flee east through India until there is no more of India left to flee, I rest a while in Thailand, then head south, where Malaysia and Singapore have determined that men of long hair shall be denied entry, and rather than succumbing to the indignity of being shorn – for the blood of a Brahmin still pulses through these veins – I jump again onto the back of the Garuda, known now as Indonesian

366

Garuda Airlines, and I fly to Jakarta, a city of great turmoil, and move quickly along narrow steel tracks on the earth to my former home of Jogjakarta, and there I see the great dance of the *Ramayana* performed beneath a full moon, and then I flee east through Java until there is no more of Java left to flee, and I stop at Banguwangi and inhale deeply and, yes, there is the slightest hint of a scent as I cross the turbulent waters, and then I see rice paddies terracing down along a great volcano, and I feel a cool breeze wafting in over the ocean, and I hear the sound of flutes deep in the forest, and I taste the nectar of jackfruit upon my lips, and I smell the fragrance of jasmine and frangipani in the air, and that's when I realize that I am home, I have returned at last, a hundred lifetimes have elapsed, and I am finally back in Bali, back where I belong.

'What's good today?' I asked the young woman behind the counter of a tiny *warong*.

Kortis looked up and a smile played upon her round, brown face. 'Frrrrruit salad good today,' she responded, the rs rolling off her tongue like a gymnast coming out of a somersault.

'What fruits are in season?' I asked, just as I had every day for the past two weeks.

'Everrrrrything in season,' said Kortis, continuing our routine. We went through this at least once each afternoon. Always the same question, always the same answer.

'Well, then, I'd better have a fruit salad.'

'*Bagus*,' she said, indicating I'd made a good choice as she cut up a banana, then added mangosteen, jackfruit, and papaya. She poured a few drops of sweet condensed milk over the top, then dusted the whole thing with grated coconut and peanuts. 'When you take me America?' Kortis asked, batting her eyelashes like a hummingbird.

'As soon as Papa gives me four goats and two cows.'

'Papa no *have* cows!' she moaned, still following the script, feigning disappointment.

'Well, you know the deal, Kortis, no goats, no marriage; no cows—'

'—no New York!' She looked at me with terribly sad eyes, then burst out laughing. 'How is *frrrrr*uit salad?'

'Fruit salad *bagus*.' She waved to me as I left the *warong* and walked along the dirt road of Legian toward the ocean. Legian was a new village, a few miles past the more established Kuta Beach, and the road was lined with palm trees, a few acacias, and sweet-smelling jasmine. Several pathways led off the road to *losmans*, guest houses that had manicured stone gardens and tiny ponds filled with water lilies. The walls were covered in hibiscus and the archways in bougainvillea, and at the sides of the entrances were shrines to the gods.

'*Salamat jalan*,' called out Wayan, wishing me a good journey as I passed the Pala Ayu. He was preparing the evening offering, a few morsels of cooked rice that he placed upon a bed of flowers. He slid a banana leaf on top of the shrine, to honor the gods who lived in the mountains and in the sky, and put another down below, to appease the demons of the ground and ocean. Almost immediately, birds flew down and nibbled at the rice – a sign that the gods were pleased. Then a dog came by, sniffed around, and slobbered up the food down below, confirming that evil, easily identifiable by its sharp fangs, would be put off for at least another day.

'*Salamat sorei*,' I called to Wayan, wishing him a good evening as I headed for the beach to watch the sunset. The Balinese weren't all that comfortable living near the beaches. They preferred it up in the mountains, closer to the gods. The ocean, with its strong undercurrents and sharp-toothed fish, was a good place to avoid. The Balinese were lousy swimmers and reluctant fishermen, and they looked at the sea not for sustenance but as a place of great danger. It didn't really take long to figure out the ABCs of Bali: up, good; down, bad. Smile, good; fangs, bad.

I learned all I needed to know about the ocean the first time I went in. Bali combined the blue waters of Greece, the white sands of Lamu, and the gentle dunes of Mauritius, and as I floated on my back, I realized this was about as close to paradise as it gets. The only thing possibly amiss was that the people were rather diminutive, they were the size of ants, in fact – *ants?* – and suddenly I realized I was half a mile out to sea, caught in a riptide . . .

I hadn't felt a thing. The riptide had snuck up on me, as silent and unobtrusive as a cat burglar, and carried me out in the undertow. My first inclination was to swim in against the current, but I quickly discovered that the more I swam, the farther away I got. My second inclination was that this was a very good time to panic. Fortunately, I remembered hearing that the way to beat a riptide is to swim parallel to the beach until you get out of the undertow, and then simply ride the waves in. That's what I did. I rode those waves like the Silver Surfer, dragged myself out of the water, and headed over to Kortis' *warong* for a double fruit salad.

I hadn't been with a woman since Martine, not counting Emmanuelle, and with Emmanuelle, counting was the whole problem. While the Balinese women were attractive, I was pretty sure that a casual toss in the hay wasn't exactly what they had in mind. No, an indiscreet night could come back to haunt me, and Bali, with its dozens of malevolent deities, was not the best place for a haunting. Better to be indiscreet with my own kind. One of my own kind just happened to be on the beach that sunset. Her name was Elizabeth, she'd been roaming around the islands for a couple of months, and she seemed very nice. By six, we were sharing a papaya; by seven we were holding hands; by eight, we were making love in my *losman*; by nine, we were making love in her *losman*; by ten, we were talking with her roommate from New Zealand; and by eleven, she was accusing me of being more interested in the roommate than in her.

'No way!' I lied.

The next day, the three of us took a *bimo*, a rickety jitney, to Ubud, an artists' colony in the mountains. Along the way, we passed through the rice paddies that stretched up and down the island. The Balinese had discovered that by terracing the hills, they could channel the rivers from the mountaintops and irrigate all the land below. If anything went wrong, everyone was affected, so they banded together to keep the rivers flowing, helping each other plant, grow, and harvest the crops. This cooperation in the paddies spread to their social lives as well, where nearly everyone becomes a dancer or a musician, a painter or a wood-carver. Bali is an island of artists – so much so that art is considered a natural part of life. Everything in Bali is art. The wooden bell placed around a cow's neck is art, the spirit catcher spinning in the wind is art, the carved handle on a hammer is art, the container for carrying betel nuts is art, the engraved frame of a weaving loom is art, the basket for carrying fruit and vegetables is art.

Elizabeth and I viewed the paintings of Ubud, the jewelry of Celuk, and the wood carvings of Mas. Alexis, having just left New Zealand, could hardly take her eyes off all the unusual sights. I could hardly take my eyes off Alexis. Elizabeth could hardly take her eyes off me watching Alexis. The next day, we walked through the monkey forest of Sange then headed toward the village of Tampaksiring. All I could think about was getting Alexis alone somehow, to tell her my feelings. We came upon a tiny fruit stand in the middle of nowhere, where an old lady sat bare breasted beneath a parasol in the burning sun. She had nothing but one jackfruit, but it was the biggest piece of fruit I'd ever seen. It was two feet long and a foot in diameter and when I purchased a hundred rupiahs' worth, the old lady cut off a chunk that could've fed ten people.

Higher in the hills, we came upon a river, where Elizabeth decided to take a dip. Alexis and I found a shady spot not far away, and I saw my chance. I broke off some jackfruit and gave it to her, then took a piece for myself and examined the strange way the meat of the fruit grew between long, tuber-like cells. I'd only eaten jackfruit that was already cut up, without all the weird stuff in between. 'So, alone at last,' I said.

'Yes,' said Alexis, looking nervous.

'I've been wanting to talk to you—'

'Oh?' she said, a little too quickly. 'About what?'

'Well, not exactly *about* anything, just, well, you know . . .'

'It must be very important if it had to wait until Elizabeth left.'

'Yes, well,' I said, biting into the jackfruit, 'I was just wondering if maybe sometime you'd like to *mmmmppphhh—*'

'Pardon me?'

'*Mmmmppphhh . . . mmmmppphhh . . .*' I said, trying to speak. I couldn't open my mouth.

'I'm sorry, could you repeat that?'

'*Mmmmppphhh! Mmmmppphhh!*' I said, a little louder. My lips were glued tight.

'*Um* . . . are you all right?'

'*Mmmmppphhh! Mmmmppphhh!*'

'What's that? You want Elizabeth?'

'*Uh-mmmmppphhh!*' I groaned, shaking my head.

'Hang on, I'll get her.'

I collapsed against a tamarind tree. This was just perfect. Not only had I blown my chance with Alexis, I'd gotten my mouth sewn up in the bargain. God was punishing me, that was pretty obvious, and I deserved it. What was I thinking, trying to hit on Elizabeth's roommate like that?

'You didn't eat that fiber stuff in the jackfruit, did you?' called Elizabeth from the river.

'*Mmmmppphhh! Mmmmppphhh!*'

She came over with a half coconut shell filled with water. 'Here, wash your lips off.'

I drenched my mouth and felt my lips cracking open a bit. Alexis had stayed at the river but now she joined us. She looked like she'd been laughing. 'Feeling better?' she asked.

I nodded.

'So, I'm sorry, what were you saying?'

'*Mmph . . .*'

Elizabeth and Alexis left for Java a few days later and I returned to Legian. My room at the Pala Ayu was nothing

371

special, but I was glad to be back in familiar surroundings. I lit a kerosene lantern, ran a cloth over the back of my guitar, then polished a silver medallion of Saraswati, the goddess of music, that was attached to the neck. I tuned the strings and was reaching for a harmonica when a strange sound came echoing across the room. '*Geck-o . . . geck-oooo . . .*'

I turned the lamp toward the wall to see a gecko – a green, six-inch lizard – staring down at me from near the ceiling. It called out again and again and I counted six, seven, and eight cries. I waited a moment, and then it called out for a ninth time, which was considered fortuitous by the Balinese. I decided to forget about the harmonica and let the gecko handle the melody. We jammed until late into the night, me, the gecko, and a couple of flying salami bugs who showed up around closing time for some tipsy harmonizing.

The next morning, I was sitting on a ledge outside my room, staring into the fronds of a palm tree – I'd become an excellent palm gazer over the past couple of years – when a voice interrupted my reverie. 'Hey, you.'

I looked over to see an attractive woman standing there with her hands on her hips. 'Me?'

'Yeah, you. I'm Susan. I live next door. I'm having a party tonight. You're playing.'

'What?'

'I heard you last night. You'll do.'

'Well, thanks – if that was a compliment – but I don't play in public.'

'Now you do. Ten o'clock over at the Kayu Api.'

'No-no-no, you don't understand—'

'You're not gonna play the temperamental artist, are you? We don't have time for that kind of bull.'

'Listen, I've been playing guitar for one year and—'

'Fine. I've got things to do. It's very simple. If you don't play, I'll make your life a living hell.'

I looked at her sculpted body, her lithe torso, her swimmer's arms, and figured she probably could do exactly that. Of course, I wasn't going to be intimidated into anything – this is my *music* we're talking about – but then I saw the look in her eyes, and decided that discretion was the better part of a good beating. 'You said ten, right?'

'On the button.'

The party was in full swing when I got to the Kayu Api. It seemed as if everyone from Legian was there and half of Kuta Beach had shown up, as well. Austrian Lothar was there, hitting on Canadian Lynn, Penny and Barbara were dancing with Dem and Milan, Razamé de la Crackers was performing magic tricks for some local kids in the corner, Linda from Hong Kong was making eyes at a handsome Javanese waiter, Greek George was drinking and laughing too loud, and Meg from Melbourne was staring at my guitar case.

Things quieted down when Balinese gamelan music came over the speakers and Isla, a zaftig New Englander, made her entrance. Isla was all done up in a Surabaya sarong, inch-thick eye makeup, a crown of gardenias, and three-dozen bangles that were stacked up her arms. She looked exactly like Dorothy Lamour in an old South Seas musical. Off to the side, her Balinese dance teacher watched hopefully as Isla went through the steps of the classic Legong dance. Isla started off tenuously, stumbling and losing her balance a few times on some difficult moves, but then she jutted her jaw from side to side, darted her eyes dramatically, and raised a leg perfectly parallel to the ground as she twirled around. Isla's teacher smiled broadly but not as broadly as Isla, who was absolutely beaming with joy. Her smile was so infectious that the whole crowd began smiling, and then applauding, and as we cheered her on, Isla did another move, and then another, and then, before anyone knew what happened, she pulled her sarong right down to her waist and began dancing bare breasted, like the Bali dancers of yore, and now her sizeable tits were bouncing up and down – in perfect time with the gamelan – as Isla twirled and beamed and took her bows.

Watching Isla reminded me of Wendy the Snake Dancer in

Mombasa, and I realized it was *Showtime* again, that I was up next, and that this time I was the whole show. No African band to back me up, not even a bunch of drunken Swedes trying to pound out a blues. No, this time it was just me, and I was terrified. I saw there was a clear path between me and the door, but then I noticed Susan staring at me and realized she'd make a scene even more embarrassing than my feeble attempts to be a one-man band. Okay, this is it, time to be exposed as the fraud I really am, there's nowhere to hide, I'm standing in front of a hundred people and I'm going to play them some totally lame songs sung in a weak voice accompanied by an inept guitar and boy, paradise sure can be miserable, and I'm tuning up, feeling sick to my stomach, and a drunken Australian surfer comes up to me and says, 'Look into my eyes, you can see for a thousand miles,' and he's right, I can see for a thousand miles, his eyes are portals down some long and windy road, and I'm on that road, singing a song, strumming a guitar, tapping my foot, blowing some harp, and it's a long road to nowhere that I'm on, a road with a thousand women and a thousand men, a road full of life and death, a road with no way on and no way off, a road that just keeps flying by, pushing me on, destination unknown, but tonight, at least, there will be applause, tonight I will feel good, tonight I'll wind up in bed with Meg from Melbourne and we'll make love to the ocean pounding against the shore, to a gecko calling out nine times in the night, to the sound of a harmonica still hanging in the air.

# 37

# The Spirit Catcher

The ocean roared against the beach at Legian. Rising over vast coral reefs, the tides swelled, swirled, surged, and crested, then dropped like a ledge against the jagged rocks. The amplitude built with each series of waves, but it was in every ninth wave that the full fury of the ocean was unleashed. Every ninth wave is the biggest. Every ninth wave comes crashing over the sea. As the sun set over an endless horizon, I watched hundreds of tiny sand crabs fighting against the incoming tide. They burrowed into the sand and held on valiantly for a second or two, then lost their grip and were funneled a little further out. As the water passed over them, they dusted themselves off and, quite comically, made a mad dash on their minuscule legs for dry land. Again and again, they repeated this sidelong dance of survival – until the ninth wave. For if they weren't on high ground when the ninth wave hit, they would be dragged out and disappear forever into the sea.

I felt a shadow and looked up to see a strange-looking man standing a few feet away. One of his eyes was glassy and rolled back in its socket, while the other had too much white around the cornea. He stared at me for a moment, then began cackling and walking backwards toward the trees. It was creepy, him edging away like that, laughing and leering, and I wondered if this was the man I'd heard the Balinese talk about, the man from the Black Magic Forest.

\* \* \*

A Barong dance was planned for that night. Wayan told me it was a special ceremony, not one of those tourist performances, and that he himself would be dancing. There wasn't much of anything around when I arrived, just a dusty open space inside a grove of trees and a few dozen villagers listening to a gamelan orchestra. The group consisted of drums, gongs, flutes, and a vibraphonelike instrument that was struck with steel mallets. The music built and released like waves in the sea, and I felt myself floating off to the hypnotic beat. A short while later, four Legong dancers appeared in shimmering, sequined sarongs and performed the traditional opening for the ceremony. Then the Barong, a great leonine figure, danced into the clearing. His head was a large wooden mask, his body a mass of cloth and hair that was slung over two men wearing striped leggings. They danced in perfect conjunction, their legs moving not precisely together but slightly apart – like a real lion – as the head and mane dipped and swayed to the music. After the Barong carved out his territory, Rangda the witch appeared, and everyone instinctively moved back. Rangda wasn't much more than a giant mask, but she was so horrific, it was hard not to be frightened. Her orange eyes bugged out in a malevolent glare, her mouth opened to reveal enormous fangs, and her tongue hung all the way to the ground, bright red, as if she'd just tasted the blood of her latest victim.

Rangda did her dance and challenged the Barong, and then the two of them were in the center of the clearing, the feet of the Barong and the hooves of Rangda kicking up great clouds of dust as they faced each other down, good and evil going at it, while children hid behind their mothers' skirts and men watched with nervous smiles. I smelled a wave of heavy incense and glanced over to see a priest blowing clouds of sandalwood into the faces of a half-dozen men as he intoned a prayer. I noticed how their faces were totally blank. One of them was Wayan. The men were led into the dance area, each of them carrying a long kris knife. The kris, a wavy, beveled blade, was sharp and jagged and annealed for maximum strength. After dancing as a group in front of

Rangda and the Barong, each of the men did an individual dance to the Barong. They held the tips of the kris knives against their hearts in a personification of the fight of good against evil. Their hands were wrapped around the pommels as the spirit of Rangda tried to force the blade into their hearts and the Barong fought back, pulling the blade away. Back and forth the battle went – played out in the biceps of the dancers' arms – while two husky men stood a few feet away, watching the eyes of the dancers and the muscles in their arms. Every once in a while, when things looked like they might spin out of control, they stepped in to grab the knife.

Last to dance was Wayan, and he entered the ring with an energetic leap. As he swung the kris in a circle and placed it over his heart, I noticed the two burly men watching him closely. The point of the blade pushed against his skin, then released, then pushed again, back and forth it went, Wayan's blank expression never altering. Then – maybe it was the raising of an eyebrow or the twinge of a muscle – the two men leapt upon him and struggled to pull the knife away. Still, Wayan's expression didn't change – he was in a deep trance – and even the strength of two men wasn't enough to stop him. The gamelan abruptly stopped, more men rushed over to grab Wayan's arms, and finally they pulled the kris away before he managed to kill himself.

The priest doused the dancers with holy water from Mount Agung and one by one, as the droplets touched their faces, they came out of their trances. All but Wayan. He was still struggling on the ground, kicking and screaming, when the priest pulled a live chicken from his satchel. He held the frantic bird in front of Wayan's face and then, in one quick motion, snapped its neck with his bare hands and shoved it into Wayan's mouth. Wayan sucked the warm blood, his body shaking uncontrollably, until he finally collapsed onto the ground. The priest disappeared, the two burly men picked up Wayan, and the crowd quickly dispersed. As I headed out of the clearing, I noticed Madé, Wayan's wife, standing by herself against a tree. She watched Wayan from a distance, then turned and walked home alone.

* * *

'Did you hear what happened?' asked Susan when I came out of my room the next morning. She was sitting in the garden, drinking a cup of *kopi susu*, the local coffee, a faraway look in her eyes.

'What, at the Barong?'

'No, no, they caught some guy, a Javanese, stealing a radio. They chased him through the fields, a whole bunch of them, and caught him ten feet from the beach.'

'For a radio?'

'I don't think the radio mattered anymore. He dumped that way back. He was running for his life.'

'What do you mean?'

Susan stared into her coffee. 'They didn't mess around. They beat him up so bad, he finally crawled to the water and tried to swim away.' She finally glanced up and I could see her eyes were red and puffy. 'His body washed up this morning.'

'They *killed* him?'

'Yeah, a bunch of local guys.'

I felt a chill down my spine. 'Was Wayan one of them?'

'Wayan . . . K'tut from down the road . . . Nyoman, the *bimo* driver . . . they were all there.'

'For a *radio*?'

'That's the way they handle things around here,' said Susan, shaking her head. 'I guess they'll sleep just fine tonight knowing there's one less thief around.'

I remembered Wayan's dance, then imagined him running amok in the middle of the night, still half-crazed from the incense and the holy water and the warm blood of a chicken. Had he been the instigator? Had he been judge, jury, and executioner? It occurred to me that the word *amok* comes from the Indonesian language, and for very good reason. The Indonesians, normally the gentlest of people, have a tendency every once in a while to go completely berserk. As far as I could tell, running amok wasn't confined to Indonesia, but it did seem to be most prevalent in the tropics. In Rwanda, the Tutsis and Hutus ran amok every couple of decades. The Nicaraguans seemed to be beset by the same phenomenon. Ninety-eight percent of the time, you couldn't ask for a nicer neighbor than an Indonesian, Rwandan, or Nicaraguan. But should they happen to run amok, it's a pretty good idea not to have one of their radios under your bed.

I wasn't running amok – not yet, at least – but I was running out of money. I thought about going to Japan, where Americans could teach English, but the prospect didn't thrill me. One night, after I had played again at the Kayu Api, Susan came over with Tamara, an Englishwoman who'd just arrived from Tokyo. 'I've got someone you should meet,' she said.

'I really enjoyed the music,' said Tamara with the hint of an east London accent.

'Thanks, but I'm really—'

'Don't let him get started,' said Susan. 'He needs a good kick in the ass.'

'Susan says you're thinking of going to Japan. You ever think of playing there?'

I moved Tamara out of Susan's earshot. 'You see, the thing is, I'm just starting out on the guitar and—'

'Yeah, but it sounds good. And the harmonica . . .'

'I'm not trying to be modest. I know I'm a good harmonica player.'

'You're a *great* harmonica player.'

'Okay, maybe I'm a great harmonica player, but the guitar, I've been playing for *one* year. I'm nowhere near ready to play clubs.'

'You're good enough, if you ask me. I've got a few contacts, if you're interested.'

'Contacts? I, *uh,* I don't know . . .'

Tamara turned back to Susan. 'You're right. He *does* need a kick in the ass.'

There was another commotion when I arrived back at the Pala Ayu that night. A big gas lantern was glowing just down from my room, some locals were chattering nervously, and

Wayan stood vigil out near the shrine, holding a ten-foot spirit catcher in the air. I remembered that look in his eyes from the night of the Barong dance, and approached cautiously. 'What's going on?'

'Terrible thing . . . terrible thing . . .' he said, pointing to the lit-up room. 'New visitor, the one arrived today . . .'

I remembered seeing a young guy checking in earlier in the day. 'Who, the Korean guy?'

'Yes, Korean . . . South Korean . . .'

'What about him?'

'He gone in ocean . . . first time . . . he dead.'

'*What?*'

'Ocean no good.'

'Wait a minute . . . he *drowned*?'

'Ocean very angry.'

'I just *saw* the guy . . .'

'Son of Korean ambassador. I keep spirit away. Spirit very angry. We do *puja* all night.'

I walked to my room, thinking how those prayers were probably a very good idea. As I lay in bed that night, Wayan's spirit catcher whistling in the wind, I began to realize just how dark the dark side of paradise could be. Bali was a place to be reckoned with.

# 38

# The Ninth Wave

Meg was a nurse who'd lived in London the past two years and was now on the last leg of her journey before returning to Melbourne. She was traveling with her friend, Chrissy, and the two of them were very sweet, but unusually naïve, I thought, for women who'd been away that long. They'd somehow made it halfway around the world without so much as a toke off a joint. We headed out to Gunug Kawi, an ancient temple where a special ceremony was taking place. The lower castes, often unable to afford cremation, temporarily bury their dead until a Brahmin dies. A prominent priest had just passed on and his family paid for 108 of the poor to be dug up and cremated alongside him. The ceremony began at his home, where the priest was loaded onto a precarious five-tiered tower. Some men went running down the street, shaking the tower in order to disorient the spirit of the dead priest so that he couldn't find his way back home and bug the relatives. At the cremation grounds, his body was placed inside a wood Brahmin bull and set ablaze. Beneath the other bodies, which were in various states of decomposition, 108 fires were lit. The bull burned for hours, its legs going first, then the head and shoulders. Finally, there was nothing left but the priest, whose body had been slung on a wire mesh inside the sarcophagus. With his charred corpse now suspended in the air for all to see, the tender of the fires came by and poked a stick into his chest cavity, releasing a geyser of fluids that spouted for the next thirty minutes.

When it was all over, Meg and I caught the first *bimo* back to Legian and fucked like crazy.

The restaurants in Legian advertised 'mushroom omelets' on their menus. Since there was only one kind of mushroom growing in Bali – psilocybin – the omelets were a rather adventurous choice for breakfast. Being listed on a menu made them seem so innocuous, however, that Meg and Chrissy decided it was time to try something different. They showed up at the Pala Ayu one morning and announced they'd just had the speciality of the house. 'Why don't you have some?' said Meg.

'Uh . . . I don't think so,' I said. I wasn't really feeling psychedelically inclined at the moment, and, even if I'd been in the mood, I was certain that those screwy little mushrooms growing all over the island would hardly do the trick.

'Oh, c'mon, why don't you? It'll be fun!' said Meg.

'Yeah, it'll be fun!' seconded Chrissy.

Fun? I'd never taken a trip in my life that was *fun*. Incredible, yes, but *fun*? It occurred to me that Meg and Chrissy had absolutely no idea what they were getting into. Even though those mushrooms were almost sure to be duds, what if something went wrong? How could I leave these girls to their own devices? Dear God, why do you torture me? 'Okay, I'll do it.'

'*Yay!!!*' they yelled. They reminded me of Lucinda and Jillian.

'How many did you eat?'

'I had three,' said Chrissy.

'I had five,' said Meg.

'Wow,' I said, trying not to sound condescending. Three? Five? Was this some kind of joke? I decided if I was going to do mushrooms, I'd at least give myself a fair chance of getting off. The forest behind the beach seemed like a good spot to find some fresh ones. 'You'll be all right for a little while?' I asked them.

'Sure, we only took them five minutes ago.'

'Okay, don't get into any trouble,' I joked as I headed down the path. It had rained early that morning, and a few drops still glistened on the frangipani that grew wild at the edge of the forest. As I entered a palm grove, I felt the sun disappear and noticed a slight chill to the air. I came upon a giant banyan tree, its dozen trunks intertwined in a magnificent maze, its branches growing like a hundred serpents into the sky, and saw some mushrooms in a sliver of sunlight. They grew up along the bark, into the crevices of the roots, and out along the ground.

The mushrooms were small, maybe the size of a quarter, with rounded, beige tops. I snapped one off and rolled it around in my hand, then picked more until I had a nice little mound. Suddenly – *fwap!* – a stick smashed down just inches from my hand. I jerked back my head to see the man from the beach, the man with the rolled-back, glassy eye. 'Hey!' I yelled, instinctively cupping my hands around the mushrooms.

'*Tidak mau!*' he yelled back, pointing to the big mound.

'What's no good? The mushrooms?'

'*Tidak mau!*' he said again.

'What? What?' The man stared at me, those bizarre eyes almost burning into my skin, then tapped his stick against my hands. 'All right, all right,' I said, reluctantly opening my palms.

His eyes widened. He knocked a dozen mushrooms out of the mound, looked again, then knocked out a few more. Then he looked at me and flashed a big, toothless grin. '*Baguuuuus.*'

'Yeah, *bagus,*' I said, forcing a smile.

The man began flapping his arms like a bird, then edged backwards into the trees. '*Salamat jalan,*' he said, with a thoroughly insane leer. '*Salamat jalaaaaan . . .*'

When Madé saw the seventy-five mushrooms I asked her to cook up for me, she begged me to stop. 'No good . . . no good!' she said. I was sorry I didn't speak Indonesian. If we were in Kenya, I would've explained to her that I was *bwana mkubwa*, that I had peed in the jungle. Madé finally gave in,

383

Meg and Chrissy took a walk, and I sat on my porch waiting for the mushrooms to come on. I sat there, feeling nothing, thinking about the effects of acid, how it would fade in and fade out at first, from one reality to another, back and forth, back and forth, like dipping a toe into the water a few times before finally taking the plunge. I waited for a sign, a little shimmer, a little wave, a little *anything*. Half an hour later, Meg and Chrissy showed up, looking down in the dumps. 'If mushrooms are supposed to be so much fun,' Meg said, 'why are we so unhappy?'

Oh, great, my nurses are on a bummer. It was just as I'd feared, they're going to need a guide, and here I am, straight as an arrow, unable to connect. 'It's okay,' I said, managing to sound both patronizing and inept at the same time, 'don't worry.'

Meg knelt down on the floor next to my chair. 'I don't understand. It's terrible. Everything is so confusing.'

I put my hand on her head and found myself actually petting her. 'There-there . . .' I said, sounding downright papal. Then I blinked. It wasn't an unusual blink, just a run-of-the-mill blink where the eyelid comes down over the cornea, brushes against the lower lid, then lazily flutters open. No, it was a blink just like the four or five hundred blinks I'd already blinked that day, or the couple of thousand blinks I blinked the day before. Except for one thing. My eyes had somehow turned completely around in their sockets and I was staring straight into my brain.

It took exactly that long to go from papal infallibility to fallen angel. In the blink of an eye, I was transported to the heart of a psychedelic maelstrom, and I wondered if I'd ever get out. I was assaulted by such a rush of stimuli that I thought my head would explode. There was a mat on the floor, a cup on the ledge, a spoon in the saucer – where did all this *stuff* come from? Had the world gone mad? It was filling my head with millions of molecules of unnecessary information. Clear out! Clear out!

I heard Meg's voice echoing off the frying pan in the kitchen. 'Can we go somewhere?'

Yes! By all means! Let's go somewhere! Anywhere but here! Somewhere cool and safe, with only one or two colors! 'Beach!' I said, pointing my arm like some mad general about to lead his troops to a massacre. It took Meg, Chrissy, and me either sixty seconds or three and a half hours to get out of the Pala Ayu, down the main road, over the little grassy patch, across the dune, and onto the sand. I lost track of time somewhere around the twelfth syllable of the word 'okay,' which Meg may or may not have used to indicate that she did or did not want to join me or whoever it was that was occupying my body. Along the way, I managed only one clear thought: There was no way in hell I could be anyone's guide. The moment I saw those billion grains of sand – each with its own story to tell – I knew I had blasted through to some whole other zone. I was so desperate to get away, I didn't even feel guilty when I said to Meg: 'I'm leaving. Don't go near the water.'

I marched along the beach, watching my feet making imprints in the sand, my knees bent, up, down, up, down, my toes digging in between the grains, my heels kicking up tiny granules behind me, the sun beating down and casting a narrow shadow, knees bent, toes digging, heels kicking, sun shining, up, down, up, down, hot, thirsty, exhausted, must rest, must rest. Finally, I stopped and turned. Meg and Chrissy were still there, staring at me with odd expressions. *Hmmm*. I had been marching in place. 'Be well,' I said, and continued on, this time more in earnest.

There was a door I had encountered on every acid trip, behind which, I suspected, were unimaginable secrets, as well as terrors too horrifying to comprehend. I'd stuck my foot through that door a few times, but always I pulled back, telling myself next time, maybe next time. But there never was a next time, because I was afraid that if I went through that door, I'd never come back. That was before. Now, madness had grabbed me by the throat and was yanking me right to the precipice. I tried to scream, but I had no voice. I tried to run, but I had no feet. I was being catapulted and felt an endless tumbling as my body went flying through that door so fast that I could barely hear it slam shut. I collapsed on the sand, far down the beach where no one else could see, and realized I'd finally done it. I had gone stark, raving mad. I was Fat Albie, Crazy Helen, and Wendy the Snake Dancer all rolled up into one tightly coiled ball. I was certain that I'd not only lost my mind, but that it was gone forever, and I sat there, waiting for someone to come and strap me into a straightjacket. Go ahead, attach electrodes to my temples, and give them a little extra juice, because this guy's lost it, this guy's over the edge, this guy's going, going . . .

Gone. I stared down at my body, which was lying fifty feet below facedown in the sand. I could see the bottom of my feet, the back of my legs, the back of my sarong, the back of my vest, and the back of my head. I saw the top of a palm tree, and marveled at how different the fronds looked from above, how the tree resembled a giant onion, unfolding and twisting and opening into itself. I saw the lush tops of acacias, the spindly tips of bamboo stalks, and the tall branches of the banyan. I flew in for a closer look, until I was almost inside the bark itself, and I moved up along the branch, watching the wood breathe as it coiled higher and higher, and then, just at the top, it began shaking and vibrating. Suddenly, without warning, the branch reared back and sprung at me with great bulging horrific eyes – its fangs dripping in blood, pieces of raw flesh wedged into its jaw, it came at me like a hood covering the horizon and took a voracious bite out of the sky.

I jerked away just in time, but something else approached. Its skull was creased with knobby protuberances, its side was dull and puffy, and then it turned and I saw one enormous eye in the middle of its head, the orb pulsating wildly back and forth, its bloody red capillaries crossing through the retina, and then it bore down on me, this monstrous Cyclops, sucking me into the sickening, glutinous matter that oozed from its veins. I tore free and soared higher as the head of a wild boar flew through the air, its jagged teeth chomping and tearing at me as I tried to hide behind a cold black cloud, and then everything sped up, I was spinning around like an electron, being assaulted by one horrific creature after another, their eyes bulging, trancelike, demonic, and I knew now where I was, I was trapped above the Black Magic Forest, in an endless orbit with the demon spirits, and I would be chased forever like this, this was to be my fate, to stare into the eyes of madness, circling around and around and around, and then I felt the circle closing, the orbit getting tighter, the speed increasing, until there was nothing but a cascade of horrific images screaming out at me, spinning, spinning, spinning, faster and faster, and then, when the whole earth shook like it would explode, I was suddenly shot out of the orbit with tremendous velocity, riding a centrifugal force that spun me over the trees and over the dunes and over the sand until I came face-to-face with a figure so welcoming, so gentle, so nurturing, that I wanted nothing more than to be cradled, to give in absolutely and totally, to shed myself of skin and bone and memory, to be cradled in the arms of my mother's mother, to give in and give in and give in . . .

The world exploded. There had been a terrible nuclear war and the fallout was carried in on the ocean breeze. I looked far down the beach and could see people scurrying away, trying to avoid the inevitable, but it was too late. The sky was an endless palette of pastels, of purples and pinks and lilacs, and this, I understood, was the color of death, it wasn't really so bad after all, just an expanse of cool billowing clouds welcoming me into my first day of the *bardo*.

To be dead is to lose all fear. Perhaps it would have been nice had some monk played a horn for me, but it didn't really matter, I didn't need anyone's help, I was already well along the journey and I knew that no car could crush me, no bullet could pierce my heart, no knife could slash my skin, there was nothing left to fear, neither disease nor poverty nor loneliness, there was nothing left to fear at all, and that's when I heard a voice beckoning me to the ocean – 'Come,' it said – and I threw my clothes onto the beach and walked down the sloping sand. The voice called again and I quickened my pace until I felt the first wave of the sea lapping at my toes. 'Come,' it said, and I felt at peace as the second wave brushed my ankles, the third crested at my knees, and the fourth reached my thighs. I waded further into the ocean as the fifth wave rose to my. hips and the sixth to my waist. 'Come,' said the voice, and I knew there was nothing to fear as the seventh wave rose to my chest and the eighth to my neck. I was at peace, I was secure, I was released, and then the ocean surged, a great wall of water bore down on me, and I welcomed it, I surrendered, I felt myself tumbling, I was beneath the sea, my body sinking to the ocean floor, and that's when another voice boomed out – 'No! It is not yet time!' – and I felt something picking me up in the water, I felt my head and neck and chest rising, and I felt myself suddenly riding the ninth wave as it built and built and built and crashed into the shore . . .

The sun was low in the sky but warm enough to heat the sand. I was lying prone, my arms stretched out over my head, my fingers kneading the sand like a kitten on its mother's breast. I felt a tiny surge of energy with each caress of the ground, the warmth rising up through my fingers, into my hands, along my arms, and into my body. Over and over my fingers captured life from the sun and sent it coursing through my veins, until finally I had the strength to sit up and look around.

I had been there four or five hours. The tide had come in, gone out, and taken my clothes along with it. I touched my face and my arms. Was I alive? Everything shimmered and glistened and pulsated – I was still on the far side of the door – but this was another room I had entered. I was aware that the sun was about to set, that there was no one left on the beach, and that it was time to go home. I walked along the shore for half a mile, then cut up toward the path that led over the dunes. I was just about to leave the beach when something called to me – not a voice so much as an essence. 'You must give something back,' it said.

Yes, an offering. The gods had guided me through this

journey and held me in their hands. I must give thanks. I bent down and removed a ring I'd gotten along the way, a silver band with red Roman glass. I held it in my hand, squeezed it in my palm, then opened my fingers and let go. The ring traveled in an arc for a foot or two, then disappeared into thin air. I ran my hand over the sand, expecting to find it lying there, but there was nothing. I stood up, looked around, and felt the ground one more time. The ring was gone. 'Thank you,' I said.

I left the beach, walked up the path, along the dune, over the stretch of grass, and onto the main road of Legian. I walked naked past the bicycle shop and several *warongs* before turning onto the path for the Pala Ayu. I found myself sitting in the chair in front of my room – the same chair where the day had begun a lifetime ago. I sat there for an hour as the sun went down and night set upon the village. I relived what had happened over and over, telling myself that I must never forget this day, not one single minute of it, but already some of the images were fading – the face of the Cyclops, the eyes of the boar – they all were fading, the door was closing . . .

I glanced down at my hand and saw something incomprehensible. The ring, the one with the Roman glass, was sitting on my finger. I couldn't understand – had none of this happened, had I never left this chair? I closed my eyes and told myself, remember, remember the tops of the trees, remember the grains of sand, remember the waves and then I opened my eyes and the ring was gone. Back and forth it went, with each blink of the eye – the ring was there, the ring was gone, the ring was there, the ring was gone – and I felt myself shifting between two realities, the door was closing, tighter and tighter . . .

And then, finally, the ring was really gone. Each time that I reopened my eyes, it was gone, and I knew the trip was finally over. I went inside my room, closed the door, and lay on my bed. The last thing I remember, as sleep pulled me under, was the sound of the ninth wave crashing against the shore.

# 39

# Perfect

When I awoke twelve hours later, a songbird was singing the most beautiful melody I'd ever heard. The sound began deep in its throat, rose to a soprano warble, and erupted into a cascade of notes. I looked across the room and noticed how the light refracted through the bamboo curtains like shadow puppets. Rama and Sita embraced. Dewi spread her wings. Ganesh reared his trunk. Then a gecko appeared. It called out nine times, scampered across the ceiling, and disappeared into a crevice in the wall. I brushed some water across my face, surprised at how refreshing it felt, then noticed how the drops glistened like tiny prisms as they fell into a basin. The room itself seemed more attractive than I remembered. A single flower graced a wooden vase. A batik pillow leaned against a bare wall.

I opened the door onto a perfect day. The air was warm, the sky clear, and a breeze from the ocean blew in with just the hint of jasmine. I heard the sound of a wooden cowbell and looked over to see a man urging on a cow with gentle taps to its rear. The cow stepped on a banana leaf, which crinkled into the ground and flipped the remnants of an offering to a dog lolling in the shade nearby. The dog lazily nibbled at the rice, then ambled over to a cooler spot under a palm tree. A girl hung a sarong off a branch and brushed her hair with boar bristles while a boy rode by on a wobbly bicycle, kicking up little mounds of sand. A man drinking palm wine followed behind, swaying to and fro and tipping an imaginary hat to three women who passed by with giant baskets of fruit balanced on their heads. They turned onto a path where an old man carved a teak box and watched over his naked grandson, who ran after a chicken that always stayed one step ahead. The chicken flapped its wings and stirred up a ripple on a pond, where a frog leapt off a water lily and disappeared into the water below. The ripple built to the edge of the pond, where it caressed the toes of an old lady who sat bare breasted beneath an acacia, weaving a purse from bamboo. Another woman ground pomegranate seeds for dyeing, while her daughter stretched bolts of cotton to dry in the sun. The cotton rolled down to a grove of trees, where two boys marched in a circle playing bamboo flutes. The boys ran back along the path to the *losman* next door, where three little girls practiced the Legong, waving their hands in the air, tiptoeing in the dirt, flashing their eyes from side to side, and I watched those eyes, big and brown and innocent, as they darted from the young boys to the old lady to the naked baby to the old grandfather, and something made sense for the first time, that it was all really quite perfect – the births and the deaths, the burials and the cremations, the offerings and the celebrations – and it extended beyond this place, it extended into something far bigger into which all of this fit, and for the first time, the drowning of a Korean and the murder of a petty thief made sense, the black quarter of Nairobi made sense, the sex safaris of Mombasa made sense, the street children of Karachi made sense, the crowds of Old Delhi made sense, the wristwatches of Kathmandu made sense, the rickshaws of Calcutta made sense, the waiters of Bangkok made sense, the soldiers of Laos made sense, Annika's abortion made sense, Martine's plane crash made sense, the whole crazy thing made sense, even if I couldn't explain a word of it, and I thought back to the marketplace in Bombay – at how angry I was when the Italian woman said, 'Isn't life perfect?' – and wished that now, at this moment, I could tell her, yes, I finally understand, it is perfect, every disappointment and failure and illness is perfect, every war is perfect, every riot and teargassing and beating is perfect, every beggar on the streets is perfect, every insane variety of the human experience is absolutely, totally, 100 percent perfect.

'What happened to you?' asked Susan when I walked out into the courtyard. 'We were getting ready to call out the bloodhounds.'

'I didn't know they had bloodhounds in Bali.'

'Turns out they don't. Plan B was to call out the geckos.'

'Have you seen Meg and Chrissy?'

'This morning. They were playing volleyball.'

'*Volleyball?*'

'Uh-huh, something wrong with that?'

'Not at all. So . . . they're okay?'

'They looked fine to me.'

'Good. That's *very* good.'

'I suppose it is.'

'And *you* look good. *Very* good.'

'*Um* . . . are you all right?'

'Never better.'

'Well, not to ruin your blissful day or anything, but I'm having another party tonight.'

'What time should I be there?'

'What? No kicking and screaming?'

'Of course not.'

'Are you *sure* you're all right?'

I was more than all right. For the first time, I felt I actually understood something. For the first time, I desired not to fight what was happening around me, but to accept it as something precious. For the first time, I felt completely at ease with my surroundings and comfortable with who I was. And how perfect it was that this should arise only weeks before my departure from the Third World. The seemingly disparate fragments of my journey had coalesced into something meaningful and I felt I could leave with the sense that I'd grown at least a little. I was going to Japan – that, I'd already decided  – but now, rather than feeling antipathy, I welcomed the opportunity. I pictured Japan as being much like the West, and with it would come a new set of challenges. I'd have to trade in my sarong for a shirt and pants, but I figured so long as I didn't iron a crease into them, I stood a decent shot at adapting. After all, wasn't anything possible? I was happier than ever before, yes, truly happy, so much so that my happiness meter was entering totally foreign territory. At first I thought it was a mistake, that the mechanism had gone haywire, or that the ocean air was too humid, or that some sand was jamming things up, but no, as I looked more carefully, I saw that the meter was functioning perfectly, it wasn't swinging around wildly at all, no, it was a nice solid line: eight, eight-point-five, nine, nine-point-five . . .

Over the next few days, people seemed to be actually flocking around me, as if to soak up the good vibes. I was at peace, content, and even a little radiant all at the same time. The mushrooms had unleashed something overwhelming, some kind of gravitational pull, and wherever I went, I was downright magnetic. Women who'd never noticed me were suddenly interested. The man at the bicycle shop offered me a free week on his best bike. Children came by to play on my porch. The old men of the village stopped to chat. The *bimo* drivers insisted I sit up front in the best seat. Kortis added extra grated coconut to the top of my fruit salad.

Meg and Chrissy came to say goodbye – they were finally leaving for Melbourne – and weren't the slightest bit angry with me for deserting them. In fact, Meg said that as soon as they got to the beach, they just relaxed and enjoyed the view. 'We had fun!' she said. Then Tamara wrote from Japan that she'd found the perfect apartment in Tokyo and had encouraging reports about the club scene. It was all falling into place . . .

More people came and went and my last few days in Bali were a nonstop party. To cap it off, I walked into a restaurant one afternoon and saw a deeply tanned woman with long black hair, an amber necklace, and seven earrings. '*Lois?*' I said, dumbfounded. I hadn't seen her for three years, not since Amsterdam, when she was still with Michael on their houseboat. She introduced me to Fantuzzi, whom she'd been with ever since. If I was a one-man band, Fantuzzi was a one-man circus. He was known everywhere for his 'blowouts,' wild tribal gatherings that drew thousands of people. He sang, danced, played guitar, acted, and probably would walk a tightwire if anyone was crazy enough to string one. Fantuzzi was an instant dose of energy, the eye of the hurricane, a nonstop performer who drew everyone along for a wild ride. Within ten minutes we were jamming, me and Fantuzzi and a whole entourage he'd whipped up over lunch: a gamelan drummer, a boy on flute, a German tambourine player, an Italian conga drummer, three Dutch sisters singing backup, and a half-dozen Balinese dancing girls. We played until we were too exhausted to continue and then we played some more. Fantuzzi finally headed for the beach and a dozen people followed him. Lois looked tired, but she went along. It was all part of the deal. She was in a traveling road show, and her boyfriend just happened to be the whole show.

It was time for one last blowout, but first, there was a certain matter I needed to take care of. I knew that everything was perfect in the universe, but there was something in my very own room that felt out of place. One thing stood out, inconsistent with the surroundings, inconsistent with the candles, the bamboo curtains, the straw mattress, the batiks, the rice paper, the guitar and harmonicas, inconsistent with who I was. I needed to make one more offering.

I went down to the ocean and watched the tide receding beneath a magnificent sunset. Then, with the final rays of light, I dug my feet into the sand, swung around a few times like a shot-putter, and let fly with a tremendous heave into the ocean. There was a big plunk in the water as a heavy object sunk, hit bottom, then bobbed up like a cork. It floated there, ever stubborn, until the next series of waves came in. The object rose, fell, bobbed some more, then finally got caught in the current. As the last sliver of the sun disappeared over the horizon, I watched as my rucksack floated out to sea. It was the final trapping of my journey, the virtual symbol of being on the road, and just like the cameras and watches, it too needed to go.

The day before my flight, I went to Denpasar, thinking about everything that had happened during my three months in Bali. The roar of a motorcycle interrupted my reverie and I looked up to see a man and a woman speeding my way. The guy was blonde, with a stubble of beard, and the woman had such a perfectly shaped head that, for an instant, I thought I was back in Stockholm – but no, I knew that was impossible. Stockholm was some whole other lifetime. Stockholm was another universe. Wasn't it?

Time stopped for one brief second. The *bimos* and the buses stopped, the people on the streets stopped, the motorcycle stopped, and I could see her clear as day: It was Annika. She looked beautiful. Her skin was tan, her eyes sparkled, and her hennaed hair blew in the breeze. What was she doing here on my final day in Bali? Was this just another coincidence? Was destiny playing its final card? No, it was a test, that's what it was. The Barong and Rangda had gotten together to have one last laugh and for an instant I felt a kris knife on my heart. It tugged one way and then the other, back and forth, and then time caught up, the motorcycle sped by, and I just kept on walking – I didn't turn, I didn't call her name, I didn't even flinch – I just kept on walking and never looked back.

That night, the Kayu Api was packed. Susan was throwing a going away party and everyone was there. I would've liked to believe, they were all there for me, but the truth is, Fantuzzi had spread the word that he'd be playing and people were coming in by dugout canoe from Borneo for the event. 'So, I'm finally getting rid of you,' said Susan.

'You wore me out, you beat me down.'

'But you surrendered.'

'Actually, surrender connotes honor. I'd have to say I capitulated.'

'I can't tell you how good that makes me feel,' said Susan, breaking into a wide smile. 'I hope I wasn't too rough on you.'

'I needed it. You helped me out, Susan. Thanks.'

'My only regret is that now I have to find someone new to torture. It's a pity. You were such a perfect subject.'

Susan floated off into the crowd while Fantuzzi warmed up the audience. After I played a set of my own material, Fantuzzi returned to whip the crowd into a frenzy. I didn't mind being upstaged at my own party – not too much, anyway – but then Fantuzzi called on me to join him. I was reluctant, but when he pointed at the harmonica, I figured why not? I hadn't played solo harmonica since Africa. Cupping the harp in my fingers was like shaking hands with an old friend. I'd almost forgotten how good it felt to touch the wood body and metal casing and to form a chamber of air with my hands. Playing with a neck brace was one thing, but this was something else, this allowed for a hundred different sounds.

Fantuzzi played a couple of verses, then looked at me and nodded. I did a little run in the lower register and bent a note into a low growl, then repeated it a few times and broke a little higher. I could feel the tone working its way up my spine as I held my fingers together and sucked a jet stream through the reeds. The tone built and built, higher and higher, coursing around a minor jazz scale and reverberating with overtones, and then it built a little more, until the reeds felt fluid, as if they were suspended in oil, and then the tones reached higher still until they exploded into a mad rush of notes, and I was gone, I was back on stage in Mombasa – I was gone – I was back on stage in Nairobi – I was gone – I was back on stage in Stockholm – I was gone – and three years of my life were in that run, three years of going up, down, and sideways, three years of searching and questioning, three horrible wonderful terrible glorious years, and the notes were coming in clusters now, punching out in staccato

396

bursts, and each note was a memory, clear and crisp and clean, of my childhood, of my mother and father, of an endless stream of people, and the notes kept building as the images flew past, trains and buses and rickshaws, mountains and deserts and beaches, hotels and houses and caves, friends and teachers and lovers, and then I began to understand one more thing, that love is wonderful, it makes the journey easier, it adds a dimension that pushes us on, but love is not the answer, the Bone Man was right, love is only one small part of something much larger, and it was then that I saw her standing in the audience, she was looking at me and smiling and listening, and the notes came now more in colors than in sounds, they were bold brush strokes, bright reds and vibrant yellows and resounding oranges, they were completing a picture, yes, how perfect it was that she should arrive on the eve of my departure, how perfect that I should confront her one more time, how perfect that destiny and fate should intermingle for one last dance.

When I arrived back at the Pala Ayu that night, Annika was waiting for me. 'Hey, stranger,' she said.

I took a long look at her, as if trying to place the face. 'New York, wasn't it? The East Side Bookstore?'

'Could be. I'm thinking maybe Greece.'

'That's right, now I remember. We kept missing each other.'

Annika smiled and moved a half step closer. 'The music sounded incredible tonight.'

'You think?'

'It just keeps getting better.'

'Well, thanks. Thanks a lot.'

'So . . . Bali . . .'

I thought for a moment about Jhochen Tole in Kathmandu, how I'd followed Annika out of the Mandarin Restaurant. 'It's a real trip,' I said.

'It's amazing, isn't it? You leaving, me just getting here . . .'

'Lots of paths cross in Bali.'

Annika smiled and looked off into the distance.

'Remember that night in Stockholm? When we wound up at Eva's and you picked me up and carried me around the apartment?'

'Yeah, I remember.'

'And that snake of hers, what was it called?'

'Frederick.'

'Frederick! Oh, God, what a team!'

'I hated that son-of-a-bitch snake.' Annika and I looked at each other under the light of a kerosene lamp and had a good laugh. 'So, you still mad at me?' I asked.

'For what?'

'Sleeping with Eva.'

Annika turned away, then looked at me slyly. 'A little.'

The lamp swung slightly in the breeze and I caught sight of her glistening eyes. 'Boy, you sure carry a grudge.'

'We've been through a lot since then,' said Annika. 'Both of us.'

'That's for sure.'

'And now you're leaving.'

'Seven o'clock tomorrow morning.'

'It's too bad.'

'Yeah, I'm going to miss it here.'

'I don't suppose you could stay longer?'

'I can't. The visas, the tickets, they're all taken care of. Anyway, you're with Wolfe.'

'That's not really serious. It's just . . .'

Her voice faded away. I reached behind a tile on the wall for my key to the room and unlocked the door. As soon as I lit a candle, I saw a gecko scamper across the ceiling. He trumpeted out his first call as Annika walked in and stood against the wall. 'You've got to watch out in Bali,' I said as the gecko called out again.

'I've heard.'

'There's an undercurrent—'

'Yeah, in the water—'

'There's an undercurrent everywhere.'

'Okay, I'll remember.'

I went over to my dresser and opened the drawer as I

398

counted the gecko's calls: four . . . five . . . six . . . 'This is for you,' I said, handing Annika an antique sarong I'd bought up in the mountains. 'It's batik, from Surabaya.'

She opened up the cloth and studied the geometric shapes, which interlocked but never touched. 'Yes, I see. There's a little tag here that says: BATIK, FROM SURABAYA.'

The gecko called out a seventh time and then an eighth and as I waited for the ninth call, I thought how perfectly ironic this was, yes, how very, very perfect, that after all this time I had finally become the man Annika could fall in love with all over again, just as it was time to leave. And we stood there like that, in the candlelight of my room at the Pala Ayu, only hours before my departure, staring at each other, a thousand memories hanging in the air, waiting for the ninth call of the gecko that never came.